RAILROAD NATION

RAILROADS PAST AND PRESENT

H. Roger Grant and Thomas Hoback, editors

INDIANA UNIVERSITY PRESS

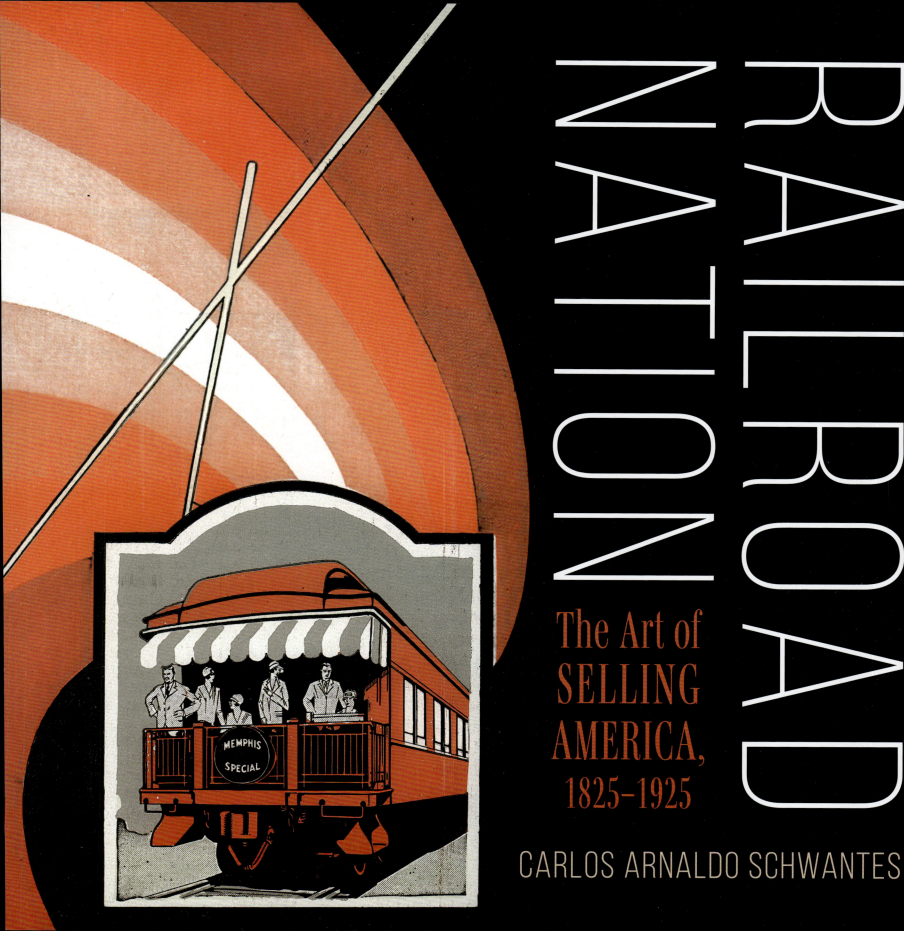

RAILROAD NATION

The Art of SELLING AMERICA, 1825–1925

CARLOS ARNALDO SCHWANTES

MEMPHIS SPECIAL

This book is a publication of

Indiana University Press
Office of Scholarly Publishing
Herman B Wells Library 350
1320 East 10th Street
Bloomington, Indiana 47405 USA

iupress.org

Manufactured in Korea

First Printing 2025

Cataloging information is available from the Library of Congress.

ISBN 978-0-253-07224-5 (hdbk.)
ISBN 978-0-253-07225-2 (web PDF)

To my granddaughter
Magdalena Victoria Schwantes
by her "Saint Louis Grandpa"

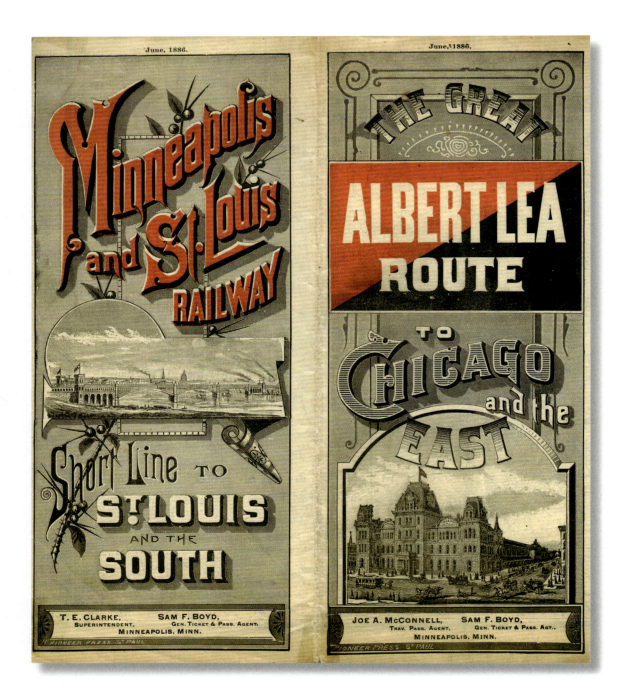

Our railways are a majestic construction, grand and awe-inspiring to behold in their wonderful winding courses, and are suggestive of vast power, great genius, and enterprise and myriad labor.

—from *West Shore Railroad Suburban Times*, September 1890, 2

The Minneapolis & St. Louis used the cover of its 1886 timetable to promote a through route between Chicago and Minneapolis via a connection in Albert Lea, Minnesota. Despite its bold and colorful imprints, the railroad remained a marginal carrier for passenger travel across the Upper Midwest.

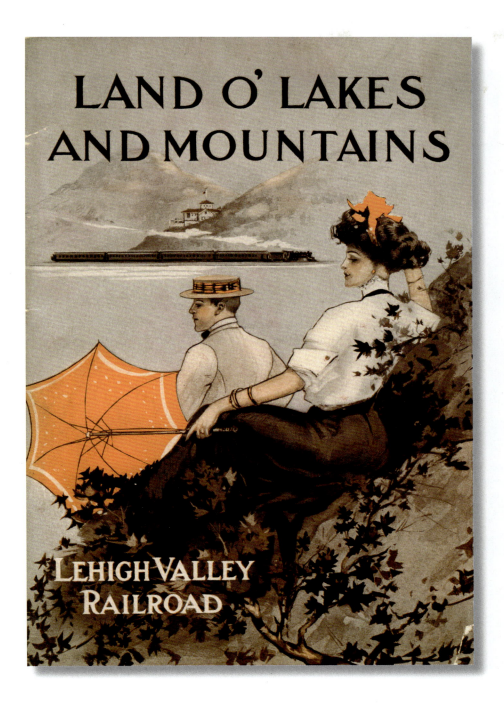

LAND O' LAKES AND MOUNTAINS

LEHIGH VALLEY RAILROAD

In a summer trip the pleasures of expectation are almost as great as those of realization, and nothing contributes to the pleasures of expectation more than a good railroad folder. No tourist ever saw such lakes or trout streams or stopped at such hotels as are described in the railroad folders.

—from *Abilene Reflector*, as quoted in *Minneapolis Register* (Minnesota), May 2, 1918

Lehigh Valley's *Land O' Lakes and Mountains* (1909) brochure emphasized the scenery along the railroad's rural right-of-way between New York City and Buffalo. Every North American rail carrier of consequence, and some marginal ones, issued comparable trackside guides to interpret the passing landscape for curious travelers.

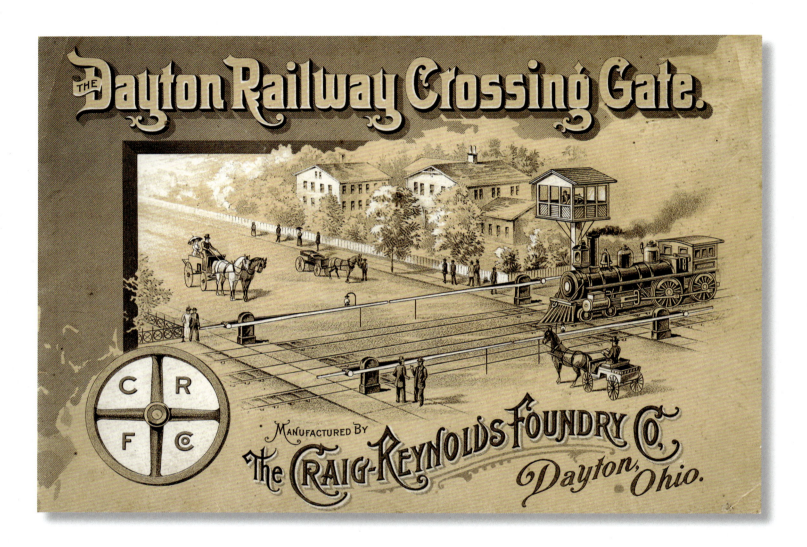

A sales brochure for the Dayton Railway Crossing Gate emphasized a common feature of transportation landscapes then and now: the intersection between tracks and roadways and its potential for accidents. In addition to the railroads themselves, industry suppliers such as Westinghouse and General Electric were major publishers of rail-oriented imprints.

In modern times, it is the railway which makes the city. The importance of any city is rated not by the amount of ground it covers or the number of people it contains, so much as by its railway connections.

—from *Railway Review*, September 20, 1879, 135

The up-to-date advertiser no longer claims impossible advantages. His is not the short line between all points and his map is not drawn to prove it. He does not claim universal superiority. People do not believe that sort of statement, no more than we believe that a patent medicine cures all ills as per advertisement.

—from George T. Nicholson, Passenger Traffic Manager, Atchison, Topeka & Santa Fe Railway, *Official Guide*, November 1899, xxvii

---

On its 1894 timetable covers, the Fremont, Elkhorn & Missouri Valley featured an enormous elk head, a bold design element likely to make its publications stand out on hotel and station racks crowded with travel publications issued by competing railroads. The largest racks, in fact, featured an array of spaces capable of displaying 110 different timetables. In New York City alone, some eight million heavily illustrated railroad folders were given away in 1903. Carriers paid $150 per thousand for the most heavily illustrated timetables, which they distributed to travelers.

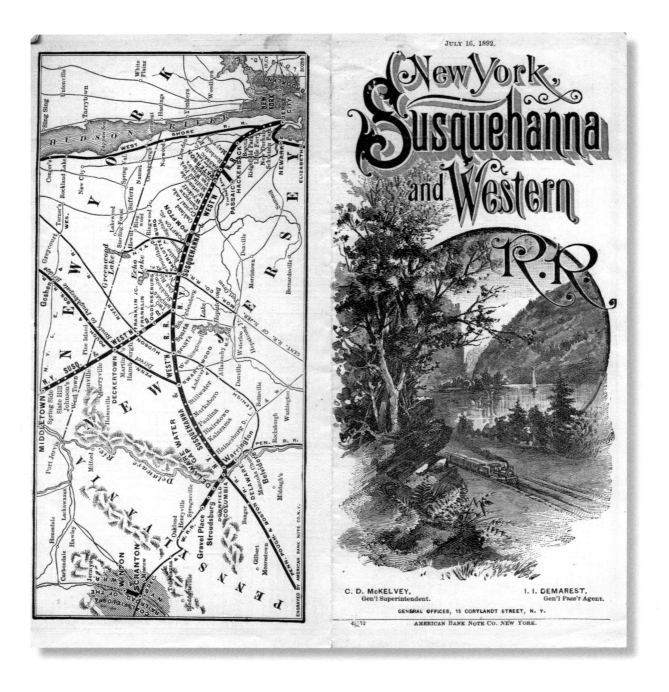

The New York, Susquehanna & Western timetable and system map date from 1892. The cartography is typical of the rail industry's indulgence in the fantasy that tracks always traced a straight line, even through mountainous terrain.

Persons are warned against planning a walking trip by a railroad map. Because a locomotive and train can level off a state, pocket a river, bulldoze a mountain range, and snub a Great Lake, it does not follow that this can be done on foot.

—from *Boston Transcript*, quoted in *Wall Street Journal*, July 30, 1910

CONTENTS

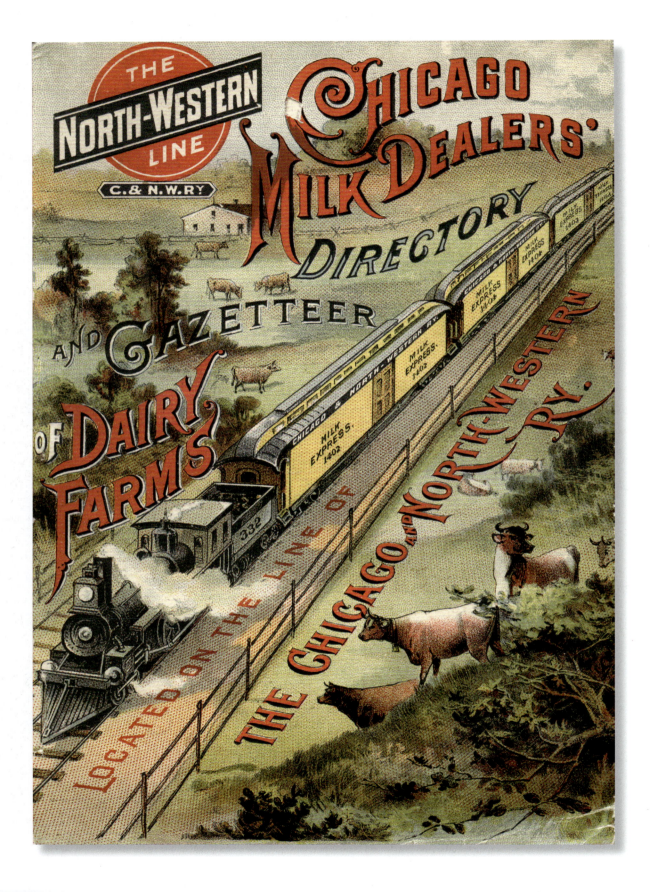

The extent to which the great railroad systems of the United States invoke the aid of printer's ink in their laudable ambition to develop passenger business is something that rather astonishes the foreign transportation manager.

—from *Daily Journal* (Montpelier, Vermont), June 23, 1899

The Chicago & North-Western's *Chicago Milk Dealers' Directory* (1892) offers a compelling example of commercial art, which although busy in its many details has become a favorite of the author.

PREFACE and ACKNOWLEDGMENTS

Several years ago, I reviewed a book, massive in size and gorgeous in appearance, by Ian Kennedy and Julian Treuherz titled *The Railway: Art in the Age of Steam*. I subsequently visited the Nelson-Atkins Museum of Art in Kansas City to savor the exhibit on which their book was based. I doubt that a more impressive collection of fine art devoted to the railroad has ever been assembled or so beautifully displayed—or ever will be again. However, I realized that railroads around the world were responsible also for a remarkable outpouring of illustrations that may not rise to the level of "fine art" but that speak to the industry's need to captivate an audience visually.[1]

The desire to publish the railroad emerged only gradually during America's post–Civil War decades, and complementing desire came improved printing technologies that enabled the rail industry's outpouring of commercial art. Words alone could be persuasive, but railroads during the 1870s and 1880s discovered that color graphics gave their publications added appeal. Companies large and small sought to enhance visually the covers of their public timetables, their most ubiquitous form of paper advertising, and also their many thousands of distinctive brochures intended to promote vacations by train or the settlement of railroad lands—the "scenery and soil," as an early twentieth-century advertisement for the Saint Louis-San Francisco Railroad cleverly phrased it.[2] Several large printing firms used the latest color technology developed in Germany in the 1890s to deliver a steady stream of the most visually appealing commercial art that money could buy.[3]

Since the 1870s, professional wordsmiths and illustrators supported by railroad dollars had crafted thousands of booklets, brochures, and pamphlets that represented American time and space as the nation's first big business sought to portray it. Railroad publications intended for general readers ranged from one- and two-page leaflets to thick items that easily qualified as books. During the summer of 1892, for example, upstate New York's Rome, Watertown & Ogdensburg Railroad issued an informative publication that "contains 228 pages, octavo size, has over 150 illustrations, and contains seven fine maps. The cost of tours, list of some eight hundred hotels and the routes and rates for over six hundred combination summer excursion tickets are also included." Anyone desiring a copy need only mail ten cents to the railroad's general passenger agent in Syracuse, New York.[4]

During the pre–Civil War days of the 1840s and 1850s, railroad publicity tended to be "rough stuff, bombastic, not logical, not even seeking to be logical," wrote Edward Hungerford, a keen student of American transportation, in 1915. "The railroads advertised 'Shortest Route,' 'Best Route,' 'Most Popular Route,' and, though people went and in many cases found they were not the shortest, the best, or the most popular route, what mattered it?" During the postwar decades, things changed: "It took advertising in the seventies and the eighties, even into the nineties and up to today, to build the fat farms and the fine towns, the budding cities that one sees from the [train] car window as today he crosses Minnesota, the Dakotas, Montana, Oklahoma, and West Texas."[5]

The multitiered literature racks common to rail stations and most reputable hotels typically displayed the artists' handiwork as a colorful array of timetables from dozens of different roads. During their vigorous competition with one another in the late nineteenth and early twentieth centuries, railroad publicists came to believe that a visually attractive cover could captivate potential travelers. Thus, the early years of the twentieth century, before America's entry into World War I in April 1917, were by any measure the golden age of railroad commercial art.[6]

While *Railroad Nation* seeks to showcase the rail industry's commitment to commercial art during the nineteenth and early twentieth centuries, I must include a chapter on the curious fate that befell the railroad as publisher when in April 1918 the federal bureaucrat appointed to oversee the newly established United States Railroad Administration abruptly terminated half a century of advertising creativity to bolster America's determination to win World War I. I have devoted an entire chapter to this strange interlude and another to the industry's struggle to resurrect its publishing legacy after March 1920, when Uncle Sam's oversight ended.[7]

Several individuals deserve credit for the different ways they influenced my thinking as this book took shape, and foremost among them was Professor William S. Greever, my history department colleague at the University of Idaho. Bill and I never actually taught together because he had retired by 1984, the year I relocated there, but through our University of Idaho connection, we discovered a mutual love of railroad history. Once a quarter for several years, we drove together ninety miles north to Spokane to spend a day with Robert Downing, retired president of the Burlington Northern Railroad, genial host, and a truly wonderful source of contemporary industry insight as well as personal railroad anecdotes.[8]

I observed that Greever kept a hardbound set of *Official Railway Guides* in his living room, but never did I realize that those massive volumes represented only the proverbial "tip of the iceberg" in terms of his personal library until one day many

years later when I unexpectedly learned that Bill had willed me his entire rail collection. He even provided the money required to ship it from Moscow, Idaho, to my Missouri home in Ballwin, near Saint Louis. Greever, by the way, earned his Harvard doctorate in American history with a study of the landed domain in the American Southwest of the Atchison, Topeka & Santa Fe Railway, but even before graduate school he had collected railroad ephemera during his World War II travels as a member of Uncle Sam's army.[9]

Helping me pack the Greever collection into fifty large boxes for shipment halfway across the United States and then in subsequent years serving as my mentor as I explored the wonderful world of ephemera and learned archival best practices was Edward Nolan, the longtime head of Special Collections at the Washington State Historical Society in Tacoma and an author of railroad histories. Ed encouraged me to showcase in *Railroad Nation* some of the items housed within the Schwantes-Greever-Nolan Collection of Travel and Transportation Ephemera, and I appreciate his encouragement.[10]

After I relocated from the University of Idaho to the University of Missouri–St. Louis in 2001, new colleagues influenced my thinking as I pondered how to create the book that has become *Railroad Nation*. Foremost was Gregory P. Ames, a veritable walking encyclopedia of railroad knowledge who was curator of the John W. Barriger III National Railroad Library from 1998 to 2011. This treasure trove of railroad history was located only a few hundred yards from my campus office, and thus on numerous occasions I tapped into Gregg's extensive fund of knowledge, which he unfailingly shared along with a helpful dash of wit. More recently, he read the penultimate draft of this manuscript and provided numerous helpful suggestions along with corrections. I think it fair to add that Gregg did not agree with everything I wrote, but as a longtime academic I always enjoyed stirring the political pot to encourage my students to think about matters of history from different perspectives. Old habits die hard in print.

I came to depend, too, on Nick Fry, Gregg's successor at the Barriger Library, for all kinds of research help. Also, at the University of Missouri–St. Louis, Professor Steven Rowan, my History Department colleague, kindly shared with me his English translations of the 1830s and 1840s accounts compiled by

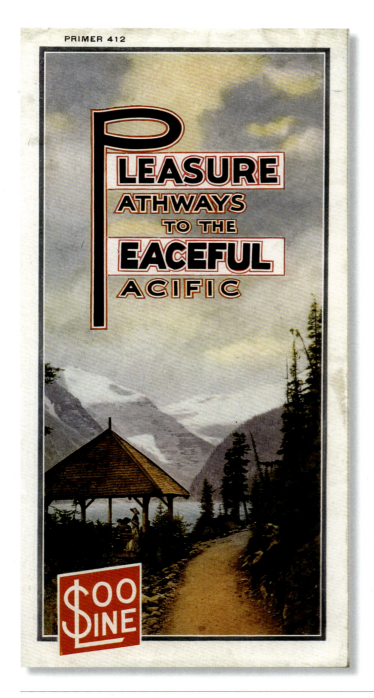

PRIMER 412

PLEASURE PATHWAYS TO THE PEACEFUL PACIFIC

SOO LINE

For readers who may recall the Minneapolis, St. Paul & Sault Ste. Marie ("Soo Line") of the 1950s as an unassuming carrier, the railroad's strong commitment to publishing early in the twentieth century may come as a surprise. Back then, the Canadian Pacific subsidiary promoted the scenic wonders of the Canadian Rockies through which its luxury trains passed between the Midwest and West Coast. One 1910 imprint had a tongue twister of a title: *Pleasure Pathways to the Peaceful Pacific.*

German and French visitors who traveled to North America to study its numerous canals and railroads.

I still correspond with Ed and Gregg via email and also communicate with another influence, Thomas G. Hoback, the now retired president of the Indiana Rail Road. I appreciate Tom's firsthand knowledge of the rail industry as well as his keen interest in its rich history. In 2014 we discovered a mutual interest in the railways of Great Britain, and during the next several years until the COVID-19 plague made international travel impossible, we enjoyed an annual pilgrimage together to spend two or three weeks exploring every corner of Great Britain with our BritRail passes. We often wondered where else we could ride so many long-distance trains for a mere thirty dollars a day.

There may be other members of the Friends of the Stockton & Darlington Railway residing in the United States, but Tom and I are both "card-carrying" devotees of the world's pioneer steam railroad. That is a primary reason why I reference early English railroads in a book ostensibly devoted to railroad publishing activity within North America. I don't think the two can be meaningfully separated, at least not during the early years. The North Atlantic was no ocean barrier to the free exchange of technical information among rail advocates in England, continental Europe, the United States, and Canada.[11]

Over the years I incurred a debt of gratitude to students who enrolled in the Railroads in American Life classes I taught at the University of Missouri–St. Louis from 2001 through 2016 and notably to Ron Goldfeder, with whom I still enjoy an occasional "railroad" working lunch and who on several occasions guided my students through the vast railroad holdings of the National Museum of Transportation in the Saint Louis suburb of Kirkwood. Students like Ron taught me as much railroad history as I may have taught them.

Here I pause to thank Don Hofsommer, the late Roger Grant, the late Peter Hansen, and other fellow directors of the Lexington Group, as well as Ray Mundy, Daniel Rust, and Alfred Runte for the ways each of them influenced my thinking about the encompassing subject of railroad history. I have been like a sponge absorbing all I could since the early 1950s when I stood in our Indiana backyard and was entranced by the Pennsylvania Railroad's daily sprint of trains along its busy main line that linked New York and Saint Louis.[12]

As for illustrations used to complement my written text, all are from the Schwantes-Greever-Nolan Collection of Travel and Transportation Ephemera, and most have never before been republished. The beauty of railroad ephemera first captivated me many years ago, and I have remained entranced by it. I used some colorful examples of railroad commercial art in my book titled *Railroad Signatures across the Pacific Northwest* (1993) and again in a book I coauthored with James Ronda titled *The West the Railroads Made* (2008). *Railroad Nation* thus embodies my lifelong fascination with the number and variety of railroad publications and my determination to dig still deeper into the topic, especially into the technical evolution of printing that made the many colorful railroad publications possible. Trade journals devoted to the printing industry are voluminous, and thus I have attempted to distill what was most applicable to railroad commercial art.[13]

At the beginning of my college teaching career in 1969, I took advantage of an opportunity to devote a few leisure hours each week to a class on letterpress printing, a craft with a rich history that dates back centuries to the invention of movable type. I enjoyed learning the art of setting type in a composing stick and in this way gained insight into the evolution of the printing technology used to produce the visually arresting rail publications.

Attached to one wall of my home office is a drawer from a California job case, and its many divisions are filled with a random assortment of movable type. This display offers an additional source of inspiration as I push forward to share with readers of *Railroad Nation* what I have gained from a lifetime of formal library and document research as well as from informal "history on the hoof" explorations into how railroads and their publications, and especially their commercial art, redefined time and space.

Again, the story of railroad publishing and its impact is multifaceted and impossibly large. The chapters of this book represent an admittedly personal distillation of an immense topic, and thus they provide an example of what one of my professors called "responsible reductionism." Readers are free to decide how "responsible" I have been in the choices I have made. As always, I alone am responsible for any errors of fact or quirks of judgment that may appear on the pages that follow.

During the 1930s and toward the era covered by *Railroad Nation*, several rail publications embraced the art deco style popular at the time, as did the Norfolk & Western on the cover of a brochure devoted to the Memphis Special, a train operated jointly with the Southern Railway.

RAILROAD NATION

The railway folder was a characteristic and highly developed expression of American literary genius. It was in the best sense educational as well. Many persons learned most of what they knew of American geography from a rapt perusal of folders while traveling or waiting for trains, and it was possible from a judicious selection of them to gain a liberal education in pictorial art and literature and American history as well as exceptional fictional instruction.

—from *Evansville (Indiana) Journal*, April 9, 1918

Tracks of Lehigh Valley traversed the anthracite coal region of eastern Pennsylvania, and thus Black Diamond, the name of its premier passenger train between New York City and Buffalo, was an appropriate description of its valued cargo. The timetable pictured here dates from 1896.

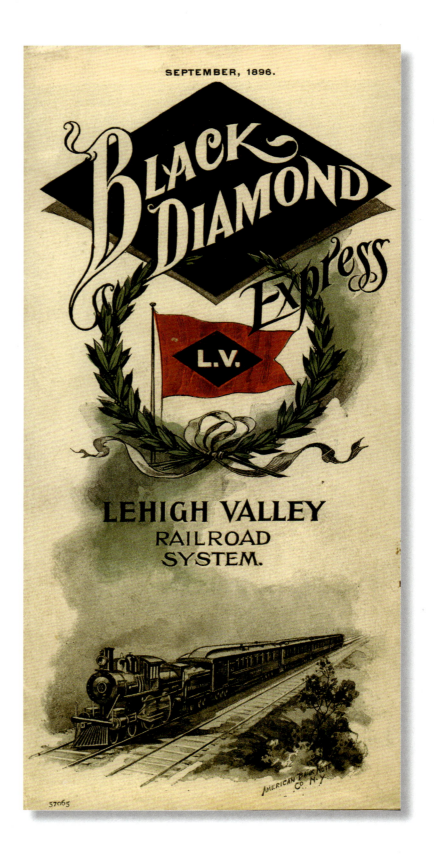

INTRODUCTION

RAILROAD IMPRINTS

As the numerous individual railroads of North America grew larger and more complex, they were of necessity forced to become paper-intensive enterprises. Just to maintain the steady flow of goods and people across time and space, managers had to develop new ways to keep track of trains as well as individual freight cars and cargoes, to monitor their employees, and to stay current with finances—and to do so in a manner that ensured accuracy, punctuality, safety, and honesty. They adapted business practices from earlier enterprises, but they also had to invent new management and accounting techniques to overcome the wholly novel spatial challenges that railroads and their far-flung operations created.[1]

Today's visitor to the historic South Street Seaport area along New York's East River can explore at leisure a typical countinghouse, a structure in which much commerce was conducted during the early nineteenth century. Perhaps the most noticeable design feature of the typical countinghouse interior was the raised platform on which the boss sat—as is exemplified by Ebenezer Scrooge in Charles Dickens's 1843 novella *A Christmas Carol*—to personally oversee the activity of his clerks as they stood at their tall desks to tally the daily flow of trade goods. The elevated promontory not only emphasized the heightened power of the boss but also facilitated his personal oversight of all work being done (or not) and amplified his words of praise or reprimand.[2]

This cozy spatial arrangement derived from the elevated quarterdeck aboard the sailing ships that hauled goods between Manhattan's acres of wharves and the distant ports of the world. This management model functioned well on land and sea so long as the boss and workers maintained visual contact with one another, as was true for a countinghouse as well as a ship. Railroads, even relatively short ones, redefined space and required the invention of a new model of oversight that worked effectively even when top managers and their employees seldom, if ever, met face-to-face. Hence the necessity for paper documents of all types to facilitate the timely flow of communication between railroad management and a company's far-flung operating employees. Information transmitted expeditiously via various paper documents was vital to the successful operation of any railroad. In short, a railroad ran on paper, and lots of it, just to keep its trains operating smoothly and safely along its rails of iron and steel.

Over the years, the railroads of North America generated many different types of paper documents—from passenger tickets, wall calendars, and advertising posters to train orders and bills of lading. In *Railroad Nation*, I intend to concentrate on two broad categories of paper documents that railroads most clearly intended for public consumption, and those publications showcase the railroad industry's investment in the incredible variety of eye-catching illustrations used to enliven their timetables and

COME BY WAY OF THE BEAUTIFUL INDIAN TERRITORY

A HEARTY WELCOME TO ALL THE WORLD

AS THE PIGEON FLIES!
Come through the Gate to Texas,
—) THE (—
CITY OF DENISON.

Rand, McNally & Co., Printers, Chicago.

Missouri, Kansas & Texas R'y.

PRIDE OF THE WEST THE MISSOURI KANSAS AND TEXAS RAILWAY.

SEDALIA ROUTE. CHICAGO HANNIBAL SEDALIA KAN. CITY ST. LOUIS JUNC. CITY PARSONS FORT SCOTT DENISON DALLAS HOUSTON GALVESTON AUSTIN

Passing through a country inhabited by a Free and Enlightened People, through a country most grand and picturesque, through wonderful cities and towns, fast filling up with a people yet to carve deep their names on a world's history.
"The Sunny Southwest."

RAND, McNALLY & CO., PRINTERS, CHICAGO.

During the final third of the nineteenth century, the Missouri-Kansas-Texas ("Katy") was notable for the variety of its imprints, some of which featured odd graphic designs and obscure messages, as does this brochure cover image from the 1870s. The same was true for Chicago, Rock Island & Pacific imprints of the era, but one of its oddball publications from the mid-1870s was mean-spirited in its support of the popular California crusade to expel Chinese immigrants.

promotional brochures. From the dawn of the railroad era in the mid-1820s until the expansive decade of the 1880s, neither type of publication was visually attractive. There were exceptions, of course, but only during the final three decades of the nineteenth century did publications intended for public consumption—that is, railroad-generated commercial art—evolve from the drab black-and-white broadsides and text-only advertisements that the early railroads placed in local newspapers to communicate train times to the traveling public. Beginning most noticeably in

the 1890s, railroad publications employed a riotous mélange of color graphics to heighten the visual appeal of public timetables and their thousands of different brochures intended to promote vacation destinations as well as to entice settlers to create farms, ranches, and towns alongside newly laid tracks. California, Colorado, and Florida were probably the three states featured most often in the turn-of-the-century promotional blitz.[3]

North of the border, the Canadian Pacific actively encouraged immigrant farmers to settle the expansive prairie landscape that evolved into the provinces of Manitoba, Saskatchewan, and Alberta—as did its biggest rivals, the Grand Trunk Pacific and Canadian Northern, a generation later. In the United States the popular phrase was "winning the West," but diverse areas of the country apart from the trans-Mississippi West, most notably Florida, also received federal land grants to encourage railroad construction and settlement. To promote the sale as well as settlement of their vast land holdings, railroads discovered that commercial art enhanced the appeal of their many imprints. The array of increasingly attractive brochures, pamphlets, and handbooks after 1880 benefited from major improvements in printing technology, especially in the use of color. Railroad imprints grew most impressive during the two decades that followed the late-1890s revolution in color printing technology. In the early twentieth century, they grew increasingly vital to company profits because an estimated 50 percent of all passenger business was "created tourist traffic." Travel frequently termed "created" or "artificial" resulted from publishing activity that encouraged Americans and Canadians who might otherwise be content to remain at home to board trains to see for themselves the attractions promoted by railroad imprints.[4]

Initially (during the forty years from 1825 until 1865, from the birth of the modern railroad until the end of the American Civil War), the young industry spent its time perfecting its methods of operations. Section I of *Railroad Nation* thus offers an in-depth look at how tracks and trains profoundly reoriented North American time and space during these years of railroad growth and maturation. One useful phrase to describe this early evolution of the industry might be "from tentative and halting beginnings to confidence and mastery." Events during these four decades constitute the historical context from which commercial art emerged in the 1870s and 1880s and subsequently flowered until squelched during the Great War in 1918.

Before the 1870s, railroads gave little thought to the use of commercial art to illustrate their messages to travelers and potential settlers of their landed domains. If they sought increased impact, during the 1850s and 1860s they employed varied fonts of movable type to create flamboyant designs borrowed from the circus posters of the day. The 1870s' addition of color images to bold and creative arrangements of type forever banished the drabness of early imprints, or so it seemed until the federal

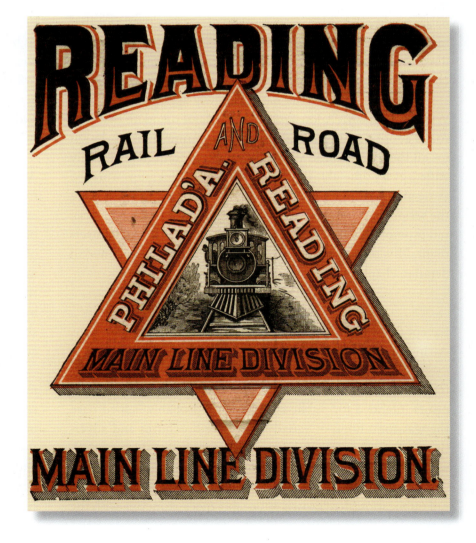

The cover ornament from an 1889 publication issued by the Philadelphia-based Reading illustrates the rail industry's late nineteenth-century transition from a heavy emphasis on creative arrangements of movable type to the increased use of pictorial art. One problem with advertisements created from typefaces was that their creative arrangement called more attention to the artwork than to the message.

government conscripted the industry for military service during World War I.

War in Europe toppled several great empires, and within the United States it upended the familiar world that American railroads and their publishing activity had done so much to create. The world of railroad graphics changed abruptly—and in many ways forever—after December 1917, when the federal government created the United States Railroad Administration (USRA). No clear precedent existed to guide Uncle Sam's new bureaucracy, one that now oversaw every detail of wartime rail operations across America—from the abandonment of marginal carriers (a first for the United States) to the food served aboard dining cars and the design of timetables and other publications that appeared on display racks. No detail, no matter how small or seemingly insignificant, escaped federal scrutiny, and that included the rail industry's decades-long patronage of artists, illustrators, and photographers to enhance their timetables, brochures, posters, and other types of promotional imprints.

In early April 1918, the nation's newly appointed rail czar, William Gibbs McAdoo, approved a federal mandate that railroads adopt a uniform and thoroughly unimaginative design for all their timetables. With rivalry among railroads officially stifled, every timetable cover in the literature racks now wore the same unappealing military drab and thus served to underscore the seriousness of the nation's latest military crusade. Likewise, rail promotional literature of all types vanished virtually overnight. This odd interlude in railroad publishing is explained in detail in chapter 19.

Except for America's World War I years, railroad publications during the opening decades of the twentieth century generally exemplified the best principles of layout and design. In fact, the industry's heavy use of commercial art to enliven its many imprints intended for public consumption probably helped pave the way for a flood of equally attractive brochures and advertisements from automobile manufacturers during the twentieth century.[5]

Several decades earlier, especially during the 1870s and 1880s, rail publications had grown noticeably more attractive with the increased use of chromolithography and better-quality coated papers. However, the color printing process of that era was both time-consuming and labor intensive because printers used successive ink-covered engraved stones, all placed in exact register atop one another, to create an image. The chromolithographs were vibrant and perhaps even stunning to eyes unaccustomed to many forms of color visual communication that we take for granted today. It is possible that chromolithographs and other rail-generated commercial art provided Americans their most insistent exposure to color printing before 1918.[6]

The desire for a quicker and simpler process than chromolithography resulted in the new multicolor printing technology developed in Germany just before 1900, but accounting for the desire of railroad management to use the newest and best color printing techniques and the latest principles of layout and design to boost the appeal of their timetables and promotional brochures entails a more complex explanation. The two motivating influences that stand out most clearly are railroad expansion across large and lightly populated swaths of the United States and Canada and the increasing amount of leisure time available to urban dwellers in both countries.[7]

In the late nineteenth and early twentieth centuries, North America's lightly populated frontier landscapes were located mainly in the western halves of both nations, but similar areas could be found in northern Michigan and across rural portions of the American South, and especially in Florida, which south of Tampa was little more than an unappealing mangrove swamp until the dawn of the twentieth century. Interestingly, in 1900 the two largest cities in Florida were Jacksonville and Key West, but railroads would soon rearrange the state's urban hierarchy by supporting the growth of Miami, Tampa, and other population centers.

The American and Canadian Wests traditionally commanded the most attention in terms of development activity, and railroad publishers did far more than the national governments of either nation to publicize to the world the positive attributes of those regions and to facilitate their settlement between the 1870s and the 1920s. Their motives were hardly altruistic: if their publications and various other forms of promotional activity could spur population growth and thus stimulate economic activity,

The undated *From the Mountains to the Gulf* brochure was issued by the East Tennessee, Virginia & Georgia, a future component of the Southern Railway.

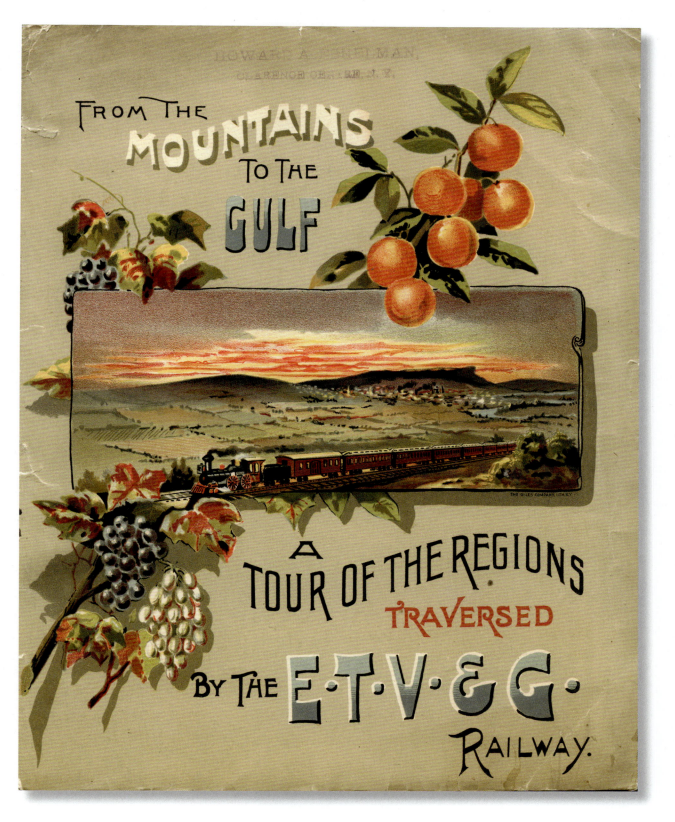

Springs Mountains and Sea Shore Resorts

Chesapeake & Ohio Ry.

Near Afton

Along the New River

W. C. Wickham, 2nd Vice President.

H. W. Fuller, Gen'l Pass. Ag't. RICHMOND, VA.

The Grand Scenic Route to the Sea.

Matthews, Northrup, & Co. Buffalo, N.Y.

railroads could then generate the passenger and freight traffic necessary to make profitable ventures of their latest extensions of track.

To that end, railroads issued thousands of different promotional brochures in English as well as in the languages of northern and western Europe to woo settlers from these favored nations as well as from populous parts of the United States and Canada. Their narrowly targeted advertising was a primary reason why, for example, Germans were prominent among the many settlers that railroads lured to North Dakota and why Scandinavians favored Minnesota and Wisconsin.

This population distribution can be attributed in large measure to the railroad as publisher. Moreover, individual railroads hired emigration agents to make certain their publications were liberally distributed at agricultural fairs and across northern and western Europe. They offered special low rates to enable migrants to continue from the Atlantic ports of both the United States and Canada to the promised lands abutting their tracks farther west.

Besides promoting settlement, railroads, after the American Civil War ended in 1865, sought to capitalize on the public's growing fondness for vacations and weekend outings. They progressively honed their publishing skills to describe with words and illustrations the delights of leisure time spent at Niagara Falls, an early and popular destination close to the main population centers of both the United States and Canada, and later, after railroads first made "wonderland" easily accessible to train travelers in the 1880s, the attractions of the more distant Yellowstone National Park, and finally, in the early twentieth century, the pleasures of Florida and the Gulf Coast.

Exaggeration became an accepted feature of railroad publishing, and it inspired some occasional good-natured commentary.

Facing, The Chesapeake & Ohio distinguished itself as a hauler of coal, and yet many of its late nineteenth-century publications promoted vacation travel. During the time span covered by *Railroad Nation*, the railroad also ran an uncommonly fine fleet of passenger trains via the West Virginia coal country to link Washington, DC, and the Norfolk area with Cincinnati.

A display rack filled with colorful railroad imprints presented a temptation to take "an armful of these folders home with you, spread 'em out on the table after dinner, and commence traveling. You can catch pike as long as the boat and bass the heft of a safe; you can pick roses the size of a bass drum or play football with oranges of the dreadnought type, plucking them from the trees while the proprietor of the grove stands by and grins—according to the folder." At the very least, the combination of verbal excess and the typical folder's numerous illustrations tempted readers to take no-cost vacations within their imaginations, as many people did.[8]

In those days real vacations, in contrast to the fantasy or paper variety, were limited to wealthy Americans and Canadians who had time and money enough to devote weeks and even months to leisure travel. The typical outing, on the other hand, consisted of a one-day or weekend trip from a crowded city to a nearby park or resort, and these short excursions appealed mainly to workers and their families who had but limited time and money to devote to personal pleasure. The workweek at the turn of the century typically included a full day of rest only on Sundays, and with the average annual wage being about $500, every penny spent on leisure activity counted.[9]

The numerous electric interurban lines that sprang up like mushrooms in the early twentieth century joined their steam railroad big brothers to issue highly illustrated brochures intended to promote one- or two-day outings and sometimes trips to more distant vacation destinations. During these years, even railroad companies usually regarded in more recent times as no-nonsense freight haulers issued colorful brochures that sought to promote vacations and outings to boost passenger revenues. One example was the Pittsburgh-based Bessemer & Lake Erie, usually thought of as little more than a conveyor belt for the iron ore that traveled across western Pennsylvania from ports on Lake Erie to the steel mills of Pittsburgh.

In sum, what I propose to offer readers on the following pages is an illustrated history, both chronological and topical, of the commercial art of railroad time and space as exemplified by the railroad as publisher. While my main purpose is to showcase a representative sampling of the incredible variety of publications issued by the railroads of North America, I believe in operating within a broadly defined historical context. To that end I will cast an occasional side glance at the art of time and space as illustrated by rail publications published in Great Britain as well as promotional brochures generated by steamship and intercity bus lines. In fact, numerous bus companies in the United States in the 1920s and 1930s were railroad owned, and their own colorful publications were influenced by their railroad overseers.

We begin with an overview chapter that looks at the evolution of American transportation during the lifespans of the two Lincolns. Father Abraham, an Illinois railroad lawyer before his White House years, was born in 1809, and his son Robert Todd Lincoln died in 1926, having recently served as president and then chairman of the board of the Chicago-based Pullman Company, famous for its railroad sleeping cars. Perhaps worth noting in terms of the years spanned by the two Lincolns, the first steamboat appeared on the rivers of the American West in 1811, and the epochal transatlantic solo flight of Charles A. Lindbergh took place in 1927—and did more than anything else to attract investors to commercial aviation, which by the 1950s had become a serious competitor to North America's railroads.

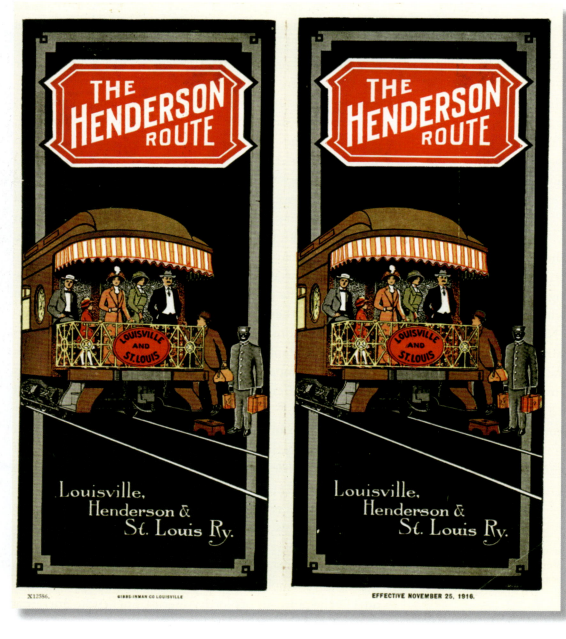

In contrast to the frilly commercial art favored by many railroads at the turn of the century, Henderson Route's 1916 timetable cover and its depiction of travelers aboard an end-of-train observation car was simple yet forceful. The Louisville, Henderson & St. Louis Railway became part of the Louisville & Nashville in 1929.

SECTION ONE

RAILROAD TIME AND SPACE

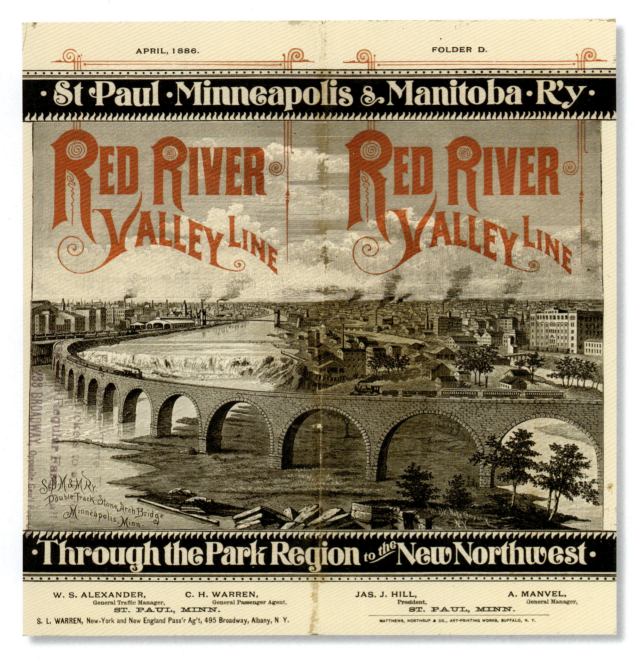

· St Paul · Minneapolis & Manitoba · R'y ·

RED RIVER VALLEY LINE　**RED RIVER VALLEY LINE**

S.P.M. & M.Ry.
Double Track Stone Arch Bridge
Minneapolis, Minn.

· Through the Park Region to the New Northwest ·

W. S. ALEXANDER,
General Traffic Manager,
ST. PAUL, MINN.

C. H. WARREN,
General Passenger Agent.

JAS. J. HILL,
President,
ST. PAUL, MINN.

A. MANVEL,
General Manager,

S. L. WARREN, New-York and New England Pass'r Ag't, 495 Broadway, Albany, N. Y.

MATTHEWS, NORTHRUP & CO., ART-PRINTING WORKS, BUFFALO, N. Y.

The St. Paul, Minneapolis & Manitoba (which in 1890 became part of the Great Northern Railway) saluted its massive stone arch bridge across the Mississippi River on its 1886 timetable cover. A counterpart to the Minneapolis engineering masterpiece was the even more technologically daring Eads Bridge in Saint Louis, which when completed in 1874 was the first in the world to use steel, a new construction material to extend tracks across the nation's greatest waterway. For years the timetable covers of the Ohio & Mississippi Railroad (later the Baltimore & Ohio Southwestern) saluted James Buchanan Eads's remarkable feat of engineering.

The Railroad mania, which is beginning to prevail in the United States with the universality of an epidemic, will divest many of our citizens of their prudence, and involve them in absurd and ruinous expenditures on Railroads, where the scarceness of population, or physical obstacles, render them inexpedient.

—from *American Railroad Journal* (1832)[1]

Railroads, as a means for transportation, have been long in use upon a limited scale; but it is only within the short period of ten or twelve years, that they have been successfully applied to purposes of general traffic.

—from *American Railroad Journal* (1837)[2]

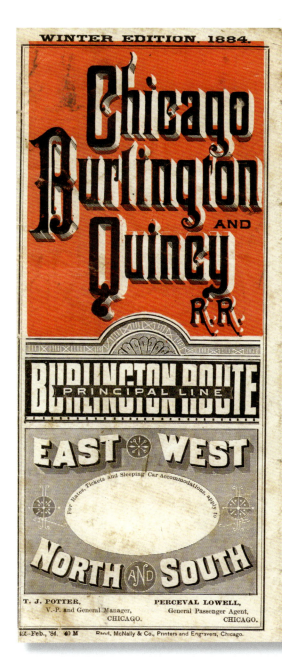

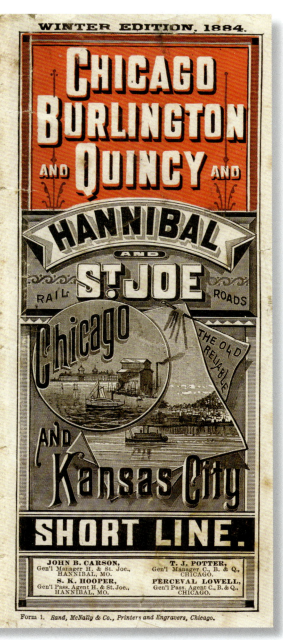

The construction of railroads is probably the most engrossing subject now occupying the attention of our people. Every portion of our country is aroused to their importance.

—from Henry V. Poor, *American Railroad Journal* (1850)[3]

The Chicago, Burlington & Quincy acquired the Hannibal & St. Joseph to extend the commercial reach of Chicago across the fertile farmlands of northern Missouri to the emerging metropolis of Kansas City.

Cover art favored for numerous rail promotional imprints, such as the Wisconsin Central's *Summer of 1888* featured here, could be described as dainty or sweet. Life on a steam railroad was grimy, greasy, and dangerous, but industry publicists, whose job it was to encourage trip planning, consciously sought to appeal to women. Wives played a major role in selecting family vacation destinations and thus were supposed to be impressed by artwork that featured women and emphasized the "soft side" of railroad operations.

When we consider that from that day to this over 150,000 miles of railroad have been built in the United States, one can comprehend the strides the railway has made up to date, but its future possibilities cannot be imagined.

—from Grenville M. Dodge, *Paper Read before the Society of the Army of the Tennessee* (1888)[4]

The Saint Louis, Iron Mountain & Southern (the "Iron Mountain Route"), part of the rail empire assembled by Jay Gould, used the printing press to encourage travel to Texas and its settlement. Austin may have functioned as the political capital of the Lone Star State, but for decades its de facto economic capital was Saint Louis, the nation's fourth-largest metropolis at the dawn of the twentieth century.

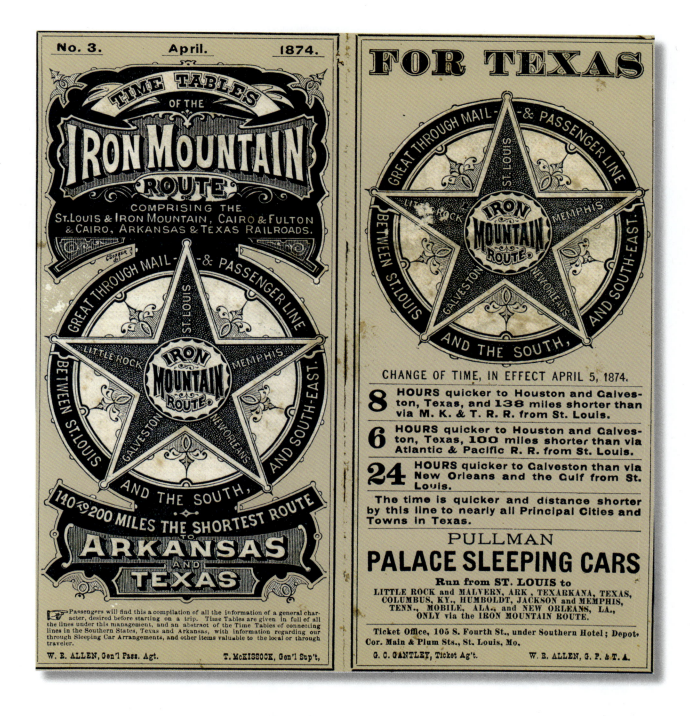

The object of the Road, to put it plainly, is to put settlers and industries along the Road, simply and solely to create more local traffic, freight, and passengers; the lands are now cheap.

—from Houston East & West Texas Railway, *Texas* (1894)[5]

" . . . THAT THIS NATION, UNDER GOD, SHALL HAVE A NEW BIRTH OF FREEDOM . . . AND THAT GOVERNMENT OF THE PEOPLE, BY THE PEOPLE, FOR THE PEOPLE, SHALL NOT PERISH FROM THE EARTH"

BUY WAR BONDS

"'Mary [his wife] insists, however, that I am going to be Senator and President of the United States, too.' These last words he followed with a roar of laughter, with his arms around his knees, and shaking all over with mirth at his wife's ambition. 'Just think, [Lincoln] exclaimed, of such a sucker as me as President!'"

—from *Memoirs of Henry Villard, Journalist and Financier, 1835–1900* (1904)[1]

Michigan's Pere Marquette used the back cover of a 1943 timetable to invoke patriotic memories of Lincoln during America's World War II fight and to urge travelers to buy war bonds.

1

TIMELINE AND OVERVIEW

THE TWO LINCOLNS AND THE AMERICAN RAILROAD

The century covered in *Railroad Nation* was a remarkable time in the history of American transportation. The emergence and evolution of rail imprints and the industry's increased use of commercial art are topics conveniently encompassed within the lifespans of the two Lincolns, father Abraham and son Robert Todd Lincoln, from 1809 to 1926, and so we begin our story here. History recalls Abraham as America's beloved Civil War president and martyr, but before he took up residence in the White House, he had already made a name for himself as a railroad lawyer in Illinois. Robert Todd Lincoln returned to his family's roots in Illinois, where from 1911 to 1922 he served as president and then chairman of the board of the Pullman Company, based in Chicago. During the years of Lincoln's stewardship, Pullman's fleet of railroad sleeping cars constituted the largest hotel chain in the world.[2]

During the decades bookended by the lives of the two Lincolns, the railroads of North America passed through several distinct phases. The first was a time devoted to the exchange of abstract ideas and isolated experiments that predated the opening in 1825 of the world's first railway of the modern era, the Stockton & Darlington in northeast England. Then followed two decades of trial-and-error experimentation, of self-trained civil engineers and tinkerers putting their ideas to work to discover which technologies might succeed and which would fail. One result was the rapid multiplication of railroads across the eastern half of the United States during the 1840s and 1850s. The coalescence of numerous locally oriented railroad lines into a North American system featuring a standardized time and track gauge took place mainly during the 1880s and 1890s. The exercise of unprecedented power by the railroad industry in the late nineteenth century culminated in the enactment of federal and state regulations during the so-called Progressive Era of the early twentieth century. By 1914 the millions of restrictions that covered nearly every aspect of railroading had achieved their purpose. While the results satisfied a cohort of meddlesome "progressive" politicians, the burden of endless regulation incapacitated the industry financially and left it starved for the investor dollars required to modernize its rolling stock and support structure. Finally, of great importance toward the end of the span of time highlighted by *Railroad Nation* was the steadily rising tide of nonrail competition, which grew ever more worrisome to the formerly imperious railroad industry after 1914.

During his early life in frontier Kentucky, Indiana, and Illinois, Abraham Lincoln witnessed the slow dawn of steam-powered transportation. The year he was born, 1809, there was none west of the Appalachians, but change was soon coming. Lincoln was a toddler when the first vessel powered by steam left Pennsylvania and paddled west along the interior waterways that blessed the nation's Middle West. It steamed down the Ohio River and along the shores of the three states that defined the life of Lincoln before the White House. Nicholas Roosevelt had overseen construction of the *New Orleans* in Pittsburgh and now served as its captain on a maiden voyage downriver to its namesake city. Although the use of steam to power anything mobile was a novelty in 1811, Roosevelt had enough confidence in himself and his pioneering handiwork to bring his pregnant wife and young daughter along as passengers. His son was born aboard the *New Orleans* near Louisville, Kentucky.[3]

During the night of December 15, 1811, Roosevelt may have had second thoughts about including his young family on a voyage subject to many unknowns and potential dangers. That night one of the strongest earthquakes ever recorded on the North American continent—centered in New Madrid, Missouri—momentarily caused the Mississippi River to run backward and thus worsened the hours of terror for settlers living along its banks. The *New Orleans*, if it continued downriver, would need to pass New Madrid and navigate a waterway that the earthquake had made unfamiliar even to veteran boatmen. Thus was the American heartland introduced simultaneously to the uncontrollable and capricious power of nature and the useful power of steam.[4]

The *New Orleans* did reach its namesake city, and during the next several years an increasing number of steamboats joined the various unmechanized watercraft already in use along the length of the natural highways formed by the Mississippi, Ohio, Illinois, Missouri, and numerous other navigable rivers of the Midwest. Exactly half a century later in 1861, the year President Lincoln entered the White House, a steamboat probed the final navigable stretch of the great river highway that extended three thousand miles inland from New Orleans when it completed a voyage from Saint Louis to Fort Benton, Montana, which could legitimately claim to be the farthest-inland port in the world.[5]

Long before steamboats achieved that milestone, mechanically minded individuals in England had harnessed steam to power yet another new mode of transportation: the railroad. That took place in 1825, a landmark year that also witnessed the completion of the Erie Canal in the United States to link the city of New York with the Great Lakes and thus enable the young metropolis to gain coveted access to the nation's foremost agricultural cornucopia. On the opposite side of the Atlantic, the trains of the Stockton & Darlington Railway showed the world what the union of steam locomotion and iron rails could accomplish. The world was never the same after 1825 whether by canal or railway.[6]

That was the year Lincoln turned sixteen, and many more years would pass before he and other midwesterners saw their first railroad or steam locomotive. For them, the natural water highways sufficed. Lincoln's first paying job was to ferry passengers to and from steamboats plying the Ohio River. Later, in 1828, he and a friend named Allen Gentry successfully guided a flatboat load of Midwest farm produce down the Mississippi River all the way to New Orleans, the southern metropolis where Lincoln witnessed his first slave auction. In 1830, the Lincoln family relocated from Indiana to unimproved land two hundred miles north along the Sangamon River near Decatur, Illinois. It was there that Lincoln gave his first political speech: he spoke in favor of improving navigation on the Sangamon River.

All across the Midwest, the pace of life noticeably increased during the 1830s, and the call for improved transportation became a common refrain. The completion of the Erie Canal in 1825 greatly quickened the pulse of the young nation. Merchants in the major port cities of the East Coast took note as commerce flowing along the Erie Canal between New York and the Midwest swelled from a mere stream into a veritable river. They grew jealous, then fearful, and finally they panicked lest their own cities—most notably the ports of Boston, Philadelphia, Baltimore, and Charleston—suffer from the stiff competition. But therein lay a major problem, and how these other cities might best solve it was by no means clear. Only one place in the entire chain of mountains that stretched from Maine to Georgia offered a feasible path for a canal between the East Coast and the Great Lakes, and that place was already occupied by the Erie

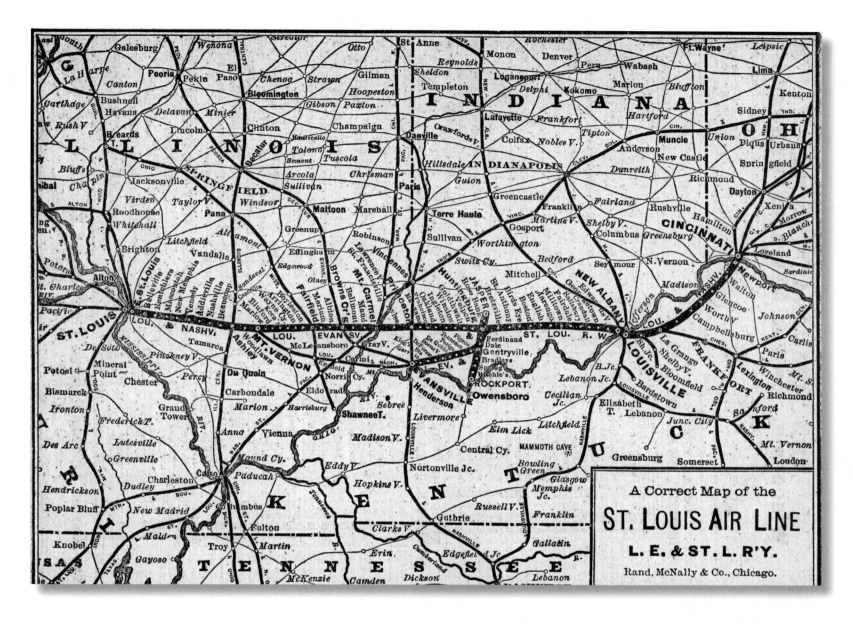

A Correct Map of the
ST. LOUIS AIR LINE
L. E. & ST. L. R'Y.
Rand, McNally & Co., Chicago.

Canal through upstate New York. Boosters of Boston, Baltimore, and Charleston placed their hopes in the railroad, though no one in the late 1820s knew whether iron wheels on iron rails could climb mountain grades. Philadelphia merchants opted for a hybrid combination of railways and canals to reach across the Appalachians to Pittsburgh, where the Ohio River provided them easy access to the fertile heartland.

In the Midwest itself, the success of the Erie Canal inspired local promoters to envision and then construct two canals that

An 1885 map of the St. Louis Air Line provides a graphic overview of the heartland area that the young Abraham Lincoln called home. The western portion of the route later formed part of the expansion-minded Southern Railway.

Great Iron Bridge of the C. R. I. & P. R. R., between Rock Island and Davenport.

The Chicago & Rock Island constructed its first bridge across the Mississippi River of wood. After it burned under mysterious circumstances in 1856, the rail line constructed the sturdier structure of iron pictured here. Abraham Lincoln served as the company's attorney.

extended across Ohio from Lake Erie to the Ohio River, and yet another canal crossed neighboring Indiana with the same objective. In 1848, Illinois completed a canal between Lake Michigan and the Illinois River to forge an important new transportation corridor between the Great Lakes at Chicago and the Mississippi River near Saint Louis.[7]

The desire to construct canals to reap the economic benefits they supposedly guaranteed turned into a veritable craze during the fifteen years after the completion of the Erie Canal, but slowly, almost as a sideshow to the transportation drama of the canal age, railroads began to gain favor. Even more than with steamboats and canals, technological uncertainties defined the early years of railroads. No one knew what innovations might work successfully during the coming years and what innovations might seem promising but lead to costly and time-consuming dead ends. Philadelphia, the nation's premier city when the Erie Canal was completed, was so concerned about the advantages the waterway conferred on New York that it hastened to implement a transportation corridor of its own to the Midwest, which turned out to be expensive and the ultimate example of a dead-end technology.[8]

Enthusiasm for canals waned after the Panic of 1837, and the youthful railroads increasingly flexed their impressive technological muscles. Nonetheless, along the natural waterways of the Midwest, no victor clearly emerged until the mid-1850s, and here the young lawyer Lincoln scored an important victory for the railroads. The case had its origins in the bridge the Chicago & Rock Island Railroad extended across the Mississippi River in 1856 to push the spatial reach of the young giant of a city emerging on the southern shore of Lake Michigan west into the farmlands of Iowa.

The problem was that Saint Louis, a much older and much larger city than Chicago in the 1850s, had enjoyed decades of prosperity as a result of its domination of the commerce that flowed along the main water highways of the Midwest, and Saint Louisans feared the newfound expansiveness of the emerging rival to the north.[9] Just as the port cities of the East Coast jealously guarded their commercial hinterlands, so did Saint Louis, which until challenged by Chicago in the 1850s possessed what was probably the most extensive commercial hinterland in the entire United States. Steamboats plying the Mississippi, Illinois, Ohio, and Missouri Rivers and numerous smaller tributaries defined its spatial reach, and where steamboats could go no farther, a series of trails extended the reach of Saint Louis overland to Santa Fe in northern Mexico, to Salt Lake City, to the mouth of the Columbia River in Oregon, and even to San Francisco Bay after the United States acquired California in the late 1840s. Not without reason was Saint Louis called "the gateway to the West."[10]

The Rock Island's new bridge across the Upper Mississippi threatened the hegemony of Saint Louis. By enabling trains from Chicago to cross the great waterway, the Illinois-based railroad gained access to some of the most fertile land in the United States, areas that needed rail transportation to awaken their full economic potential. Moreover, Iowa's relatively flat prairie landscape encouraged railroad builders to continue laying track west all the way to the Missouri River and beyond. That meant Chicago could use its railroads to amputate Saint Louis's lucrative steamboat trade north of the railheads at Rock Island on the Mississippi River and at Omaha on the Missouri River. Perhaps it is coincidental, but probably not, that a Saint Louis–based steamboat, the *Effie Afton*, crashed into the new railroad bridge at Rock Island only days after it opened. The resulting fire destroyed the wooden structure and sent the embers floating gently down the Mississippi past Saint Louis, much to the delight of legions of steamboatmen who called the Missouri metropolis home. This was the basis for the lawsuit Lincoln argued for the railroad.[11]

Later as president, Lincoln signed two major pieces of railroad legislation, both of which greatly benefited Chicago and vastly expanded its commercial hinterland at the expense of Saint Louis. The first measure, in 1862, provided federal support for the construction of the nation's first transcontinental railroad, which proposed to connect Omaha with Sacramento. Lying due west across the prairies of Illinois and Iowa from Chicago, Omaha could easily be linked to the eastern half of the United States by means of a continuous line of tracks connecting through the metropolis growing rapidly along the southwestern shore of Lake Michigan. The second measure, in 1864, provided federal support for a second transcontinental railroad to be built between Lake Superior and Puget Sound on the Pacific coast. Lying still farther north, it too would become a natural tributary of Chicago and further extend its commercial hinterland across an area once claimed by Saint Louis and the huge fleet of steamboats based there.[12]

In April 1865, at the time of Lincoln's assassination, the United States had been bound together once again by force of arms, though only weeks had passed since General Robert E. Lee and a last major Southern army had surrendered at Appomattox in Virginia. With the return of peace, the nation could focus its attention on improving its existing railroads and constructing thousands of miles of new lines to develop vast swaths of lightly populated land in the West and South. The decades from 1865 until 1915 would be the heyday of railroad empire builders James J. Hill in the Northwest, Henry Flagler in Florida, and several others.[13]

All the while, the comfort of long-distance train travel across the sprawling network of railroads that blanketed the United States, Canada, and Mexico noticeably improved. At the forefront was George Mortimer Pullman, the Chicago innovator who made his reputation and his personal fortune by building and operating a huge fleet of railroad sleeping cars. So comfortable and so extensive was his network of "palaces on wheels" that the Pullman name became synonymous with the sleeping car, and all would-be competitors fell by the wayside. At the time that President Lincoln's son Robert Todd became president of the company, Pullman operated a fleet of cars that numbered in the thousands.[14]

When Robert Todd Lincoln died in 1926, the most comfortable way to travel anywhere in North America was aboard a Pullman car, but during his eleven-year tenure as head of the

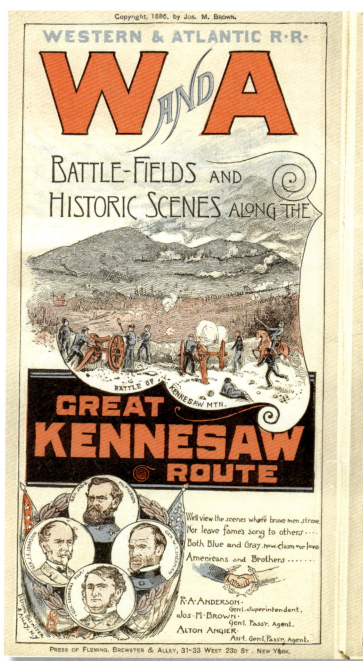
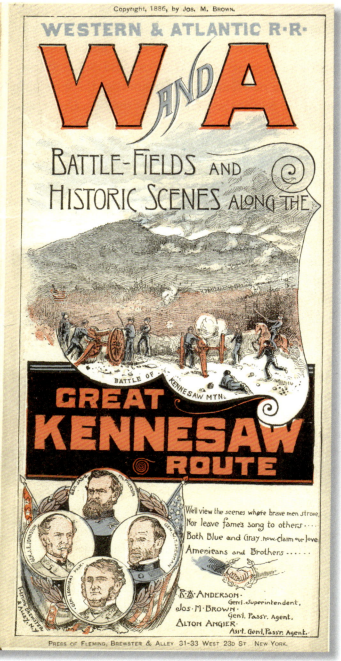

North or South, tourism to Civil War battlefields was popular among railroad publicists in the late nineteenth century. In 1862, Western & Atlantic tracks between Atlanta and Chattanooga were the setting for a wartime drama that Walt Disney later immortalized in a 1956 film titled *The Great Locomotive Chase*. The railroad issued this colorful commemorative brochure in 1886.

company, the railroad industry of North America had changed dramatically, and not necessarily for the better. Ten years earlier, in 1916, the network of rail lines across the United States had reached its peak mileage. In December of the following year, the United States government took over operation of the railroads as a wartime measure, and even after World War I ended in November 1918, Uncle Sam kept his hand firmly on the throttle until March 1920, when the federal government ended its hamfisted conscription of the railroads and returned them to their investor owners.

By March 1920 it was abundantly clear that the exuberant era of railroad expansion was finished, and, in fact, the industry's golden age was past. Each year during the 1920s, highway competitors—private automobiles, intercity bus companies, and finally intercity truck lines—took an increasingly large bite out of railroad profits, at first most noticeably for local passenger trains but toward the end of the decade also for freight, the railroad industry's bread and butter. After Charles A. Lindbergh thrilled the world by becoming the first person to fly solo across the Atlantic, from New York to Paris, during the summer of 1927, the United States became "air-minded" as never before, and Wall Street investors rushed to bankroll a host of new commercial airlines that in future decades would only add to the competition railroads increasingly faced.[15]

By the late 1920s, railroads no longer dominated everyday life as they formerly had; nonetheless, during the nearly 120 years spanned by the lives of the two Lincolns, the railroads of North America had dramatically reordered both time and space. The world was never to be the same. How one of the most remarkable transformations in world history unfolded is documented by railroad imprints. Section I of *Railroad Nation* offers an overview of several milestone events during the first century of North America's railroads that are key to an understanding of railroad time and space, while section II illustrates how the industry's remarkable outpouring of commercial art encouraged spatial reinvention and heightened time consciousness.

During the 1920s, the Chicago & Alton inaugurated trains called Abraham Lincoln and Ann Rutledge. They connected Lincoln's hometown of Springfield many times daily with Chicago and Saint Louis. The railroad offered free stopovers to enable travelers to tour central Illinois sites related to the martyred president. Ann Rutledge was allegedly Lincoln's first ladylove. The brochure cover pictured here dates from 1937 and salutes the railroad's introduction of diesel locomotives to power the Abraham Lincoln.

The Iron Mountain Route, like the Missouri-Kansas-Texas, also based in Saint Louis, indulged in some truly whimsical artwork. It is possible that both railroads employed the same artist in 1894 to emphasize their speedy connections to Texas and the Southwest.

In this country our railroad experience has been short, and we have much to learn yet in reference not only to their construction, but their management.

—from *American Railroad Journal* (1849)[1]

2

COMING TO TERMS WITH THE WONDER OF THE AGE

The decades of the 1830s and 1840s were a time of boundless possibilities for most Americans. A band of religious zealots popularly known as Millerites predicted the return of Christ and a fiery end for a sinful world in 1844, but America's prevailing optimism silenced all but the most persistent naysayers. Proposals for improvement in all fields of endeavor regularly stirred the national consciousness, and some gained their advocates a measure of popular support. Some "scientific" claims that to subsequent generations may seem preposterous appeared credible enough during that era of boundless possibilities to warrant serious investigation.[2]

Vigorously advancing one such idea was John Cleves Symmes Jr., who asserted that the earth was hollow and open at both poles. Inside the sphere was located the best farmland imaginable. The "holes at the poles" assertion gained enough traction on Capitol Hill that in 1836 the seemingly rational members of Congress funded a four-year expedition by the United States Navy that circumnavigated the globe between 1838 and 1842, in part to assess the validity of Symmes's hollow earth assertion. At southerly latitudes the ships found plenty of ice but no evidence to support the "holes at the poles" claim. The frozen rim

of Antarctica called Wilkes Land recalls Charles Wilkes, the commander of the United States Exploring Expedition.[3]

Many of the seemingly preposterous ideas of the age were tested by on-site observation, as was true for the Wilkes Expedition, or by trial and error, or both. Formal training in civil engineering was limited to the ranks of America's military, and scientific understanding was for the most part still rudimentary. University-trained "experts" did not yet dominate the national marketplace of technological ideas. As a result, American technology in the 1830s and 1840s was amazingly democratic in its accessibility and eclectic in its potential applications, two characteristics that contributed to a sense of boundlessness and optimism in the young republic.[4]

To evaluate firsthand the frothy mix of technological wonder and potential humbug, European observers regularly sailed to North America, while Americans traveled to England, the world's "Mother of Railroads," to learn what they could by observing early English practices and railways in action. No one thought of these observers as industrial spies, and fortunately they were not at all secretive about their intentions or their observations. The result was the detailed documentation of North American

TRIAL OF TREVITHICK'S ENGINE ON A CIRCULAR RAILWAY, IN A FIELD NEAR THE NEW ROAD, LONDON, 1808.

The progression from Richard Trevithick's Circular Railway, the steam-powered curiosity displayed in London's Euston Square during the summer in 1808, to bona fide steam railways like the Stockton & Darlington and Liverpool & Manchester in England and the Baltimore & Ohio in the United States took place over the span of a single generation.

railroads in their infancy—the successful experiments no less than the humbugs and technological dead ends. Among the perceptive European observers of the era were Michael Chevalier from France and Anton von Gerstner from Germany. The massive reports each man compiled for his national patron provide a wealth of details on the state of the railroads built in the United

States and Canada during the 1830s and 1840s, the golden age of trial-and-error "engineering." No one could yet say with assurance what inventions or applications might work and what assuredly would not, especially in terms of railroad technology.[5]

Chevalier's fellow countryman Alexis de Tocqueville is far better known today for his own personal observations published in the 1830s as *Democracy in America*. By contrast, Chevalier's firsthand account of the technological democracy that prevailed in America in the 1830s is largely forgotten, but it is nonetheless exceedingly valuable as a study that preserved for future generations the many exciting possibilities of that pioneering era of railroads. Complementing Chevalier's numerous observations from the French perspective were those of his German contemporary Franz Anton Ritter von Gerstner, who was likewise fascinated by American transportation and communication technology during the 1830s and who published his own evaluation in a thick volume called *Die inner Communicationen* (1842–1843).[6]

As with technology, no prior organizational model prevailed in terms of how best to manage a railroad once tracks were on the ground and trains streamed along them. Some observers as late as the 1840s speculated that it was humanly impossible to manage competently a railroad any longer than 150 miles.[7] That was because an effectively managed enterprise of any size in the 1830s and 1840s typically consisted of managers and employees who worked within shouting distance of one another. As noted earlier, export-import businesses located on the New York waterfront adopted the face-to-face management model that prevailed aboard large sailing ships, an intimate relationship with which they would have already been thoroughly familiar. That is, to oversee his roomful of clerks, the managing partner of a typical countinghouse stationed himself atop a raised platform analogous to the quarterdeck of a ship. No employee was beyond his line of sight. Railroads, on the other hand, required the successful management of an extended workplace, an unprecedented spatial challenge that lent itself to as much managerial trial and error as did the evolving technology of tracks and locomotives.[8]

The American historian George Rogers Taylor published an account of the era of Chevalier and Gerstner in his book *The Transportation Revolution, 1815–1860*. The title is certainly a fitting description of how new transportation technologies, some of them originally quite rudimentary, evolved and soon became powerful enough to redefine dramatically the spatial relationships within the young American republic. This revolution was wrought mainly by steamboats, canals, and railroads, three modes of transport that borrowed from and amplified the attributes of one another. It was the steamboat, not the railroad, that first familiarized Americans with the almost magical power of steam to propel vehicles, and it was the Erie Canal and its surveyors and builders that did much to impart a modicum of mathematical consciousness to a generation of self-trained tinkerers who would be attracted to the subsequent "science" of railroad building. With not one American school apart from West Point equipped to teach formal courses in civil engineering, the construction of the Erie Canal functioned as a hands-on university to train "students" to go forth and supervise the construction of other canals, much as America's first true railroad, the Baltimore & Ohio, did for the building and operating of other railroads after it commenced running trains in 1830.[9]

Five years later, in mid-1835, the *American Railroad Journal* announced that trustees of the Rensselaer Institute in upstate New York had approved the formation of a school of civil engineers, a landmark event in the history of American railroads. "This is the first school of the kind ever organized on this continent. The Royal Military Academy at Woolwich, England, and the Polytechnic, in Paris, have branches nearly similar." The journal added that "a very spirited corps of 6 or 8 young gentlemen have already entered the division and will probably offer themselves for the degree of Civil Engineer in October."[10]

In 1825, when the Erie Canal was completed across New York from Albany on the Hudson River to Buffalo on Lake Erie, it easily formed the showpiece of the nation's transportation revolution. Though cargo traveled along the canal at the slow pace defined by mules and horses, the waterway efficiently surmounted the once-formidable Appalachian Divide by means of a series of locks and thus became a conduit for a new and lucrative stream of commerce between the agricultural states bordering the Great Lakes and the Atlantic seaport of New York City. How the Erie Canal wrought a spatial transformation that redefined basic economic and social relationships up and down the Atlantic Seaboard is aptly described by historian W. J. Rorabaugh in his book *The Alcoholic Republic*. He explains how the products of field and orchard grown in western Pennsylvania and Ohio that once found their most lucrative market as whiskey, hard apple cider, and other easily transported alcoholic beverages could travel profitably to markets in New York City via the Erie Canal as regular agricultural commodities.[11]

A common belief at the time was that "trade was like water" in that it invariably flowed along the path of least resistance, and thus New York City's easy access to the grain fields and orchards of the Midwest via the Erie Canal frightened rival ports along the Atlantic Seaboard, and their responses likewise worried New York, which, in the words of a Baltimore newspaper in 1835, was "alarmed for her Western Trade, and well may she be. Pennsylvania has the shortest, cheapest and quickest line of communication between the West and the Atlantic, and we venture to assert without hesitation that her immense line of Canals will in a short time be as much thronged with trade as those of New York now are."[12]

The merchants of the Atlantic port cities refused to concede a market this lucrative to New York City without a technological response of their own. Boston, Baltimore, and Charleston all chose to embrace the fledgling railroad as their economic savior, while the region surrounding the nation's capital in Washington chose to construct the Chesapeake and Ohio Canal. Philadelphia, which was the nation's foremost city before the Erie Canal and which had the most to lose in terms of its commerce with the Midwest, sought to surmount the Appalachian Mountains that bisected Pennsylvania, but without the topographical advantage exploited by builders of the Erie Canal across upstate New York. The canal and railroad technologies of the day could not breach the mountain barrier alone. Thus, Philadelphia and the state of

OPENING OF THE STOCKTON AND DARLINGTON RAILWAY, SEPTEMBER 27, 1825.

Pennsylvania bankrolled a creative yet peculiar hybrid system that combined a series of canals with inclined-plane railroads.[13]

In the early 1830s, it was by no means certain that railroads offered a significant advantage over canals and navigable rivers. The experts had not yet proved that iron wheels on iron rails could climb a grade of any consequence. Many an early railroad enterprise in the United States was built only to supplement the nation's waterways. Hence, the corporate title of Baltimore's railroad, the Baltimore & Ohio, spoke to the city's intention to extend tracks west to the Ohio River and its agricultural hinterland. The name of another early railroad referenced both the Delaware and Hudson Rivers. Even something so basic as the rails themselves became the subject of a great deal of trial and error in the 1830s. While some contemporary observers thought in terms of tracks on the ground, others insisted that iron rails should rest on raised supports formed from wood or granite blocks.[14]

Another fundamental question was whether the rails themselves should be made completely of iron. Wood was exceedingly plentiful in the young American republic, and thus to save construction dollars the body of a rail could be fashioned cheaply from wood and topped with a bearing surface of strap iron. Rails of this type were common on the railroads of the United States before the Civil War.

It is significant that in Great Britain, where American observers traveled in the 1820s to see for themselves the latest advances in railway construction and operation, the railway track from that day to this is called "the permanent way," while early railroads in the United States were so cheaply constructed from materials readily at hand that the word *permanent* could never describe any aspect of their right-of-way location or their infrastructure. One railroad advocate in the mid-1830s urged builders to avoid the expense of using cuts and fills to cross undulating terrain and said that if the tracks "were to be extended several miles to avoid crossing a hill, as they are cheaply made, the increased length is no great evil." One mile of track in the United States cost only about one-fourth as much as in Great

Britain. The impression prevailed in England that the typical American railroad was a "light and flimsy affair," but Yankees turned such criticism to their advantage when they noted, for example, that "our stations have been built for use, not show, and are more convenient, but less costly, than the English." As time passed, American railroads would spend millions of dollars to upgrade many of their early and frugally built rights-of-way and stations.[15]

Tracks, bridges, stations, and all other features of the American railroad landscape were to a surprising degree fashioned from wood, and hence they were ephemeral, destined to be replaced by better structures once more money was in hand. Trees were so numerous across Pennsylvania ("Penn's woods"), for example, that some observers claimed squirrels could easily cross from one end of the state to the other without leaving the treetops. In an 1846 essay that compared British and American practices, the *Edinburgh Review* observed that the railroads of the United States had substantially reduced the cost of construction by building few viaducts and tunnels, unlike lines built in the United Kingdom: "Where the lines have to be conducted over streams or rivers, bridges are constructed, in a rude but substantial and secure manner, of timber, which is supplied from forests at the road side, subject to no cost save that of hewing it. The station houses, booking offices, and other buildings, are likewise slightly and cheaply constructed of timber."[16]

Wood also provided cheap fuel for American locomotives. Even as late as the 1860s, railroads occasionally switched between wood and coal to explore further the problems associated with each and to determine which offered the most cost-effective way to power the trains. A foreign visitor described the ride behind a wood-burning locomotive: with wood as fuel, "there is an incessant shower of sparks, destructive to dress and comfort, unless all the windows are shut; which is impossible in warm weather." Yes, early American railroads appeared insubstantial to British observers, but worth noting is the claim voiced in 1832 that small "railroads made entirely of wood and even conforming nearly to the natural surface of the country, have, in [a] large number of cases repaid their cost, even in a few months."[17]

America's self-anointed railroad experts learned valuable lessons from their trial-and-error methods, and, more importantly, they did not hesitate to share what they learned with one another. Their preferred method was to publish their thoughts and observations not in huge volumes such as Chevalier and von Gerstner prepared for their respective European governments but in pamphlets, following a long-standing American tradition. Numerous pamphleteers had fostered the American Revolution, and a subsequent generation of wordsmiths had prepared and published arguments for and against the construction of the Erie Canal. Long before the first spade of earth was dug to inaugurate the construction of the Baltimore & Ohio Railroad, pamphleteers had been busy exchanging with any willing readers their ideas on the value of railroads. In other words, the work of publishing about the railroad began well before America had a bona fide railroad in operation.[18]

Several landmark events took place at the dawn of the 1830s. Britain's Liverpool & Manchester Railway formally opened on September 15, 1830, with festivities attended by Arthur Wellesley—the Duke of Wellington, current prime minister, and hero of the Battle of Waterloo with his victory over Napoleon in 1815—but the day was marred by one of the first passenger fatalities of the railway age when British statesman William Huskisson accidentally stepped into the path of one of the railway's steam locomotives. A few months earlier, on the opposite side of the Atlantic, a Baltimore & Ohio horse-drawn coach had completed the thirteen-mile journey to Ellicott's Mills on May 22, 1830, to open America's own pioneer railroad. The Maryland community, now renamed Ellicott City, is recognized as the site of the oldest surviving rail station in North America, which dates from 1831.[19]

Also, on July 4, 1831, the Western Hemisphere's first serial publication devoted to railroads, the *Rail-Road Advocate*, launched a brave publishing venture that lasted less than a year. Based in Rogersville, a village in the hills of East Tennessee and a location several hundred miles from the nearest tracks, the plucky journal frequently filled its eight pages with news of canals and other internal improvements to supplement its meager coverage of railroad happenings. On one occasion it filled an entire page with a copy of the fifth annual report of the Liverpool

& Manchester Railway. Though it is unlikely that anyone living in Tennessee had seen a railroad, no one could accuse the *Rail-Road Advocate* of being insular.[20]

In early 1832, a few months before the demise of its Tennessee predecessor, a second landmark publishing venture appeared as the *American Rail-Road Journal*. Like the rail industry itself, the new publication was "an experiment, and by many deemed one of doubtful issue." The paucity of rail news and paid subscribers was troublesome and on occasion forced the brave venture to add filler that bore no relationship to railroads. The journal suspended publication for several weeks in 1837 "for the reason that we cannot collect money enough to pay the compositors and pressmen for printing it."[21]

The 1830s issues of America's second rail publication are fascinating reading because its successive issues not only discussed railroad innovations that worked as intended but also speculated about various possibilities that never panned out. If early locomotives could not surmount a grade of any consequence,

a common belief, then why not use water-filled locks to raise or lower locomotives and cars hydraulically. Steep inclines that used cables powered by stationary steam engines offered yet another intriguing way to surmount a steep grade, one that Pennsylvania used to cross the Appalachian Divide, which separated Philadelphia from Pittsburgh.[22] The *American Railroad Journal* was based in New York City, and it grew and matured along with the industry it covered. The publication remained in business into the early twentieth century, and its successive issues provide an invaluable historical record that spans many decades. During the nineteenth century, when railroad construction energized the United States and forged new spatial relationships, industry trade journals were published in Boston, Philadelphia, Chicago, Saint Louis, and Cincinnati, in addition to New York City.[23]

Cincinnati, once the most populous city in the Midwest until surpassed by Saint Louis and then Chicago, was home to the *Railroad Record*, which kept readers abreast of the frenzy of railroad construction activity that took place across the nation's heartland during the 1850s. The heyday of railroad-oriented journalism was probably from 1880 until 1915, after which many formerly successful publications merged or shut down their presses as the industry's earlier enthusiasm waned as a result of federal and state regulatory measures.[24]

TRANSPORTATION TIPPING POINT

The merits of canals versus railroads became the subject of a lively public debate in the 1830s and 1840s, but improvements in technology tipped the scales: "Canals may carry cheaper, but railroads are quicker, and what is of not less importance, can be used every month of the year, while canals are closed for at least five months, or nearly half of the year, and so long are useless to the producer or manufacturer."*

* *American Railroad Journal*, July 31, 1845, 491.

Railroad locomotives offered another intriguing challenge to America's many natural-born tinkerers and spurred the publication of numerous additional pamphlets. A generation of mechanics and self-taught engineers enthusiastically embraced the quest for greater power and efficiency by seeking ways to adapt steam power to the primitive conditions that prevailed on the railroads of the United States, such as curves much sharper than any found along the "permanent way" of England. The hallmarks of America's early railroads derived from an inescapable reality within the United States: it was a huge country compared to Britain or France. But despite geography and limited budgets, Americans were eager to forge a transportation network that unified their new nation and facilitated its military defense. With little money to do so, they rushed to construct their infrastructure as rapidly and as cheaply as possible.[25]

One result was that the high-pressure steam engines used to power their steamboats were prone to horrific explosions, and their trains derailed with alarming frequency. Such accidents were almost always regarded as minor setbacks in a nation that prized speedy transportation and that was thus willing to tolerate the attendant risks, though foreign visitors were often appalled by the crudeness they experienced aboard American trains.[26]

In the words of novelist Charles Dickens, who visited North America during the first half of 1842 and published his observations later that same year, "On, on, on—tears the mad dragon of an engine with its train of cars; scattering in all directions a shower of burning sparks from its wood fire; screeching, hissing, yelling, panting; until at last the thirsty monster stops beneath a covered way to drink, the people cluster round, and you have time to breathe again." Not only did travelers from abroad find train accommodations rudimentary—"shabby," in the words of Dickens—and the ride rough but they thought many of their fellow travelers were exceedingly rough in dress and in public manners. A frequent complaint was that American males constantly spat tobacco juice in the stations and aboard the cars.[27]

In 1866, the *American Railway Times*, a Boston-based publication, reflected on the "future of the railway system." Taking note of the phenomenal growth of the nation's rail lines since 1830, its editor dared to predict that "at the close of the present century we shall have at least sixty thousand miles of railway in operation in the United States." He was a poor prophet. A mere four years later, in 1870, the national total had already topped fifty thousand miles, and it would continue to rocket upward to 193,000 miles in 1900 and ultimately to approximately 254,000 miles at the industry's network peak in 1916.[28]

Major feats of engineering, especially the construction of bridges and tunnels to overcome the technological shortcuts required to get America's early railroad tracks on the ground as cheaply as possible, became sources of industry pride. An 1878 timetable cover for the Hoosac Tunnel Route saluted the Fitchburg Railroad's expensive and multiyear achievement (1851–1873) of boring nearly five miles through the mountain barrier in western Massachusetts to connect Boston with the railroads of upstate New York.

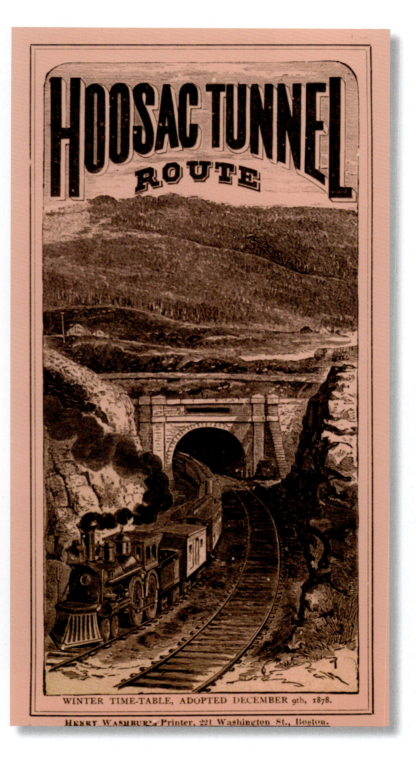

Although the Colorado & Southern was most closely identified with the Centennial State, when its tracks linked the Rocky Mountains with the Gulf of Mexico, they forged a new spatial relationship and offered fresh vacation possibilities, as is illustrated in the 1927 brochure titled *Our American Riviera*.

In 1838, the idea of a Pacific railway had ceased to be novel and the execution of the project was freely suggested, predicted, and urged in newspapers and magazines from that time.

—from John P. Davis, *The Union Pacific Railway* (1894)[1]

3

SPATIAL REORIENTATION

PASSAGES TO ELSEWHERE

In December 1852 the Pacific Railroad of Missouri set in motion the latest expression of America's Manifest Destiny: "Yesterday witnessed the starting of the first locomotive in North America west of the Mississippi—the pioneer in whose tracks soon will follow others, and whose first breath is the omen pointing to the grand system which is to develop the almost infinite resources of a country so vast as that lying between the Mississippi and the Rocky Mountains." The whistle shriek of the locomotive announced to Saint Louisans "that the moment of departure had arrived, and after the bell had tapped the last call, the driving wheels commenced revolving, and locomotive, tender, three cars with iron rails, engineer, passengers and all were on the road toward sun-down."[2]

The search for an easy passage to India was not new in the railroad era. In 1492 it had fired the imagination of Christopher Columbus and his Spanish patrons, King Ferdinand and Queen Isabella. North America, of course, inconveniently blocked his way, but might it be possible to discover an easy water passage *through* North America itself? In 1776, the dream of a Northwest Passage motivated the third voyage of Captain James Cook, who

at the behest of the British government searched the Northwest coast of America in hopes of finding its Pacific outlet and then sailing east through the waterway back to the North Atlantic and home to England. Cook failed, but the quest continued. America's third president, Thomas Jefferson, sponsored an epic exploratory expedition led by army captain Meriwether Lewis, and in the early 1800s it threaded its way west from Pittsburgh and Saint Louis, up the Missouri River, across the Rocky Mountain backbone of the continent, and down the Columbia River through the future states of Oregon and Washington to reach the Pacific Ocean, where they spent the winter of 1805–1806. The following spring the expedition headed back to Saint Louis. Its three-year odyssey revealed that the Northwest Passage—whether defined as a waterway extending from sea to sea or as an easy overland passage through the Rocky Mountains—was pure illusion. Nonetheless, the ongoing quest for a Northwest Passage generated an impressive library of publications.

The underlying desire to find an easy way to cross North America endured, and by the middle 1850s, the successes of railroad builders working east of the Mississippi River opened the way for the new exploration of an old idea by means of a transcontinental railroad with trains running from one coast

WEST BOUND ROUND TRIP
SUMMER FARES
1912

WESTERN TRIPS
for
EASTERN PEOPLE
1912

"See America First"
GREAT NORTHERN RAILWAY
National Park Route

"See America First"
GREAT NORTHERN RAILWAY
National Park Route

of the United States to the other. "There are certain steps in the progress of our railroads that mark great events in the history of these works. One of these was the opening of the Rock Island and Chicago Railroad to the Mississippi River." Even if the *American Railroad Journal* got the carrier's name wrong, the ability of railroads to reorient long-standing spatial relationships and shrink travel times and distances was certainly worth noting. "From New York, the depot of western produce, to Rock Island, the distance by water must exceed five thousand miles; by railroad it is only about one thousand." Two years later, the Ohio & Mississippi opened to Saint Louis to provide the Baltimore & Ohio a through connection from the Chesapeake Bay to the Mississippi River, the acknowledged dividing line between East and West within the United States.[3]

Publications from the 1840s and 1850s devoted to the pros and cons of the railroad phase of the long-running quest for a Northwest Passage would fill a small library. Asa Whitney emerged in the late 1840s as the most indefatigable promoter of federal support for a transcontinental railroad, but skeptics were quick to claim that he had "no experience in railways nor in engineering to correct or control his theories. Having committed himself to his project, all the vast intermediate unknown between the Mississippi and the Pacific, became mere plastic material in his hands, to be mounded into any shape to suit his fancy. He saw no obstacles because he did not appreciate what constituted such." Whitney, according to the *New York Journal of Commerce* in 1849, was "enthusiastic to the highest degree," and with "untiring energy" he succeeded in placing his views "before almost every person in the country. The subject of a railway to the Pacific is one of universal interest."[4]

Whitney, however, was not the first person to envision a railroad to the West Coast. As early as the 1830s, a few visionaries had claimed that a rail line across the Rocky Mountains was feasible, but the idea of a transcontinental line gained significant traction only in the late 1840s and early 1850s, when Whitney tirelessly promoted it. An aroused Congress not only debated the merits of his proposal but also funded an army examination of five potential east–west routes as well as a north–south route along the Pacific slope. Thirteen massive volumes known collectively as the *Pacific Railroad Survey* appeared during the mid-1850s. Within the United States they easily qualified as the greatest publishing effort to date devoted to railroads.[5]

One journal wholly caught up in the transcontinental railroad fever of the mid-1850s was the *Railroad Record* of Cincinnati. In addition to its usual weekly publication, in the mid-1850s it published a serial supplement devoted entirely to the promotion of a transcontinental railroad, preferably one that began in Texas and followed a southerly route to California. This was an ingenious ploy intended to benefit Cincinnati, which expected to connect with the proposed route via Cairo, Illinois, and a rail line extended across Arkansas. What made it especially clever was that it bypassed a rival city, Saint Louis, which until the late 1850s was clearly the front-runner in the race to serve as the nation's railroad gateway to the West. In 1855 there were about four hundred railroad companies in North America, with 18,374 miles in the United States (mostly located east of the Mississippi River) and another 877 miles in Canada.[6]

Saint Louis was actually a latecomer to the railroad game, but when it became a bona fide player in 1851, it put its bold ambitions on full display: its leading citizens launched not just one but two Pacific railroad projects. Originally, both were subsumed under the name of the Pacific Railroad of Missouri, but eventually the South West Branch emerged as a transcontinental aspirant that called itself the Saint Louis-San Francisco, or Frisco. Before Missouri's audacious display of rail enthusiasm in the early 1850s, no American railroad had dared to use the word Pacific in its corporate title. In fact, before the Frisco settled on its name, it had earlier called itself the Atlantic & Pacific. Though Missourians

During a span of thirty years (1820–1851), Missouri's bombastic United States senator Thomas Hart Benton served as the chief spokesman for the American West on Capitol Hill. In his later years, he became a thunderous promoter of a railroad to the Pacific coast (and beyond) from his hometown of Saint Louis.

his exceptionally bombastic style of oratory to the national debate. Not without reason was the Missouri senator sometimes referred to as the "Old Thunderer." Benton has been in the Senate since Missouri became a state in 1821, and over the course of six terms he had accumulated considerable seniority—and not a few enemies. For years prior to 1849 he had advocated federal construction of an overland passage that would combine roads and waterways to link Saint Louis with the distant mouth of the Columbia River, which for many years was the only outlet to the Pacific the United States possessed.

About the same time that Benton became a convert to railroads, the United States acquired California with its magnificent port of San Francisco. The discovery of a precious mineral at much the same time was electrifying news, even across the Atlantic Ocean in England, where that nation's leading railway journal, *Herapath's*, wrote in early 1849: "It is almost impossible to discredit the numerous accounts which reach us, but if they are to be believed, California is a continent of gold." That was an exaggeration, of course, but the journal noted correctly that "the poor man has already become rich, the labourer is placed on an equality with the master, and even the Governor is left to cook his own dinner."[8]

For Benton the purpose of a transcontinental railroad was clear, as he stated with his usual bombast in a speech he gave to the thousand delegates attending a railroad advocacy meeting in Saint Louis in October 1849. Benton's favored project must serve as nothing less than a link in a commercial chain that would connect his hometown, Saint Louis, with India.[9]

Benton was right about one thing: no private investor was likely to come up with money to bankroll a railroad that would trace its way across the lightly populated "Great American Desert" unless it had a destination in mind that could somehow promise a reasonable return on the investment. The fabled wealth of India could do that.

When printed in pamphlet form, Benton's enthusiastic support for a transcontinental railroad further contributed to the growing mountain of documents produced during the great national debate. Discussion of a railroad to the Pacific coast was a popular topic during the 1850s, with much talk devoted to gaining a better understanding of the topography of the American West,

had no miles of track on the ground until 1851, they knew how to dream big dreams, and the nation's first railroad to the Pacific coast was not the full extent of their grand ambitions. Why terminate in California? Why not extend the reach of the Missouri metropolis across the Pacific Ocean all the way to India? The city of Saint Louis, commonly described as the gateway to the West, might also have become the gateway to the Far East.[7]

Missouri's influential United States senator Thomas Hart Benton was a late convert to the idea of a railroad between Saint Louis and the Pacific, but when he did embrace the proposal in 1849, he did so with his usual over-the-top enthusiasm and added a region about which most Americans knew little. Benton's son-in-law, John C. Fremont (nicknamed "the Pathfinder"), twice explored the dry landscape between Missouri and California in 1843 and 1844, but his hasty assessments of the region—initially that "the country is little better than a sandy desert" and then that it was little short of a paradise—proved of mixed value to promoters of a Pacific railroad. Critics of Fremont, of Benton, and even of the idea of a transcontinental railroad responded with strong words, blasting some of their geographic assertions, both positive and negative, as "purest fiction" that "no sane or well-informed man, will for a moment doubt."[10]

The wrangling continued for the better part of the 1850s, accompanied by much spread-eagle oratory, pulpit-pounding assertions, and calls for immediate action: "Men of energy, rouse ye!" Some Americans thought a Pacific railroad too expensive; others questioned whether two decades of technological experimentation and the resulting improvements had made it feasible. In any event, publications devoted to the topic consumed considerable paper and ink, at least until the Civil War erupted in April 1861 and diverted the nation's attention to the question of its survival.[11]

Federal legislation authorizing a railroad to the Pacific was enacted during some of the darkest days of the American Civil War. However, little construction took place until the conflict ended in April 1865. Then the "whole nation, released from war-like pursuits," was animated to complete the "great national thoroughfare." One western news correspondent who observed the progress of construction west from Omaha gushed: "There is nothing connected with the Union Pacific Railroad that is not wonderful." An elaborate final-spike ceremony joined Union Pacific and Central Pacific tracks at Promontory, Utah, in 1869.[12]

When the nation's first transcontinental railroad was completed in 1869 between Sacramento and Omaha, the railroads of Chicago stood ready to fill the gap across Iowa between West and East. As for the Pacific Railroad of Missouri, its tracks finally did reach Kansas City in 1865, only months after the Civil War ended and after fourteen years of incremental advances and harrowing setbacks. The pioneer rail aspirant to the Pacific never did

live up to its name: its tracks reached Pueblo, Colorado, at the foot of the Rocky Mountains but could advance no farther. There would be no Saint Louis–based "Passage to India."[13]

Historically, Saint Louis had enjoyed the lucrative commerce that flowed along four great water highways of the Midwest: the Mississippi, Missouri, Illinois, and Ohio Rivers. The several railroad lines built west from Chicago during the 1850s and 1860s progressively amputated the northward commercial reach of Saint Louis by steamboat. Despite the historic river-oriented commerce lost to Chicago railroads, the Missouri metropolis could conceivably restructure its economic reach by building a web of rail lines to link Saint Louis manufacturers with promising new markets in the Southwest: most notably in the state of Texas but also in Arkansas, Louisiana, and Oklahoma. In the late 1860s these railroads, with track either on the ground or in the planning stage, reoriented the compass of opportunity and once again illustrated the power of railroads to transform spatial relationships. The first Saint Louis railroads reached Texas in the early 1870s, and while they were a far cry from the "Passage to India" that Senator Benton had once envisioned, by linking with rail lines already built in Texas, they soon functioned as a "Passage to Mexico." Not too many years passed before Pullman sleepers ran through between Saint Louis and Mexico City, and for a time the Missouri metropolis served as the nation's foremost rail gateway to Mexico.[14]

It is worth noting that the president of Mexico, Porfirio Diaz, welcomed the Yankee railroads that built across the border and deep into Mexico. An increasing number of critics claimed with justification that Diaz had become a dictator, and the railroads built into Mexico functioned as three straws permitting American capitalists to suck Mexican commodities north to enrich the Yankees but giving little in return. Diaz fled to Paris in 1910 at the commencement of a revolution that plunged Mexico into a bloody Civil War that lasted ten years. The Magón brothers, who were the most vocal critics of Diaz and who had functioned as spark plugs to ignite the uprising that sent him into exile, were both based in Saint Louis. The spatial relationship made possible by the railroad links forged between Saint Louis and

FRISCO to Florida

FRISCO to Florida

FRISCO LINES

FRISCO LINES

The Sunnyland

Kansas City-Florida Special

The spatial relationship emphasized in the *Frisco to Florida* brochure (1915) was made possible after American railroads standardized track gauge and car dimensions in the 1880s to facilitate the interchange of freight and passenger cars. It was natural that many geographic allies later combined to form the large systems that came to dominate the industry by 1900. Half a century earlier, Senator Thomas Hart Benton was so focused on the construction of a rail line west from Missouri to the Pacific coast that it seems unlikely he gave thought to a route that connected Saint Louis and Kansas City with Florida, such as the Frisco and Southern later forged with their joint operation of through passenger trains. Besides, during Benton's 1850s, Florida did not amount to much as a destination. Ocean bathing was still popularly regarded as a weird fad, and the rise of the state's famed citrus industry was a post–Civil War development.

Mexico City facilitated the flow of freight and passengers as well as revolutionary ideas.[15]

In the case of George Edward Kessler, the railroad facilitated the outreach of a much sought-after idea generator. Quite unexpectedly, on a day in 1901 oil gushed forth from a well being drilled near Beaumont and blackened the Texas sky. The geyser of black gold heralded a new era for Texas, especially after wildcat drillers discovered an abundance of oil pooled below the ground in other parts of the newly wealthy state. Stock jobbers headed north to the city that effectively functioned as the financial and cultural capital of Texas, Saint Louis, to lure investors large and small into the oil game, and so too did newly rich Texans in search of a way to give their rough-and-ready state a more refined edge aesthetically. The man most often sought out to do the refining was the Saint Louis–based city planner and landscape architect named George Edward Kessler. Municipal parks and urban boulevards in major cities in Texas traced their origins to Kessler's touch of aesthetic genius.

Indicative of newly forged rail connections to destinations elsewhere was the Atchison, Topeka & Santa Fe's 1908 promotion of travel to England and Europe via its trains across the western United States.

The spatial bonds that railroads forged between Saint Louis and the Southwest and Mexico are but one regional example of the transformative power of tracks and trains. Another example, this one of global significance, involved the "Passage to India," but not the one Senator Benton and others imagined extending across the Pacific from the West Coast of the United States. On the opposite side of the globe, another proposed "Passage to India" pitted the empires of Great Britain and Russia against each other in a spatial cold war that used railroads and steamships as weapons of choice. History remembers this imperial test of wills as the Great Game that was played out in late nineteenth-century Persia. India was long regarded as the crown jewel of the British Empire, and regular steamship service maintained a bond between the mother country and her wealthiest colony. But Russia seemed poised to disrupt their cozy relationship by extending railway lines south into Persia, a threatening gesture because to the east lay India, which at the time included the future nations of India, Pakistan, and Bangladesh. A political cartoon of the day depicts a decidedly unhappy Persian cat being squashed by a Russian bear and a British lion.[16]

The bear and the lion never engaged in outright military conflict in Persia (Iran), but the Great Game was a rehearsal for what followed in the early twentieth century as Great Britain and Russia sought to use railroads to extend the imperial reach of London across Africa from the Cape of Good Hope north all the way to Cairo and that of Moscow east across Siberia all the way to Russia's Pacific port of Vladivostok. These bold ventures, and many more modest ones, generated plenty of publishing by and about the railroads.

During a span of fifty years, from 1830 until 1880, North America's railroads sought to overcome the idiosyncrasies of their early years, and finally they achieved the agreement necessary to standardize time and track gauge between 1883 and 1886. There was more to be accomplished, of course, even in respect to railway nomenclature. In the late 1880s the industry still could not agree on what terminology best described the man "whose vocation is to operate a locomotive." The six main contenders were *engineer, engine driver, driver, locomotive engineer, locomotive runner,* and *runner.* The *Official Guide* threw its support behind the adoption of a seventh term, *engineman,* but dismissed two new contenders, *locomotor* and *enginor,* the latter term a favorite of the *Railway Register.* "The attainment of uniformity and precision is our only object in discussing railway nomenclature," emphasized the *Railway Register,* which was happy to debate the issue.

While editors sparring over nomenclature may seem like a frivolous matter today, the extended debates over time and gauge were deadly serious, and a span of several decades saw considerable printer's ink used in the search for agreement.[17]

James J. Hill used two enormous ships to extend the reach of the Great Northern Railway west from the end of its tracks in Seattle across the Pacific to Japan, China, and the Philippines. In an odd way the Great Northern Steamship Company represented the embodiment of the dream of a "passage to India" expressed in the late 1840s and 1850s by Senator Thomas Hart Benton.

"ON TIME"

Although this General Motors advertisement appeared in the late 1940s and was used to promote its diesel locomotives, the emphasis on accurate timekeeping was as old as the rail industry itself.

There is no "Standard Rail-Road time" in the Confederate States, but each rail-road company adopts independently the time of its own locality, or of that place at which its principal office is situated. The inconvenience of such a system, if system it can be called, must be apparent to all, but it is most of all annoying to strangers to the fact. From this cause, many miscalculations and misconnections have arisen, which not unfrequently have been of serious consequence to individuals, and have as a matter of course, brought into disrepute all Rail-road Guides, which of necessity give the local times.

—from *Hill & Swayze's Confederate States Rail-Road and Steam-Boat Guide* (1862)[1]

4

GOD'S TIME VERSUS RAILROAD TIME

Time is an elusive matter for most people. We live our lives in terms of the passage of time as recorded by clocks, watches, or smartphones, but when trying to pin down exactly what time is, the average person easily becomes lost in a thicket of abstract philosophy and complex physics. As Saint Augustine famously observed in his *Confessions*, "What then is time? Provided that no one asks me, I know. If I want to explain it to an inquirer, I do not know."[2]

The dilemma of time confronted the superintendents of North America's largest railroads in the early 1880s. Across the United States and Canada, the rail industry's steady expansion since the 1830s had created a monumental headache for operators and travelers alike. Superintendents needed to find a practical solution to the problem of local time reckoning across a complex network of tracks that had expanded far beyond the wildest imaginations of industry pioneers in England and the United States in the 1820s and 1830s.[3]

When the Baltimore & Ohio spiked down its first tracks in the late 1820s, the entire nation moved at a slow and undemanding pace. Its centers of population large and small resembled self-contained islands scattered across the land, and communication and transportation among them moved at the leisurely pace dictated by Mother Nature or by the brute strength and stamina of animals and humans. That is, one primary means of travel was by water along the coast and inland lakes and rivers, and wind and water currents supplied the power needed to travel from one place to another. Humans used bodily strength as needed to supplement or overcome the forces of nature. Fur traders traveled across the breadth of North America from bases in Montreal and Saint Louis by means of the continent's waterways and when necessary used their own strength to portage their canoes or paddle upstream against the current. Options for travel overland depended on human feet or the plodding pace of a variety of horses, mules, and oxen. Even with the coming of steam power to inland waterways, the reckoning of time remained informal, and especially so when compared to the precision later demanded by railroads. Train scheduling demanded accuracy to the minute to prevent collisions.[4]

The primary time concern for travel and commerce by water or overland by freight wagon or stagecoach was the season of the year. John Butterfield launched the first stagecoach route across the American West in 1858 to connect Saint Louis and San

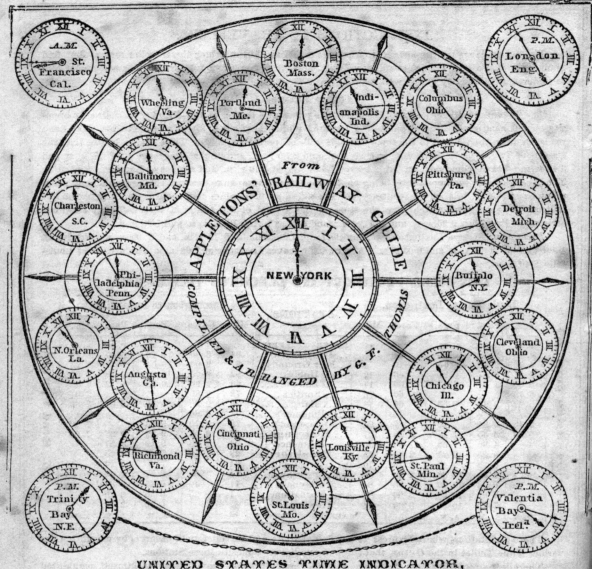

UNITED STATES TIME INDICATOR,

Showing the Difference of Time between the various Cities of the United States: including San Francisco, California; Trinity Bay, Newfoundland; Valentia Bay, Ireland; and London, England.

It will be perceived, by glancing at the "Indicator," that when it is noon at New York, it is 12 minutes past 12 00 at Boston, 25 minutes past 1 00 at Trinity Bay, 24 minutes past 4 00 P. M. at Valentia Bay; when it wants 15 minutes of 9 00 A. M. at St. Francisco, Cal., it wants 5 minutes of 5 00 P. M. at London, England. Thus, by a little calculation, the reader will readily perceive the difference of time between the several points, and obviate the necessity of moving the hands of his watch to be in time.

There is no standard railway time in the Union, each Railway Co. adopting the time where its principal office may be located; we would, therefore, suggest to the traveller the necessity of consulting the "Indicator," and, if possible, to be at the depot some few minutes previous to the departure of the trains.

To Travellers.—As our object is to publish a *reliable Guide*, regardless of expense, we would thank the travelling community if they will notify us of the incorrectness of a Time Table, and we will not only exclude it from the "Guide," but notify the public of the same.

Appleton's *Time Indicator* (1860) perhaps qualified as an example of railroad art, but its attempt to clarify a confusing "system" of timekeeping was without doubt mentally challenging for rail travelers.

Francisco. His horse-drawn coaches, in fact, pioneered commercial passenger travel across the western half of the United States. Butterfield's contract with the federal government allowed him to vary his transcontinental timetable according to the seasons—lengthening travel time during winter and shortening it during summer. Anyone who chose the Butterfield option to or from California instead of an ocean passage by water around Cape Horn or across the Isthmus of Panama had to be prepared for nearly a month of hard travel. With baggage limited to twenty-five pounds, some travelers who undertook the long and dusty journey chose to fill their luggage to capacity with bottles of whiskey in hopes of anesthetizing themselves during the lengthy crossing of the desert Southwest.

The first steamboat did not appear on rivers west of the Allegheny Mountains until 1811 and Nicholas Roosevelt's famous voyage of the *New Orleans*. Timekeeping for a steamboat journey, as with travel by stagecoach, need not be precise, and it was often measured in terms of days, not hours or minutes. No disaster resulted if a steamboat reached the wharves of Saint Louis or Memphis a few hours late, or even several days late. Avoiding disaster on the railroads, on the other hand, demanded precision in timekeeping. The time-honored practice for train operating crews was to compare their watches for accuracy at the beginning and ending of each run, and woe to the conductor who attempted to save a few dollars with the purchase of an inferior brand of watch not approved by management. Such parsimony could cost a penny-pincher his job. Roving watch inspectors punished indifference to safe timekeeping practices.[5]

Another key feature of timekeeping on both sides of the Atlantic was the division between secular and sacred time. That is, how did people keep Sunday sacred and still run a railroad? In the new American nation, and even earlier in colonial days, a simple solution had been to shut down businesses on Sunday. The same pious thinking prevailed during the nation's post–Civil War years. In 1884, for example, the Massachusetts rail commissioners recommended "that the managers of the Boston & Albany Railroad carefully consider whether there is any need of many of the freight trains which are now run on the Lord's day, with the object of greatly reducing their number." William E. Dodge, a partner in a successful transatlantic metals trading firm based in New York, recalled that churchgoers stretched heavy chains across some streets to halt the noise of traffic on Sunday mornings. Dodge was an uncompromising advocate of strict Sunday keeping by railroad managers. As a member of the board of directors of the Central Railroad of New Jersey, he promoted its shutdown on Sundays, and when management ignored his pious proposals, he resigned in disgust. When the Jersey Central later went bankrupt, Dodge believed that God had vindicated his strict reckoning of secular and sacred time.[6]

The matter of limiting or halting Sunday train service entirely was a particularly contentious matter for the railroads of New England. The region's Puritan founders were noticeably strict when it came to matters of sacred time. They did not, for example, promote the celebration of Christmas, which they considered too Catholic in origin ("Christ-Mass"). Instead, Thanksgiving was their special time for gift giving. The Puritan Sunday was most notable for all the things a person could not do.[7]

For many descendants of the Puritans, that meant no trains on Sunday because they were "the harbingers of evil to whatever town or villages they enter. The peace and quiet which has prevailed on the Lord's day from time immemorial, flies before the shriek of the locomotive, and in their stead come the clatter of the train, the hurrying and rush of porters, passengers, omnibuses, cake and apple vendors, and the confluence of village idlers." History records that the desire to ban railroads from operating trains on Sunday achieved only mixed results.[8]

Henry Varnum Poor, editor of the *American Railroad Journal* during the 1850s, noted in 1854 that "in none of the New England States are Sunday trains run. Several reach Boston early Sunday morning from New York, but none leave it, or any other New England city, on that day. Throughout all these States there is one day in seven when even the locomotive reposes quietly in its stall, and the senseless machine pays its homage to a law ordained for the good of man alone. As we leave New England we find a greater laxity."[9]

As railroads grew larger, practical considerations overcame local objections. Could, for instance, a trainload of live cattle remain idle for twenty-four hours on a siding or in a rail yard to await the end of Sunday before resuming its journey to the stockyards of Chicago? The same issue confronted railroads that hauled perishable fruits and vegetables from Florida and other parts of the South to markets in the North. In the end, matters of practicality overcame rigid Sunday-keeping practices on America's rail lines. In fact, Sunday became a favorite day for railroad-sponsored outings that enabled workers and their family members to escape at least temporarily the noise and grime of the city. Trolley and electric interurban railways invented the amusement park in the late nineteenth century to offer a Sunday safety valve to workers occupied earning a living during the week's other six days. With the annual wage for factory workers averaging around $500 at the dawn of the twentieth century, the nickel carfare each way to access the pleasures of a free trolley park was affordable.[10]

Apart from the contentious issue of the proper observance of sacred time, railroads found themselves wrestling with how best to keep accurate track of the passage of time regardless of the day of the week. This was a matter that crept up on rail managers as their industry grew larger and more complex between the 1830s and the 1870s. Initially they adapted rail operations to the practices that prevailed in the slow-paced world of the 1820s and 1830s as defined by the isolated, scattered, and largely self-contained communities. It was a world in which time reckoning depended on the standard a local community set for itself. Thus, dozens upon dozens of different time standards prevailed across North America. The maddening multiplicity of local times made little difference when the leisurely paced world required two days to travel between New York and Philadelphia.[11]

The result was that early railroads each chose a time standard for themselves. Usually that was the time that prevailed in the community in which a company located its general offices—in Baltimore, for instance, in the case of the Baltimore & Ohio. But not always: as the young Atchison, Topeka & Santa Fe extended a line of tracks west across the lightly populated prairies of Kansas, it chose as its standard of time that of Jefferson City, the capital of Missouri and a community the Santa Fe never reached. Why Jefferson City? Because the Santa Fe's primary connection

was originally with the Pacific Railroad of Missouri, which did run its trains according to Jefferson City time. For the Santa Fe, that was a practical solution, while for the Missouri railroad based in Saint Louis, it was probably a matter of good politics.[12]

As the tracks of more and more railroads interconnected to extend the range of train travel for Americans and Canadians, they created an annoying challenge for through travelers using the trains of two or more separate companies. Travelers changing trains in a large city might discover as many as four different time standards used by the railroads that intersected there. Traveling salesmen often used watches that featured two sets of hands, one set to local time and the other changed as needed to one of the sixty or more local time standards that prevailed across North America. Thus, when changing trains in a major junction city like Cincinnati or Indianapolis, a through traveler might miss the outbound train because of the idiosyncratic differences that typified railroad time standards before November 1883. Dozens of local variations in time, while inconsequential during railroading's pioneer days, had grown maddeningly complex and ever more disruptive by the early 1880s.[13]

North America's worsening time muddle prompted the superintendents of several separate lines to seek a common solution by forming a new organization, the General Time Convention, in hopes of addressing the dilemma. During meetings held in different cities of the United States over a span of several years, they politely listened to a variety of self-proclaimed experts on time, and that included students of physics whose proposals were so abstract and unworkable in the daily operations of a railroad that the superintendents summarily rejected them all. What the superintendents sought was a way of reckoning time that could be easily understood and safely implemented by the ordinary folk they employed as engineers, conductors, train dispatchers, and the like.[14]

The upshot was that railroads—*and railroads alone*—willed the United States and Canada onto standard time on a special Sunday, November 18, 1883, by providing an organizational scheme so simple and convenient that it continues to be used today. Seldom, if ever, do we remember its railroad origins or the individuals who conceived the system of timekeeping that railroads adopted. "Last Sunday, the 18th, has become a historical

The *Official Guide* supplied travel information for well over a century. Its thickness, less than an inch in 1869, bulked up over the years to at least three inches during the late 1920s before it slimmed down slightly during the Great Depression of the 1930s. Its size mirrored the evolution of rail travel across North America.

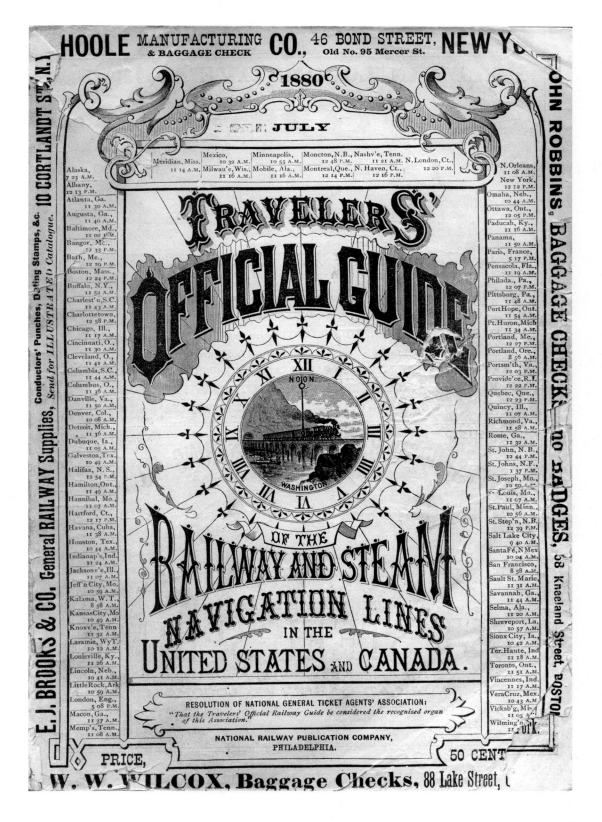

KEEPING WATCH OVER THE RAILROADS

Accompanying the standardization of time in 1883 was the need for train crews to maintain accurate watches to adhere closely and thus safely to rules, timetable details, and a dispatcher's orders. Makers of the highly accurate watches demanded by railroads included the American Watch Company of Waltham, Massachusetts, which in 1857 began to use machines to make hundreds of standardized parts that skilled operatives assembled into a railroad watch. Ten years later, the American Watch Company accounted for half of all watches used by onboard crews, with at least seven other makers accounting for the rest.*

With railroad watches came frequent inspections to ensure their accuracy. In addition to a railroad's own inspectors, local jewelers handled periodic checkups. A locomotive engineer or conductor who dared to purchase an inferior timekeeper could be subject to severe discipline. A watch off by thirty seconds might seem a trifling matter, but "thirty seconds equal half a mile, and more to the locomotive engineer of a high-velocity special or a twentieth century flyer." Half a mile deviation from a railroad's carefully timed schedule might mean the difference between safe operations and a costly accident.†

* *American Railroad Journal*, January 12, 1867, 29. Providing an illustrated summary is Shawn M. Hearne, *The Railroad Timekeepers* (Baltimore: B&O Railroad Museum, 1999).

† Webb C. Ball and his watch inspection service, newspaper advertisement, 1910, reprinted in James B. Morrow, *The Man Who Holds a Watch on 125,000 Miles of Railroad* (Oxnard, CA: Meredith, n.d.), 3. After a horrific wreck in 1891 caused by inaccurate timekeeping, Ball, a Cleveland jeweler and keen student of time measurements, gained recognition for the exacting standards he applied to clocks and watches, and dozens of railroads hired Ball and his employees to oversee their official clocks and employee watches. Eventually, some railroads created their own cadre of inspectors. Hearne, *Railroad Timekeepers*, 6–7. Some leading railroads, most notably the Pennsylvania, furnished accurate watches to locomotive engineers as a part of their equipment. *American Railroad Journal*, January 12, 1867, 29.

Facing, One of the many Howard Watch advertisements, this example from 1911 featured a conductor and his ever-present watch. A passenger conductor was always the boss of the train, and within his domain he was the master of railroad time and space as well as a model of sartorial splendor.

The Howard Watch

Sometimes you see a prosperous looking passenger inquire the time, and you wonder why he does not take out his own watch to compare with the conductor's.

It is not that he has no watch—but because he is ashamed of the time he is carrying. He has no confidence that it is anywhere near correct and he tries to save his dignity by not making a comparison.

What do you think of the type of man who will carry a cheap and uncertain timepiece because it doesn't have to be seen?

It is quite different with the HOWARD owner. He is ready to match time with all comers.

The HOWARD is the closest rating watch in the world—and worth all it costs to any man of accurate habit and orderly mind.

A HOWARD Watch is always worth what you pay for it. The price of each watch—from the 17-jewel (*double roller*) in a Boss or Crescent gold-filled case at $40 to the 23-jewel in a 14-k solid gold case at $150—is *fixed* at the factory and a printed ticket attached.

Not every jeweler can sell you a HOWARD Watch. Find the HOWARD jeweler in your town and talk to him. He is a good man to know.
Drop us a postal card, Dept. D, and we will send you "The Story of Edward Howard and the First American Watch"—an inspiring chapter of history that every man and boy should read.

E. HOWARD WATCH WORKS, Boston, Mass.

date as being the occasion of the great transformation of American time standards," noted the *Railway Review*. The Chicago-based publication added that "Professor Charles F. Dowd of Saratoga, N. Y., who originated the theory of the new system, and W. F. Allen, of the *Travelers' Official Guide*, for urging its practical application and obtained its adoption, have reason to be proud of their connection with so important an innovation."[15]

Many ordinary Americans in 1883 resented railroad power as showcased by their preemptory rearrangement of something so basic as the God-given system of sun time by squeezing the hours of the day into just five zones that spanned the continent from Nova Scotia to California. Railroads ignored the protests, and with the new timetables they issued on the Sunday "with two noons," a majority of North America's rail carriers switched from local "sun time" to the continent's new system of standard time and accepted no compromise with any previous ways of reckoning the passing hours.[16]

Some railroads, most notably those that served the city of Pittsburgh and the state of Michigan, did not join the realignment, at least not immediately. "Those railways which chose to conservatively await the actions of others are reassured by the ease with which the change was made," reported the *Railway Review*. "No accidents or annoyances occurred anywhere, as far as we have heard, because of the change, and wonder is universal at the timidity which put it off so long."[17]

After considerable huffing and puffing by the nation's newspapers, both for and against standard time, the remaining holdouts, both the railroads and the communities they served, grasped the wisdom inherent in the new system of timekeeping. The rail network of the United States and Canada gained a new measure of uniformity and operated its trains according to the system sketched out by members of the General Time Convention. For practical reasons, the junctions between the five time zones occurred at railroad division points, places where crews handed off their trains to one another and synchronized their watches for accuracy.[18]

After the 1883 transformation of timekeeping, railroad timetables both public and employee served as unalloyed statements of one industry's power to transform time and space. Only God, or so it often seemed during America's informal debate of the monumental time change, was more powerful than the railroads, and maybe even the heavenly deity was no longer the boss of time across the United States and Canada.

Perhaps never before or since in earth's history has an obscure, self-appointed, and wholly informal organization such as the General Time Convention held such all-encompassing and lasting power to influence the daily lives of millions of people. The government of the United States did not formally enter the picture until more than three decades later, when in early 1918 it asked Americans to observe daylight saving time to conserve natural resources vital to the nation's recent commitment to a crusade to "Make the World Safe for Democracy," also known as World War I.[19]

The impact of the General Time Convention did not end in 1883. Rather pleased by their success in implementing standard time, the railroad superintendents elected to reconvene to discuss additional matters of mutual importance to their industry, such as how the dimensions of freight cars could be standardized to facilitate their easy handoff from one railroad to another as they transported goods the length of North America. In the end, the 1880s could be labeled the decade of standardization. Not only did the General Time Convention and its successor organization standardize key elements of railroad operations and equipment but the rail carriers worked together to eliminate the impediments imposed by nonstandard widths between the rails—the gauge question. The standardization of track gauge and train timekeeping went hand in hand to create the integrated rail system that formed the basis for the world's largest common market in the late nineteenth century. In addition, standardization encouraged the combination of small and locally oriented railroads to form the several large and highly competitive systems that emerged as publishers of significance.[20]

Facing, The Missouri Pacific realized that Americans needed to understand "railroad time," and to that end, it published an explanation in the mid-1880s and distributed it to the traveling public.

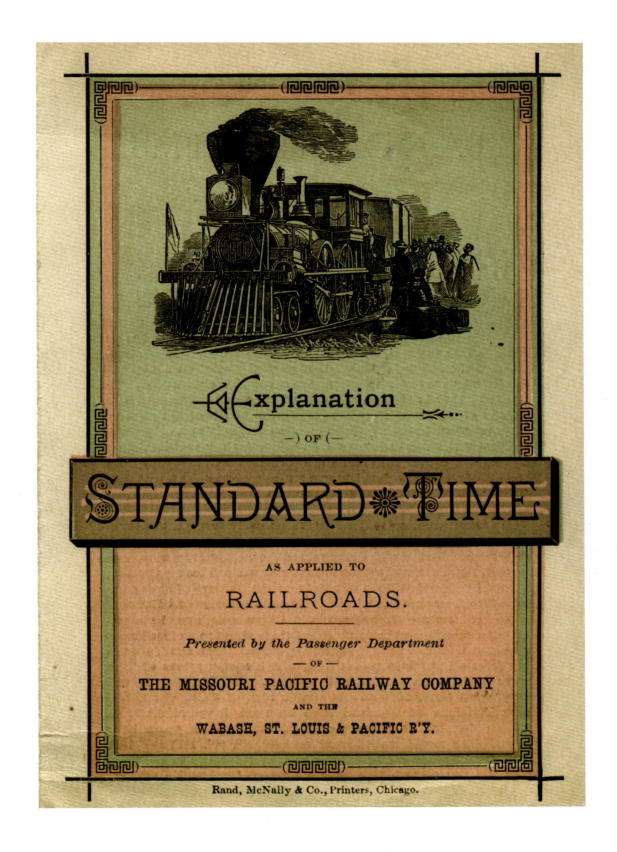

Explanation

-) OF (-

STANDARD TIME

AS APPLIED TO

RAILROADS.

Presented by the Passenger Department

— OF —

THE MISSOURI PACIFIC RAILWAY COMPANY

AND THE

WABASH, ST. LOUIS & PACIFIC R'Y.

Rand, McNally & Co., Printers, Chicago.

The St. Louis-Chicago Line, Wabash Railway

THE above view shows a stretch of the many miles of the rock ballasted double track recently constructed by the Wabash Railway between St. Louis and Chicago; grades have been reduced, the curves have been eliminated and the distance shortened—producing a track straight, level, direct and as smooth as good ballast and 90-lb. steel rails can make it.

It is safe to predict that by the next census there will be uniformity of railroad gauges throughout this country, which will be especially beneficial to the southern states in expediting and improving the transportation of freight, etc. The change is being rapidly made.

—from *Nebraska State Journal* (Lincoln), August 20, 1885

A Wabash timetable image from 1917 emphasized tracks that extended to the distant horizon. Tracks represented the silent partner in a world dominated by locomotives, especially the iron horses powered by steam. Artwork (including photographs) that featured locomotives, a kinetic form of industrial sculpture, far outnumber those depicting the tracks, though a compelling argument can be made for the aesthetic appeal of a line of tracks extending across the landscape to a vanishing point.

5

THE BATTLE OF THE GAUGES

"The locomotive forces itself on every one's attention. Its shrill cry is heard before it turns adjacent curves, and its rumbling wheels keep up their strange music several minutes after the train has whizzed past the station. Its smoke is a daily and its glaring headlight a nightly spectacle. By comparison, the roadbed is quiet and unostentatious." Quiet and unostentatious, yes, but the lengthy battle over the proper track gauge, the space between the rails, was anything but hushed.[1] It inspired much publishing about the railroad and numerous heated exchanges. In Britain and in North America, "it was waged with an intensity worthy of a better cause. It was the means of evoking much personal feeling, and caused the estrangement of many friends."[2]

The debate, which in North America extended across several decades until the mid-1880s, was not about the advantages likely to result from a uniform standard and its contribution to a uniform system of tracks; rather, proponents of uniformity disagreed about what measurement North American railroads ought to adopt. "No man can doubt the desirableness of one uniform gauge." A time-honored way to argue any cause in the United States was to write advocacy pamphlets and submit letters to newspapers.[3]

With the conclusion of the Civil War in April 1865, the national debate over the legality of secession and slavery ended. During the following two decades, however, Americans remained divided over matters of standardization, both of time and rail gauge, despite the positive benefits that uniformity would likely confer on the reunited states. When individual carriers implemented gauge standardization, their newfound unity contributed to a fully functional web of rail lines, one that after the mid-1880s extended from coast to coast and from the deserts of central Mexico to the tundra of northern Canada. Not only did the standardization of gauge make this latest form of industry-wide integration possible but the creation of a North American track network encouraged railroads to expand the scope and variety of their publications. A railroad based in Boston, for example, had incentive to publish a run of ten thousand or more tourist brochures to promote leisure travel to a world's fair held a thousand miles away in Chicago in 1893 or in Saint Louis in 1904. Likewise, it made sense to blanket northern and western Europe with settlement brochures, many written in local languages, to encourage migration to the Americas. Trains met the ships that docked in New York or Halifax to transport immigrants through to the plains of Kansas or Saskatchewan or to any other destination. In short, improved transportation and the railroads' stepped-up commitment to publishing went hand in hand during the late nineteenth century.

Arguably the most fundamental space on any railroad is the distance between the parallel rails, a measurement called gauge. With the adoption nationwide of a uniform or standard gauge of four feet, eight and a half inches during the "standardization decade" of the 1880s, the several hundred railroads of the United States and Canada for the first time created a North American network. The idea seemed logical when finally implemented, but it required a major reorientation of rail industry thinking to achieve it. Unlike standard time, which was implemented on most railroads on a single Sunday in November 1883, the standardization of gauge was accomplished only slowly over a span of six decades on a piecemeal basis by individual carriers.

Early railroads of North America had been fiercely independent, and most of them could not care less what track gauge a neighboring line might adopt because running through passenger trains and interchanging freight had not yet been considered. As early as the mid-1850s, a few forward-thinking individuals took note of the problem created when two railroads of different gauges intersected: "Breaks of gauge have produced sad results. The break of gauge compels break of bulk everywhere, and this amounts to a *tax* imposed upon transportation." The author concluded his essay with a thunderous denunciation of the local orientation of railroads, which impeded the creation of a national system: "The question of gauge, as it has been used in this country, is a humbug without palliation."[4]

During the mid-1850s, no fewer than six different gauges prevailed on railroads across the United States, each with its

The cover of a Bessemer & Lake Erie 1911 timetable was unusual in its depiction of a section of rail, but the visual emphasis made perfect sense given the railroad's close ties to the steel industry, which once centered in Pittsburgh. The robust heart of steel production in the early twentieth century originated a greater tonnage of rail freight than any other city in North America.

GAUGE, WHEN MERE INCHES MAKE A BIG DIFFERENCE

There is no compelling logic behind the emergence of four feet, eight and a half inches as the standard for North American railroads. As the *Railroad and Engineering Journal* observed in 1890, Horatio Allen, an early-day engineer, recommended in 1829 that the South Carolina Railroad adopt a gauge of five feet. "It was a great misfortune," averred the respected publication, "that the gauge for all American railroads was not made 5 ft. The extra width of 3½ in. would now be an immense advantage in the construction of both cars and locomotives. As the weight, size and capacity of these has grown the value of this 3½ in. of space between the rails has increased in about the same ratio."*

* *Railroad and Engineering Journal*, March 1890, 113. When the Stockton & Darlington Railway opened in 1825, its rails were originally set four feet, eight inches apart, with their outside dimensions being five feet. A valuable discussion of gauge by British engineers present at the creation of the nation's first modern railways in 1825 and 1830 appears in *Railway World*, September 8, 1877, 845. For an extended discussion that carefully weighs the pros and cons of different gauges, see *Railway Times*, April 8, 1871, 105–107. Britain's remarkable Isambard Kingdom Brunel originally adopted for his Great Western Railway, which linked London and Bristol, a broad gauge of seven feet, the broadest implemented on Earth, though "God's Wonderful Railway" was later reduced to standard gauge to facilitate the interchange of traffic with surrounding carriers. J. C. Bourne, *The History and Description of the Great Western Railway* (n.p., 1846); L. T. C. Rolt, *Isambard Kingdom Brunel* (1957; repr., New York: Penguin Books, 1989). The early 1890s brought a finish to Brunel's idiosyncratic standard and a lengthy retrospective look at "the battle of the gauges" from *Railway World*, October 4, 1892, 1014–1015. *Railway World* described the gauge controversy of 1840s Great Britain as "ancient history" but added that "during its continuance it was waged with an intensity worthy of a better cause. It was a means of evoking much personal feeling, and caused the estrangement of many friends. It cost the companies vast sums of money, and has very materially hampered the finances of the Great Western Railway to the present day. From the very outset, however, this result of the sturdy independence of Isambard Brunel was doomed."

advocates.[5] The lack of agreement on track widths resulted in a jumble of gauges that was a primary stumbling block to the creation of a continent-wide rail system: "The more the railroad system of the country becomes consolidated, the more is felt the want of continuous connections. A difference of gauge is an exclusion, nearly as embarrassing as an open stream across the route of a public highway."[6]

In addition, early carriers could not even agree on basic terminology because advocates of a variety of broad gauges insisted on labeling every other option narrow gauge. Perhaps the least confusing term is the *Stephenson gauge* because industry pioneer and self-trained technological genius George Stephenson borrowed the gauge of four feet, eight and a half inches commonly used by coal mines in his home area around Newcastle, England,

and applied it to his later railroad projects, like the Liverpool & Manchester Railway, which opened in 1830. The origin of the odd dimensions legitimated by Stephenson as *standard gauge* remains a mystery, despite the claim widely circulated on the internet that it derived from Roman chariots, an assertion that sounds convincing but is utterly fraudulent.[7]

The fact remains that many pioneering railroaders had trouble grasping the wisdom of adopting a single gauge for North America to facilitate the interchange of cars and thus simplify and speed the movement of freight and lengthen the distance that could be covered by through passenger trains. When the tracks of the Indianapolis & Cincinnati Railroad were opened in late October 1853, they extended ninety miles from Indiana's capital city toward Cincinnati, but the company apparently was in no hurry to continue construction east another twenty miles from Lawrenceburg and across the state line into the Ohio metropolis. Instead, a steamboat plied the Ohio River to make the connection. It was much the same story when the first railroad was built south from Chicago toward Saint Louis. Its tracks stopped in Alton, Illinois, and for a time through freight and passengers used Mississippi River steamboats to complete their journey. At other locations, ferries transferred rail cars across the nation's waterways. Bridges were expensive, and many early lines could not afford to construct them. Often, a river landing marked the end of the tracks, and early railroads often expressed no interest in extending them to the opposite bank. The primary purpose had been to supplement steamboat traffic, not to supersede it, and that goal had been achieved at the water's edge. Once again, gauge made little or no difference because its intent was to intersect with river traffic and not with another railroad.[8]

When the tracks of two different gauges did meet, often a matter of pure serendipity, the bodies of any through freight cars had to be lifted off one set of wheel assemblies (called trucks) and onto another, or at worst, through cargoes required a crew of laborers to transfer the load between cars of different gauges by hand. For bulk items like corn or wheat, the transfer might require hours of labor-intensive shoveling for each car. A third alternative was a "convertible" axle that could be shortened or lengthened to facilitate the transition between gauges, but these did not work well or prove popular.

Legislation that President Lincoln signed in 1862 mandated a gauge of four feet, eight and a half inches for the nation's first transcontinental railroad. Plenty of people within the industry continued to refer to these dimensions as *narrow gauge* because they remained convinced that rails spaced five feet; five feet, six inches; or even six feet apart provided a better option. At the time, incidentally, a bare majority (53%) of the 33,248 miles of rail line in the United States conformed to standard gauge; the other half used a hodgepodge of track gauges that ranged up to six feet.

Just two months after the Civil War ended in 1865, the *Railroad Record* celebrated the completion of a broad-gauge route that extended via Cincinnati to link New York and Saint Louis, a distance of 1,200 miles. There was "no parallel to it in magnitude and facilities in this or any other country." This trunk line was expected to act as a magnet that attracted nearby lines to the six-foot standard, and when linked they would form a large and fully functional alternative to other gauge options. The reach of the broad-gauge system could easily be extended. It was not to be, and during the early 1880s all three railroads that formed the broad-gauge alternative between New York and Missouri abandoned their idiosyncratic fight and joined the trend toward one standard for all of North America.[9]

By the 1870s, when it seemed that a uniform gauge might at last form an interconnected system across the northern portion of the United States, advocates of three feet or three feet, six inches between the rails unexpectedly rose to prominence, insisting that the narrower gauge offered the same advantages but cost less to construct. Their arguments persuaded economy-minded builders to add miles of narrow-gauge track to the national total, and not all of it was built to serve mining regions in Colorado or other remote areas of the mountain West. Perhaps because of its position at the crossroads of the continent, Saint Louis formed the belt buckle for several different railroads that adhered to a gauge of three feet. At one time a narrow-gauge trunk line extended across the nation's midriff from Ohio to Texas.[10]

Enthusiasm for narrow-gauge tracks lasted from the early 1870s until their appeal fizzled out in the mid-1880s, although several more years passed before a few penurious holdouts raised

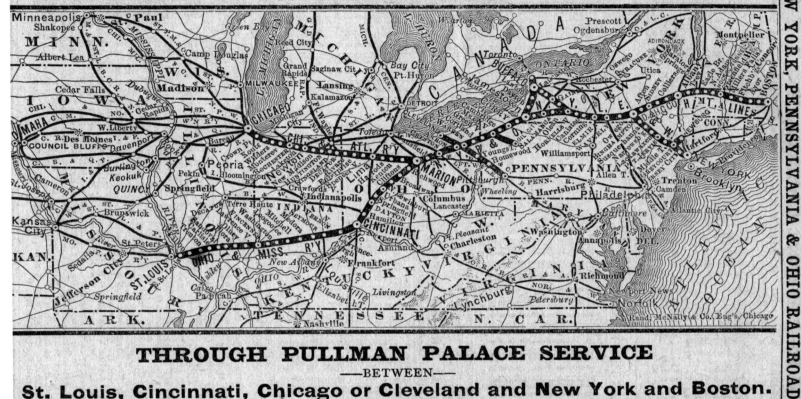

THE CONNECTING LINK BETWEEN THE WEST AND EAST.
SOLID TRAINS
—BETWEEN—
CHICAGO or CINCINNATI and NEW YORK.

NEW YORK, PENNSYLVANIA & OHIO RAILROAD.

THROUGH PULLMAN PALACE SERVICE
—BETWEEN—
St. Louis, Cincinnati, Chicago or Cleveland and New York and Boston.
Ask for Tickets via THE NEW YORK, PENNSYLVANIA & OHIO RAILROAD.
THIS IS THE "CHAUTAUQUA ROUTE."

the dollars needed to complete the conversion. One of these was the Lake Erie & Western, which extended narrow-gauge tracks across Ohio, Indiana, and Illinois. A lack of funds stalled the midwestern carrier's conversion to the standard gauge system that now prevailed across the United States, even in the South, a longtime regional holdout for broad-gauge tracks. Because it required new bridges and other alterations to the infrastructure, widening a narrow-gauge railroad to standard size involved

A map published in 1885 depicted the route of the formerly important Great Broad Route with a track gauge of six feet that connected the East Coast with the heartland cities of Cincinnati, Saint Louis, and Chicago via the tracks of the Erie, Atlantic & Great Western; Cincinnati, Hamilton & Dayton; and Ohio & Mississippi railways.

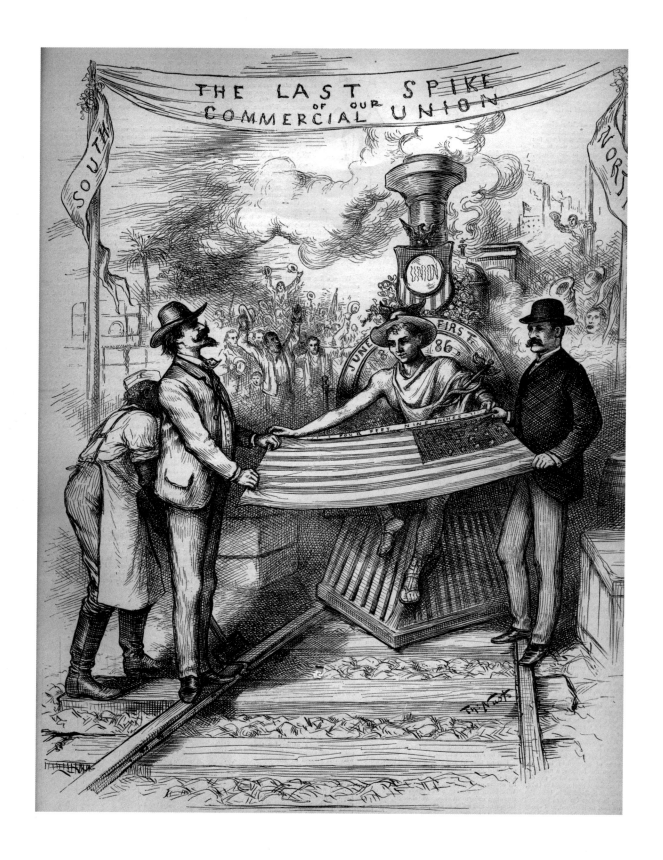

far greater expense than reducing broad-gauge tracks. Only in scattered mining regions of the West did the three-foot gauge continue to make sense.[11]

During the standardization decade of the 1880s, one significant group of holdouts remained stubbornly committed to the increasingly idiosyncratic gauge of five feet. These were the railroads of the South, which had always marched to a decidedly different drummer, and the North's Civil War military triumph in 1865 had not altered that. Many of the region's rail lines had been built originally to facilitate the movement of crops from inland fields to coastal ports—to bypass the rapids and falls that limited river navigation between the South's broad coastal plain and its rolling Piedmont uplands. The localism and lack of any meaningful rail interchange persisted for decades across the South, though a broad gauge of five feet between the rails was most often cited as the region's de facto standard.

After months of preparation, on a single day in late May 1886 southerners moved their tracks inward a few inches and joined the rest of North America's standard-gauge network. *Harper's* magazine celebrated the landmark event with a cover image that showed North and South properly and fully unified at last through the medium of the railroad. Fruit, lumber, and cotton from the Deep South could travel for the first time to nearly every corner of North America without encountering any cumbersome breaks in gauge.[12]

The remaining exceptions—most notably a few short railroads in Maine that used a two-foot gauge, mountain railroads in Colorado that continued to use a three-foot gauge, and some isolated narrow-gauge lines in California—did not amount to much in the overall network of railroads that henceforth used standard-gauge track. In short, the gauge question that had bedeviled railroads since the earliest days was effectively settled—at least for North America. Other parts of the world less affected by railroads waited a while longer. Australia to this day uses several different track gauges, as does India.[13]

With increased standardization came a noticeable increase in the railroad publishing activity that emerged during the post–Civil War years. The late 1860s had witnessed an outpouring of land-promotion literature from Jay Cooke and Company, the Philadelphia banking firm responsible for transforming the Northern Pacific's enormous grant of land into the dollars required to pay for the railroad's construction from the Upper Great Lakes to the Pacific Northwest. Likewise, the completion of the first transcontinental railroad at Promontory, Utah, in 1869 had made it relatively easy to cross the United States in the comfort of a train, but one popular antidote to the High Plains landscape, which many travelers found boring, was the railroad handbook that described the passing scenery (often with the addition of a few jokes and entertaining anecdotes).[14]

With the adoption of standard time in the 1880s and the integration of the American South into the standard-gauge network, long-distance travel grew much easier and more comfortable than it ever had been. A person could board a train in New York or Philadelphia and continue all the way to Florida; it was the same for travel between Chicago and San Francisco or Los Angeles. Finally, the decade of the 1880s witnessed a burst of construction never topped during any comparable span of time, and additional miles of track meant an expanding array of travel options and a growing number of rail publications to advertise them.

Getting to the Pacific coast grew immeasurably easier after the Union Pacific and Central Pacific joined forces to complete in 1869 the first line of tracks that linked the Midwest with California. This combination dominated transcontinental travel during the 1870s, but the competition increased noticeably after 1883. On February 5, a combination of several allied railroads opened the Southern Pacific's Sunset Route across the desert Southwest to link San Francisco and Los Angeles with New Orleans. A few months later, on September 8, Northern Pacific officials staged an elaborate final-spike ceremony in Montana to inaugurate a third travel option to and from the West Coast, the first by a single carrier.

The Atchison, Topeka & Santa Fe had slowly but steadily extended its tracks west from Kansas to California, but in 1888

SPATIAL FRAUD: WHEN A FEW EXTRA MILES MADE A BIG DIFFERENCE

Railroad space took many different forms, as illustrated by a particularly bizarre case of mismeasurement in the state of Pennsylvania. Public timetables invariably included detailed enumerations of the mileage between stations, and with the cost of rail tickets typically based on the number of miles a passenger traveled, accuracy affected the pocketbooks of travelers and railroads, albeit inversely. Eduard Schenk was a Pittsburgh civil engineer who frequently rode the train to Youngstown, Ohio, a journey of sixty-four miles, or so he claimed. The Pittsburgh & Lake Erie insisted that the two cities were spaced sixty-eight miles apart and charged him accordingly. The discrepancy of four miles incensed Schenk, who disputed both the railroad's calculations and the extra ten cents it repeatedly charged him (and all other passengers who made the journey). As a member of a profession that prized numerical precision, he protested to the Interstate Commerce Commission (ICC) in Washington, DC. He complained that, because of its mismeasurement, the railroad reaped a bonus of thousands of extra dollars annually from its passengers.

The ICC in 1907 ordered the Pittsburgh & Lake Erie to survey the distance anew, and much to the railroad's chagrin, it discovered that Schenk was correct. Having won his point, he declined to pursue further legal action. However, the government of Pennsylvania took note and subsequently mandated that every railroad in the state must remeasure every mile of track for accuracy. Even small spatial errors, whether intentional or not, could add up to a big financial windfall for the carriers.*

* *Pittsburgh Press*, April 21, 1907; *Pittsburgh Daily Post*, April 21, 1907; *Courier* (Harrisburg, PA), May 7, 1907. I am indebted to Gregory P. Ames, who collected a file of items related to this curious event and shared it with me.

it opened a new route east from Kansas City to Chicago to form a fourth transcontinental line within the United States. North of the border, the completion of the Canadian Pacific Railway on November 7, 1885, provided yet another transcontinental option.[15]

Each new transcontinental railroad meant increased competition. Options for through travel aboard the trains operated by several different railroads heightened the interest of individual carriers in boosting patronage by publishing endless streams of promotional literature.[16]

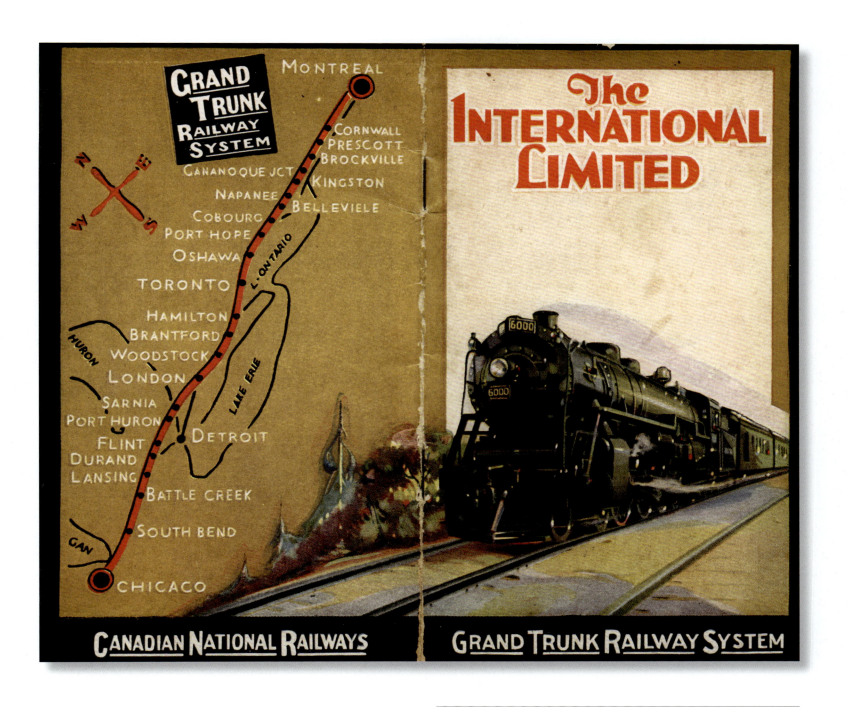

The adoption of a common gauge for the United States and Canada during the 1880s made it possible for the Grand Trunk's International Limited to run between Montreal and Chicago without needing to transfer passengers and freight at the international border. This Canadian National brochure dates from 1926. Likewise, a common gauge enabled the Missouri Pacific to run through trains between Saint Louis and Mexico City and for a time positioned the Missouri metropolis as the nation's premier rail gateway to Mexico.

The desire to publish the railroad only intensified with the completion of several additional transcontinental lines: the Great Northern in January 1893; the Chicago, Milwaukee & St. Paul (Milwaukee Road) in May 1909; and the Western Pacific in August 1910.[17] In fact, with the Western Pacific, rail magnate George Gould aspired to complete a truly transcontinental line of tracks from Baltimore to San Francisco via Saint Louis, a first for the United States. The construction of the Wabash Pittsburgh Terminal, the eighty-six-mile link that buckled Gould's coast-to-coast system together and gained it access to an area of heavy industry that generated more freight tonnage than any other location in the United States, proved ruinously expensive, however.[18]

With the completion of the Western Pacific in 1910 and the closure of a short rail gap in western Pennsylvania, the ego-driven empire builder achieved his goal of linking several lines to form the first and only railroad that ran from Atlantic to Pacific under one ownership. The unwieldy combination endured only a few months before financial troubles began to bedevil each of Gould's rail lines, and one by one they entered receivership. The Gould empire collapsed. "George Gould had made many enemies and when the final break came he had no friends to come to his aid. His system snapped at both ends and the Gould era of railroading was over."[19]

Nonetheless, the individual railroads Gould intended to form links in his coast-to-coast chain engaged in a variety of publishing activities—ranging from very little for his Western Maryland and Pittsburgh & West Virginia lines to significant contributions to railroad literature and commercial art for his Wabash, Denver & Rio Grande and Western Pacific holdings. But excelling the literary output of all other Gould properties was the Missouri Pacific System, which together with its subsidiary railroads produced a visually stunning array of illustrated pamphlets and brochures.[20]

The western transcontinental railroads of the United States that were completed between 1869 and 1888 all possessed landed empires to sell to settlers. Those lines completed between 1893 and 1909 were not similarly endowed, but that did not diminish their interest in publishing the railroad. The Milwaukee Road, perhaps because it was a latecomer and could claim no land grants of its own, was nonetheless an especially vigorous promoter of settlement and vacation opportunities in the areas it served. The color cover of a promotional brochure that showed a farmer plowing gold coins from the Montana soil, symbolism every agrarian understood, attracted widespread attention and earned the railroad's boosters some friendly derision from the local press.[21]

With the introductory chapters of section I, I sought to provide chronological context for railroad publishing activity during its first century. In section II, I seek to highlight their most popular promotional themes and to showcase the rich legacy of commercial art that resulted from publishing the railroad. During the industry's first century, its output of pamphlets, booklets, posters, and illustrated calendars and timetables was so prodigious and varied that I can offer only a representative sample of their commercial art on the pages that follow.

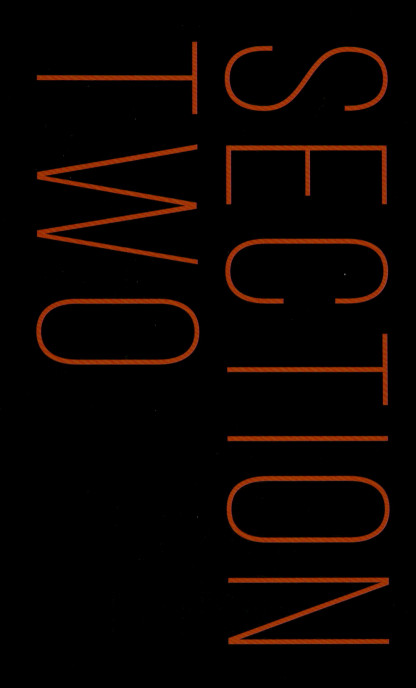

SECTION TWO OWL

RAILROAD COMMERCIAL ART

A Florida East Coast brochure from 1921 provided a unique perspective on the railroad. Maps featuring an elevated perspective (a bird's-eye view) were common among steam railroads—and even among some electric interurban railways—but this brochure takes the idea to new heights.

What is considered the most artistic railroad folder in the world will soon be received by patrons of the Atchison, Topeka & Santa Fe Railway. It revolutionizes similar publications, is published at Chicago monthly, and contains fifty-six pages of the finest book paper.

—from *Albuquerque Weekly Citizen*, December 19, 1896

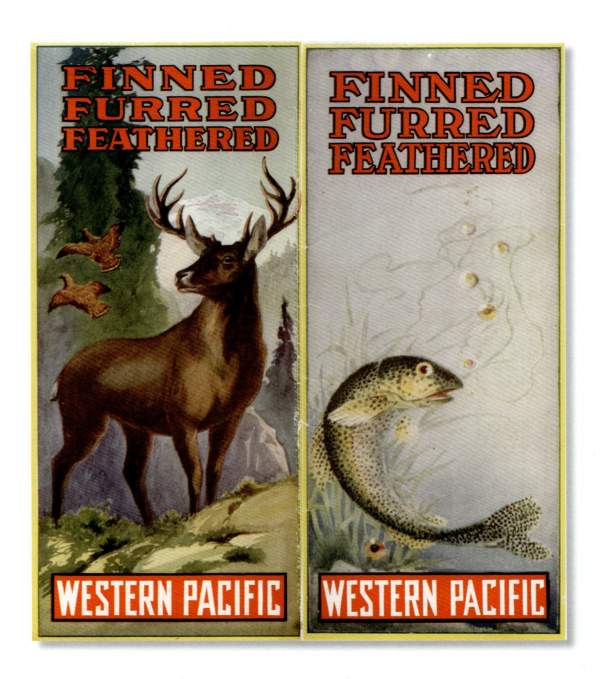

The Western Pacific's *Finned, Furred, Feathered* brochure cover (circa 1915) was one of many rail industry imprints intended to encourage hunting and fishing.

"Finned, Furred, Feathered" describes the fish and game as well as the resorts and outdoor attractions of the Western Pacific Railway in California. A useful feature of the folder is an outline map, showing that famous stream, the Feather River, between Oroville and Portola, together with tributary creeks, distances, river crossings and roadways.

—from *Official Guide*, August 1914, xxix

One of the most artistic railroad booklets ever circulated in this section is one just gotten out by the Passenger Traffic Department of the Southern Railway, entitled "The Land of the Sky." It is extensively illustrated, many of the splendid views, which as is well known, are among the finest in the world, being shown in elaborately colored pictures.

—from *Nashville Banner*, May 15, 1912

Southern Railway published a new *Land of the Sky* brochure annually, each of which featured different artwork on its cover. Among the railroads of North America, the publication of an annual series of brochures was common. For example, the Northern Pacific published *Wonderland*, and the Bangor & Aroostook had *In the Maine Woods*.

However, if you want a first-class description, get one of the railroad guide-books; for be it known to all ordinary "pencil-pushers" that when one of these railroad guide-book writers gets up steam, "pulls the throttle valve wide open," and starts out on a descriptive tour, ordinary scribblers "lost their right of way," and should very prudently "side-track" themselves.

—from *Des Moines Register*, September 1, 1883

The Crosbyton–South Plains, a Texas short line with big ambitions for the agricultural transformation of its High Plains location near Lubbock, was among the smallest of North America's railroad publicists. Its imprint *The Farmer and the Railroad* appeared in 1912, one year after the company commenced running trains, and was longer by a few pages than the rail line itself, which totaled thirty-nine miles. The Atchison, Topeka & Santa Fe purchased the diminutive carrier in 1915.

6

THE COMPASS OF OPPORTUNITY

"One is simply amazed at the vast of amount of money, energy, patience and persistency there is expended in setting forth the resources, advantages, capabilities, and wonders of this part of the continent," Emma Adams wrote in 1888, describing the "wild delirium for 'improvements'" she observed along the Pacific coast of the United States. Railroad publicists were prominent among the many self-anointed boosters who sought to reorient the nation's compass of opportunity in a westerly direction. It was the same in other regions of the United States, and especially in the heartland, where Saint Louis battled to protect its traditional dominance of an Upper Midwest commercial hinterland from post–Civil War inroads by the much younger city of Chicago. Sensing that they were losing the economic contest to the urban upstart on Lake Michigan, merchants in Saint Louis sought to use several newly constructed rail lines and their promoters to reorient the city's compass of opportunity away from its traditional Upper Midwest markets and toward the Southwest, a young and commercially dynamic region that was ripe for development.[1]

Why did Chicago become known as the hog butcher of the world and Saint Louis gain fame for its beer? The answer lies in the tangled history of the transportation-defined spatial relationships that entwined this pair of cities during the middle decades of the nineteenth century. Their historical rivalry offers a case study of the transformative power of different modes of transportation, especially the railroads, as expressed in new miles of track and the resulting flood of promotional publications. Together, tracks and booster tracts would reorient spatially the compass of opportunity. In other words, while the process of publishing the railroad turned the publicity spotlight onto hitherto unknown vacation and settlement opportunities, railroad booklets and pamphlets, like the tracks themselves, simultaneously contributed to spatial reorientation within the United States and Canada.

Saint Louis was by far the older of the two cities, predating the emergence of the lakeside village of Chicago in the 1830s by a full half century. Missouri's largest city (until surpassed in population by Kansas City in the 1990 federal census) profited enormously from its geographical location at the center of one of the world's most extensive systems of aquatic superhighways—a commercial system made even more profitable by the forests, rich soil, and mineral wealth that lay within easy reach of the steamboats and other forms of water transport used to carry passengers and freight. Lead from mines in Wisconsin, a state that was likewise a valuable source of lumber, traveled down the Mississippi to Saint Louis, as prized cargoes of furs moved down the Missouri from the High Plains and Rocky Mountains.

In some ways the Missouri River was the most remarkable of all the interior water highways, and therein lay the basis for Saint Louis's claim to be the nation's "Gateway to the West."[2] That assertion was valid for decades until the end of the 1850s, and during those years the Missouri metropolis grew prosperous because of the many steamboats that called it home. To the north, Chicago developed no strong connection to the inland rivers, not even with the 1849 completion of the Illinois & Michigan Canal that gained it physical access for the first time to the great rivers of the West. The city turned instead to railroads to extend its commercial reach inland from Lake Michigan. Its expanding network of tracks invariably reached the rivers long dominated by the Saint Louis–based fleet of steamboats, and at various river-and-rail intersections like Rock Island, Illinois, and Sioux City, Iowa, trains diverted cargoes formerly headed south along the Mississippi and Missouri Rivers and sent them east to Chicago and the Great Lakes.

Saint Louis, rather than yield to the Windy City, used its own expanding network of tracks to reorient its compass of opportunity. That is, it struck out in a new direction toward Texas and the Southwest, a developing region that Chicago would find difficult to dominate. Coincidental with the opening of the first rail routes between Saint Louis and Texas in the mid-1870s, Saint Louis brewers like Anheuser-Busch purchased refrigerated cars to ship ice-cold beer to thirsty residents of the Lone Star State.[3]

Aiding Saint Louis in its newfound commercial quest was the Southwest System of railroads assembled by Jay Gould and based in Saint Louis. One component of the Gould empire was the historic Pacific Railroad of Missouri, soon to become better known as the Missouri Pacific. Its historic orientation was to the west, though its reach to the West Coast stalled in Colorado, well short of tidewater. Offering a direct route to Texas was the Saint Louis, Iron Mountain & Southern, another Gould property that in future years would become a vital component of the Missouri Pacific System.

The vigorous publishing of the railroad, whether by the Missouri Pacific or Iron Mountain, became a hallmark of Gould's quest to dominate the Southwest, and no one emerged as a more bombastic wordsmith in the service of his master's cause than Logan Uriah Reavis. His several booster brochures and books brimmed with breathless enthusiasm for all the features of the Southwest served by the Gould railroads and for Reavis's personal mission to relocate the capital of the United States from the District of Columbia to the centrally located Saint Louis.[4]

The Gould lines and other Missouri-based railroads prospered because of the dynamic growth of the Southwest, and their numerous booster brochures benefited from the new and improved printing technology exported from Germany. Many of the imprints became masterpieces of railroad commercial art. During the early 1890s, a terminally ill Gould relinquished control of his Southwest System to his son George, a man possessed of even greater ambition than his father. He was determined to be the first person in American history to extend rail lines from one coast to the other, but a rickety assemblage of seven separate railroads extending east to west as the Western Maryland, Pittsburgh & West Virginia, Wheeling & Lake Erie, Wabash, Missouri Pacific, Denver & Rio Grande, and Western Pacific proved unwieldy and soon collapsed. Gould lost millions of dollars in his ego-driven quest. By contrast, his brother Edwin seldom made newspaper headlines, as George often did, and he presided successfully (and apparently contentedly) over the fortunes of the St. Louis Southwestern (the "Cotton Belt Route"), a railroad that extended from Saint Louis south across Missouri and Arkansas into the forests, cotton fields, and oil patches of eastern Texas.

Facing, The Saint Louis, Iron Mountain & Southern was tireless in its efforts to redirect the compass of opportunity to Texas and Arkansas. Like many of the transcontinental rail lines farther west, it possessed a large federal grant of land in Arkansas that it desired to see settled and made productive. *Arkansas Fills the Bill* dates from the early twentieth century.

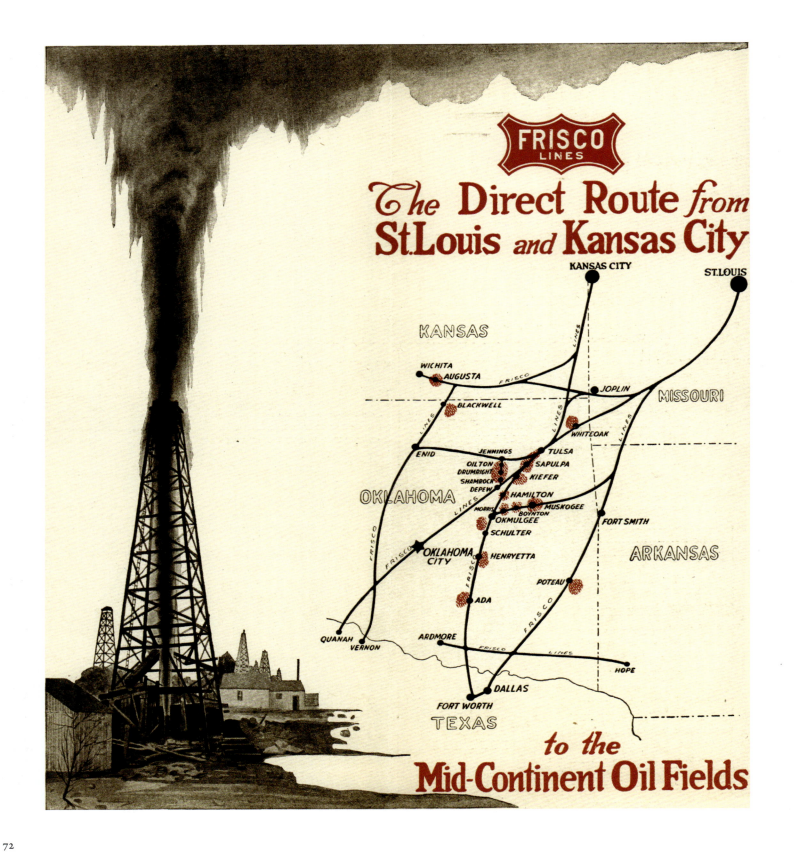

FRISCO LINES

The Direct Route from St. Louis and Kansas City
to the Mid-Continent Oil Fields

Especially after the early twentieth century and the discovery of "black gold" beneath the soils of Texas and later Oklahoma, the urge to "sell the Southwest" to prospective settlers and vacationers only grew more compelling, as did the publications issued by the several Missouri-based railroads that reached south from Saint Louis and Kansas City to reorient the compass of commercial opportunity. These companies included the Missouri Pacific and the affiliated St. Louis, Iron Mountain & Southern, the Cotton Belt, the Missouri-Kansas-Texas ("Katy"), the St. Louis–San Francisco ("Frisco"), and the Kansas City Southern.

It might be tempting to believe that the most vigorous development of the cities and hinterlands of America's "last frontier" (apart from Alaska), aided as always by railroad publicists, occurred in the far western states and territories during the late nineteenth century. In fact, the new state of Oklahoma (1907) and its most vigorous phase of promotion came later, in the early twentieth century, as did the railroad boosting of the hitherto isolated Ozark Plateau of southern Missouri and northern Arkansas. *Oklahoma, the Twentieth Century State* was one of several brochures issued by the Passenger Department of the Rock Island Lines, which sought to focus the attention of immigrants and other potential settlers on its mid-American service region.[5]

During the boom times of the early twentieth century when America's network of tracks continued to grow by additional thousands of miles each year (until it reached a historic mileage peak in 1916), no one could predict with certainty where a railroad's ambitions might lead. For sure, ever-creative wordsmiths and commercial artists stood ready to generate popular enthusiasm for any new vacation destinations and business opportunities.[6]

Their visionary talents were by no means limited to the American Southwest. Southern Florida was ripe for railroad development, as was western Canada, where the Canadian Pacific and two additional transcontinental railroads sought to extend the reach of the nation's two wealthiest and most populous provinces, Ontario and Quebec, across North America to British Columbia on the Pacific coast. But why stop there? Some enthusiasts predicted the construction of a rail line north through Canada's Yukon Territory all the way to Alaska, perhaps with some sort of link to Russia's newly completed trans-Siberian route. Such optimism seemed oblivious to mountain ranges perpetually clad in snow or storm-tossed miles of open ocean.[7]

Redirecting the compass of opportunity generated intense competition not only among cities and regions but also among the rail rivals that served them and benefited most directly from what the different areas of the United States and Canada had to offer. If rail publications typically featured intense and insistent language, it was because of the serious battles waged among rail competitors—at least until the rise of serious highway competitors during the 1920s forced railroads to redirect their combative energy to the newcomers and away from rail industry rivals.

During the heyday of vigorous competition among railroads, from the 1870s until the federal takeover of the industry in 1918, publishing remained of paramount importance, but so did the hands-on examination of the claims advanced by individual carriers. Even if wordsmiths who published the railroad could not convince potential settlers to move to farms or trackside communities in the Dakotas or Colorado, the railroads themselves could bring the fabled products of those states and others to curious audiences, aboard special display cars. The Northern Pacific was one pioneer in the creation of a traveling agricultural exhibition. Its latest car, which toured the United States in 1910, featured a variety of "soil and scenery" exhibits typical of state and county fairs: "The car will be accompanied by representatives of the passenger and immigration departments of the Northern Pacific and by a lecturer who will supplement the exhibits by illustrated talks." During its travels (mainly through the South and East), it paused in numerous small towns and opened its doors to the local farmers and merchants to better acquaint them with the opportunities available along its tracks in the Northwest. The hands-on displays proved very popular. "This is a very direct method of advertising, and it appears to possess strong merits as a means of reaching the parties most likely to be interested."[8]

Another form of publicity that emulated the hands-on approach of the display cars was the Road Improvement Train that Southern Railway operated throughout its service territory. The idea was to demonstrate how rural dwellers might improve the country roads, many of which at the dawn of the twentieth century amounted to little more than dirt traces that quickly devolved into muddy quagmires after a rain. The Southern was joined by other major American railroads, most notably the Illinois Central and the Frisco, both of which operated Good Roads trains on tracks through their respective territories.

Management reasoned: "The importance of good roads to the development of the farming industry cannot be overstated." Indeed, farm-to-market roads would benefit railroad freight haulers, but rail executives in 1910 or 1911 could not envision that their advocacy for better rural roads would within a decade result in a national network of all-weather highways that facilitated intercity bus and truck competition and encouraged ownership of private automobiles?[9]

Emulating the railroad publicists was a new generation determined to publish the highway. Before components of the expanding network of federal highways were first numbered in 1926—with Route 66 gaining lasting fame—long-distance roads were named. The Lincoln Highway was perhaps the best-known example because it was first to span the United States. Each of the named routes (or "trails") competed for motorists by issuing special publicity brochures not unlike those the railroads had used earlier to reorient the compass of opportunity.[10]

Facing, The Southern Pacific, which was based in San Francisco, extended across the continent from Los Angeles to New Orleans, and in the 1920s it was eager to redirect the compass of opportunity to Texas. Otherwise, several Saint Louis–based railroads would dominate the Lone Star State. The Texas & Pacific, a major player across Texas, might seem locally based, but, in fact, it was controlled by Gould interests based in Saint Louis, and for years it functioned as a Missouri Pacific subsidiary. All railroads mentioned in this caption now form part of the Omaha-based Union Pacific.

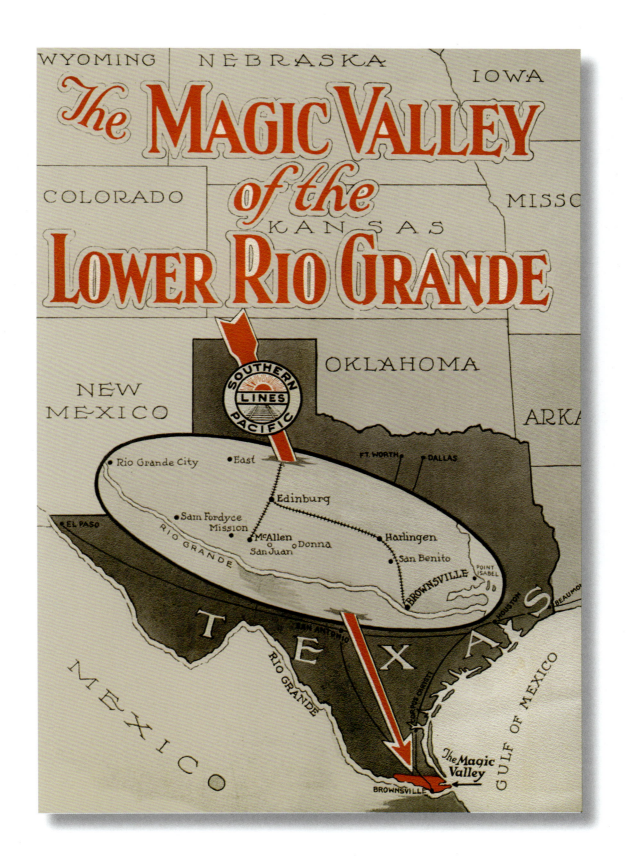

Across The Continent Through Canada

GRAND TRUNK SYSTEM

During the second decade of the twentieth century, a time of unusual prosperity in Canada, the Grand Trunk thought the time was right to extend its tracks across Canada to the Pacific coast. The Canadian Pacific had been the nation's first railway to do so, three decades earlier in 1885, when it completed a line between Montreal and Vancouver. The date of the Grand Trunk System brochure pictured here is 1917. Alas, for Canada's ambitious latecomers, success proved elusive. Consequentially, the Confederation government acquired and combined several struggling carriers to form the Canadian National Railways. Ironically, Canada's two gigantic railways are today major players within the United States, the Canadian National having acquired the historic Illinois Central and the Canadian Pacific, the Kansas City Southern.

I congratulate you most heartily on the completion of the transcontinental railway on Canadian soil. May it prove a permanent bond of union between the eastern and western portions of this great Dominion.

—British Columbia premier William Smithe, quoted in *Victoria (Canada) Daily Times*, November 23, 1885

7

RAILROAD IMPERIALISM AND NATION BUILDING

Few nations owe more to a single railroad than Canada owes to the Canadian Pacific. Without a "grand national highway" of tracks that extended six thousand miles from coast to coast to weld together its scattered provinces and territories, there might be no nation of Canada, or at least no Canada as it is geographically configured today. Appropriately, commentators described the spatial configuration of its ten provinces as resembling a linear train of railway cars. Both physically and symbolically, the railroad played an inordinately large role in fostering the national growth of the Dominion of Canada after its formation in 1867 and, more importantly, in keeping it from falling apart, as some prominent Americans greedily hoped it would. Here was an example of the power of railroads to reorient the compass of opportunity—that is, to rearrange existing spatial relationships—on a grand scale.[1]

Even after the American Civil War ended in 1865, the US secretary of state, William H. Seward, remained peeved with Great Britain for its pro-Confederate sympathy during the early years of the conflict. He was willing to settle the national grievances if Britain transferred to the United States one or more of its

colonies located north of the international border. Two years later he acquired the Russian colony of Alaska in a deal that was widely criticized as "Seward's Folly." A newspaper cartoon of the day showed the secretary of state bringing home to the United States a big chunk of ice. Such criticism, however, was both shortsighted and unfair because Seward saw America's interest in Alaska in geopolitical terms: with its acquisition of Alaska, the United States might be able to wrest the colony of British Columbia from Canada's grip to create an American land bridge that extended along the Pacific coast all the way to the Arctic Circle and beyond. Deprived of an outlet on the Pacific, the new nation of Canada might remain so weak that it would simply fall into American hands like a piece of ripe fruit, an analogy that dates from that era of geopolitical uncertainty.[2]

It is more than coincidental that the American acquisition of Alaska and action by the British Parliament in London to create Canada occurred within days of one another. To make certain that the westernmost colony of British Columbia remained out of American hands and tied its future firmly to the new nation, Canada promised to extend a railway to the Pacific coast. Passengers and freight using the new corridor would serve to unite the scattered provinces of former British North America. It was in many ways a rash promise—and it proved to be an exceedingly expensive and difficult one to fulfill.

British Columbia took the bait, and with the driving of a final spike at Craigellachie on the Pacific Slope in 1885, Canada's central government finally made good on its promise. Builders of the Canadian Pacific Railway surmounted numerous challenges as they extended a line of tracks west from Quebec and Ontario across the rugged Laurentian Shield north of Lake Superior, across the prairies, and finally over the Rocky Mountains to reach the newly created community of Vancouver. The creation of the transcontinental nation by means of the Canadian Pacific was truly a milestone in the annals of railroad time and space.[3]

Canada experienced further tribulations during the depression decade of the 1890s, and those included nearly becoming a battleground during a heated dispute in 1895 between the United States and Great Britain over the location of the international boundary between Venezuela and British Guyana. One supposed reason many of Canada's early railroads adopted a broad-gauge standard of five feet, six inches was to make it difficult for its nearest neighbor, the much more populous United States, to invade it, as it had done during the War of 1812. The nations of Russia and Spain had both adopted broader-gauge tracks than prevailed across most of Europe, supposedly to forestall the threat of invasion. During the continent's early years of railroad construction, residents of both Russia and Spain retained vivid memories of the attempted Napoleonic conquests just twenty years earlier. Likewise, Canada's Intercolonial Railway purposely chose a long and roundabout route between Montreal and Halifax to prevent this vital link in Britain's globe-girdling imperial lifeline, the All Red Route, from straying too close to the border with the United States. The occasionally frosty relations between the North American neighbors warmed noticeably after the peaceful resolution of the Venezuela Boundary Dispute in 1899, an odd event that finally ended Canada's fear of a military invasion from south of the border.[4]

With the dawn of the twentieth century and the return of prosperity, Canada's heightened national confidence encouraged the launch of two additional rail projects that sought to duplicate the success of the Canadian Pacific as a transcontinental carrier. One was the Grand Trunk Pacific, and the other was the Canadian Northern, both of which headed bravely west from the Great Lakes to the Pacific coast. Both projects ran into serious financial trouble and, along with the historic Grand Trunk line based in Ontario and Quebec, ended up as wards of Canada's central government. The resulting combination emerged shortly after World War I as the Canadian National Railway, a sprawling network of tracks that formed North America's second truly transcontinental rail highway.[5]

A word of explanation is needed here. South of the Canadian border, residents of the United States had for decades used the term *transcontinental railroad* in a glib and inaccurate way to describe the several lines that ran overland from the Midwest to the Pacific coast. In the 1850s, the Pacific Railroad of Missouri had promised to build a railroad to the Pacific from Saint Louis. It was the first American railroad to use the word Pacific in its corporate title, but its stated aim was never to cross the United States from one coast to another. Even the much-heralded "first transcontinental railroad" completed at Promontory, Utah, in May 1869 was far from spanning the continent. Its eastern terminus was Omaha, Nebraska, and initially its tracks did not physically connect to the railroads on the opposite bank of the Missouri River that would provide it access to Chicago and the eastern United States.

Most of America's original "transcontinental" railroads did not truly span the continent, except for the Southern Pacific, which connected New Orleans on the Gulf of Mexico with Los Angeles and San Francisco on the Pacific coast. Again, the Union Pacific's original eastern terminus was Omaha, while for the Atchison, Topeka & Santa Fe and the Chicago, Milwaukee, St. Paul & Pacific it was Chicago, and for both the Great Northern and the Northern Pacific it was Saint Paul, Minnesota.

Historically, the rail network of the United States was divided into two large spheres, with carriers operating in either

Facing, The date for the Panama Railroad map is 1900. The interoceanic rail link was completed in 1855, and during the early twentieth century, construction of the Panama Canal would progress toward its completion in 1914. The Panama Railroad operates today as a subsidiary of the Canadian Pacific Kansas City Limited, itself the result of a merger that dates from 2023.

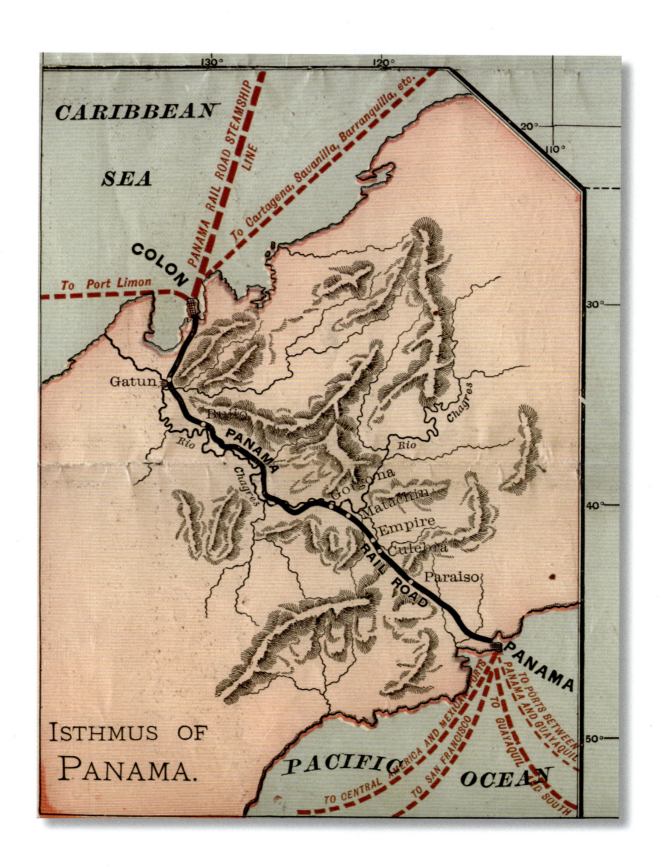

CARIBBEAN

SEA

COLON

To Port Limon

PANAMA RAIL ROAD STEAMSHIP LINE

To Cartagena, Savanilla, Barranquilla, etc.

Gatun

Bujio

PANAMA

Rio

Chagres

Gorgona

Matachin

Empire

Culebra

Paraiso

RAIL ROAD

Rio

Chagres

PANAMA

TO PORTS BETWEEN PANAMA AND GUAYAQUIL

TO GUAYAQUIL AND SOUTH

ISTHMUS OF
PANAMA.

PACIFIC OCEAN

TO CENTRAL AMERICA AND MEXICA

TO SAN FRANCISCO

the eastern or western halves of the nation—and it is still basically that way today. The most important intersections between the two halves were Chicago and the Mississippi River cities of Saint Louis, Memphis, and New Orleans. There were a few exceptions to this geographical division. The Wabash Railroad based in Saint Louis spanned the Midwest from western Missouri to upstate New York, and the Chicago-based Illinois Central breached the Mississippi barrier with tracks that extended west to Sioux City, Iowa, and with another line farther south that linked the Mississippi capital of Jackson with Shreveport in northwestern Louisiana.[6]

Finally, credit for being first to link the Atlantic and Pacific Oceans belongs to the Panama Railroad, all forty-eight miles of it completed in 1855. Short though it was, few enterprises were more difficult to construct or earned more profit per mile than the rail line across the isthmus: "The road pays larger dividends than any other in the world." In terms of its construction, the "malarious, pestilent, fever-breeding air" of the steamy isthmian jungles provided a more formidable challenge than the modest elevation of three hundred feet that divided the two oceans until the completion of the Panama Canal in 1914.[7]

Around the globe, no other railroad this short achieved a more monumental reinvention of time and space. California joined the United States in 1850, but for the next five years a commercial connection with the rest of the Union required sailing ships to complete the dangerous and time-consuming voyage around South America's Cape Horn. Trains of the Panama Railroad could complete in a single afternoon an interoceanic journey that had formerly required several months at sea.[8]

As with the so-called transcontinental railroads across the western United States, the two large railroads that spanned Canada needed to populate and develop the lands along their tracks. That required them to launch major publishing programs that at times seemed to issue colorful new brochures almost monthly. Like the brochures published by American railroads, the Canadian ones promoted settlement on one hand and vacation opportunities on the other. Publicists transformed Banff and Lake Louise, located along Canadian Pacific tracks high in the Rocky Mountains, into star attractions, as the Canadian National later did for Jasper National Park.[9]

Moreover, the Canadian Pacific emulated the major railways of Great Britain and built a series of outstanding hotels along its tracks from coast to coast. These properties operated under the Canadian Pacific brand for many years.[10] The railroad's portfolio at one time also included a fleet of steamships and Canadian Pacific Air Lines. Unlike in the United States with its populist fear of monopolies, north of the border the Canadian Pacific remained free to fashion a comprehensive transportation system.[11]

Offering an interesting counterpoint to the Canadian example of the role transcontinental railroads could play in nation building is Brazil, the largest nation in South America but not one that stretched across the continent from coast to coast. West of the Andes Mountains and along the Pacific coast lay several large Spanish-speaking nations, including Peru and Colombia. There would be no transcontinental railroad for the Portuguese-speaking nation, and thus it had little incentive to populate its vast interior. For decades, most Brazilians lived close to its Atlantic coast. To promote the development of its interior, the national government based in coastal Rio de Janeiro created a new inland capital of Brasilia in 1956 and dramatically reoriented the compass of opportunity. The move, though bold, did little to foster the kind of rail networks that developed across the United States, Canada, or even Mexico, another bicoastal nation. To this day the scattered railroads of Brazil serve mainly as natural resource conveyor belts to transport iron ore and other products from inland sites to port cities along the Atlantic coast.[12]

Of all South American nations, only Argentina developed a large and truly comprehensive railroad network. It was much the same across the South Atlantic in the nation of South Africa. Elsewhere on the African continent, rail lines were scattered, and most served the same function as the natural resource haulers of South America.[13]

In the case of Canada, railroad imperialism had successfully welded a nation together. The same was true for Russia's trans-Siberian railroad completed in 1904. But several other grandiose projects, like Cecil John Rhodes's proposed Cape to

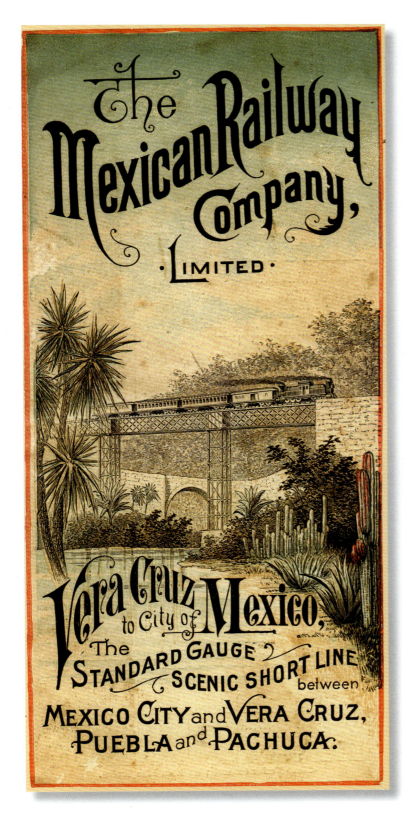

Cairo railroad stretching the length of Africa and Germany's ambitious Berlin to Baghdad railroad, were clearly examples of railroad imperialism intended to benefit a colonizing nation. Rhodes died in 1902, well before he could see his project through to completion, and it never was finished; the colony of German East Africa (now the nation of Tanzania) lay perversely situated between an otherwise continuous string of British colonies and stubbornly blocked the railroad of its national rival because Germany had colonial ambitions of its own in Africa.[14]

A more successful example of railroad imperialism was the extension of three American railroads running south from the international border with the United States and deep into Mexico, a process that one American contemporary in 1882 lauded as the "railway invasion of Mexico." Two of the rail corridors extended south from the Texas cities of Laredo and El Paso, and the third ran deep into Mexico from opposite the Arizona border city of Nogales.[15]

President Porfirio Diaz allowed Yankees to build railroads in Mexico to develop the nation. After revolutionaries overthrew the increasingly dictatorial Diaz in 1910 and thereby launched a decade of civil war, the nation's railroads were forcibly joined to a sprawling government system called the National Railways of Mexico, though in more recent years these same lines were privatized and allowed once again to fall under Yankee control—or even more recently, under Canadian control. Herein lies another irony that makes history intriguing: in April 2023, the Canadian Pacific (headquartered in Calgary, Alberta) acquired the Kansas City Southern, which operated an extensive network of tracks in Mexico.[16]

My referencing the Kansas City Southern and Mexico invokes thoughts of Arthur Stilwell, a remarkable railroad visionary based in Kansas City, Missouri, at the dawn of the twentieth century. His expansive geopolitical thinking encompassed the

Gulf of Mexico, the West Coast of Mexico, and even Asia, all linked by his railroad creations to the agricultural resource-rich Midwest. Stilwell was one of a handful of Americans—most notably Henry Plant and Henry Flagler in Florida, Henry Villard and James J. Hill across the Northern Tier states and territories, and William Barstow Strong of the Santa Fe across the Southwest between Chicago and Southern California—who more or less single-handedly and successfully reoriented railroad time and space.[17]

Stilwell's first big project was to extend a rail line south from Kansas City to the Gulf of Mexico to provide an ocean outlet for the farm products of the Midwest. This successful enterprise became known as the Kansas City Southern. Stilwell next desired a rail outlet for Kansas City on the Pacific Ocean. By laying a ruler across a map of North America, he observed that the shortest rail route to the West Coast from Kansas City and the agricultural cornucopia of the Midwest was to the sleepy Mexican fishing village of Topolobampo. His ambitious Kansas City, Mexico & Orient line was never completed during his lifetime, and it never was to be completed as Stilwell envisioned it. A line of tracks from Wichita south to the Mexican border ended up being acquired by the Atchison, Topeka & Santa Fe, while farther south in Mexico itself one challenge after another thwarted the railroad builders.[18]

One of their biggest challenges was to run a line of tracks through the Sierra Madre and the Copper Canyon, a chasm five times larger than Grand Canyon in the United States, though not as colorful. The Chihuahua-Pacific finally completed a line of tracks from Chihuahua to Topolobampo and, with the Copper Canyon forming a major attraction, managed to sustain the operation of a tourist-oriented train, which in the early twenty-first century was the sole survivor among the many passenger trains that had once served travelers in Mexico.

The irony is that although Stilwell never realized his ambition to connect Kansas City with the Pacific coast, his first brainchild, the Kansas City Southern, did acquire a major portion of the privatized National Railways of Mexico and was thus able to weld together a through line of tracks extending from Kansas City south to Mexico City via a Laredo, Texas, international gateway. The reconfigured Kansas City Southern thus had tracks in place to benefit from the cross-border flow of traffic made possible by the North American Free Trade Agreement, which linked the United States, Canada, and Mexico. The agile railroad, for years the smallest of the seven big carriers that dominated rail traffic across the United States and Canada during the initial decades of the twenty-first century, also profited from the rehabilitation and successful operation of its short transcontinental subsidiary in Central America, the historic Panama Railroad. After the expansion-minded Canadian Pacific acquired Kansas City Southern in 2023, it formed an international north–south corridor that complemented its historically significant east–west transcontinental line across Canada and thus gave a new meaning to the concept of railroad empire building.[19]

Facing, The Chicago & Eastern Illinois was a midwestern railroad that reached no farther south than Evansville, Indiana, on the Ohio River, yet after the United States' victory in the Spanish-American War of 1898, it proudly promoted the nation's newly acquired overseas empire, as did its competitor, the Illinois Central, which with tracks extending from Lake Michigan to the Gulf of Mexico had an obvious economic incentive to do so.

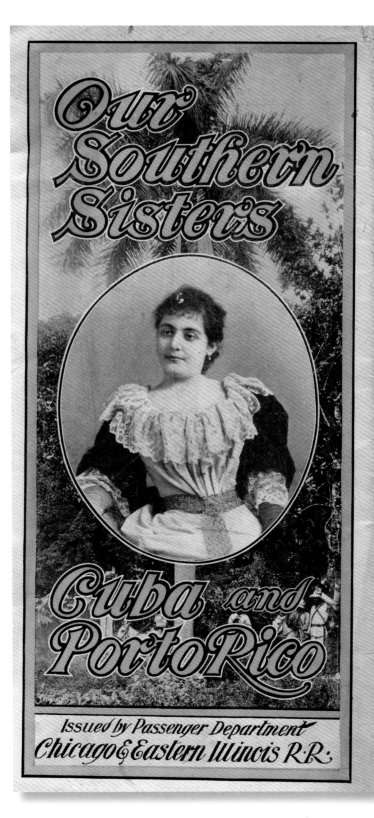

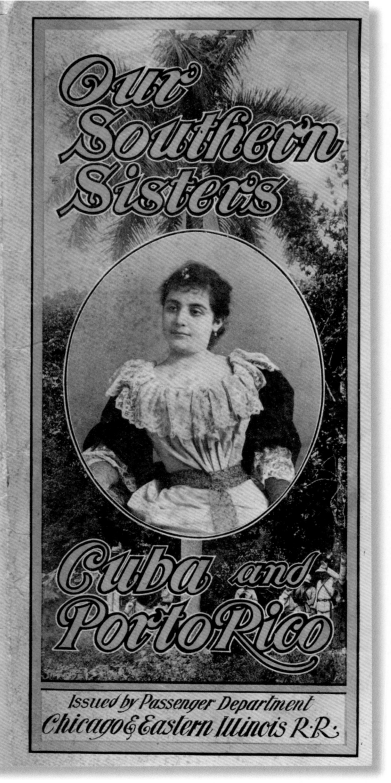

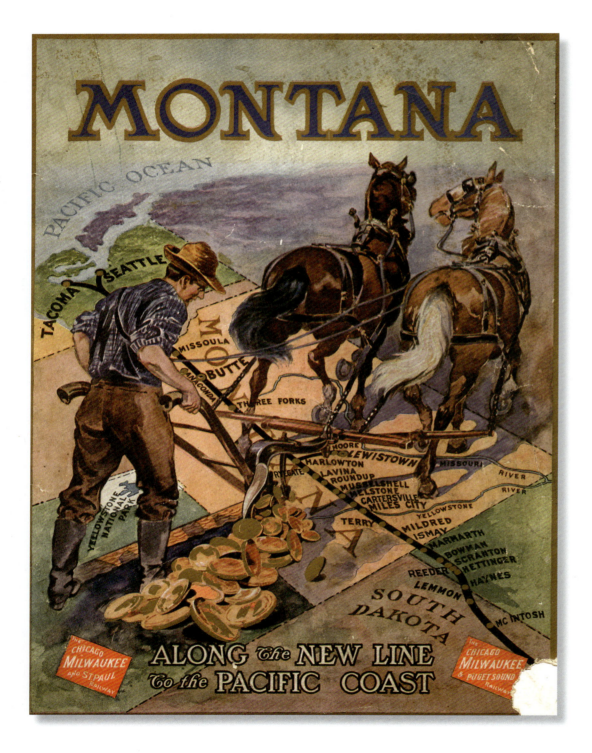

But the building of a railroad is one thing, and the development of traffic is quite another. Long before our rails crossed the Dakota-Montana line we had a force of experienced immigration agents in the field prospecting, not for gold, nor silver, nor copper, but for business.

—from the *Milwaukee Railway System Employees' Magazine* (1914)[1]

The Chicago, Milwaukee & St. Paul (later known as the Milwaukee Road) was a latecomer among the transcontinental railroads of the United States, and thus it received no federal land grants to encourage its construction. Undeterred, the exceedingly prosperous carrier based in the Upper Midwest (which counted members of the oil-rich Rockefeller dynasty among its directors) plunged boldly west from South Dakota to the Pacific coast, filled with ambition to transform the landscape along its right-of-way. Perhaps its most famous imprint, fifteen thousand copies of which the railroad distributed in 1910, showed a farmer plowing gold coins from the soil of Montana.

8

MAGICIAN'S WAND

LANDSCAPES REPACKAGED FOR HOMESEEKERS

Landscapes do not interpret themselves. The same area, especially if it were remote from centers of population and unfamiliar to most Americans or Canadians, had the potential to become fertile farmland or remain a desert wasteland, depending on its interpreters. The Northern Pacific's transformation of the Great Plains landscape that federal cartographers had initially disparaged as the "Great American Desert" was perhaps the single most dramatic example of an unappealing and seemingly peripheral part of the United States repacked by railroad publicists as a desirable commodity, a process easily likened to the transformative power of a magician's wand. Additional landscapes that benefited from a railroad-inspired metamorphosis include the chilly and remote northern reaches of Michigan, Wisconsin, and Minnesota; the fetid mangrove swamps of southern Florida; and the arid West, which stretched a thousand miles from eastern Washington and southern Idaho to New Mexico and Arizona, places that two or three generations of rail publicists assiduously worked to repackage as appealing prospects for settlers.

In numerous instances, even before the initial mile of a new rail line had been spiked into place, company wordsmiths, photographers, and illustrators had already coupled clever and always positive prose with visually arresting images. On the pages of their countless booster pamphlets, swamps became scenic lakes and chilly prairies became temperate fertile fields poised to yield lucrative crops of corn or wheat once settlers plowed them. One writer for *Sunset*, the Southern Pacific's booster magazine, described the process of landscape transformation as "transplanting the Garden of Eden," a reference to the unspoiled paradise mentioned in the opening chapters of the Bible.[2]

The earliest railroads in the United States and Canada typically connected a pair of significant cities, or an urban entrepôt with its established hinterland. Hence, it was easy for entrepreneurs to observe and anticipate how much traffic a newly constructed railroad might expect to haul. If nothing else, a promoter could stand alongside a road and simply count the number of freight wagons and passenger coaches as they passed. Rail construction in the northeastern United States peaked before the Civil War, and because much of the region had already been developed, the railroad as publisher had no reason to promote additional settlement there or highlight agricultural opportunities awaiting newcomers to the New England states. But in the West or South, plenty of opportunities awaited railroads that sought to develop

MAGICIAN'S WAND: TRANSFORMING THE GREAT AMERICAN DESERT

"The great American Desert was once a shivering subject for a dreary winter evening talk, but the great trackless waste has become in a large proportion the garden of the west in fertility. . . . With the turning up of the soil, come the natural atmospheric influences, and the rains followed. Trees were planted and flourished, and Paradise replaced dreariness. And so, year after year, the tide of prosperous settlement verges westward, and the rain advances the same." The arguments of boosters sounded good on paper, but the claim that rain followed the plow proved spurious and harmed many trusting settlers.*

* A. T. Sears and E. Webster, *Sears and Webster's Railway Guide* ([Chicago]: Sears & Webster, 1879), 18.

and later to encourage trackside development. The purpose of a land grant was to take a commodity the federal government possessed in abundance, the public domain, and use individual swaths to launch new railroads. In return, railroad companies sought to use their grants of land to raise the dollars needed for construction. In 1850, Uncle Sam possessed public lands totaling nearly a billion and a half acres, much of it inaccessible and unappealing to settlers despite earlier grants to support wagon roads and canals. The construction of railroads could and would transform the public domain. The federal land giveaway originated with the Illinois Central during the 1850s. The program continued for the next two decades, until late 1871, and was used to support the construction of rail lines in Florida, in the southwestern states of Missouri and Arkansas, and most prominently in the states and territories of the Far West. In all, rail builders in twenty-seven states received bequests of federal land.[3]

On a map, a typical land grant resembled a linear checkerboard of alternating mile squares of railroad and government land. The reasoning was that when rail lines were fully operational, the value of agricultural lands within ten to twenty miles of the track corridors would rise in value, and thus the squares of land retained by the federal government would double or triple in value. Proponents argued that because railroad construction increased land values, Uncle Sam would lose nothing from his giveaway program. Federal gifts of land came with strings attached, however. A railroad needed to lay tracks and commence running trains within a specified number of years, or else it would forfeit its bequest. In addition, many grants obliged railroads to carry the mail and other federal traffic at a significant discount.[4]

Despite variations over the years until Congress discontinued land grants in the early 1870s, every rail recipient gained real estate to transform into investment capital. Thus, land grants provided rail lines and other beneficiaries a compelling incentive to promote settlement along their tracks. That was as true for land giveaways in Illinois, Missouri, and Florida as it was for the railroads of the Great Plains and Far West, which have been the primary focus of historians writing about this topic. The emphasis was logical because no railroads within the United States received more munificent gifts of land than the

lightly populated landscapes. During the late nineteenth and early twentieth centuries, such areas still abounded across the United States and Canada and offered moneymaking opportunities as well as serious financial challenges to newly built railroads.

The initial challenge was to populate the countryside through which newly laid tracks passed. Opportunity came with land grants the federal government gave to several dozen fortunate railroads outside the Northeast to support initial construction

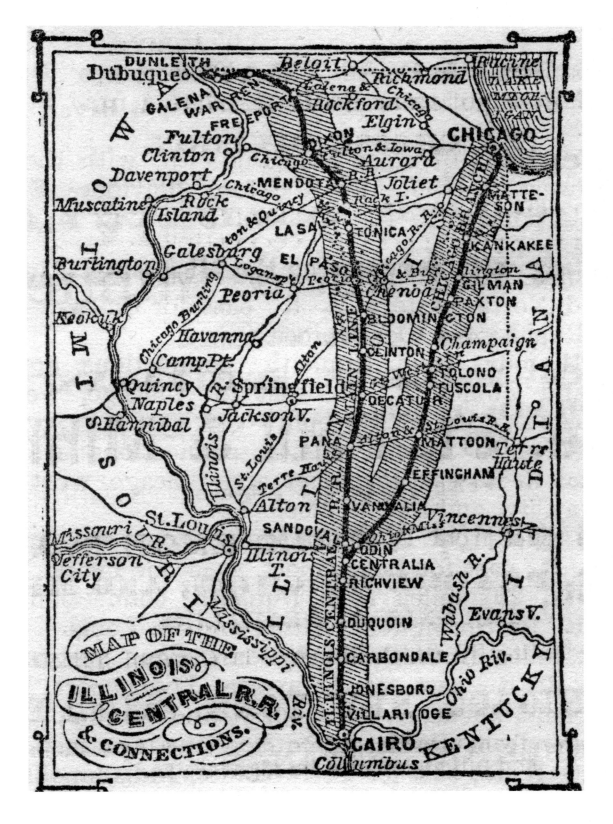

The Illinois Central, aided by its powerful patron in the United States Senate, Stephen Arnold Douglas, was in the early 1850s the pioneer recipient of the federal government's land giveaway to encourage railroad construction.

western carriers, with the nation's single largest grant ever going to the Northern Pacific, which in the 1860s proposed to extend its tracks across the northern tier states and territories between Lake Superior and Puget Sound. In 1862 Congress passed legislation to support the two companies that promised to build the nation's first transcontinental railroad, and then two years later, in July 1864, it doubled down on its bet that a second "Passage to India" would unify and benefit the United States, presuming the Union won the Civil War, an assumption that was by no means certain during the bloody battles that took place that year.[5]

The corridor of land that Congress granted the Northern Pacific was larger in area than all six New England states combined. Specifically, the railroad received 25,600 acres per mile in the territories and 12,800 acres per mile in the states. Apart from Wisconsin and Minnesota, its proposed right-of-way ran through the territories of Dakota, Montana, Idaho, and Washington, and thus the Northern Pacific would qualify for the higher giveaway most of the distance to the Pacific coast.[6]

The challenge facing the Northern Pacific was to transform its landed empire of forty million acres into construction dollars. That would not be easy. Americans held much of its vast donation in low esteem. Grasslands of the Great Plains had in the not-too-distant past been officially disparaged as the "Great American Desert." Thus it became necessary for boosters to convince skeptics that the area was worth settling—or, more generally, that dollars spent constructing a rail line across such an unpromising landscape would provide a reasonable return to investors. Wordsmiths needed to work their topographical magic.

The prominent Philadelphia banking firm of Jay Cooke & Company rose to the challenge after it agreed in 1870 to manage the sale of bonds to underwrite the cost of Northern Pacific construction. Its marketing strategy included a vigorous promotional campaign that intended to transform a landscape widely perceived as desolate, if not worthless, into a new paradise on Earth. As a result, believers and nonbelievers alike came to refer to Northern Pacific lands as "Jay Cooke's Banana Belt," a reference to the exaggerated claims made by Cooke's many booster pamphlets.[7]

American eagerness to construct new railroads during the post–Civil War decade created a gigantic financial bubble that burst in 1873, with ruinous results for Jay Cooke & Company. Two years later the Northern Pacific itself failed, as did eighty-nine other railroads during the depressed times of the 1870s. Economic distress temporarily halted construction of the Northern Pacific's main line and left the western and eastern ends of its track separated by a gap of 1,500 miles. The railroad, but not Jay Cooke & Company, eventually recovered its financial footing, and by 1881 its construction was underway again. Railroad executives and other luminaries, including former president Ulysses S. Grant, rode aboard special trains to Garrison, Montana, the site of an elaborate final-spike ceremony held in September 1883.[8]

The Panic of 1873, which destroyed Jay Cooke & Company and bankrupted the Northern Pacific, did not stop the presses, however. The person who gained control of the woebegone Northern Pacific in the early 1880s and guided the railroad's main line to completion in 1883 was a German immigrant named Henry Villard, an ambidextrous visionary who combined the skills of a seasoned journalist with those of a bold and daring financier. The annual reports the Northern Pacific issued during the Villard years were unusually entertaining and easy to read even without financial literacy, and no doubt Villard himself composed large portions of their text. Even after Villard departed the company in late 1883 (because he had overplayed his financial hand), the Northern Pacific remained for many decades one of the biggest railroad promoters in the history of the United States. North of the border, the land settlement activities of Canadian Pacific kept many additional printing presses busy.[9]

Facing, This Northern Pacific timetable dates from spring 1883, a landmark year in the history of transcontinental railroads. In September in an elaborate ceremony held near Garrison, Montana, the driving of a final spike completed the railroad's main line between the Great Lakes and the Pacific coast. The community of Garrison burnished the name of William Lloyd Garrison, one of the most famous American advocates for the abolition of slavery and the father-in-law of the ambidextrous Henry Villard, an American journalist as well as the entrepreneur who did the most to open the Northern Pacific's transcontinental line, a dream twenty years in the making.

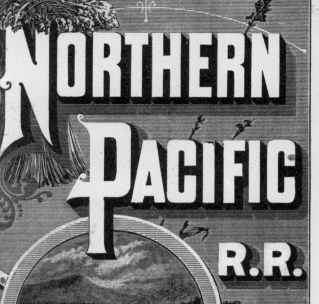

NORTHERN PACIFIC R.R.

MINNESOTA, DAKOTA, MONTANA, IDAHO, WASHINGTON & OREGON.

CHAS. B. LAMBORN,   P. B. GROAT,
Land Commissioner,   Gen'l Emigration Agent,
St. Paul, Minn.

7-April-'83.   Rand, McNally & Co., Printers, Chicago.

NORTHERN PACIFIC R.R.

MINNESOTA, DAKOTA, MONTANA, IDAHO, WASHINGTON & OREGON.

H. HAUPT, General Manager,
J. T. ODELL,   GEO. K. BARNES,
Sup't Transportation,   Gen'l Pass. and Ticket Agent,
St. Paul, Minn.

Rand, McNally & Co., Printers and Engravers, Chicago.

The Pennsylvania was prominent among the railroads that welcomed immigrants from northern and western Europe to East Coast ports in the United States during the 1880s, though like most other carriers serving the Northeast it was not a big promoter of settlement along its tracks.

Railroads treated settlement promotion with utmost seriousness. "The land, the timber and the minerals along the line of the Houston East and West Texas Railway are unexcelled in all the South, West, North or East. It cannot be described to do it full justice. To see it is the only way to determine its real value." The tone of the Texas railroad booklet sounds stilted and exaggerated to modern ears, but rhetorical excesses were common during the late nineteenth and early twentieth centuries, the golden age of railroad land promotion and publishing activity. With railroad encouragement, potential settlers boarded special trains and set out by the thousands to view the new lands for themselves.[10]

Among the pioneers of the railroad colonization of the West was George S. Harris, land commissioner for the Burlington & Missouri River line. During the 1870s, this railroad alone deployed some 250 agents across the eastern half of the United States and throughout England, Scotland, Sweden, and Germany. Its boosters flooded Europe with hundreds of thousands of pamphlets printed in several different languages, all of them intended to attracted settlers. Large railroads of the American West even stationed agents at departure points like Chicago to monitor closely the flow of immigrants and provide management with frequent tallies of how many carloads of prospective

homeseekers the various competing lines hauled. For certain, no other institution, and not even the national governments of the United States and Canada, compared with the railroads in their zeal to promote settlement. With a landed empire greater than that of any other railroad in the United States, publicists of the Northern Pacific were responsible for a remarkable outpouring of booster literature. Dozens of titles were freely available at any one time, and the railroad added new imprints almost monthly.[11]

The Northern Pacific's most famous publication was its *Wonderland* series, the thick and beautifully illustrated books the railroad issued annually for about twenty years between 1890 and 1910 to promote both travel and settlement. Among other examples of the Northern Pacific's yearly flood of land settlement publications was *Words of Praise from the New Settlers, or Central North Dakota along the Northern Pacific Railway* (1901), which was essentially an illustrated compilation of testimonials from prosperous settlers. Lands granted to the Northern Pacific accounted for nearly one-quarter of the area of North Dakota, a greater percentage than that of any other state, and this helped to fuel the railroad's long-running booster campaign. Not only did the Northern Pacific's emigration department publicize the rewards that awaited agrarians who settled its lands but its booster literature also listed opportunities awaiting any business

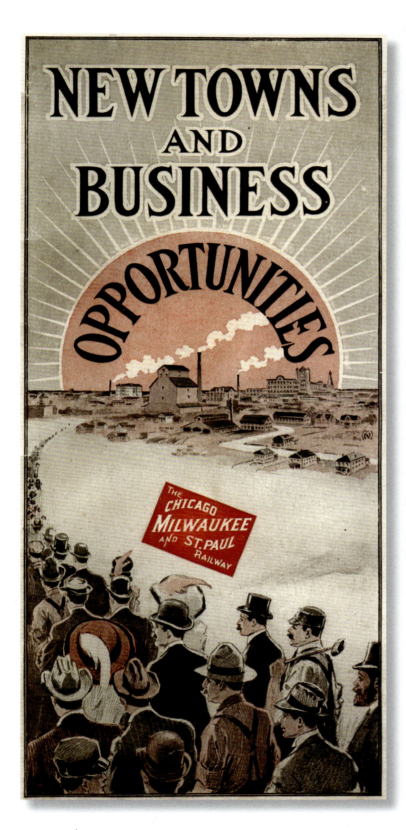

owners, doctors, and lawyers willing to settle in the country towns that emerged along its tracks.[12]

Even carriers lacking substantial grants of land, such as the Minneapolis & St. Louis Railway, promoted western settlement. Its publication *Homes and Farms in South Dakota* highlighted the opportunities awaiting settlers of that state: "The many illustrations with which the pages of this publication are filled are proof of the fertility of the soil and of the substantial character of the farms which have already commenced to dot the landscape, as well as the business opportunities which the new towns are affording." Farther west, the Denver & Rio Grande promoted *Fertile Lands of Colorado*, a publication that as of 1909 had already gone through ten editions, "with statistics and information revised down to date."[13]

Rail publications intended to promote settlement adhered to a predictable pattern over the years, using engravings and line drawings as illustrations early on and then featuring lavish chromolithographs and numerous black-and-white photographs in later years, with a verbal text that exuded enthusiasm and was usually punctuated by statistics carefully chosen to predict how good an area's prospects were likely to be in the coming years. In their earnest presentations on a variety of topics, rail publications often grew predictable, as if their creators adhered to an industry-wide template. There were creative exceptions, of course, as the Soo Line's *North Dakota, Story of a Grain Wheat* proved. This unusual form of boosterism consisted of a series of ten colored postal cards, each one illustrating a different phase of the journey of a grain of wheat—its cultivation, harvesting, and milling. A small pamphlet accompanied the postcards.[14]

Another inventive technique was to package booster literature as a narrative easily read and enjoyed. One of the best examples of this form of creativity came from *Sunset* magazine's

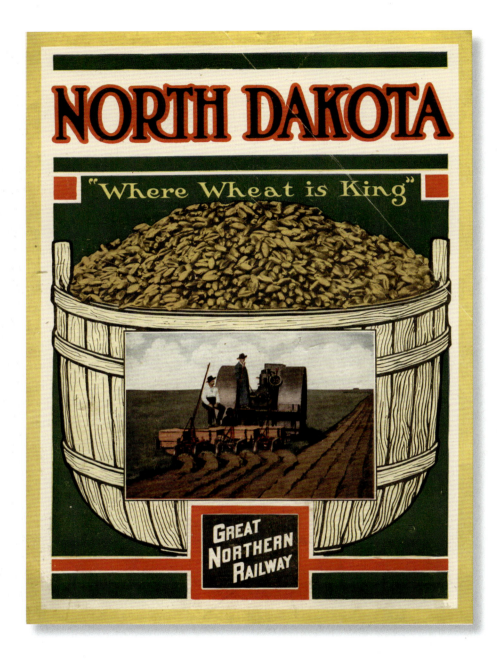

NORTH DAKOTA

"Where Wheat is King"

GREAT NORTHERN RAILWAY

The Great Northern was a prominent promoter of Montana and Dakota farmlands. Congress split the sprawling Dakota Territory into two states in 1889, with the Great Northern, Northern Pacific, and Minneapolis, St. Paul & Sault Ste. Marie focusing their booster activities on North Dakota and the Chicago, Milwaukee & Saint Paul and the Chicago & North-Western doing likewise on South Dakota. In terms of the new spatial relationships their rails forged, main lines ran east to west across the Dakotas, and none of these rail companies sought to develop an equally significant north–south corridor. The Great Northern published its brochure around 1911 to promote North Dakota wheat.

Homeseekers' Bureau, based in Portland, Oregon. To promote the development of Washington's fertile Yakima Valley, the Homeseekers' Bureau issued a narrative brochure titled *The Old Timer and The Homeseeker,* which featured these two representative types on its front cover. The old-timer's self-imposed task was to share his story of success and upward mobility as a farmer and grocer after he relocated to the Yakima Valley in 1897. The homeseeker, a skeptical individual who wanted to test Pacific Northwest booster claims for himself, was, appropriately enough, from Missouri, the Show-Me State.[15]

Their question-and-answer dialogue took place in the smoking compartment of a Pullman car. The newcomer studied the desert landscape of eastern Washington as it passed his train window and then exclaimed aloud in disgust, "Well, of all the God-forsaken countries I have ever saw! If the West is all like this, none of it for me." This provided the opening for the old-timer to work his persuasive magic, recorded at length on the brochure's next several pages. Here, in short, was a fresh and exceedingly clever way to package the often dull and highly predictable recitation of statistics and enthusiastic claims.[16]

Finally, despite the variety of brochure titles, railroad publicists in the early twentieth century did not seek to reach all nationalities in their appeal to potential immigrants. They ignored Asians, South Americans, and Africans, and even their focus on Europe was selective. In a discussion of "the nationality best suited to become settlers," held in 1922 at the annual conference of the American Railway Development Association in Denver, the colonization agent for the Duluth, South Shore & Atlantic admitted that, in his quest to populate Michigan's Upper Peninsula, the immigrant from northern Europe "is best suited for settlement here." He did not seek homeseekers from other areas. He reasoned that settlers from Scandinavia were best equipped to endure the harsh

THE SOUTHERN
HOMESEEKER
AND INVESTORS GUIDE
QUARTERLY   SEPTEMBER, 1916

IN PIEDMONT VIRGINIA

NORFOLK & WESTERN RY.
ROANOKE   VIRGINIA

F. H. LA BAUME   W. C. SAUNDERS
AGR'L & IND'L AG'T.   GEN'L PASS'R AG'T.

Within the United States, the rail industry's quest for homeseekers was most pronounced west of the Mississippi River, but farmlands in the post–Civil War South also beckoned to newcomers and were promoted by several of the region's railroads, most notably by those wishing to build new lines in Florida but also by established carriers such as the Norfolk & Western in Virginia, which issued this imprint in 1916.

winters typical of the Upper Peninsula. For the same reason, the Northern Pacific favored immigrants from Germany and Scandinavia to populate its landholdings in North Dakota and other northern tier states.[17]

Representing the inverse, perhaps, of publications intended to lure European settlers to the American West were railroad pamphlets and broadsides that advertised periodic openings of Indian reservation lands to new settlers. Although the Milwaukee Road constructed its Pacific Extension long after the federal land giveaway had ended in 1871, it nonetheless expected to benefit from the West's population growth when in 1909 its publications touted the opening of Flathead, Coeur d' Alene, and Spokane reservation lands in the states of Montana, Idaho, and Washington to outside colonists. The Northern Pacific's appeal was simple: "Uncle Sam will give you a home in the Flathead Indian Reservation of Western Montana." Farther east that same year, 1909, the Minneapolis & St. Louis Railway promoted the opening of the Cheyenne River and Standing Rock Indian Reservations in South Dakota and emphasized the ease with which prospective settlers could reach these areas via its "splendid through trains from St. Paul and Minneapolis." With a brochure titled *Isn't It Time you Owned a Farm?*, the Chicago & North-Western in 1911 announced the availability of three thousand federal homesteads on the Pine Ridge and Rosebud Indian Reservations.[18]

As with any form of advertising, it was possible to overstate the value of a product. Unlike exaggerated claims for household products like laundry soap or headache remedies, the overstatement of the value of railroad land on the High Plains resulted in human tragedy when settlers found success elusive if not impossible to attain. It is likely that the railroads promoting the settlement of eastern Montana truly believed the popular but unproven and ultimately specious

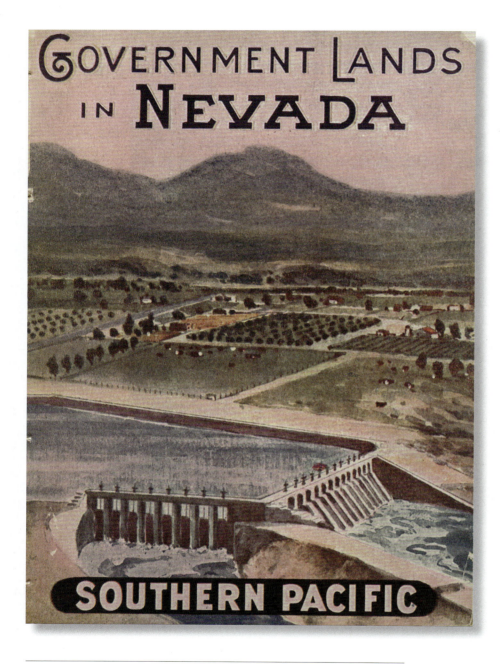

A Southern Pacific imprint from 1908 promoted federal lands that irrigation projects had opened in the deserts of northern Nevada. Irrigation combined with the convenience offered by rail transportation also transformed desert landscapes into farmlands in other parts of the West, most notably in Arizona and across southern Idaho, where the Oregon Short Line was without a rail competitor.

argument that "rain follows the plow." That is, if settlers tilled the virgin soil, the process of plowing would create the added rainfall needed to grow lucrative crops of edible grains in an area that formerly had supported only native grasses.

It was a theory convincing enough that railroads vigorously promoted it, thousands of settlers acted on it, and everyone lost when an unusual cycle of wet years ended in 1918 and parched the soil and souls of trusting settlers, who abandoned farms in eastern Montana by the thousands. Railroad development programs would continue well into the twentieth century, though never with the same tragic results as happened in the badlands of eastern Montana.[19]

In their quest for competitive advantage as well as settlers to populate their land grants, railroads learned that their publications needed eye appeal. Graphics became important, perhaps even more so than verbal arguments about soil fertility and rainfall. The use of color steadily gained favor and even took a quantum leap to new levels of attractiveness shortly before 1900 when American printers installed the state-of-the-art color printing technology only recently pioneered in Germany. One legacy of seven or eight decades of railroad promotional zeal is a wealth of colorful brochures. In fact, the list of railroad publications devoted to settlement is so long that no one has ever bothered to identify and catalog them all. Remember, too, that every copy of a brochure that somehow survived until today represents only a single example of print runs that typically numbered in the tens of thousands. Settlement promotional brochures, moreover, offer only one striking example of the way the railroads of North America functioned as publishers intent on redefining the landscapes along their tracks. A related activity that may have generated an even larger body of ephemeral literature was the railroads' promotion of tourism, representative samples of which are displayed in the following two chapters.[20]

The back cover of a Plant System brochure (circa 1900) used color graphics to emphasize the defining role the railroad played in the early twentieth-century landscapes of northern Florida and southern Georgia. The Atlantic Coast Line acquired the Plant System in 1902 and thus became a major player in the development of the Sunshine State, along with the Florida East Coast and the Seaboard Air Line Railroad. However, only during the state's 1920s boom did the Seaboard extend tracks south to Miami, as the Florida East Coast had done a quarter century earlier.

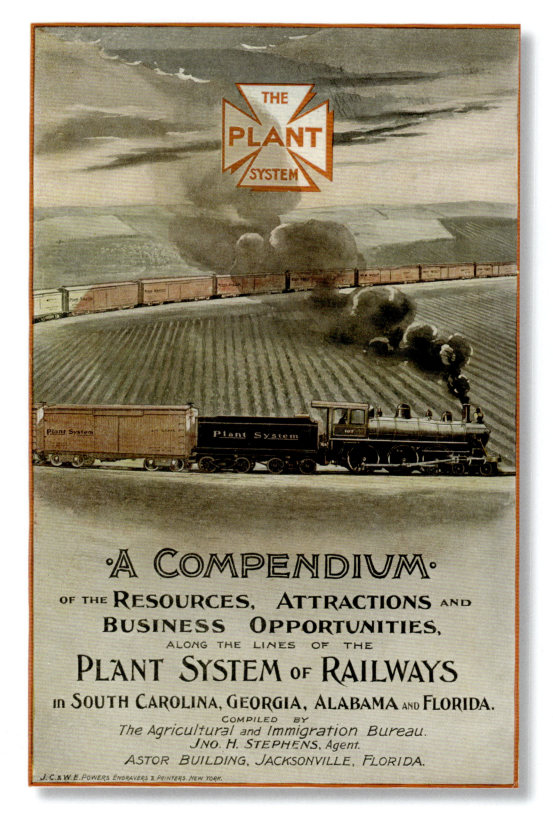

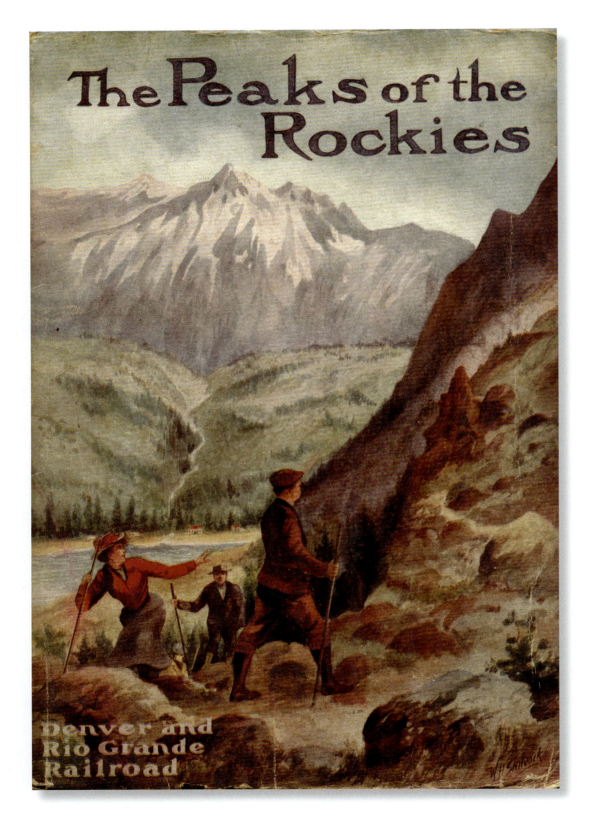

The barriers of time and space are now so broken that the invalid, flying from the east winds of New England, can sit at ease viewing the play of the seals on the Pacific coast, or bask in the breezes that blow o'er the Haytien seas, with the comfortable assurance that speedy communication keeps him in touch with the stock market and the home circle.

—from *Railway World* (1891)[1]

The Denver & Rio Grande operated an extensive network of tracks among the Rocky Mountain peaks, with many miles built to the nonstandard gauge of three feet between the rails, an economy measure appropriate to the sharply uplifted terrain. The Rio Grande had good reason to advertise the beauties of Colorado, which along with Utah formed its service area. Colorado and California were the two states in the American West that most inspired the railroad as publisher, with boosters of the Chicago, Rock Island & Pacific; Missouri Pacific; Chicago, Burlington & Quincy; and Union Pacific all contributing to the veritable flood of imprints. Florida inspired the same enthusiasm among the railroads of the Southeast. *The Peaks of the Rockies* dates from 1911.

9

INVENTING NEW VACATION DESTINATIONS

Railroads relentlessly sought ways to build traffic. At the dawn of the twentieth century, long-distance travel was a rail monopoly across much of the United States, apart from its inland and coastal waterways. However, with their passenger trains, railroads competed vigorously with one another. Along highly competitive routes such as between Chicago and New York or between New York and Florida, they sought to lure travelers aboard their trains, and the same was true of their pursuit of tourists. To appeal to travelers, many of whom were business executives and traveling salesmen, publicists emphasized the interior environment and range of comforts featured aboard a railroad's finest trains, while the emphasis for tourists was on vacation landscapes in addition to the onboard amenities they would enjoy during their journey.[2]

Just as they had combined words and compelling imagery—verbal and visual texts—in pamphlets intended to transform indifferent landscapes into what settlement promoters insisted would become attractive and desirable farms, orchards, and ranches, railroads as publishers also sought to fashion compelling new vacation destinations. The list of favored possibilities evolved over the years and grew longer as railroads extended their reach into hitherto isolated areas of North America—southern

Florida, for example—and as the idea of an annual vacation grew popular among the nation's middle class.[3]

The pursuit of leisure did not come naturally to many Americans until the post–Civil War decades. According to a Wisconsin Central vacation brochure titled *Summer of 1888*, "Matthew Arnold, the great English author and critic, charges Americans with being in too much of a hurry to fully enjoy life. We do not know, he asserts, how to take recreation, simply because we never take it." Railroad publishers were determined to promote a new lifestyle that would allow time for pleasure outings and vacations. Issued in 1909, *The Trip of My Life* promoted scenery along the Soo-Pacific Route between the Great Lakes and Pacific coast: "It will be at once a most valuable souvenir, and for those who have not enjoyed the pleasures of the trip, an inducement to go and see for themselves."[4]

Early on, railroad publications favored the upstate New York destinations of Saratoga Springs and Niagara Falls—the former as a setting for the rich to display their attainments, to see and be seen, and the latter as a romantic layover for honeymooners. In the Far West, the coming of railroads transformed curiosities

The Delaware, Lackawanna & Western's *Mountain & Lake Resorts* was typical of the many rail imprints issued during the early twentieth century to promote a variety of vacation destinations. Railroads made their latest ones available during the early spring months to inspire individuals and families to start their summer planning. They encouraged ticket agents to familiarize themselves with vacation possibilities, especially those located along their own tracks, and to serve as knowledgeable travel advisers.

of nature into the nation's first national parks, beginning in 1872 with Yellowstone and its bubbling mud pots and spouting geysers. Upon the completion of the Northern Pacific's transcontinental line eleven years later in 1883, an occasion for unprecedented fanfare to accompany the driving of a final spike in Montana, vacation travelers with sufficient money and time could easily make the overland trek in comfort and style by using the railroad's posh sleeping and dining cars. America's wealthiest families could luxuriate aboard their private rail cars during the lengthy journey.

During the subsequent four decades, transcontinental railroads of the United States and Canada all promoted national park destinations of their own, publishing activity encouraged by the standardization of gauge across North America. First in the United States was Yellowstone, and no other national park attracted more railroad interest. "The American who has not visited the Yellowstone Park has not seen that part of his country which is at once the most wonderful and the most beautiful," claimed the editor of the *Official Guide* in 1905. "It is difficult to say whether one is more impressed by the strange phenomena of the hot springs and geysers or by the grandeur of the Canyon, for while each is a manifestation of the powers of nature, the sensations experienced in viewing one and the other are not comparable, although both are certainly awe-inspiring."[5]

No railroad was better positioned geographically to promote Yellowstone as a vacation destination than the Northern Pacific after the completion of its transcontinental line in 1883. Among its target audiences were affluent residents of the eastern United States. The Northern Pacific could not monopolize park patronage for long, however. With its geysers, mud pots, fumaroles, and other curiosities, Yellowstone became a tourist magnet exploited by several other railroads. The Oregon Short Line, a Union Pacific subsidiary, extended its tracks north from

The Milwaukee Road created the Gallatin Gateway to foster tourism to the nation's oldest national park. Though the Montana location was remote from Yellowstone itself, the railroad transported travelers into the park aboard special buses it called Gallagators. The brochure cover featured here dates from 1926, one year before the railroad's opening of its luxurious Spanish-style Gallatin Gateway Inn.

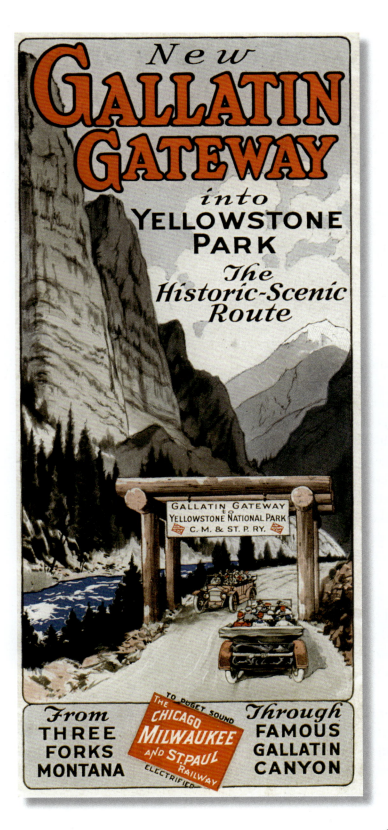

Utah to the town of West Yellowstone, where it erected a handsome depot. Travelers on Chicago, Burlington & Quincy trains accessed Yellowstone from Cody, Wyoming.

A latecomer to the Far West, the Milwaukee Road, soon listed Washington's Mount Rainier National Park among its primary scenic attractions, which included Yellowstone too, even though the nearest entrance to the national park lay seventy-five miles south of the transcontinental corridor the railroad finished to Seattle and Tacoma in 1910. Years later, in June 1927, the Milwaukee Road opened a new station and a Spanish colonial hotel called the Gallatin Gateway Inn and promoted motor trips between trains that paused there and the national park. The railroad called the special company-operated motor coaches Gallagators.[6]

For several decades these railroads had park patronage all to themselves. The coming of the first automobiles to Yellowstone in 1916 was initially not welcomed by rail carriers or park administrators.[7]

Other railroads saw commercial value in national park patronage and became instrumental in creating several additional parks. Santa Fe and Arizona's Grand Canyon became synonymous, while it shared California's Yosemite National Park patronage with the Southern Pacific. Oregon's Crater Lake was another national park that Southern Pacific wordsmiths and commercial artists promoted, and various of its publications highlighted the lake's scenic wonders, which included dark blue water within a deep volcanic caldera that made it the "eighth wonder of the world" according to President Theodore Roosevelt.[8]

The Great Northern Railway became the chief sponsor and main beneficiary of the creation of Glacier National Park, an area of spectacular Rocky Mountain scenery easily viewed from the windows of its trains across northwestern Montana. A subsidiary company built several imposing lodges within the park itself to foster tourism.[9]

Railroads that served the national parks of the West—and for several decades all of America's largest and most impressive national parks were in the western half of the United States—enjoyed a privileged status among vacation seekers, but rail lines less favored by nature and geography enthusiastically embraced and promoted a variety of leisure destinations that lay close to

their tracks. Early each year, well before travelers could solidify their summer vacation plans, the railroads of the United States and Canada issued an array of attractive brochures. The Bangor & Aroostook, a railroad located as far north as one could travel in the eastern United States, annually issued a thick volume called *In the Maine Woods* during the twentieth-century decades before World War II. The publication appealed especially to male readers eager to escape the stuffy confines of their offices in Boston and New York and exercise their hunting and fishing skills in one of the largest wilderness areas located east of the Mississippi.

A brochure issued by the Wisconsin Central, *Summer of 1888*, made a virtue of staying close to home: "Such an idea as going east to the crowded watering places to spend the sultry days of summer or to seek hunting and fishing, long ago became obsolete in this part of the moral vineyard, and attention has been turned to our own resources for out-door enjoyments. It is not boasting to say that within five years Wisconsin has become the center of attraction for more pleasure-seekers, health-seekers, hunters and fishermen than any other State in the Union, not excepting even California." The language spoke to the desire of an increasing number of Americans to indulge in the formerly unknown pleasures of a vacation. For the wealthy, that might mean a national park trip that lasted several weeks, while for the rising middle class it might mean spending a few days at a resort closer to home: "The less fortunate of America's millions will be well satisfied with an evening on the beach within reach by trolley, or a steamboat ride on the river, down the coast or across the lake over the week-end."[10]

An in-between option for budget-conscious Americans, and one promoted mainly by railroads serving the Northeast, was to enjoy the outdoors as a *Summer Boarder*, the title of a

Facing, The Boston & Albany issued a thick annual guide to describe summer homes available in the Berkshire Hills of western Massachusetts. The railroads of New England encouraged summer boarders, devoting many pamphlets to the topic. Such boarders were not common in the hot and humid South, except in the uplands, where elevation and mountain breezes provided Mother Nature's gift of air-conditioning. Publicists promoted the Blue Ridge Mountains surrounding Asheville, as well as the North Carolina city itself, as a refreshing summer retreat, an area the Southern Railway successfully labeled "The Land of the Sky."

1904 pamphlet issued by the New York Central. Rural board-inghouses and summer rental homes were forerunners of the popular bed-and-breakfast accommodations of recent years. The boarder eager to escape the heat and grime of the city could bring "generous profits and many pleasures to the farmer," insisted the New York Central's wordsmith. Likewise, there were "city folks" eager to enjoy the "freedom and wholesomeness" of the "quiet country" who could afford the modest cost of two weeks at a rural boardinghouse.[11]

After North America's nearly complete conversion to standard-gauge track in the mid-1880s, the uniform rail network encouraged train travel by vacationers from the cities of the Northeast and Midwest to formerly distant destinations in northern Florida, in Texas, and along the Gulf Coast. *Sunny San Antonio, the Winter Playground of America*, a booklet issued by the Missouri-Kansas-Texas Railroad in the early 1920s, said, "While the North is thinking in terms of biting winds and blinding snow, San Antonio is indulging in the joys of existence in a temperature usually attributed to the ideal days of Summer." Like all such booklets, any interested vacationer could easily acquire a copy by mailing a request to the railroad's home office, which for this railroad was Saint Louis.[12]

For residents of the East Coast and Midwest, one of the newest vacation playgrounds created by railroads in the late nineteenth century was Florida, which had received several federal land grants to encourage the construction of new rail corridors. Boosters saw an alluring opportunity to promote Sunshine State attractions, real and imagined. As a result, they composed numerous beautifully illustrated pamphlets that in number and variety nearly equaled rail imprints highlighting the attractions of California and Colorado.

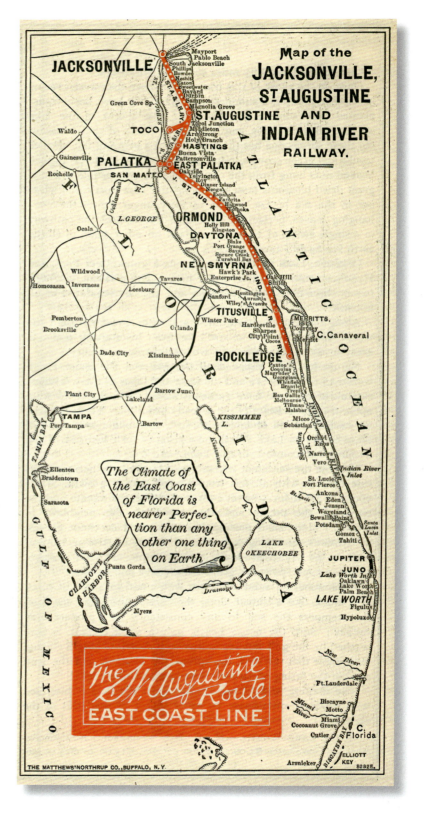

A turn-of-the-century map shows the Flagler railroad, soon to be renamed the Florida East Coast, extending halfway toward Key West. Miami was an afterthought that proved to be an unexpected economic bonus.

Henry Plant and his railroads concentrated on development of the peninsula's West Coast, while Henry Flagler did likewise on the East Coast. The invention of modern Florida was largely the work of the two Henrys. Their respective railroads and related development activity, which included the construction of several luxury hotels intended to lure affluent guests to Florida, served to showcase the transformative power of their steel highways. Plant's main sphere of activity was the region between Tampa and Jacksonville, and his holdings included several small railroads that became the "Plant System," which in the early twentieth century he sold to the expansion-minded Atlantic Coast Line.[13]

Flagler came to Florida later, and his commitment to railroad building lasted longer and was more extensive than that of the other Henry. Flagler, in fact, seemed only to stumble into Florida railroad construction by accident after his first and highly successful career as an ally of John D. Rockefeller in building Standard Oil. The creation of a trust that made Standard Oil such a fearsome and lucrative monopoly was probably Flagler's idea. After he cashed out, he used his Standard Oil millions to acquire a short and struggling railroad that connected Jacksonville and Saint Augustine. Flagler is supposed to have purchased the property to transport his sickly wife to the salubrious climate of Saint Augustine. In one sense, his purchase was a failure because his wife soon died, but Flagler took the railroad, renamed it the Florida East Coast, and began a quest to extend a line of tracks from Jacksonville to coastal destinations ever farther south. The railroad's intended reach kept changing. Initially, Flagler seemed satisfied to terminate his line of tracks in the Palm Beach area, a stretch of beach on which he built two luxury hotels to create a palm-lined oasis for the very rich, a southern counterpart to the socially aloof enclave of Newport, Rhode Island.[14]

Legend has it that a woman named Julia Tuttle who lived farther south in Fort Dallas persuaded Flagler to continue laying tracks from Palm Beach to her village, renamed Miami. At first the tiny settlement may not have appeared too promising, surrounded as it was by endless swamps and nearly impenetrable stands of mangrove. The Florida East Coast reached Miami, but why stop construction there? Flagler's ambition was not yet satisfied.

WHERE IS MIAMI?

With their development activity focused on opposite coasts of Florida, Plant and Flagler remained friendly rivals. One day, shortly after Florida East Coast tracks reached the village of Miami, Flagler is supposed to have wired his rival from his base in Saint Augustine, "Can't you pay me a visit in Miami?" Plant, then in New York City, hastened to reply, "Accept with much pleasure, but where on earth is Miami?" Flagler responded, "Follow the crowd." Indeed, crowds of newcomers brought by railroads enabled both Miami and Los Angeles to emerge in the early twentieth century as America's newest big cities.*

* *New York Tribune*, reprinted in *Pensacola News*, April 7, 1900. See also Bruce Henstell, *Sunshine and Wealth: Los Angeles in the Twenties and Thirties* (San Francisco: Chronicle Books, 1984).

Flagler's latest quest was to push a line of tracks farther south from the village of Miami to the remote site that in the early twentieth century ranked after Jacksonville as Florida's second-largest population center: Key West. That entailed the monumental feat of extending an additional 128 miles of track beyond the peninsula and across forty-one islets and the ocean currents that separate them, an engineering challenge numerous observers considered impossible and derisively labeled "Flagler's Folly."[15]

Flagler had not grown fabulously rich by making stupid investments. By building one bridge after another, the Florida East Coast leapfrogged across the sandy islets. Flagler succeeded in completing his Oversea Railroad to Key West in 1912, and soon passenger trains forwarded by the Pennsylvania Railroad to the Richmond, Fredericksburg & Potomac, to the Atlantic Coast Line, and finally to the Florida East Coast at Jacksonville were transporting guests south to Key West from New York, Philadelphia, and other cities of the Northeast. For passengers, it was always a thrill to view miles of open ocean along both sides of the track. When trains finally eased to a stop in Key West, travelers could easily board one of the ships that waited trackside to transport them ninety miles farther south to Havana and to the hedonistic pleasures of Cuba. One of the through trains from New York to Key West was aptly named the Havana Special.[16]

Even more interesting, and potentially profitable, was the spatial relationship that existed between the end of Florida East Coast tracks in Key West and the soon to be completed Panama Canal (1914). "The most important event in the recent history of transportation will culminate during the present month with the opening of the Panama Canal," observed the editor of the *Official Guide*. With its Atlantic entrance conveniently located due south of the Florida peninsula, ships transiting the canal could transfer their cargoes in Key West for fast and convenient forwarding by rail to urban markets farther north.[17]

The elderly Flagler did not live long enough to witness the formal opening of the Panama Canal or to see ships from the West Coast exchange cargoes with Florida East Coast trains at Key West. Flagler had built for himself and his third wife a mansion in Palm Beach, an imposing structure of marble and gilt-edged furnishings that is today open to the public as the Henry Morrison Flagler Museum. One day the eighty-three-year-old Flagler tripped on his mansion's grand staircase and set in motion the downward spiral that is often the fate of the elderly who suffer a serious fall. He died in 1913, one year before the opening of the Panama Canal.[18]

Though the two Henrys provided the rail infrastructure needed to spur development of the southern two-thirds of Florida, neither man lived to see the incredible boom that took place there during the 1920s. Miami became a metropolis, and Florida itself saw its statewide population rapidly increase. Railroads thrived during these boom years. Shortly before the stock market crash of late 1929 and the onset of the Great Depression, the Seaboard Air Line Railroad completed one of the nation's last new stretches of track from its existing line in central Florida south to Palm Beach and Miami. Though a latecomer to the Florida boom, its luxury trains competed head-to-head with the best accommodations and schedules the Atlantic Coast Line and the Florida East Coast had to offer.

The growing appeal of Florida destinations and the state's balmy winters encouraged railroads to add luxury trains from midwestern cities such as Chicago and Detroit to those already running from the Northeast. Thus, joining the seasonal parade of trains to Florida were those operated by the Illinois Central, Chicago & Eastern Illinois, Louisville & Nashville, and several other railroads. Because their competition grew increasingly fierce, railroads that ran Florida trains sought to win customers from competitors by annually publishing colorful promotional booklets, their variety and print runs only increasing during the 1920s boom. Less visible but nonetheless important to the development of modern Florida were railroad brochures showcasing the state's many agricultural allurements. The Florida East Coast even operated an exhibit car to familiarize people with all the Sunshine State had to offer.[19]

A decade of transformation that could aptly be described as the "transportation revolution of the 1920s" witnessed the rising tide of automobiles and intercity bus and truck competitors. This was also the decade of Florida's great land boom. Carl Graham Fisher, who made his fortune in the automobile industry and was among the founders of the Indianapolis Motor Speedway, came to Florida to develop a sandy barrier island into Miami Beach. To connect his home city of Indianapolis with his new Florida playground, Fisher actively promoted the construction of the motor corridor soon to be known as the Dixie Highway.[20]

The hurricane of 1927 punctured some of the inflated expectations generated by the Florida boom, but it was the terrible hurricane of 1935 that obliterated Flagler's Oversea Railroad and forever ended train service to the Florida Keys. High winds

Agricultural commodities ostensibly had little to do with vacation travel. Often two separate departments within a railroad were responsible for advertisements, but an Atlantic Coast Line imprint from 1934 devoted to Florida oranges and grapefruit was no less attractive than the many imprints used to promote winter vacations in the Sunshine State.

claimed the lives of nearly five hundred people trapped when the fury toppled a rescue train into the storm surge. Bridges that survived intact enabled the state of Florida to extend a highway, US 1, south along the former railroad right-of-way. Greyhound buses, and not the trains of the Florida East Coast, continued to offer commercial passenger transportation between Miami and Key West. US 1, an Eastern Seaboard counterpart to the Midwest's Dixie Highway, began in Maine and encouraged motorists from the populous Northeast to drive their own cars south to Florida.[21]

While Florida and western portions of the United States and Canada garnered the most attention from railroad publishers, between these two geographical extremes lay lightly populated areas originally overlooked by settlers and vacationers alike. Such locales grew more appealing as railroads constructed additional miles of track and then sought new frontiers to promote.

One such area was Michigan's rugged Upper Peninsula, where, in dramatic contrast to Florida, the winter snowfalls often totaled *several dozen* feet. Like Florida, it had its railroad boosters eager to repackage the landscape to attract new settlers, but had it not been for copper and other natural resources, Michigan's extreme hinterland—in terms of both geography and climate—would have remained an exceedingly difficult destination for railroads to promote.

The mountains of southern Missouri, eastern Oklahoma, and northwestern Arkansas, like Michigan's Upper Peninsula, remained off the beaten track for the stream of settlers and other opportunity seekers headed farther west during the nineteenth century. California had remained a favored destination since its gold rush of the late 1840s. The Great Plains and their seemingly endless miles of fertile farmland had enjoyed a settlement boom during the 1880s.

By contrast, farming the Ozark Plateau of Missouri and Arkansas was in many ways an afterthought. As in Michigan's Upper Peninsula, it was mineral wealth that initially spurred the development of a tristate area rich in lead and zinc. The Kansas City Southern, Katy, Missouri Pacific, and Frisco lines all extended track corridors into the Ozarks to make them fully accessible to small farmers, and the publishing activities of these railroads sought to make the formerly isolated area appealing to settlers and vacationers alike.

In addition to the usual array of attractive pamphlets intended to attract homeseekers, the Frisco ventured one step further and issued a monthly magazine to showcase its development activity and to encourage settlers to establish new homes and farms in areas served by its trains. Half a century earlier, one of the Frisco's predecessor railroads had received a huge grant of federal land in the Ozarks to encourage construction between Saint Louis and Springfield, Missouri, and potentially all the way to its namesake city of San Francisco. In early years the Frisco's land grant had been much like a gift of ice in the winter, and few settlers found the area appealing given that the farmland of the Great Plains just to the west of the Ozark Plateau was more extensive, fertile, and thus easier to transform into productive agricultural landscapes. Even better, the Great Plains homesteads could be gotten free or nearly so. Only decades later would railroads be able to shine the spotlight of opportunity on the Ozarks.

One feature of the Ozark Plateau that grew increasingly attractive with the coming of railroads was its elevation, which while moderate in comparison to the high Rocky Mountains nonetheless offered Midwest vacationers relief from heat, humidity, and grime, all typical discomforts of summer in the region's industrial cities. A large group of rail publications attests to the industry's desire to promote pleasurable escapes year-round.

Facing, The Long Island Railroad dominated a service area that extended a hundred miles east from New York City. Because it was so closely linked to America's most populous city, it enjoyed a near monopoly of freight and passenger traffic across its service area. Nonetheless, the railroad competed with many others for summer vacation traffic, and its colorful brochures sought to promote Long Island's beaches and other attractions. This one dates from 1925.

ALONG THE SUNRISE TRAILS OF **LONG ISLAND**

1925
Issued by the General Passenger Department
LONG ISLAND RAILROAD
P. H. WOODWARD,   C. G. PENNINGTON,
General Passenger Agent   Ass't Gen'l Passenger Agent
PENNSYLVANIA STATION, NEW YORK

Now that the Northern Pacific Railroad is finished, the inviting regions of the Great Northwest, hitherto remote, are made easy of access. The tide of travel flows naturally with a strong current through this new and pleasant channel, and to pilot the wayfarer, this Guide-Book has been written.

—from *The Great Northwest: A Guide-Book and Itinerary* (1883)[1]

Summer or winter, American railroads mitigated the harshness of heat and freezing temperatures by transporting those who could afford it to more salubrious climates. This Southern Railway brochure was typical of rail imprints that promoted winter escapes to Florida, the Gulf Coast, and Texas, as well as to the Carolinas, California, and Mexico.

10

MATCHLESS PLEASURELANDS AND SEASONAL VARIATIONS

The invention of electric light bulbs during the early 1880s provided "bottled sunshine" to extend the length of the day and shorten the gloom of night. In the same manner, railroads affected time-honored seasonal cycles by making summer pleasures available throughout the winter months and diminishing the physical discomforts occasioned by summer heat and humidity. That is, railroad publicists promoted winter escapes to balmy climates and summer retreats to cooler locations during the years before the widespread use of air-conditioning. In a related manner, rail imprints encouraged seekers of good health to discover the pleasures of hot springs and restorative hotel spas. Finally, there was the novelty of new vacation destinations: "Americans are notorious for their traveling propensity, and they are constantly seeking new fields of diversion; therefore places of interest that are graphically described and vividly illustrated are certain to influence a desire to visit them." Railroad publicists needed to invent "matchless pleasurelands" of all types and then regularly promote their new destinations and leisure activities lest vacation travelers become jaded.[2]

The rail industry's desire to sell summer destinations to prospective vacationers was especially intense during the decades that predated the widespread use of residential air-conditioning, a technological trend that first grew popular during the 1960s. For affluent residents of New York and the New England states, a summer escape might mean leisure travel to the thousands of hotels, spas, and summer boarding houses that awaited them in coastal Maine, the mountains of Massachusetts, New Hampshire, and Vermont, or the Adirondacks of upstate New York. Options available to midwesterners in search of relief from the region's often oppressive summer heat and humidity included train journeys to the woodlands and lakeside retreats of Michigan, Wisconsin, and Minnesota. Some families owned modest lakeside cabins, while other summer visitors pampered themselves at the Grand Hotel on Michigan's Mackinac Island.[3]

Elevation provided relief too. One especially popular destination in the South was Asheville, North Carolina, and its surrounding mountains. The Southern Railway issued annual *Land of the Sky* booklets that featured cover art evocative of the Blue Ridge Mountains. In the Midwest there was Eureka Springs, an Ozark Mountain village just south of the border that separated Missouri and Arkansas. Its central location allowed residents of Saint Louis, Kansas City, and other northern population centers easy access by train. Likewise, the Frisco Line promoted itself as the "Cool Route" that afforded Texans an easy way to

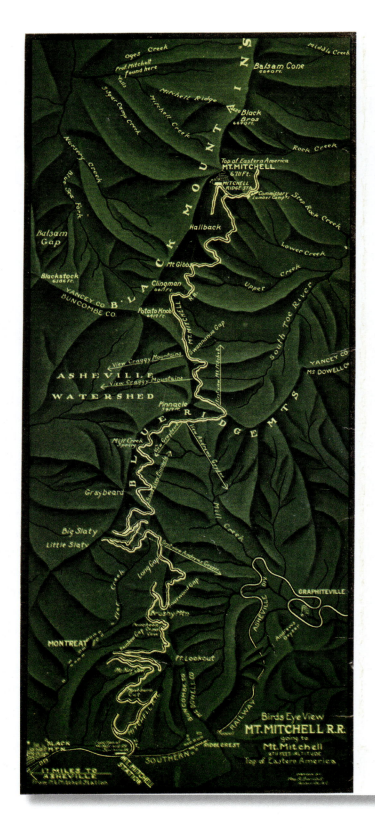

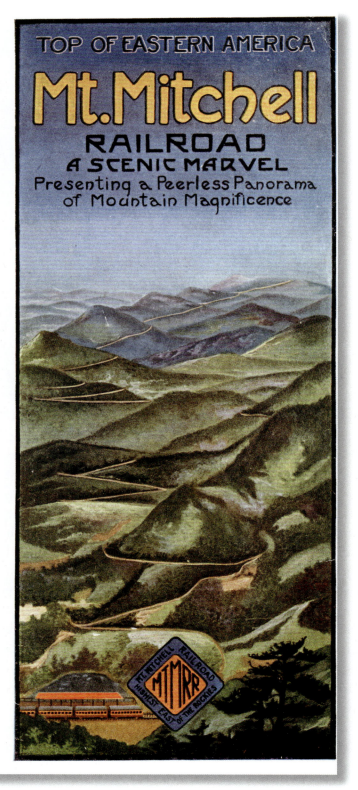

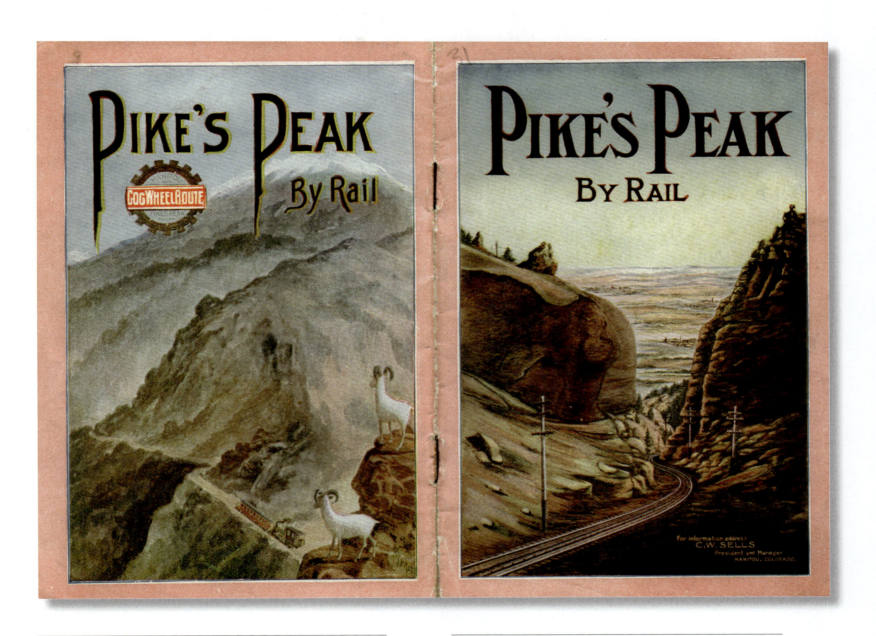

Facing, Western North Carolina's Mount Mitchell Railroad conveyed tourists to the top of the tallest peak in the United States east of the Rockies; at 6,684 feet, it was taller by four hundred feet than New Hampshire's much better known Mount Washington. The Carolina carrier was abandoned in 1921, but a cog railroad still conveys passengers to the peak of Mount Washington. This imprint dates from 1916.

Above, West of Colorado Springs is the still-operating cog railroad to the summit of Pikes Peak (14,115 feet). It is a survivor among the several tourist-oriented rail lines that hauled sightseers to mountain promontories. This example dates from 1903.

AIR-CONDITIONING AND ITS IMPACT ON RAILROAD PUBLISHING

In our air-conditioned age it is difficult to appreciate the desire Americans had to escape the heat and humidity of summer in earlier times. The annual summer search for a cool retreat was an activity mainly of the affluent, however. For Americans of limited means, the invention of electric fans during the early 1890s offered a convenient and relatively inexpensive way to cool homes and offices until the advent of true air-conditioning. Another inexpensive option was to board one of the open-sided trolley cars common at the turn of the century and enjoy a cooling breeze during the ride out to one of the nearby parks operated by electric railways. The usual fare was five cents each way. The evening ramble was supposed to be conducive to a good night's sleep.*

Some five hundred trolley parks—ranging from amusement venues to bucolic retreats along the shore of a small lake or in a shady grove of trees—once existed across the United States. Electric railways, in fact, invented the modern amusement park long before Walt Disney improved upon the idea. The concept of the roller coaster, a popular feature of any "electric park," supposedly derived from a coal-hauling railroad in eastern Pennsylvania that offered tourists thrill rides down its mountain incline.†

The link between the introduction of mechanical air-conditioning during the 1930s, the decade that saw the first air-conditioned passenger trains, and the annual outpouring of railroad imprints devoted to remaining cool and comfortable during the summer's heat and humidity should be obvious. By the 1960s it had become possible to enjoy comfortable summer days at home and in the office instead of boarding a train for the mountains or northern lakes.‡

---

* Gail Cooper, *Air-Conditioning America: Engineers and the Controlled Environment, 1900–1960* (Baltimore: Johns Hopkins University Press, 1998); Marsha E. Ackermann, *Cool Comfort: America's Romance with Air-Conditioning* (Washington, DC: Smithsonian Books, 2002); Salvatore Basile, *Cool: How Air Conditioning Changed Everything* (New York: Fordham University Press, 2014).
† Jennifer Sopko, "Amusement Parks, A Confluence of Transportation, Industry and Topography," *Ephemera Journal*, September 2022, 1, 6–13.
‡ "Air-Conditioning in Transportation," *Railway Age*, September 17, 1932, 387–388; "Passengers Unanimous in Approving Air-Conditioned Service," *Railway Age*, September 17, 1932, 396–397, 405.

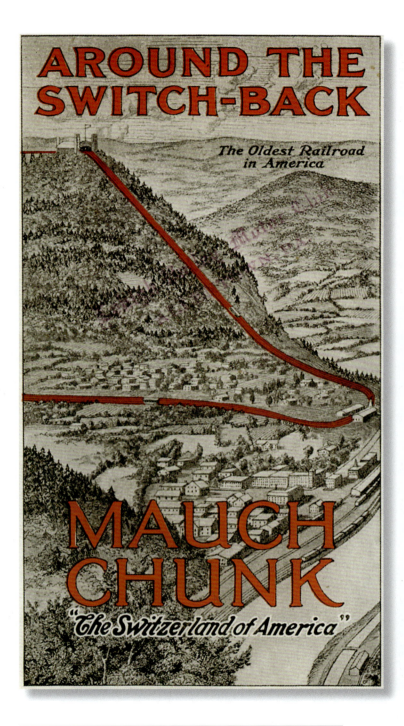

The Mauch Chunk Switchback Railway, a Pennsylvania hauler of anthracite coal from 1827 to 1932, also provided thrill rides along its serpentine tracks. The mountain railroad supposedly provided the inspiration for the amusement park's ever-popular rollercoaster rides. The company published this graphic around 1920.

escape the heat and humidity of summer and trek north to the elevated retreats of Eureka Springs or other lesser-known resorts. An annual flurry of railroad publications also urged residents of Saint Louis, Chicago, and other midwestern cities to head west by train to the cool heights of Colorado and other areas of the Rocky Mountains.[4]

Canadians benefited naturally from their northern nation's mild summer climate, but the nation's railways nonetheless promoted vacation escapes to the many lakes and extensive woodlands of Ontario and Quebec or to coastal resorts in New Brunswick and Nova Scotia. Brochures circulated freely south of the border to lure vacationers, anglers, and hunters north, and the railroads of both nations sought to make the annual trek in search of coolness as easy as possible. Finally, rural and village families all over the United States and Canada earned extra dollars by catering to summer boarders, and several rail companies published thick directories that listed the variety of getaway possibilities. The New York, Ontario & Western updated the vacation guide *Summer Homes* for 1916. In some years past, the railroad had been among the first in the United States to issue its summer guide featuring mountain resorts, all located within easy reach of the residents of the New York metropolitan area.[5]

Railroad publicists realized that during the winter and spring months, individuals and families were already thinking about summer vacation possibilities and would likely peruse several different travel brochures to decide where to spend their seasonal escape. The railroads of the United States and Canada fiercely competed for summer vacation travelers, and that became no less true for winter travelers, for whom Florida, Southern California, Arizona, Texas, and the Gulf Coast all proved to be popular destinations. Over the years, railroad publicists successfully transformed the Rocky Mountains of Colorado into a popular wintering destination for outdoors-minded Americans and those health seekers who hoped to benefit from sunshine, bright blue skies, and crisp air in a snowy setting. The Denver & Rio Grande, for example, sought to capitalize on the transformation of the Centennial State from a popular summer-only

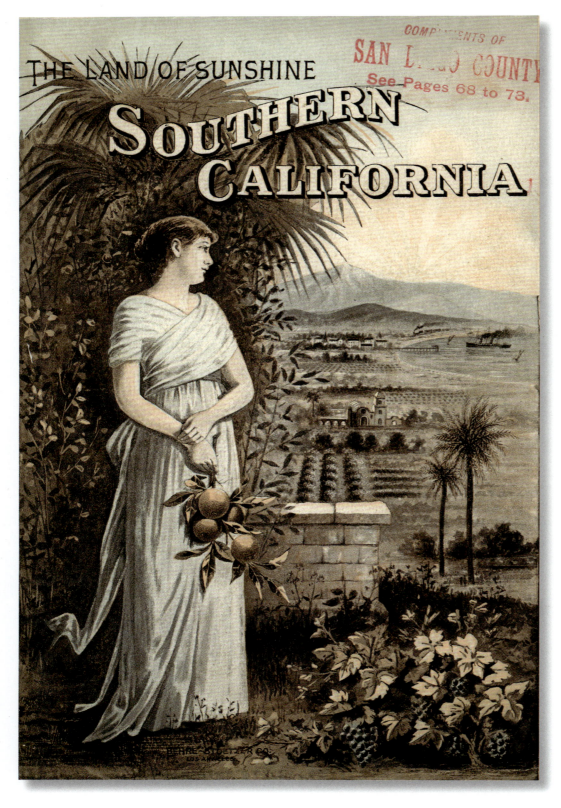

The Atchison, Topeka & Santa Fe competed with the Southern Pacific and later the Union Pacific to promote Southern California. The Santa Fe reached Los Angeles in 1887, but it was a newcomer compared to the Southern Pacific, which arrived in 1876 and had completed a transcontinental line between Los Angeles and New Orleans in 1883. The third and final entrant, in 1905, was the Salt Lake, Los Angeles & San Pedro, the brainchild of copper baron William Andrews Clark. The Union Pacific acquired the railroad in the early 1920s and thereby gained a direct entrance into a booming part of the Golden State. Among the Santa Fe's nineteenth-century imprints was *The Land of Sunshine, Southern California.* The Union Pacific issued its own attractive *California Calls You* in 1913, several years before the Omaha-based carrier formally added the line between Salt Lake City and Los Angeles via Las Vegas to its track network.

The Rutland, a railroad based primarily in Vermont and a major conduit for milk traveling from the state's many dairy farms to customers in New York City, joined with other New England carriers to advertise the region's many vacation destinations. The Rutland's favored attractions were located, of course, in Vermont's Green Mountains and along Lake Champlain.

destination into a winter playground with its publication *Winter Days in Sunny Colorado*.[6]

Also defying the popular urge to head south to escape a northern winter was the Boston & Maine, which sought to make a virtue of its northern New England service area. "In the region of the White Mountains and their foothills, and in the Rangely Lakes, a temperature several degrees below zero is not unusual, but it is a clear and crisp atmosphere, stimulating and wholesome." Winter sports including sleighing, skiing, snowshoeing, and ice fishing were popular, "and there is none of the slush and fog which distinguishes the Winter season in other regions."[7]

Finally, even if the passenger trains of individual railroads did not run through to popular tourist destinations, the Pullman Company of Chicago operated a large fleet of luxury sleeping cars that did. These accommodations cost a little more than coach tickets, but they were a popular means of travel among those who could afford them. Moreover, the Pullman Company could easily shift its fleet as needed, running cars to northern retreats during the summer months and then reversing direction and sending them south to Florida and other warm-weather destinations during the winter travel season.

In addition to settlers and vacationers, a third group best described as health seekers traveled by rail in their hunt for the healing waters of mineral springs, many of which supported the construction of one or more sanitariums and hotel spas. Many vacation-oriented rail publications included lengthy chapters that catered specifically to seekers of better health, which included millions of Americans during the late nineteenth and early twentieth centuries, an age that also featured numerous and unregulated patent medicine cure-alls guaranteed to relieve sufferers of afflictions that ranged from pimples to lockjaw.

While many vacation imprints extolled the natural wonders of the national parks, the healing properties of hot springs and spas, or the relaxation offered in rural retreats, Illinois Central publicists highlighted the attractions of Chicago and New Orleans, the two great cities that anchored the railroad's northern and southern ends. This image appeared on the back cover of a brochure issued in 1912.

Facing, The Baltimore & Ohio issued a beautiful brochure to advertise the many resorts located along or near its tracks. These included the elevated ones in the mountains of western Maryland and northern West Virginia as well as heartland retreats farther west in the hills of southern Indiana.

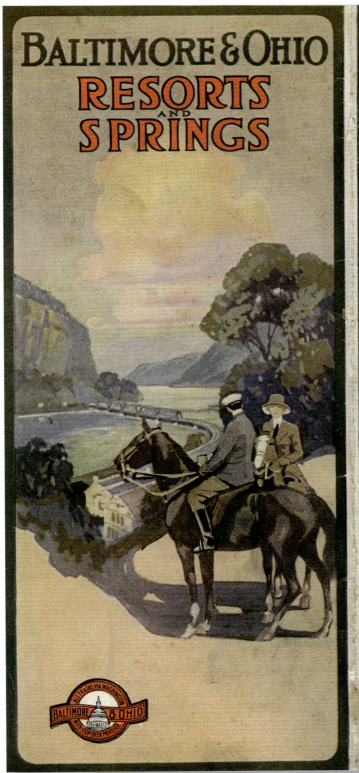
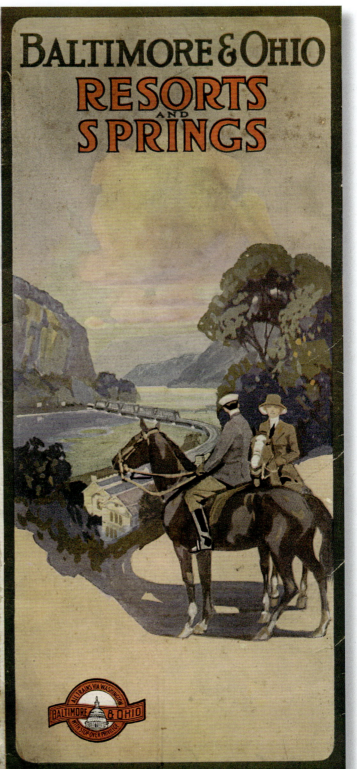

In a Union Pacific brochure issued in 1892 and ostensibly devoted to the resorts of the West, the matter of improved health received extensive coverage. The imprint reminded "weary mortals" in search of a natural restorative that "the entire Rocky Mountain region is a sanitarium. It has the sun, the mountain breeze, the crisp, mild air, which combine to invigorate and heal." The railroad's wordsmith emphasized that "the invalid reaches a point, especially if his trouble is pulmonary, where a trip such as is suggested above, means a new lease of life to him. If he pauses, it will soon be too late." The same timeless come-on sold real estate and numerous other purchases over the years.[8]

After the completion of the Chicago, Milwaukee & Puget Sound to the Pacific coast, additional rail companies took advantage of the new spatial relationships its main line across the Northwest offered to health seekers. For example, in late 1910 the White Sulphur Springs & Yellowstone Park Railway opened for traffic to serve the farmers and ranchers of Montana's hitherto isolated Smith River Valley and to make the medicinal waters of its hot springs more widely available as a health restorative. "The water will be bottled and distributed throughout the country. It is extremely beneficial for stomach and kidney troubles." Such places were popular because the flow from a mineral spring could be captured for use by hotels and resorts that specialized in soothing frayed nerves, a common complaint in the late nineteenth and early twentieth centuries but a malaise many people today prefer to treat pharmaceutically.[9]

One of America's most popular and enduring destinations for health seekers was Hot Springs, Arkansas, a mountain retreat that, unlike many similar resorts, continues to flourish today, perhaps because it features an unusual national park. The mineral waters of Hot Springs enjoyed their greatest fame when the world was innocent of tranquilizers and other nerve-calming prescription drugs. Attesting to its widespread popularity was Missouri Pacific's operation in the mid-1920s of sleeping cars through to Hot Springs from Chicago, Saint Louis, Memphis, New Orleans, Omaha, and Kansas City.[10]

The stress of running a business during the late nineteenth and early twentieth centuries seemed particularly to afflict steam railroad and electric interurban railway executives. Henry Villard, the individual largely responsible for the completion of the Northern Pacific transcontinental across the northern states in 1883, suffered several bouts of nervous exhaustion from overwork. His preferred cure was to return to his native Germany and use the soothing waters of Baden-Baden to aid his recuperation. Many other harried executives found an extended stay in Hot Springs, Arkansas, to be more accessible and affordable.

The Arkansas community had numerous counterparts across the United States, and railroad publicists took full advantage of their locations, promoting them as health-restoring destinations. The railroad publicist for Excelsior Springs, Missouri, was the Milwaukee Road, and for Colfax, Iowa, it was the Rock Island. For French Lick and West Baden Springs in Indiana, it was both the Baltimore & Ohio and the Monon, which operated through Pullman cars between there and Chicago in its train titled the Red Devil.[11]

"Hunter Hot Springs" was the title of a 1910 Northern Pacific effort to boost a Montana resort known for its medicinal value. Largely forgotten today are the many other mineral springs and bucolic retreats that promoted rest cures for frazzled nerves and, largely because of railroad publicity, became magnets for health seekers. Railroad ephemera attests to a lengthy list of formerly flourishing vacation haunts devoted to better health.[12]

Over the years, individual railroads emerged as well-recognized publicists for one or more favored vacation destinations, and their publicists annually issued a flood of updated travel literature to promote various on-line attractions, including some old favorites as well as appealing new destinations. The Canadian Pacific Railway devoted numerous booklets to various Rocky Mountain parks—notably Lake Louise and Banff Springs—easily accessible via its transcontinental trains. "This magnificent mountain region rivals, and some measures surpasses, the scenery of Switzerland. Some of the features especially attractive to mountaineers are the enormous glaciers, which lie between the mountain tops."[13]

Most of the several hundred railroads that operated within Canada and the United States did not enjoy the passenger patronage national parks generated, but most companies sought to promote and capitalize on vacation possibilities near their own

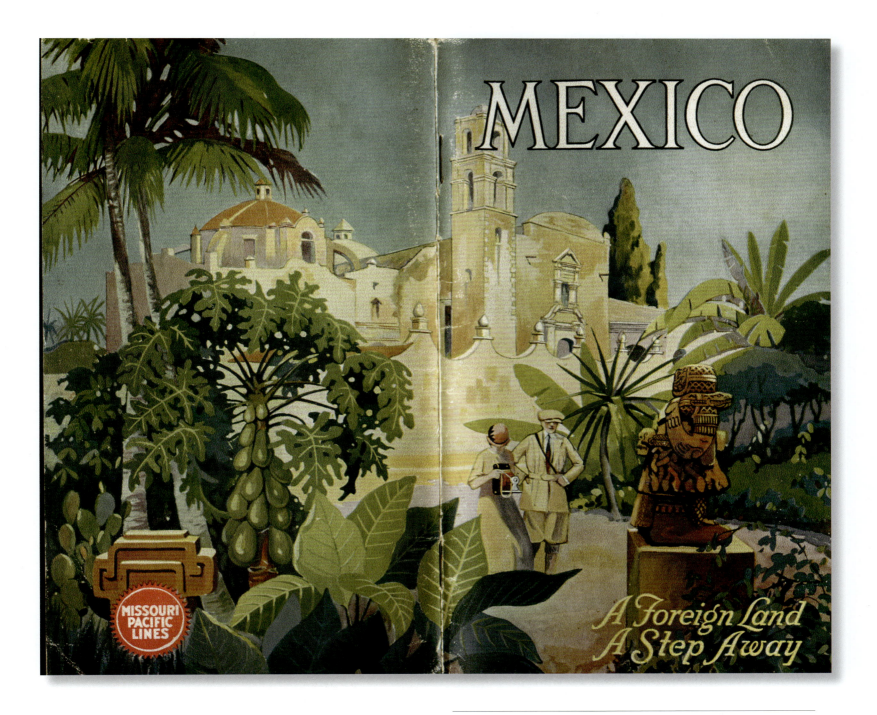

MEXICO

MISSOURI PACIFIC LINES

A Foreign Land
A Step Away

The Missouri Pacific viewed itself as a major conduit between the American heartland and the vacation attractions of Mexico. In the early twentieth century before the revolution that convulsed Mexico between 1910 and 1920, the Missouri Pacific ran through trains between Saint Louis and Mexico City and printed bilingual travel brochures in both English and Spanish.

tracks. One site for the Erie was Cambridge Springs in northwestern Pennsylvania; for the Southern, it was Asheville, North Carolina, and the "Land of the Sky"; and for the Seaboard, it was Southern Pines, another popular North Carolina destination. During the opening years of the twentieth century, the Rock Island System issued the annual booklet *Colorado under the Turquoise Sky* to showcase the many hotels, camps, and scenic attractions awaiting summer visitors to the Rocky Mountains. Southern Pacific publicists added scenic Lake Tahoe, though not a national park, to the railroad's long list of Far West attractions.[14]

Saint Louis–based railroads forged ties to cities in the Southwest and even promoted winter vacations in balmy places as far distant as Mexico City. The Missouri Pacific promoted train service through to the Mexican capital with bilingual brochures in both English and Spanish. The rail lines that served New York

Right, The Western Maryland always seemed to operate in the shadows of the Baltimore & Ohio, the far-older railroad also based in Baltimore, but in the early twentieth century, it competed with all rivals for vacation traffic to resorts nestled atop the Blue Ridge Mountains of Maryland.

Facing, In their endless quest to discover and promote new vacation attractions, the railroads of the continental United States began to boost Alaska travel in the late 1880s. That was when steamships first conveyed tourists from Seattle up the Inside Passage to Alaska, where its compelling glacial wonders could be viewed from the comfort of a deck chair. In 1898, the discovery of gold in Canada's Yukon Territory heightened the appeal of the remote region for both fortune seekers and tourists, and after 1900 when the narrow-gauge tracks of the White Pass & Yukon first linked steamships that called at coastal Skagway, Alaska, with Whitehorse in the Yukon's interior, the diminutive railroad formed a 107-mile-long conduit for mineral wealth headed south to the Pacific Ocean and tourists trekking inland in search of outdoor adventure. This brochure dates from 1914.

ALASKA
WHITE PASS & YUKON ROUTE
AND THE
YUKON TERRITORY

"THE YOSEMITE VALLEY IS BEAUTIFUL,
THE YELLOWSTONE PARK IS WONDERFUL,
THE CANYON OF THE COLORADO IS COLOSSAL,
AND ALASKA IS ALL OF THESE."
—*Burton Holmes*

ALASKA
WHITE PASS & YUKON ROUTE
AND THE
YUKON TERRITORY

"THE YOSEMITE VALLEY IS BEAUTIFUL,
THE YELLOWSTONE PARK IS WONDERFUL,
THE CANYON OF THE COLORADO IS COLOSSAL,
AND ALASKA IS ALL OF THESE."
—*Burton Holmes*

City favored winter playgrounds as far south as Florida and Cuba or closer ones in central North Carolina's Southern Pines and Pinehurst. "New Orleans has a winter climate which is almost perfect; it is a city of gardens and flowers, full of historical interest and of the most agreeable environment," or so the Southern Pacific claimed in its 1909 booklet *Winter in New Orleans*. For residents fleeing the snows of Chicago, Saint Louis, and other midwestern cities, winter days in New Orleans were promoted in booklets issued by rival carriers such as the Missouri Pacific, Illinois Central, Louisville & Nashville, and Southern.[15]

Using similar seasonal logic, railroads promoted Florida as a place of escape during the frigid months of winter. All through the late 1890s and into the early twentieth century, Henry Flagler's Florida East Coast Railway expanded the array of pleasure possibilities as it extended tracks south from Saint Augustine to Palm Beach, to Miami, and ultimately all the way to Key West. Henry Plant did the same thing for Tampa and Florida's Gulf Coast. Farther up the Gulf Coast and into the seaside fringes of Alabama and Mississippi, both the Louisville & Nashville and Illinois Central lines promoted the delights of a winter escape.[16]

While it could be expected that large railroads like the Illinois Central and the Louisville & Nashville (in addition to the Pennsylvania, Santa Fe, Atlantic Coast Line, and several others) would emerge as major publishers, some regional railroads with modest passenger operations added to the early twentieth-century parade of beautifully illustrated vacation brochures. In 1906, Western Maryland's *Where to Spend the Summer* listed more than three hundred hotels and boarding houses in or near the Blue Ridge Mountains and a hundred more for the Alleghenies, all within easy reach by train of Baltimore, Washington, and Philadelphia residents eager to escape the heat and humidity of a summer in the city. That same summer, the passenger department of the Rutland Railroad published *Across the Island and Beyond* to call the attention of vacationers to the attractions of Lake Champlain, western Vermont, and northern New York. "The country traversed by this line has a magnificent Summer climate and most attractive scenery."[17]

In 1907, the Astoria & Columbia River Railroad presented the "attractions and amusements" of Oregon's Clatsop Beach in the distinctive form of a paper clamshell, "which being opened discloses a portfolio of views of scenery along the route of that line and on the shore of that charming resort." One attraction the railroad's die-cut novelty did not emphasize was ocean bathing, hardly a pleasurable activity in the chilly waters of the Pacific Ocean, whose current swept south along the Northwest coast after brushing Alaska. The Atlanta, Birmingham & Atlantic was a regional railroad that accessed the southeastern coast, and in a similar fashion to its Oregon counterpart, it issued a vacation brochure in 1907 titled *Seashore and Mountain*. At least the temperate Atlantic waters along the Georgia coast near Brunswick were likely to be conducive to ocean bathing. Another regional carrier, the Gulf & Ship Island Railroad, connected with the Illinois Central's posh Panama Limited in Jackson, and its train called the Mississippian forwarded Pullman cars from Chicago to winter resorts along the Gulf Coast.[18]

As with brochures promoting settlement, railroad publishing for vacationers gained appeal over the years with the same application of the latest color printing technology, although target audiences for the two basic genres of rail publications were vastly different. Both brochure types, vacation and settlement, arguably attained their peak attractiveness during the years just before America's entry into World War I in April 1917, which in numerous unanticipated ways proved to be a watershed event in the history of railroads and their publishing activities.

Thousands of people take wonderful trips through the country with the aid of the illustrated railway folder. Thousands make that trip in imagination, lack of funds preventing them from making it otherwise. But the fact that they are unable to visit the wonderful places so vividly and interestingly portrayed by picture and description does not detract from their enjoyment.

—from *Buffalo Evening News* (New York), April 16, 1918

The cover of this Canadian Pacific brochure was bold, like the big-game hunters the railway hoped to attract to Canada's extensive outback. One need not journey far north from Toronto or Montreal or from Great Lakes outposts like Sault Sainte Marie to enter the forbidding wilderness country defined by the Laurentian Shield and its many lakes, granite outcrops, and mosquitos.

11
PRINT WORKS

Railroads emerged as North America's most diligent publishers because they needed to make the traveling public, potential tourists, and prospective settlers aware of what they offered. During the early years, that meant giving free rail tickets to local newspapers in exchange for their publishing a schedule of train times or creating a timetable broadside to be tacked to a wall of a station or other public place.

Gradually it dawned on railroad managers that timetables intended to convey train times to the traveling public might also serve as a means of mass communication. Around their basic and functional listing of train times, various railroads began to include advertisements for vacation or land settlement opportunities. Many travelers, after all, enjoyed following the progress of a train journey by noting the passing stations as listed sequentially in the timetable, but with a timetable already in hand, a traveler might be tempted to study various promotional advertisements too. Early schedules occasionally featured engravings to stimulate interest, while later ones enhanced their appeal by including artistic line drawings and photographs. The first illustrations were limited to black and white, but later ones featured an imaginative array of colors.[1]

American railroads during the 1850s and 1860s discovered value in publishing low-cost or free booklets and pamphlets that covered topics ranging from trackside sights to land settlement possibilities. The monthly *Official Guide of the Railways*, which dated from 1868, was not just a reliable compilation of rail timetables for North America; for years it featured a front section called General Railway Information, which highlighted and occasionally reviewed the contents of the latest rail travel brochures. The brief descriptions were especially useful to ticket agents, who among their many duties were expected to serve as travel consultants. That is, "a railroad passenger representative must be all things to all people." He must "know his railroad geography—the points of interest in the country where one can go for education or recreation, for scenic attraction or rest." In sum, "his prime motive is to create a desire to travel—to travel by train in comfort and safety"—and to promote the attractions of his railroad "in a compelling way."[2]

A stash of attractive timetables and travel brochures under the ticket counter or on a nearby literature rack greatly aided an agent's solicitation work. Of necessity, the several dozen publications on display always represented the proverbial tip of the

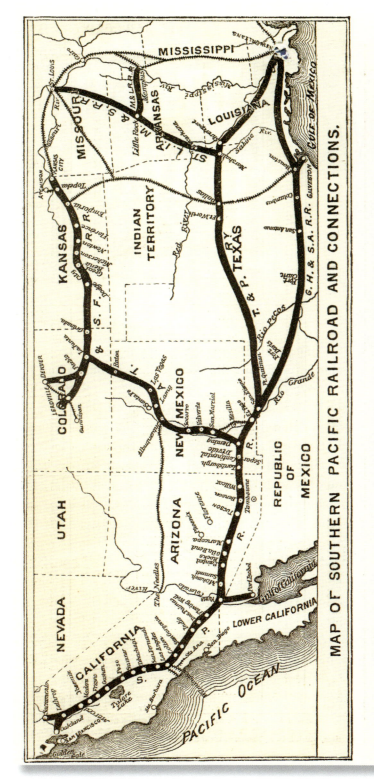

MAP OF SOUTHERN PACIFIC RAILROAD AND CONNECTIONS.

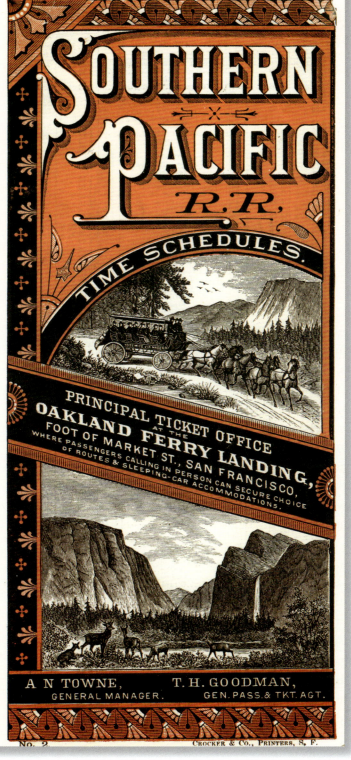

APRIL 20th, 1883.

SOUTHERN PACIFIC R.R.

TIME SCHEDULES.

PRINCIPAL TICKET OFFICE AT THE
OAKLAND FERRY LANDING,
FOOT OF MARKET ST., SAN FRANCISCO,
WHERE PASSENGERS CALLING IN PERSON CAN SECURE CHOICE
OF ROUTES & SLEEPING-CAR ACCOMMODATIONS.

A N TOWNE,   T. H. GOODMAN,
GENERAL MANAGER.   GEN. PASS. & TKT. AGT.

NO. 2.   CROCKER & CO., PRINTERS, S. F.

iceberg. Had a person attempted to collect just one copy of the annual outpouring of new promotional literature issued by the railroads of North America, the resulting hoard could have filled a small room. Furthermore, individual print runs might yield five to ten thousand copies of each publication. In addition to its various booster booklets, a larger railroad might issue tens of thousands of public timetables per month. The Pennsylvania Railroad in 1903 distributed an average of ninety-six thousand timetables just within New York City every month, while the monthly timetable giveaways at the New York Central and also the New York, New Haven & Hartford totaled seventy-eight thousand each. At the turn of the century, New York's hotel and station racks also began to stock timetables from abroad, with one of the more exotic folders featuring Russia's newly completed Trans-Siberian Railway.[3]

In 1909, for example, American railroads spent about $16 million for stationery and printing, a sum greater than they spent for steel rails. Such huge expenditures annually led one trade journal to comment that printing was "as essential to railroading as steam and steel."[4]

In 1896, the passenger department of the Union Pacific System offered at least twenty different publications, each available for the payment of ten cents or less in postage. Available titles ranged from *Prune Culture* and the *Evolution of Artificial Light* to *Outdoor Sports and Pastimes* and the *Evolution of the Locomotive.* Just in 1901, the rival Northern Pacific distributed at least twenty-two different giveaway brochures, pamphlets, and leaflets, including two written in German. The number and variety of its publications continued to climb until a decade later the Northern Pacific offered nearly forty free brochures, twelve intended for travelers and tourists and twice that number for homeseekers, all in addition to special playing cards and souvenir postcards, both

available for a small fee. The Soo Line, which forever seemed to dwell in the shadow of James J. Hill's Minnesota-based Great Northern and Northern Pacific lines, emerged in the early years of the twentieth century as a significant publisher of brochures devoted to outdoor vacation possibilities in northern Minnesota, Wisconsin, and Michigan; settlement possibilities on the Great Plains; and the Rocky Mountain scenery of Canada, through which its luxurious trains passed between Chicago and destinations on the Pacific coast such as Vancouver and a trio of American cities, Seattle, Portland, and Spokane. Given the abundance of different imprints available, the year 1912 could well have represented the apex for publishers of the railroad.[5]

It is fortuitous that printing press technology improved during these same years and could serve the railroad industry's insatiable thirst for commercial art to illustrate its many different publications. In an informal way, the two industries served to reinforce each other. By 1910 it was possible for the editor of the *Official Guide* to claim:

> The art of color printing, which has reached a high stage of perfection, has rarely been better exemplified than in a new publication just issued by the passenger department of the Oregon Short Line, "Where Gush the Geysers." The remarkable coloring of the rocks and waters of the Yellowstone Park lend themselves to this treatment, and advantage has been taken of these features to produce a book of splendidly executed cuts, every one of which is an artistic gem. These pictures alone tell the story, and the accompanying text has been made appropriately brief and crisp, just enough to give necessary information.

In his description of the text, the editor draws a subtle distinction between the straightforward phrasing increasingly preferred in twentieth-century America and the elaborate prose and orotund way of speaking so typical during the previous century. More important, perhaps, was the Oregon Short Line's use of illustrations that in the eyes of many observers approached the level of fine art.[6]

During the colonial and postrevolutionary years of the United States, printing had been exemplified by the well-known

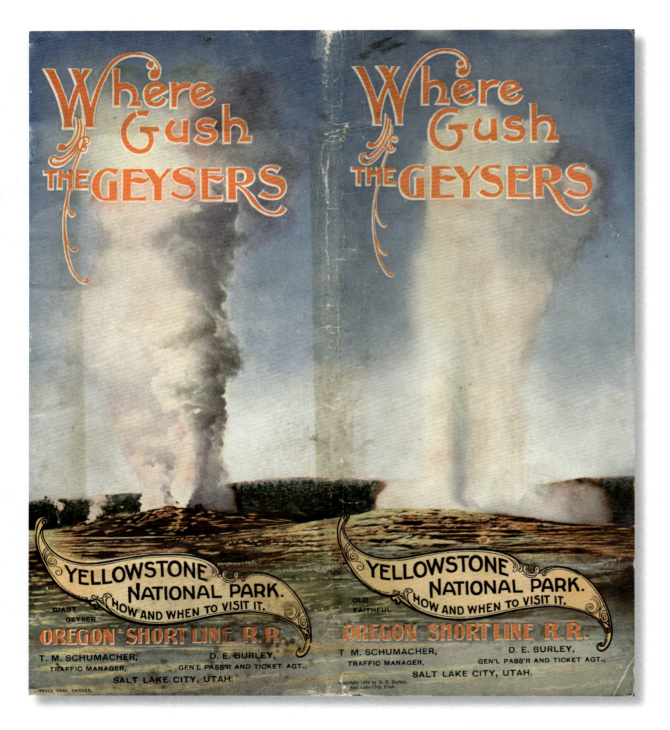

The Oregon Short Line dominated southern Idaho and provided the Union Pacific access from its transcontinental tracks at Granger, Wyoming, to the Pacific Northwest and to the western entrance to Yellowstone National Park.

Facing, Each issue of the New York Central's *Four-Track News* combined stories of general interest to the traveling public with rail industry puffery. Its most popular number featured Elbert Hubbard's "Message to Garcia," a drama set during the Spanish-American War of 1898. With a succession of print runs that totaled more than eleven million copies, it may have been the all-time publicity champ among rail promotional literature.

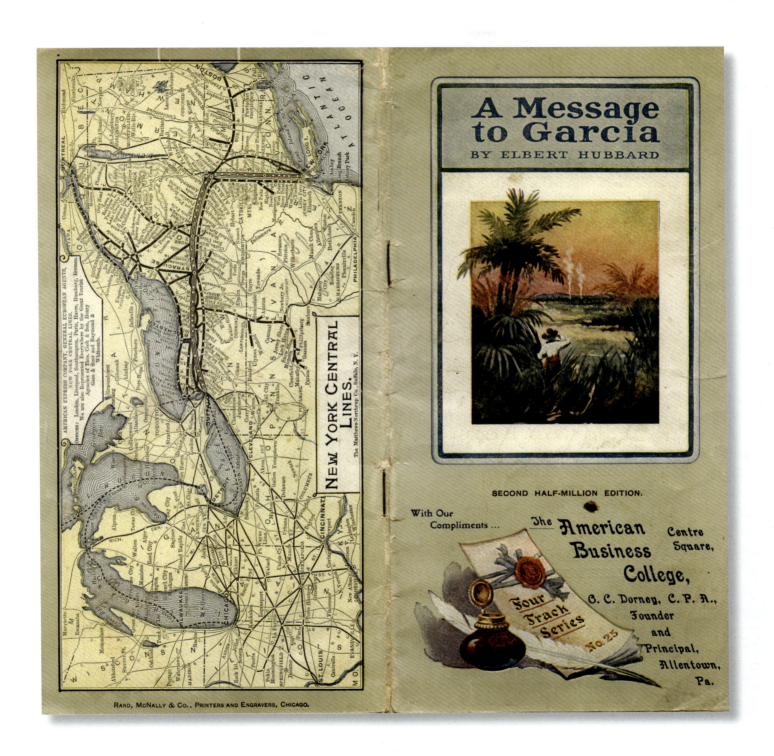

A Message to Garcia

BY ELBERT HUBBARD

NEW YORK CENTRAL LINES.

AMERICAN EXPRESS COMPANY, GENERAL EUROPEAN AGENTS, NEW YORK CENTRAL LINES. Offices: London, Liverpool, Southampton, Paris, Havre, Hamburg, Bremen. We are also Represented Everywhere by the Great Tourist Agencies of Thos. Cook & Son, Henry Gaze & Sons and Raymond & Whitcomb.

The Matthews-Northrup Co., Buffalo, N. Y.

RAND, McNALLY & CO., PRINTERS AND ENGRAVERS, CHICAGO.

SECOND HALF-MILLION EDITION.

With Our Compliments ...

The American Business College, C. C. Dorney, C. P. A., Founder and Principal, Centre Square, Allentown, Pa.

Four Track Series No. 25

story of Benjamin Franklin and his printing press in Philadelphia. The typical press of Franklin's day used human muscle to print one large sheet of paper at a time. With patience and determination, the slow and laborious process of folding printed sheets of paper into signatures and then gluing or stitching them all together would yield a booklet or pamphlet. Additional copies required repetition.

Equally laborious was the task of hand-setting individual pieces of type to form words, sentences, and paragraphs, all in proper sequence and with the expectation that the printer would not mix up the letters *p* and *q*, for instance, because all characters had to be set upside down to make a correct impression when the inked type contacted a sheet of paper. Printers were ubiquitous across North America, and many of them published a daily or weekly newspaper in addition to accepting a variety of special printing jobs. If in one community newspaper subscriptions failed to keep food on the family table, a printer often loaded a hand press and a case of movable type aboard a buckboard or other type of wagon and moved on down the road in search of publishing success in another location.

As for any artwork, it was limited mainly to wood engravings. The *American Railroad Journal*, a pioneer publication that appeared in the early 1830s, added a stylized woodcut of a locomotive to its masthead. Every few years it modernized its simple illustration with a more up-to-date locomotive woodcut.

The challenge was to mass produce any form of illustration. In some mid-nineteenth-century publications, type alone enhanced the visual impact. A variety of large and bold letters that screamed at readers was aptly described as "circus type" because it was used most frequently on broadsides intended to lure patrons to the extravaganzas staged by P. T. Barnum or one of his circus competitors. At the time, railroads paid local newspapers to print their passenger train schedules, or more often they traded rail transportation for the timetable inserts. The Interstate Commerce Commission later outlawed exchange when it mandated that railroads must pay cash to newspapers for any timetable publicity.[7]

Engravings and loud arrangements of movable type gradually yielded to more polished forms of public communication as printing technology improved, and better-quality commercial art was included in booklets and pamphlets, some of which commonly had print runs of ten thousand copies or more. George H. Daniels, the famed publicist of the New York Central System and its *Four-Track News*, printed and reprinted more than eleven million copies of Elbert Hubbard's "Message to Garcia," the most popular publication to result from the Spanish-American War of 1898.[8]

At the turn of the century, the Pennsylvania Railroad often required a million copies of its system timetables to distribute at stations and hotels along its tracks. Large companies like the Pennsylvania and the New York Central typically printed local or regional timetables in addition to the large ones that covered the entire railroad. In the early twentieth century, the New York Central was, in fact, a loose assemblage of carriers, and thus individual regional timetables appeared under the names Big Four, Michigan Central, Lake Shore & Michigan Southern, Peoria & Eastern, Pittsburgh & Lake Erie, West Shore, and even Rutland, all in addition to New York Central & Hudson River.[9]

Three large printing firms produced most railroad timetables and brochures. These were Matthews, Northrup & Company of Buffalo and Poole Brothers and Rand, McNally & Company, both of Chicago. The oldest was Rand, McNally, founded in 1868. One of its cofounders was George Amos Poole, who two years later joined his brother William H. Poole to launch a Chicago printing house of their own. Matthews, Northrup dated from the 1890s and like its Midwest competitors specialized in writing, designing, printing, and binding railroad brochures.[10]

These three firms dominated railroad imprints, though on the West Coast the aptly named Homeseekers' Bureau of the Harriman Lines unleashed a publishing blitz unprecedented and perhaps never equaled by another railroad within the United States. For five years, until upper management summarily terminated the publishing venture in September 1911, representatives of the Southern Pacific, the Union Pacific, and their several subsidiary railroads cooperated with local boosters of West Coast communities to create an unprecedented outpouring of publicity brochures. Each one featured a combination of sprightly prose, the liberal use of illustrations, and eye-catching cover

The contrast between the cover art and the sober information contained therein may appear whimsical, even incongruous, but the promotional creativity showcased in several of the Homeseekers' Bureau publications, like that for Sunnyside, Washington, could likely be attributed to program director William Bittle Wells, who numbered among the first graduates of Stanford University's Classics Program.

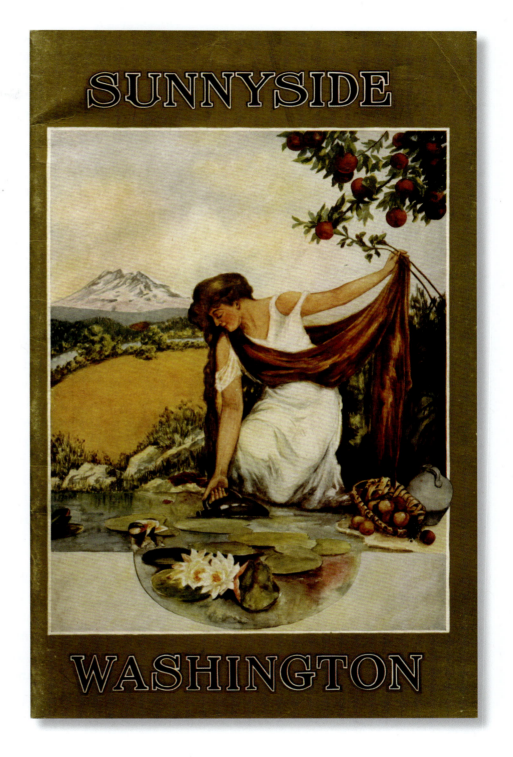

art. Some of their most imaginative cover images featured toga-clad Greek and Roman figures juxtaposed with scenes of Pacific Northwest irrigated farms and town development activity.

From his office in Portland, Oregon, William Bittle Wells oversaw a publishing venture that during its short life issued more than twelve million copies of more than a hundred different booster brochures, a monumental outpouring of rail literature by any calculation. Moreover, Wells insisted that the writers and illustrators he hired to create community booster pamphlets avoid formulaic prose and copycat layout and design.[11] In addition to the many brochures that promoted Pacific Slope communities—and not just places in Oregon, Washington, and Idaho but also numerous cities and counties in California—the vast rail empire dominated by Edward H. Harriman published *Sunset* magazine, which remains popular today as a general interest publication devoted to life on the West Coast.[12]

The popular writer Stewart Holbrook recalled that the railroad booster pamphlets he read as a young Bostonian in the early 1900s, which likely included some issued by Harriman's Homeseekers' Bureau, "somehow left the impression that one could have a decent living in Oregon and Washington simply by eating the gorgeous scenery." Indeed, the Homeseekers' Bureau brochures devoted to Hood River, Oregon, and other orchard communities of the West Coast featured life-size representations of locally grown fruit on their covers, all in delicious colors.[13]

Words alone were inadequate and were "apt to fall on barren ground unless accompanied by proof," or so many railroad publicists had come to believe during the 1890s. "The camera, the engraver, the artist and the color press make it easy to furnish this proof." Supplying photographs for railroads to illustrate their publications were commercial photographers like Asahel Curtis of Seattle. In mid-1929 when the Milwaukee Road changed the schedule of its Olympian to provide passengers with daylight views of the Bitterroot Mountains, which formed the boundary between Montana and Idaho, it contacted Curtis: "We find that our stock of photographs covering this territory is rather limited, and we wish to have some new ones made, this year, if possible." The railroad publicist emphasized that it had been criticized in the past because "most of our photographs contain no life," and it asked Curtis to include, "so far as possible, persons and animals, or both." Some larger railroads, including the Pennsylvania, maintained in-house photographers.[14]

The increased availability of small and easily portable cameras during the early twentieth century created an opportunity for amateurs to become an additional source of photographs. "The edition for 1906 of *In the Maine Woods*, published by the passenger department of the Bangor & Aroostook Railroad, is more replete than ever with illustrations of the delightful and wholesome camp life to be enjoyed in that region." As the *Official Guide* noted, "The advent of the camera in the hands of the amateur has enabled the publishers to secure many unique and surprising photographs of wild game, as well as of campers, who proceed in their own method to enjoy life in the woods."[15]

Likewise, professional illustrators were vital to publishing the railroad. Their outpouring of commercial art may have attained its visual apogee in a brochure that the Milwaukee Road issued in 1912 to promote the settlement of Montana's grasslands after its 1909 completion of 1,400 miles of track west from Mobridge, South Dakota, to Seattle and Tacoma on Washington's Puget Sound. The brochure's color cover showed a farmer and a team of two spirited horses plowing gold coins from the fertile Montana soil, a visual metaphor no prospective settler could possibly misunderstand.[16] Already by 1911, the railroad's ceaseless promotional activities had encouraged an estimated hundred

thousand settlers to relocate to the fifty thousand square miles of territory tributary to its new line of tracks. This area "has a productive capacity for the support of many millions, and with the land hunger that now possesses the American people it will not be many years before these vast reaches of country will be thickly dotted with the houses of contented and prosperous settlers and a new empire will be added to the trade and commerce of the American nation." The prose by wordsmith Mark H. Salt appeared in the *Buffalo Courier* and other daily newspapers in 1911, but the passionate words were typical of rail promotional essays at that time.[17]

Every transcontinental railroad employed wordsmiths, and so, too, did numerous other lines that announced grand aspirations spanning lengthy swaths of North America but that in the end settled for more realistic regional goals. A prime example of that reorientation was Jay Gould's Southwest System, based in Saint Louis, whose multifaceted publishing activity was discussed at length in chapter 6. One component, the St. Louis Southwestern, or "Cotton Belt Route," which was headed by Gould's son Edwin, took note of the transformation of eastern Arkansas after the introduction of rice cultivation and did its best to promote it: "This is comparatively a new industry in that State, and so favorable have the soil and climatic conditions proven that there are now many farms which annually produce enough rice for all of the weddings from the time of Adam and Eve down to the present day."[18]

Collectively, the big three national publishers, Poole Brothers; Rand, McNally; and Matthews-Northrup, together with smaller regional ones like the Homeseekers' Bureau, were responsible for a mind-boggling variety of railroad literature. "Where ten years ago travelling passenger agents sought out tourist, delegate, and invalid with meager literature, to-day the prosperous

Facing, The cover art of this 1905 Cotton Belt timetable saluted the Arkansas and Texas crop that was so important to the prosperity of the St. Louis Southwestern that it became the railroad's familiar moniker.

SEPTEMBER 1905
St. Louis Southwestern Ry. Co. of Texas.

COTTON BELT ROUTE

BETWEEN
ST. LOUIS
CAIRO
MEMPHIS
AND
ARKANSAS
LOUISIANA
AND
TEXAS.

J. W. FLANAGAN,
G. P. & T. A.,
TYLER, TEX.

F. H. BRITTON,
PRESIDENT,
ST. LOUIS, MO.

W. E. GREEN,
1ST V.-P. & G. S.,
TYLER, TEX.

SECURITY PRINTING CO. OF ST. LOUIS.

SEPTEMBER 1905
St. Louis Southwestern Railway Company.

COTTON BELT ROUTE

BETWEEN
ST. LOUIS
CAIRO
MEMPHIS
AND
ARKANSAS
LOUISIANA
AND
TEXAS.

E. W. LA BEAUME,
G. P. & T. A.,
ST. LOUIS, MO.

F. H. BRITTON,
V.-P. & G. M.,
ST. LOUIS, MO.

W. E. GREEN,
GEN'L SUPT.,
TYLER, TEX.

SECURITY PRINTING CO. OF ST. LOUIS.

masses with trunks packed and suit-cases in hand, make insatiable demands for information. Pamphlets giving the latest views and accommodations are rushed through the presses." While many such publications were intended for the traveling public and could easily be classified among the vacation or land settlement imprints described in earlier chapters, some printed items defy easy categorization. One example was the Rock Island's *Theatrical Guide*, a publication that described "Show Towns" along its track, provided a list of "theaters, opera houses and halls" in each one, and gave "particulars as to the seating capacity, dimensions of stage, hotel rates and the many details which are essential to the successful management of a theatrical trip."[19]

In the early 1920s, the Southern Railway's passenger department issued *Chickamauga, a Famous Battlefield.* Civil War sites were for a time a popular topic among railroad publicists, with Gettysburg and other notable battlefields being the subject of one or more rail pamphlets. As for the Southern Railway's *Chickamauga* folder, "it described graphically and vividly the battles of the Civil War at Chickamauga, Lookout Mountain, Missionary Ridge and other points in that vicinity famed for the historic stand maintained by the Blue and the Gray."[20]

The tracks of the Atchison, Topeka & Santa Fe traversed "an immense amount of territory and it offers diversified scenery and resorts, and the industries reached by its lines are innumerable and of great variety." Consequently, the Santa Fe issued a yearly panoply of booklets and pamphlets devoted to topics as diverse as the West its trains served. In 1901, this literature ranged from the typical, and somewhat formulaic, tourist and settlement brochures, such as *To California and Back* and *A Colorado Summer,* to specialized publications that encouraged homeseekers to examine for themselves the attractions of the Rio Grande Valley, the Texas Gulf Coast, and numerous other areas. Among the

Santa Fe's many offerings was at least one publication that fit no stereotype: "A highly-colored booklet, with many illustrations, describes the 'Moki Snake Dance,' and is written by Walter Hough, Ph. D."[21]

With the supposed end of the American frontier during the 1890s, railroad publications devoted to the Native Americans of the West increased in popularity. At much the same time on the opposite side of the continent, a popular new topic for the eastern railroads to promote was golf. The Long Island Railroad was one of many carriers responsible for beautifully illustrated booklets devoted "to the various links located along its lines." To its summer 1930 publication titled *Vacationland Accommodations,* Maine Central Railroad added a list of golf courses available in its service area. At the dawn of the twentieth century, the Oregon Railway & Navigation Company had promoted *Restful Recreation Resorts,* one of numerous rail imprints across the United States that emphasized sedentary pleasures, but by the 1920s the publishing emphasis had shifted noticeably to active vacations that featured hiking, horseback riding, snow skiing, and golf.[22]

Few railroads devoted more attention to golf than the Atlantic Coast Line and its spirited competitor the Seaboard Air Line Railroad. These two rail lines and the other carriers that served the South lavished attention on the growing array of golf-oriented resorts their trains reached in Florida, Georgia, and elsewhere. The Southern Pines area of North Carolina was a favorite topic for Seaboard publications, which urged northern golfers to head south and continue their sport during the balmy winter months in the Carolinas.

During these same years of heightened interest in various outdoor activities, vacations on dude ranches in the Rocky Mountains increased in popularity. Northern Pacific, one of many railroad promoters of this new form of recreation, noted in its booklet *National Forest Vacations in the American Rockies,* "Dude ranches are real ranches, so-titled because they are equipped with cabins, cottages, or ranch-house rooms enough to entertain summer guests. The title 'dude' simply distinguishes the welcome visitor from the seasoned old-timer. All newcomers from the city are 'dudes' to the Westerner." Not to be left out of this lucrative new recreation market, the New York Central Lines published a folder called *Westward Ho,* which featured

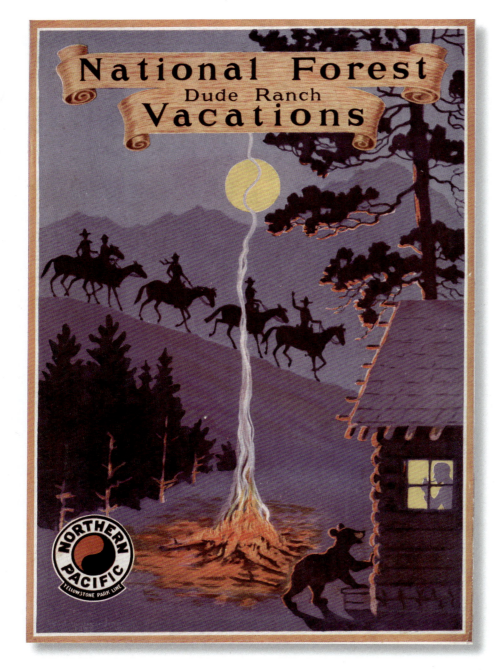

The federal government's Department of the Interior oversees America's national parks, while the Department of Agriculture oversees the National Forest. While the early national parks were viewed as national treasures because of the scenic wonders they contained, national forests played a distinctly secondary role as scenic attractions and hence as compelling vacation destinations. Their role was to serve as a source of lumber, a commodity of great economic value, but logged-off land was not scenic even when replanted with young trees. The Northern Pacific, however, dared to promote national forest vacations, at least as part of its desire to lure tourists outdoors to dude ranches accessible from its trains across the West.

and the Great Northern Railway published a booklet intended to address regional prejudice head-on. The imprint was titled *Western Trips for Eastern People*, and its cover featured two stylish women exploring the mountain West with a camera.

Railroads across North America published a large number of brochures that featured women travelers on their covers. The visual text seemed to say that although rail operations were gritty, noisy, and perhaps intimidating, a journey by train and the recreation pleasures that awaited travelers at their vacation destinations represented the height of good taste and smart behavior. Numerous railroad brochures depicted fashionable golfers on their covers, with a surprising number of these sports enthusiasts being women.

Some vacation attractions remained popular year after year, but railroad publicists and their printer allies required a steady stream of new imprints. In its 1884 brochure titled *A Bouquet from the Garden of the Gods*, the Chicago, Burlington & Quincy promoted new attractions likely to boost passenger traffic: "The great seaside resorts on the Atlantic coast have for nearly two generation been the Meccas of summer travelers." And spending weeks enjoying the surfside social whirl at Newport, Rhode Island; inland at Saratoga Springs in upstate New York; or at

dude ranches of the Far West, all far removed from the railroad's service territory in the Northeast and Midwest.[23]

The dude ranch was just one of the peculiarities of the West that travelers from the East Coast found fascinating—or distasteful. Yes, the latter perception was a matter of concern for railroads eager to promote the western half of the continent,

The Harvey Company's Indian Detours provided transcontinental travelers aboard the trains of the Atchison, Topeka & Santa Fe an optional sightseeing break in New Mexico. The brochure titled *Harveycar Motor Cruises* dates from 1929.

some other upscale resort served to confirm a family's elevated social standing: "Halcyon days were those for the comparatively favored few who could afford the time and money to be spent in such delightful manner." The Burlington proposed to expand the social scene to include "watering places" in the mountains of Colorado and to attract Americans of more "limited time and money."[24]

During the "prosperity decade" of the 1920s, when more Americans than ever had money to spend on vacations, railroad publicists tirelessly sought to create a fresh array of attractions and to advertise them as widely as possible. Among these were the Southern Pacific's Apache Trail motor trip along the scenic highway between Globe and Phoenix, Arizona, which the railroad linked with the through sleeping cars it ran west from New Orleans. The Union Pacific's 1920s counterpart was its tour of Death Valley's desert scenery via rail and motor bus. The Santa Fe advertised off-train excursions to Indian pueblos in New Mexico, the Petrified Forest in Arizona, and the Grand Canyon National Park area. Travelers rode aboard "Harvey-cars," limousines operated by the Fred Harvey Company, which originally gained fame for its quality restaurants and hotels located along Santa Fe tracks between Chicago and California and Texas.[25]

Finally, it is noteworthy that railroads need not actually serve the areas they publicized if in some way they perceived a benefit.

The Milwaukee Road, which extended its tracks no closer to Colorado than Omaha and Kansas City, nearly five hundred miles short of the Centennial State, nonetheless published a 1912 brochure titled *Colorado, the Nation's Playground*. Even earlier, in 1903 and 1904, railroads of the United States and Canada were so eager to capitalize on travelers thronging to the Saint Louis World's Fair, physically the largest such global extravaganza ever held and the beneficiary of an unprecedented flood of rail publicity, that carriers with tracks ending a thousand miles from Saint Louis—the Boston & Maine, to cite one example—nonetheless issued publicity brochures to motivate fairgoers to make their journey by train.[26]

In terms of printing and publishing, no rail imprint ever communicated with a larger number of readers than a public timetable, and when dozens of different copies plus resort brochures, each free for the taking, were displayed together on a large rack, they provided a cornucopia of information. The print run for a thick timetable folder issued at least twice yearly—and sometimes even monthly—by a large railroad like the Pennsylvania could easily total millions of copies annually. As important as colorful publications devoted to "soil and scenery" were to railroad publishing, none compared with the public timetables in importance.

The Union Pacific's *Pathway to the Setting Sun* dates from 1914 and uses simple imagery and bold colors to salute the railroad and its many accomplishments across the West.

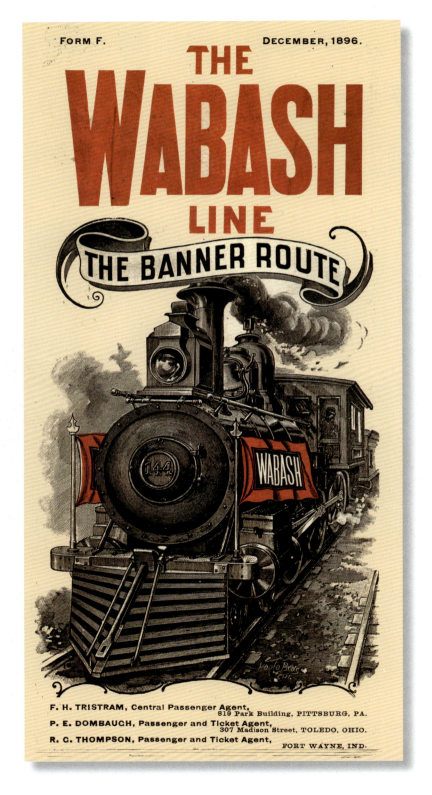

Mr. Fogg was quite ready. Under his arm might have been observed a red-bound copy of Bradshaw's "Continental Railway Steam Transit and General Guide," with its timetables showing the arrival and departure of steamers and railways.

—from Jules Verne, *Around the World in 80 Days* (1873)[1]

The cover panel of a Wabash timetable published in 1896 suggests the compelling visual impact of an onrushing locomotive.

12

TIMETABLE TYRANNY

THE CLOCKWORK RAILROAD

The first half of the nineteenth century was a time of heightened number consciousness. At sea, that meant more precise nautical charts for mariners sailing the North Atlantic. This accomplishment was one of the many useful contributions of Matthew Fontaine Maury, a pioneer in the compilation and analysis of nautical big data that could then be used to develop accurate charts for trade routes around the globe. On land, a cadre of surveyors, early practitioners of a numbers-intensive craft, discovered that work on the Erie Canal gave them enough familiarity with numbers and complex calculations to claim the title of engineer.[2]

When the Erie Canal was completed in 1825, a school of civil engineering for civilians did not exist in the United States. Significantly, the first school to grant that degree was the Rensselaer Polytechnic Institute, which was located in Troy, New York, an industrial city conveniently close to the eastern portal of the Erie Canal. The number of American schools that taught civil engineering increased only slowly between the mid-1830s and the post–Civil War era.

Like the Erie Canal, early railroad construction in America heightened the demand for trained civil engineers, or at least for craftsmen comfortable with numbers and precise calculations. Not surprisingly, an informal cohort of the technically literate crossed the North Atlantic in both directions to study the latest developments in the infant railroad industry—Americans to England and Germany, French and English observers to the United States—and to then compile written reports for the governments or railroads that sponsored their journeys. These documents are descriptive, but they also brim with numbers and calculations their compilers hoped would add to the growing body of knowledge about all aspects of railroad construction and operations on both sides of the Atlantic.[3]

During the early years, the daily operation of passenger trains generated a new set of numbers that took the form of a timetable. "The teaching of the higher branches of mathematics in all our public schools prepared the way for railroad timetables." The newspaper claim was meant to offer lighthearted criticism of the wealth of information densely displayed between the covers of a typical folder: "It cannot be seen why people love to strain their eyesight and intellects over puzzle pictures, rebuses and problems where there is the timetable to be had everywhere for the asking. You can get a whole week's enjoyment out of it, and then not be half through." During long winter nights, rural families "may discipline their minds with a railroad timetable."[4]

Today's travelers, especially those in their twenties and thirties, are accustomed to using electronic timetables on the internet that require users to input only the beginning and ending cities to receive a listing of arrival and departure times. But with early timetables, as with most other aspects of railroad operations in the 1830s, the key words are *experimental* and *tentative*. America's most significant railroad pioneer, the Baltimore & Ohio, issued what might constitute the first rail timetable in the United States on May 21, 1830. It was an inconspicuous advertisement printed in small and difficult-to-read type by a Baltimore newspaper, the *American and Commercial Advertiser*.[5]

At that time and for years to come, railroad timetables consisted of newspaper notices that listed local train arrival and departure times. Occasionally a printer dressed up one of the newspaper timetables by adding a stylized woodcut of a locomotive or a railroad passenger carriage, but most such notices were simple additions to the dense mass of type that typified the layout and design (loosely speaking) of news journals printed before the Civil War. This uncomplicated arrangement underscored the local orientation of American railroads at the time. It also presented a problem to travelers from distant locales, who would not have access to a local newspaper and its listing of train times.[6]

George Bradshaw recognized the need for something more encompassing, and thus on October 19, 1839, the Manchester printer issued the world's first compilation of timetables for several separate British railways. *Bradshaw's Railway Time Tables and Assistant to Railway Travelling* was small, easily portable, and inexpensive. Not long afterward, several similar timetable compilations appeared in the United States. Most were intended to serve regional needs only, but even this improvement represented a big step forward for the growing number of travelers by rail.[7]

The typical American timetable guide of the 1840s and 1850s was diminutive like Bradshaw's compilation and thus easily portable. Schedules published by individual railroad companies

The drab cover of an 1887 timetable issued by the Baltimore & Potomac, a Pennsylvania Railroad affiliate, was typical of the era before the widespread use of color by North American railroads.

also began the practice of listing train times and station stops sequentially in columns that corresponded to the direction of the journey: down for outbound travel and up for the return. The arrangement was easy to follow for most travelers, though it remained confusing to others. One of the most creative solutions before computers was a timetable dial, a cardboard device that prefigured the modern electronic listing of flight arrival and departure times only.[8]

Some early rail guides went a step further and, in addition to providing train schedules, took note of the gauge of the track, the type of rails used (wood or iron), and a railroad's chosen standard of time. The biggest problem with early guides, or so critics often claimed, was that some treated timekeeping in a slapdash manner. That is, they listed train times that were neither accurate nor up to date, or else they did not list them at all. One guide published in 1848 explained the omission by candidly stating that train departure times could not be displayed "with any degree of accuracy." Changes to schedules "[were] not unfrequently made without much regard to system," and often a frustrated publisher learned of new train times only twenty-four hours before their implementation. For travelers who depended on accurate timetables and guides, errors by publishers meant "vexatious delay and uncalled for disappointment." As in matters of track gauge and standards of time before the 1880s, the words that best describe early-day American train travel might be *capricious* or *idiosyncratic*.[9]

Dealing with unprecedented difficulties and facing challenges to accuracy never before or since encountered by any timetable compilers within the United States was *Hill & Swayze's Confederate States Rail-Road and Steam-Boat Guide*, which struggled to print current timetables for passenger trains across the breakaway South even as the armies of the North progressively recaptured swaths of the rebellious states. After the army of General Ambrose Burnside gained control of much of eastern North Carolina, the Hill & Swayze guide continued to print a list of stations served along ninety miles of Atlantic & North Carolina track between Morehead City and Goldsboro, but it left arrival and departure times blank. It struck a patriotic tone by noting that New Bern, for many years the North Carolina capital, was "now, alas, in the possession of our enemies."[10]

The *Travelers' Official Railway Guide for the United States and Canada* was born in June 1868. In physical size and intent, its originators modeled their publication after *Bradshaw's*, the respected timetable guide published in Great Britain since 1839. A passion for accuracy set the *Official Guide* apart from the slapdash timetable compilations that enraged travelers when misinformation caused them to miss a train, often the only one during the next twenty-four hours. The *Official Guide* was for good reason known as the "Railroad Man's Bible." Beginning in 1873, William F. Allen oversaw the issuance of the *Official Guide* twelve times per annum for the next forty-three years without missing a deadline. During those decades it gained a measure of fame as the biggest monthly publication in the world. Allen was the secretary, too, of the General Time Convention, which in November 1883 succeeded in implementing his passion for order and accuracy by gifting residents of North America with (railroad) standard time.[11]

The *Official Guide*'s first issue of 140 pages was only slightly larger physically than many predecessor publications, but being North American in coverage meant that as the number of railroads increased, as their mileage expanded, and as their passenger trains multiplied, so too did the thickness of the monthly *Official Guide*. The increased bulk meant that it was not the sort of aid to travel that the typical passenger cared to lug around in a valise or carpetbag. Its main purpose was to provide railroad ticket agents at any station in North America with accurate and up-to-date information about passenger train schedules and their accommodations anywhere tracks extended within the United States, Canada, and Mexico—and even within Cuba and Central America.[12]

Initially, the *Official Guide* had numerous competitors at the local and regional level and also a few at the national level. In 1868 there was no certainty that the newcomer would outlast any of the older publications, including its main competitor, Appleton's *Railroad and Steam Navigation Guide*, which dated from 1848. At least four additional timetable compilations, all national in coverage, vied for the attention of rail travelers. The Chicago printer Rand, McNally & Company added yet another competitor to an already crowded field when it bought Gilbert Baldwin's

THE REMARKABLE WILLIAM FREDERICK ALLEN

W. F. Allen was indefatigable in his commitment to bring order to the time chaos that prevailed across the United States before 1883. While other "fathers of standard time" dealt with its theoretical dimensions, Allen more than anyone else was doggedly determined to see a simple solution implemented in practice. That was at first a discouraging task. For fifteen years, from the *Official Guide*'s initial issue in 1868 until December 1883, the first one after North American railroads adopted standard time, the monthly publication navigated successfully through a hodgepodge of local variations. Allen, editor of the *Official Guide* from 1873 until 1915, frequently advocated a better system of time reckoning. In the *Century*, a magazine forum more widely accessible to general readers than the *Official Guide*, Allen complained two months before the historic changeover that "railroads using the various standards cross and interlace each other in such a puzzling manner as to render any ready acquisition of knowledge of the standard by which each is governed a sheer impossibility. Studying a map of the system is like tracing the intricacies of a labyrinth." Allen, more than any of his peers, became relentless, even obsessed,

with the pursuit of order, and the longtime editor of the *Official Guide* deserves to be recognized as Father Time himself, the man who finally brought clarity to North America's time labyrinth.*

When the two leading proponents of standard time, the General Time Convention and the Southern Time Convention, met together in April 1883, representatives of only fifty-six of the more than five hundred railroads then operating across North America attended. The formidable task of winning support from the full industry, or at least from a sizable majority of railroads, was handed to Allen, secretary of the General Time Convention since 1875. After seven months of ceaseless persuasion, he had succeeded in winning the support of all but a handful of holdouts, and railroad standard time was adopted on November 18, 1883.†

But there was more. As Allen explained in a 1909 presentation to Harvard's School of Business Administration, "The success of this movement revealed to the railway managers the possibility of bringing about other reforms by the same methods, and of this they were quick to avail themselves." During the years after 1883 they standardized train operating rules, matters of signaling and safety, dimensions of rolling stock, policies that governed the interchange of cars among separate railroads, and statistics and accounts. Imposing order on hundreds of railroads scattered across the United States and Canada was a formidable task, but the successful implementation of standard time no doubt encouraged Allen and other proponents of standardization.‡

* *Century*, September 1883, 796–797

† *Official Guide*, December 1923, xxix. The *Proceedings of the American Association of Passenger Traffic Officers* for 1948 contains a lengthy discussion of the *Official Guide* (pp. 55–59) and its impact on railroads and writers interested in railroads, such as Lucius Beebe in his *Mixed Trains Daily: A Book of Short-Line Railroads* (New York: E. P. Dutton, 1947).

‡ W. F. Allen, "Railway Operating Associations," *Railway World*, February 12, 1909, 128–132. At this time Allen served as secretary of the American Railway Association, successor in 1891 to the General Time Convention.

William F. Allen was born in Bordentown, New Jersey, in 1846, and after an early hands-on career as a rodman with the Camden & Amboy and West Jersey railroads, in 1872 he joined the *Official Guide*, where he remained until his death in 1915. His younger sibling, Edwin S. Allen, succeeded him as manager of the *Official Guide* and remained on the job until his death in 1927. The Allen brothers were a remarkable pair of timekeepers.

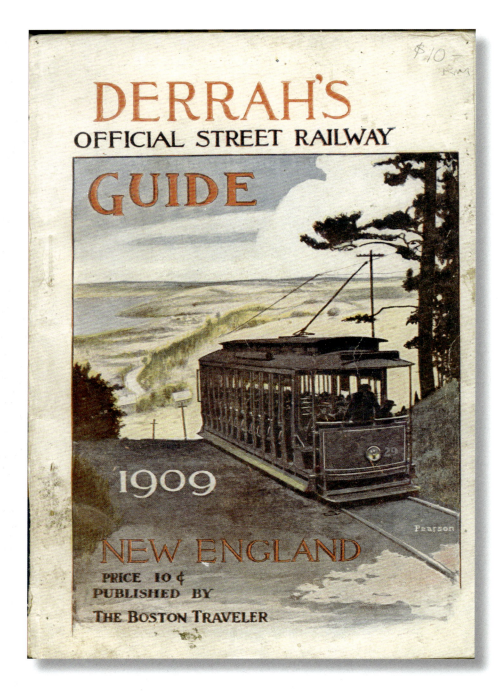

Derrah's Official Street Railway Guide of 1909 was one of an annual series of timetable and travel books intended to encourage New England outings aboard the region's electric trolleys. The region's formerly extensive network of electric tracks is gone today, except for the pieces that appear in museums.

Free Railroad Guide in 1871 and transformed it into the *Western Railway Guide*.[13]

By the time the United States joined World War I in early 1917, most of the competitors to the *Official Guide* had fallen by the wayside, but that vital reference tool grew so bulky—totaling approximately 1,800 pages by 1929—that it was impractical for traveling salesmen and others to carry copies for ready consultation. During the 1920s, portable regional timetable guides became the specialty of the Russell firm of Cedar Rapids, Iowa. Its various monthly publications occupied a secure niche for decades, and in addition to providing regional rail schedules in an easily portable format, they listed times for electric interurban railways and intercity bus lines. The Russell firm eventually distinguished itself by publishing an intercity bus guide for North America that in its scope, accuracy, and heft compared favorably to the *Official Guide of the Railways*.[14]

Monthly copies of the *Official Guide*, along with preserved copies of North America's once numerous local and regional guides, recall a time when thousands of passenger trains, both locals and expresses, were a ubiquitous feature of daily life, and they likewise document the changing fortunes of the continent's biggest business for at least a century. Abroad, the venerable Bradshaw gained such widespread fame as a reliable guide that Jules Verne showcased its value in his early 1870s novel *Around the World in 80 Days*. Arriving on the publishing scene at much the same time (1873) but surviving longer than the Bradshaw guide were quarterly (later monthly) timetable compilations published by England's foremost proponent of organized travel, Thomas Cook. When after more than a century the financially struggling Cook enterprise decided to jettison its monthly timetable guide in 2013, a former compiler named John Potter purchased the publication, which he continued from his Northamptonshire home as the *European Rail Timetable* until he sold it in 2024. With the help of volunteers, he tabulated the comings and goings of fifty

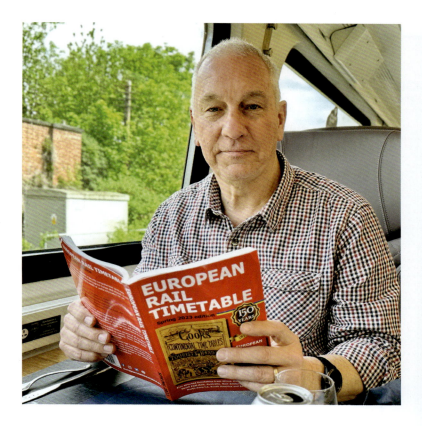

During our annual rail pilgrimages to the United Kingdom, Tom Hoback and I always sought to enjoy a meal or two with John Potter, publisher of the *European Rail Timetable*, the linear successor to guides issued by Thomas Cook, his former employer. I took this picture of Potter and his salute to Cook's one hundredth anniversary in May 2023 while the three of us enjoyed lunch aboard a luxurious Welsh train (an experiment for the operator) between LLandudno Junction and Cardiff.

thousand trains in a monthly guide nearly six hundred pages long. I hasten to commend Potter's heroic commitment to the rail industry's traditional paper timetables despite the world's headlong rush to embrace computers and electronic databases.[15]

The railroad timetable itself was a remarkable publication, and during the century after its inception in the 1820s with the appearance of the first modern-era rail lines in England and the United States, it evolved into the most powerful medium of communication between the rail industry and ordinary Americans.

TIMETABLES: PERFORM OR PAY

During the 1860s, published timetables became an important feature of any journey by rail, and their listing of arrival and departure times accurate to the minute implied a contract with the traveling public. Some railroads, perhaps as a result of unpredictable disruptions during the Civil War years, lapsed into relaxed timekeeping habits typical of the earlier era of steamboats and stagecoaches, which brought a reprimand from the *American Railway Times* in 1866: "We are aware that it is nearly impossible to run passenger trains with clock-like precision at all times, but we are confident that more precision in fulfilling the promises of time cards and advertisements than is usually done, is perfectly practicable. There is great looseness in this respect on some of the lines, and we should not object to the operation of a law requiring railway companies to comply with their promises or contracts with the public, or pay a forfeit for non-performance."*

* *American Railway Times*, May 10, 1866, 78. In addition to the vast array of public timetables, there were employee timetables "of which the passengers know nothing. These schedules are made out for the conductors and engineers, and show the exact second at which each train is due at each station, along the whole line of the road." [Helen Hunt Jackson], "Wait!," *Arizona Sentinel* (Yuma), May 29, 1886. The acclaimed writer and poet's use of the word *second* to describe railroad timekeeping represented artistic license, but it does describe well the attention to detail demanded of train operating crews.

CINCINNATI NORTHERN R. R.
BETWEEN CINCINNATI, VAN WERT, CLARK'S LAKE AND JACKSON
Read Down   Read Up

8 Ex. Sun.	16 Ex. Sun.		Miles	STATIONS	7 Ex. Sun.	17 Ex. Sun.	
pm	am				am	pm	
4.05	6.45		0	Lv. CINCINNATI .Ar	11.25	7.15	
4.22	7.02		5.6	".. Winton Place .."	11.00	6.45	
5.32	8.05		33.5	" MIDDLETOWN "	10.03	5.48	
5.48	8.22		39.2	"... Franklin ..."	9.50	5.34	
5.54	8.31		41.0	"... Carlisle ..."	9.45	5.29	
6.02	8.40		45.0	"... Germantown .."	9.32	5.16	
6.12	8.50		50.3	".. Farmersville .."	9.22	5.06	
6.22	9.00		54.8	"... Igomar ..."	9.11	4.56	
6.27	9.05		57.5	".. W. Alexandria .."	9.05	4.50	
6.40	9.20		64.7	"... Lewisburg ..."	8.52	4.38	
6.52	9.32		70.6	".. W. Manchester .."	8.40	4.25	
6.57	9.37		72.7	"... Castine ..."	8.35	4.20	
7.05	9.47		77.0	"... Savona ..."	8.26	4.11	
f7.11	f9.53		79.8	".. Ft. Jefferson .."	f8.20	f4.05	
7.25	10.05		85.2	"... Greenville ..."	8.08	3.55	
7.30	10.10		85.9	"D. & U. Crossing.."	8.05	3.50	
f7.37			90.4	"... Meekers ..."	f7.56		
7.42	10.25		93.3	"... Ansonia ..."	7.50	3.35	
7.55	10.35		98.0	"... Rossburg ..."	7.40	3.24	
8.03	10.43		102.0	".. New Weston .."	7.32	3.15	
8.07	10.46		103.1	"... Gilberts ..."	7.29	3.12	
8.15	10.55		107.5	"... St. Henry ..."	7.20	3.04	
8.23	11.05		112.0	"... Coldwater ..."	7.11	2.56	
8.35	11.25		117.7	"... Celina ..."	7.00	2.45	
f8.46	f11.35	2	124.0	"... Tama ..."	f6.48	f2.34	1 Ex Sun
8.55	11.45	Ex Su	128.2	"... Rockford ..."	6.40	2.27	
9.05	11.55		133.9	"... Ohio City .."	6.30	2.15	
9.20	12.10		141.2	Ar.. VAN WERT .Lv	6.15	2.00	
	am					pm	
12.15	6.20		141.2	Lv. VAN WERT .Ar	1.55	7.55	
12f24	f6.29		146.4	"... Cavett ..."	f1.45	f7.40	
12.30	6.35		149.4	"... Scott ..."	1.40	7.35	
12.36	6.41		151.4	"... Haviland ..."	1.35	7.30	
12.45	6.50		156.1	"... Latty ..."	1.25	7.20	
12.52	6.57		159.6	"... Paulding ..."		7.10	
1.05	7.08		165.8	"... Cecil ..."	1.05	6.55	
1.15	7.18		171.4	"... Sherwood ..."	12.53	6.45	
1.28	7.30		178.6	"... Ney ..."	12.38	6.30	
1.40	7.45		185.1	"... Bryan ..."	12.25	6.20	
f1.47	f7.53		188.7	"... Pulaski ..."	12f17	f6.10	
2.00	8.05		195.6	".. West Unity .."	12.05	6.00	
2.10	8.15		200.7	"... Alvordton .."	11.55	5.50	
2.20	8.25		205.1	"... Waldron ..."	11.45	5.40	
2.28	8.35		208.9	"... Prattville .."	11.37	5.32	
2.40	8.45		214.5	"... Hudson ..."	11.25	5.20	
f2.49	8.52		219.5	"... Rollin ..."	11 f12	5.08	
2.57	9.00		223.6	".. Manitou Beach ."	11.05	5.00	
3.02	9.05		225.8	"Addison Junction ."	11.00	4.55	
3.14	9.18		231.6	".. Cement City .."	10.48	4.43	
3.22	9.25		234.0	".. Clark's Lake .."	10.40	4.35	
f3.30	f9.35		239.0	".. Ackerman Lake.."	10 f30	4.25	
f3.32	f9.38		240.2	"... Lyonette ..."	10 f27	f4.22	
3.45	9.50		244.3	Ar.. JACKSON ..Lv	10.16	4.10	
pm	pm	am			am	am	pm

Note.—Trains 16 and 17 have Coaches between Cincinnati and Jackson. Mich.

The Cincinnati Northern's 1918 schedule, simple in its display, illustrates how a timetable works. It lists station stops for the trains that ambled across a rural landscape between Jackson, Michigan, and Cincinnati, Ohio. Passengers could follow the progress of their trains by reading down along the left side or up along the right. It seems straightforward, but published schedules on large railroads were often complex and confusing to casual users when trains split to continue to multiple destinations or when different rail routes intersected.

Earlier forms of transportation, such as steamboats and stagecoaches, had not required such precise measures of timekeeping, nor would their rudimentary timetables evolve into the kind of complex and colorful documents that railroad timetables became in the late nineteenth and early twentieth centuries. The downside was that some travelers resented the "timetable tyranny" that forced them to conform their comings and goings to the dictates of the railroad potentates as expressed in print. "The railway time books and guide books in Europe are made for the people; in America they are made for the railroad companies," or so claimed Luke Sharp, a prominent Detroit journalist, in a lengthy essay syndicated across the United States in 1889.[16]

By the 1880s it was nearly impossible to imagine embarking on a train journey of any length without a current timetable in hand. Travelers compulsively toted one or more of these ubiquitous paper documents during their journey—even if train times were conveniently posted on the walls of every station. Some people, even if they never boarded a train, acquired the latest railroad timetables to enjoy a no-cost journey of the imagination, a late nineteenth-century version of armchair travel that one "mental tourist" labeled "time-table vacations." Luke Sharp, the Detroit journalist, noted one advantage of living in America in 1889: "You get your time-tables for nothing. Now in England they make you pay a penny for even the smallest time-table of a railway." The railroads of America "[flooded] the country with time-tables as free as the waters of the Detroit River."[17]

The American public's easy access to display racks featuring dozens of different timetable giveaways was subject to abuse by the "timetable fiend," the common term applied during the late nineteenth century to individuals who compulsively raided display racks in rail stations and hotels but had no intention of making a journey except in their imaginations. "Thousands of people take wonderful trips through the country with the aid of the illustrated railway folder. Thousands make that trip in imagination, lack of funds preventing them from making it otherwise." Luke Sharp, who memorialized his own timetable obsession, did not expect many readers to "enter into my enthusiasm on the time-table business, but then thoroughly sensible people miss a lot of fun in this world. Anyhow, they don't amass as many time-tables as I do." Sharp concluded with these words: "A time-table tourist has all the fun and has no bills to pay." The *Omaha Daily News* added in 1918: "Just because the trip is imaginary does not detract a whit from the pleasure."[18]

Timetable users of either variety, actual travelers or fantasy tourists, found the publications to be information cornucopias, especially after railroads at the dawn of the twentieth century abandoned the previous unwieldy format, which when fully unfolded was the size of a bedsheet or wall poster, in favor of the more compact and easily handled folder. "As artistic advertising material many of our American railroad timetables take a high place. Some of the cover designs are of high artistic merit and are excellent examples of fine engraving and printing." As important as creative cover artwork was, ranking high among the most conspicuous features of nearly all system timetables issued after 1900 was its centerfold map, an exercise in cartographic fantasy that frequently contrasted noticeably (and sometimes humorously) with the precision demanded of train arrival and departure times.[19]

THE TRAIN DISPATCHER GAVE THE WRONG ORDER.

The newspaper cartoon depicts a harried railroad dispatcher who has mistakenly sent two trains on a collision course. This grim scenario did not happen often, but dispatchers bore a heavy responsibility. The job, which featured a passing resemblance to a three-dimensional game of chess, required a good memory, a passion for details, and the ability to keep multiple trains running on time and passing one another safely.

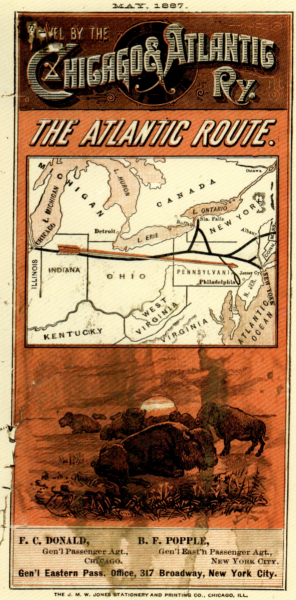

Railroad maps are more interesting than any other kind. A railroad map can make the state of Illinois twice as long east and west as it is north and south, without the slightest inconvenience. Only on a railroad map may New York, Nashville, Butte, Mont., and San Antonio be shown upon the same parallel of latitude.

—from *Birmingham Times* (Alabama), February 24, 1911

The Chicago & Atlantic in 1887 was a former broad-gauge line that linked another broad-gauge railroad, the New York & Erie, to Chicago. Its timetable cover combined a system map with stylized but dramatic artwork to suggest track straight as an arrow, which it was not.

13
RAILROAD CARTOGRAPHY AS THE LIE OF THE LAND

Maps formed a highly visible component of the publishing legacy of the railroads of North America. In the twentieth century it would be a rare system timetable that failed to include a map. Promotional brochures, especially those devoted to land settlement, featured numerous maps too. Even before the Milwaukee Road opened its Pacific extension to Puget Sound in 1909, it had already published a variety of brochures to acquaint the public with its new line, and many additional publications soon followed. One was grandly titled *The Rediscovery of America*, and another was the more prosaic *Fruit Growing in Washington*, which featured a large-scale map of the railroad's newly accessed service area.[1]

One of the most creative uses of a railroad map—in this instance, one that featured the newly completed route of the Northern Pacific Railway—appeared in a publication issued in the mid-1880s by the American Baptist Home Mission Society. In bold text the caption read, "The New Highway Across the Continent," while below it in smaller type was this warning: "While Sin is moving West by Steam, it will never do for Christianity to go afoot." Here is one of the best and most succinct statements I have seen on the power of railroads and their maps to alter existing spatial relationships.[2]

Maps intended for public consumption—each one a visual statement of a railroad's reach—varied greatly in quality, but some attained an elevated level of artistic creativity. One Northern Pacific map featured a prone figure of an Indian with a map of the railroad superimposed along his backbone. Central of Georgia timetable covers showed the palm of a human hand overlayed with a map of the railroad, with various branches extending along the outstretched fingers. In early Chicago Great Western timetables and advertisements, a map of the tracks emulated the veins of a maple leaf. In addition to various design embellishments, many railroad-published maps represented a curious form of cartographic fantasy that most members of the traveling public accepted but did not necessarily believe.[3]

Early timetables seldom featured cartography, but that changed after the Civil War. When the large timetable maps of the late nineteenth century were printed in color, the result was a visual statement that truly qualified as a work of commercial art.[4]

The largest railroads also created numerous specialized maps for in-house use, such as those intended for civil engineers

HOW TO LIE WITH MAPS

Maps were an integral part of publishing the railroad. Toward the end of the nineteenth century, railroads favored a public timetable format that consisted of one large sheet of paper printed on both sides. The blanket sheet was awkward to use, but its reverse side provided space for an enormous route map. These maps, often printed in bold colors, sometimes placed the issuing company's rail lines within the context of half the United States or within its entire national boundaries. The format was unwieldy even when folded into a supposedly manageable size, and any attempt to reference either the map or the train schedules aboard a crowded passenger car must have tried the patience and dexterity of users. Shortly before the dawn of the twentieth century, the railroads of the United States began to jettison their old-fashioned blanket sheet format in favor of a compact and much more manageable multipage booklet for their public timetables. It was virtually obligatory to include a system map as the center. In addition, system-wide timetables sometimes featured maps of station locations for Chicago or New York or some other important feature a carrier wished to emphasize visually.*

Promotional brochures usually included maps, often of the railroad that issued them but also of destinations such as Yellowstone or Yosemite National Parks. Railroad maps varied widely in accuracy, ranging from highly detailed cartography that benefited company civil engineers to maps that clearly exaggerated topographical features to persuade travelers that the issuing railroad trumped its competitors by offering the shortest and straightest route between two places. It would not be an exaggeration to describe these maps as representing the "lie of the land."†

* *Standard Union* (Brooklyn, NY), July 23, 1903. Whether given to artistic license or not, railroad maps proved to be a useful teaching tool, or so claimed one New York educator: "So far as the study of maps goes, I can get better results from the use of time-tables than from all the geographies in the market." Only the studious few appreciated the academic geography texts, but "just set a dozen boys around a pile of time-tables and tell them to locate certain cities, lakes and rivers, and they will work like beavers and come out letter perfect every time. For most children time-tables and accompanying maps are a source of unfailing interest, both in and out of school hours." *New York Times*, reprinted in *Champaign (IL) Daily Gazette*, December 20, 1902.

† Providing an excellent study of the liberties that railroads took in creating maps intended for public use is Gregory P. Ames, "Forgetting St. Louis and Other Map Mischief," *Railroad History* (Spring–Summer 2003), 28–39. See also Mark Monmonier, *How to Lie with Maps* (Chicago: University of Chicago Press, 1991); Monmonier, *Drawing to Line: Tales of Maps and Cartocontroversy* (New York: Henry Holt, 1995).

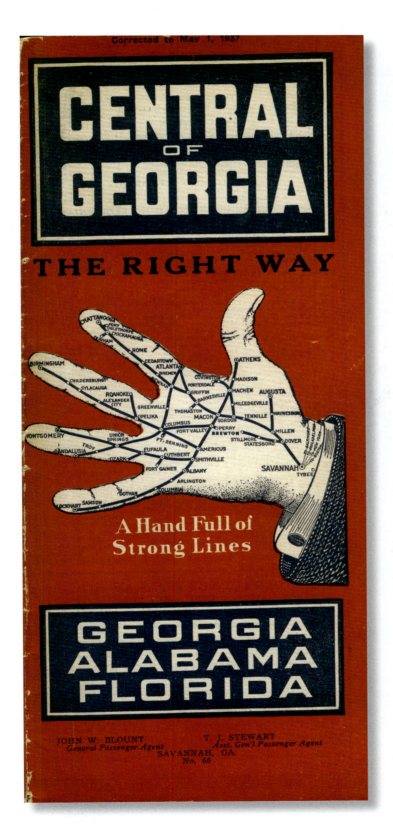

The Central of Georgia discovered that the seemingly random configuration of its lines across the South conformed nicely to the outline of a human hand to embellish the otherwise dull cover of a 1932 timetable. In a similarly creative visual, the Chicago Great Western superimposed a map of its tracks across Iowa and other states of the Upper Midwest over a maple leaf, with tracks representing veins.

and surveyors. The cartography was detailed and highly accurate, in contrast to rail maps intended for public consumption, which were often little more than colorful complements to railroad boosters' claims. That is, a rail line that traced a serpentine course through the mountains, as did the tracks of the Kansas City Southern through the hilly terrain along the border between Arkansas and Oklahoma, could appear deceptively straight on a timetable map drawn by a skilled cartographer. The railroad, in fact, named one of its trains the Flying Crow to emphasize the beeline its tracks made (on the map at least) south from Kansas City to the Gulf of Mexico. At the dawn of the twentieth century, it was not uncommon for major railroads to add the words *air line* to their corporate title to imply that their tracks traced the shortest distance between two major destinations, as the Piedmont Air Line (part of the later Southern) supposedly did across Virginia and the Carolinas.

Another artful trick of cartographers was to highlight one railroad's track network within a regional web of connecting lines, but with tracks of competitors lightly drawn or not included at all. In other words, the typical railroad map intended to "inform" the traveling public might best be described as bolstering the "lie of the land." Nonetheless, in their variety and artistic creativity these maps constituted one of the most creative and colorful contributions to publishing the railroad.[5]

The manifold excesses of railroad mapmakers provoked a response from the *New York Herald*, which in 1895 lampooned the entire dubious enterprise:

"This won't do," said the General Passenger Agent, in annoyed tones, to the mapmaker. "I want Chicago moved down here half an inch, so as to come on our direct route to New York. Then take Buffalo and put it a little farther from the lake.

Facing, Visual elements included on the cover of a 1903 Kansas City Southern timetable included a map of tracks that headed straight south to the Gulf of Mexico, the route of a train it called the Flying Crow. It was a clever and creative example of marketing because, in fact, KCS tracks followed a serpentine course through the Ouachita Mountains of eastern Oklahoma and western Arkansas. No responsible railroader was about to label a train, especially one that crossed the Bible Belt, the Flying Serpent, because that would surely suggest the devilish snake that tempted Eve in the biblical account of the Garden of Eden. That said, for a time the Monon Railroad did operate across its home state of Indiana a passenger train called *The Red Devil.*

Above, A Northern Pacific route map superimposed over the body of a prone Indian appeared as an advertisement in *Harper's Weekly* in 1900. The railroad used the same odd imagery in other publications, but it left viewers to interpret any possible symbolism. Likely a viewer's perception in 1900 differed greatly from that of today's readers.

"You've got Detroit and New York on different latitudes, and the impression that that is correct won't help our road.

"And, man, take those two lines that compete with us and make 'em twice as crooked as that. Why, you've got one of 'em almost straight.

"Yank Boston over a little to the west and put New York a little to the west, so as to show passengers that our Buffalo division is the shortest route to Boston.

"When you've done all these things I've said, you may print 10,000 copies—but say, how long have you been in the railroad business anyway?"[6]

The *Official Guide,* which was highly valued for the month-by-month accuracy of its timetables, also published thousands of railroad maps over the years. The high standard of accuracy that defined train arrival and departure times did not apply to the railroad-supplied maps that accompanied them. Some maps qualified as reasonably accurate, while others offered a visually entertaining counterpoint to the uniform enumerations of train times. The maps varied from small and simple representations to two-page spreads for larger railroads like the Pennsylvania and the Atchison, Topeka & Santa Fe. Occasionally a map projected future intentions of a railroad, as a dotted line branching across Missouri from the Santa Fe's main line to Saint Louis once did. The railroad never achieved its Saint Louis ambitions, but the city's massive Union Station did contain a Fred Harvey restaurant, one of only two not located along Santa Fe tracks.[7]

NAMES ON THE LAND

Going hand in hand with railroad cartography were names that appeared on maps. In the United States east of the Mississippi River, rail lines usually came after settlement. When railroads of the Atlantic Seaboard were constructed during the 1830s and 1840s, existing communities dictated their choices of route locations, destinations, and the place names on their maps. The same was true when new rail lines began their hurried march across Ohio, Indiana, and other states of the Midwest during the 1850s.*

It was different west of the Mississippi. The region's first rail line, the Pacific Railroad of Missouri, was launched only in 1851 and made scant progress from Saint Louis toward the West during the next ten years. I say "West" in the most general sense possible, because Kansas City, an obvious destination along its proposed route to the Pacific coast, did not exist when ground was broken along the Mississippi River on a memorable July 4 at the start of the 1850s. In other words, across the American West, railroad construction often preceded city and town building. Railroads chose names for the locations of their new depots and stations and then appended them to their maps. The first building of many raw settlements of the Great Plains and other areas of the West was often a feature within a landscape soon defined by depots, roundhouses, shops, and water tanks.†

As perturbing as deliberate map distortions might be, for a community to be omitted entirely from a railroad map was an ominous sign. It often signified a place in decline because without a railroad connection, the prospects of a village or town were grim. Ghost towns of the United States were not limited to spent mineral bonanzas of the Far West, though the names of the midwestern ones have long been forgotten, in contrast to those of Nevada, California, and elsewhere that continued to intrigue a loyal cadre of ghost town aficionados. Some are even preserved in a condition of arrested decay as state parks.‡

* The classic history is George R. Stewart, *Names on the Land: A Historical Account of Place-Naming in the United States* (1945; repr., Boston: Houghton Mifflin, 1967).

† H. R. Williams, vice president of the Milwaukee Road, named station stops along its extension from South Dakota to the Pacific coast. Among his choices were Othello, Washington, for his favorite Shakespeare play and Avery, Idaho, for Avery Rockefeller, a major shareholder. Both communities became division points that for several decades witnessed the daily handoff between the steam and electric locomotives that powered the Milwaukee Road's through trains. In all, Williams named thirty-two station stops across the state of Washington alone, including Ralston, which he named after Ralston Purina Company, the Saint Louis maker of his favorite breakfast cereal. See Carlos A. Schwantes, *Railroad Signatures across the Pacific Northwest* (Seattle: University of Washington Press, 1993), 123–124; John C. Hudson, *Plains Country Towns* (Minneapolis: University of Minnesota Press, 1985).

‡ Ames, "Forgetting St. Louis and Other Map Mischief," 31–32. Among the ghost towns preserved as state parks are Bodie in California and Bannock in Montana.

By contrast, *Bradshaw's* compilation of timetables just for the railways of Great Britain and Ireland in April 1910 was a densely packed tabulation that extended across nearly a thousand pages and was almost entirely unleavened by maps, advertisements, or information about the carriers. The list of timetables opened with a map of the Great Western Railway and closed with ganged advertisements that occupied more than two hundred additional pages, while between these two features was an unrelenting listing of times for tens of thousands of trains. The mass of numbers must have been daunting to any reader afflicted with numerophobia, or the pathological fear of numbers.[8]

Over the years, railroads updated their system maps as the result of new construction or the latest merger—or in some cases, a separation forced by the onset of hard times and bankruptcy. That was the early twentieth-century fate of the Frisco and the Chicago & Eastern Illinois, which had at one time issued a single map to depict their sprawling but ultimately unwieldy combination of tracks across Illinois, Missouri, and the Southwest.

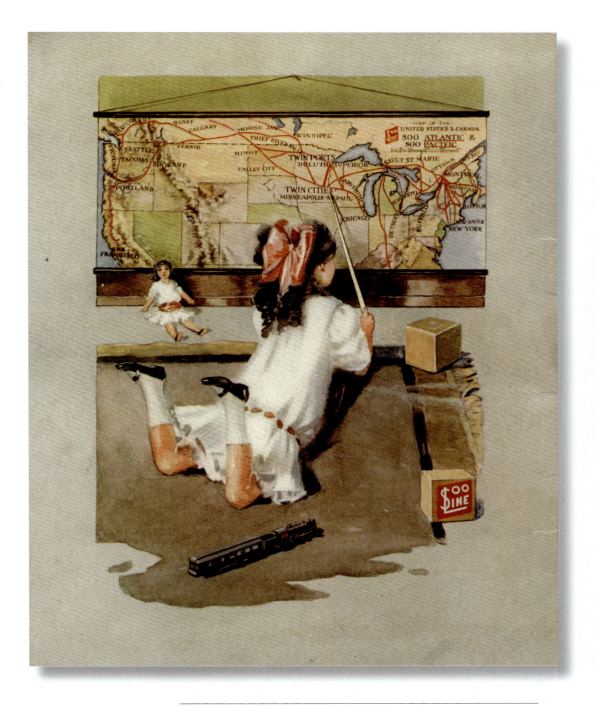

The back cover image of the Soo Line's *The Trip That Sue Took* offers a creative look at the familiar subject of railroad maps. In terms of railroad publishing, the pre–World War I imprints of the Soo, Katy, and Iron Mountain are among my favorites in terms of their variety and visual creativity.

Avoiding the usual lines followed in preparing a railway folder, the Missouri Pacific—Iron Mountain System, sends an epitome of art and literature, representative of the St. Louis World's Fair.

—from *Lincoln Star* (Nebraska), May 23, 1904

The delicate motifs and pastel colors used on the front cover of Baltimore & Ohio's Chicago Fair booklet of 1893 seem to foreshadow coming trends within the art world. The art nouveau movement, a style most closely identified with the Czech artist and illustrator Alphonse Mucha, dates from the same year and grew increasingly popular over the next three decades.

14

MEET ME IN SAINT LOUIS
AND ELSEWHERE

RAILROAD WORLD'S FAIRS

During the latter half of the nineteenth century, the cities of Chicago and Saint Louis waged a bitter war of words—at least it was bitter from the perspective of Saint Louis, where local publications occasionally referred to Chicago as "the enemy." The jealousy frequently expressed by Saint Louis toward the younger but much faster growing city dated back to the late 1840s, when Missouri senator Thomas Hart Benton sparred with his Illinois counterpart Stephen A. Douglas to determine which state and city ought to emerge as the nation's rail gateway to the West. Though both men were loyal Democrats, they were passionate adversaries when promoting Saint Louis or Chicago.[1]

Over the intervening years up to 1904, the municipal rivalry played out in various symbolic displays that transcended mere words. After Chicago successfully hosted an impressive world's fair in 1893, Saint Louis determined that its own world's fair of 1904 should be even bigger and more impressive than anything Chicago had done. It had to be superior in every possible way because the municipal ego of Saint Louis, the nation's fourth-largest city, demanded it. The fairground occupied by the 1904 extravaganza was, in fact, twice the size of Chicago's World Columbia Exposition. In its geographical expanse, the Louisiana

Purchase Exposition was the largest in the history of world's fairs. That same year, 1904, George Gould opened a station in downtown Pittsburgh for his intended transcontinental railway. A special band saluted the inaugural train, bound via a Wabash connection west to Saint Louis, with the hit song of the day, "Meet Me in St. Louis, Louis, Meet Me at the Fair."[2]

The concept of a world fair dates from the 1850s, when the first one was held in London. During subsequent years, fairs, some officially sanctioned and others not, competed to display the latest and greatest technological achievements of the age. Fair organizers usually chose a theme to justify the huge effort and expense the extravaganzas entailed. Centennials provided a good pretext for a celebration, and the United States held its first officially sanctioned world's fair in Philadelphia in 1876 to commemorate the hundred-year anniversary of the signing of the Declaration of Independence. The Philadelphia-based Pennsylvania Railroad publicized America's first official world's fair, but hardly with the same vigor that animated rail publicists of subsequent fairs in Chicago and Saint Louis. The visual impact

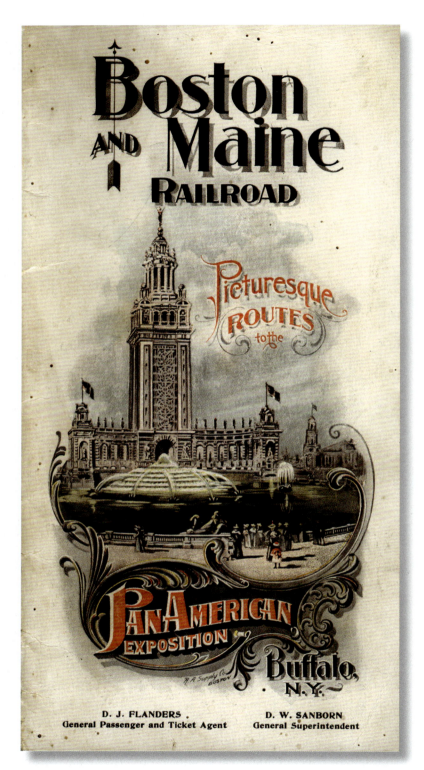

of their many 1893 and 1904 pamphlets and brochures was far greater than that of the 1876 advertisements. Like the evolution of timetable graphics, the latest world's fair publications were a tribute to advances in color printing technology and to railroads' greater awareness of the impact of their advertising.

Chicago's great fair of 1893 celebrated the four hundredth anniversary of the epochal voyage of Christopher Columbus to America, albeit a year late. Likewise, when Saint Louis held its fair in 1904 to celebrate the centennial of the Louisiana Purchase, it missed the actual date by one year. But never mind, a world's fair enjoyed enormous popularity in those years regardless of the time and place. Saint Louis, as host of only the third officially sanctioned world's fair held within the United States, nearly popped its municipal vest buttons as it swelled with hometown pride.[3]

At both the Chicago and Saint Louis world's fairs, the railroads of the United States put their many technological achievements on public display. One unmistakable message was that their tracks had redefined North America's time and space. World's fairs also spurred railroad publishing. Each of these special occasions was a potential revenue bonanza for the railroads that conveyed millions of passengers to and from the fair's host city. Timetables and brochures heightened the popular enthusiasm for joining the crowds of fairgoers.[4]

For Philadelphia's 1876 centennial, the primary beneficiary had been the Pennsylvania Railroad, a hometown institution. During the next quarter century, numerous railroads across the United States awakened to the revenue-enhancing possibilities of a world's fair. The Louisiana Purchase Exposition

The Northern Central and Pennsylvania railroads highlighted Philadelphia's Liberty Bell in an 1876 publication devoted to the first world fair held in the United States, a celebration of the centennial of American independence. The nation's railroads did not yet see the value of advertising such occasions or doing so with the use of expensive color graphics such as chromolithography. That changed when Chicago hosted the World's Columbian Exposition in 1893, and thus America's second officially sanctioned world's fair witnessed a variety of colorful rail imprints.

of 1904 resulted in a veritable avalanche of promotional publications from the nearly two dozen railroads that served the city and from others that did not. The Boston & Maine was a New England carrier that did not run its trains within a thousand miles of Saint Louis, but it sought to claim a share of the fair-generated traffic by publishing special brochures.

Prominently displayed at the World's Columbian Exposition in 1893 was New York Central's locomotive No. 999, reportedly the fastest in the world. Two weeks before joining the fair exhibits, No. 999 attained a speed of 112 miles per hour, though that "terrific speed" was never confirmed by scientific instruments. Nonetheless, the claim conferred bragging rights on the New York Central. Also among the railroad displays in Chicago was the Mississippi, an antique locomotive that belonged to the Illinois Central but that was built in 1834 by the Stephensons, father and son, in England. The contrast between these two locomotives highlighted the progress made by railroads over the decades, and showcasing examples of technological progress was one purpose of a world's fair. In addition, the Chicago fair served as a coming-of-age party for the Windy City, and the 1904 fair celebrated the emergence of the modern metropolis of Saint Louis.[5]

World's fairs and similar expositions were held in subsequent years in major American cities such as

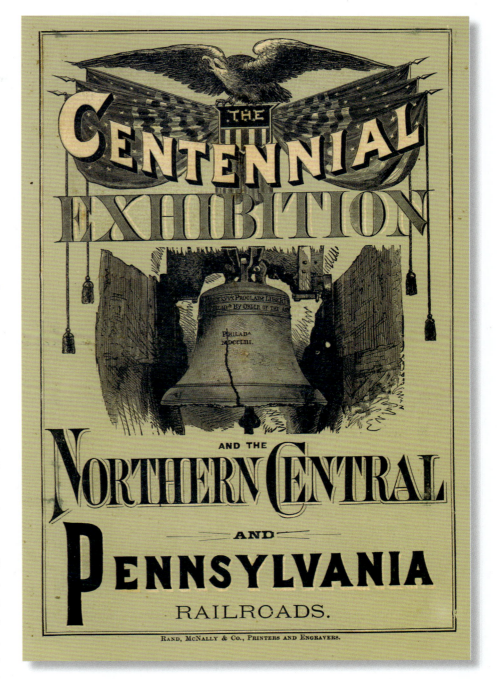

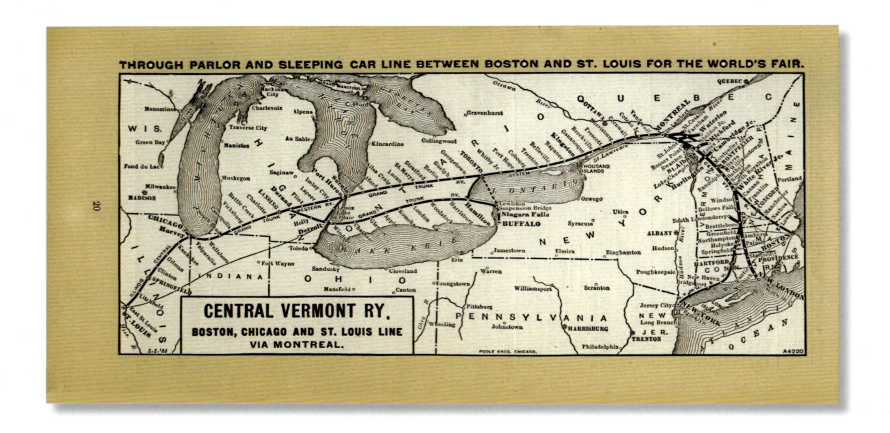

Above, The Central Vermont's map of the route across southern Canada to the Saint Louis Louisiana Purchase Exposition of 1904 suggests that although the railroad was New England based, it still hoped to profit from fair traffic. No major railroad in the United States, in fact, missed the opportunity to promote the nation's third officially sanctioned world's fair. The result was a prodigious outpouring of paper documents, from timetables to special brochures, that saluted America's fourth-largest city and its extravaganza, one that occupied more physical space than any other world's fair held in the United States or abroad.

Facing, Like many railroad counterparts, this Baltimore & Ohio Southwestern brochure sought to encourage travel to the Saint Louis fair. The colonnaded building featured in the left panel is today the Saint Louis Art Museum, one of a handful of structures to outlast the 1904 extravaganza, which also gave the world the ice cream cone. Located at the base of the area now called Art Hill are the Cascades, an exposition centerpiece that inspired Scott Joplin to compose a ragtime favorite called "The Cascades." His most popular composition was the "Maple Leaf Rag," composed in 1899 and named for a gentleman's club in his hometown at the time, Sedalia, a railroad center in western Missouri.

Seattle, San Francisco, San Diego, Chicago, and New York. One reason for their existence, apart from the opportunity to display the technological wonders of the age, was to give fairgoers a stateside substitute for international travel. In Saint Louis that meant an odd and controversial display of a group of Indigenous people from the Philippines, an American possession acquired recently during the Spanish-American War. By the 1970s, global airlines afforded an increasing number of American travelers the opportunity to go abroad and see the real wonders of Egypt or the peoples of the Philippines for themselves. The appeal of hosting a world's fair in the twenty-first century lessened further when cities lost money hosting one of these extravaganzas.

I have always been fascinated by improbable historical connections, and one such noteworthy chain of events links the largely forgotten World's Industrial and Cotton Centennial Exposition, a world's fair of sorts held in New Orleans during the first half of 1885, and the glitzy attractions of Las Vegas 140 years later. The story begins with some samples of copper-bearing ore that the territory of Arizona displayed to fair visitors, among them William Andrews Clark. Unlike most casual observers, he recognized the mineral specimens from the United Verde Mine for their potential value. Clark already qualified as a "copper baron" because of his holdings in Montana mines, which included the gigantic Anaconda Copper Company, and now he spied another potential moneymaking bonanza in Arizona.[6]

His eyes did not deceive him, and in 1888 he traveled to Arizona and purchased control of the United Verde Smelter Company in an area now known as Clarkdale. The company's mine was located farther up the slopes of the Mingus Mountains at Jerome. Construction of the Verde Canyon Railroad hauled Clark's copper to a connection with the Santa Fe and thus to distant markets.[7]

Clark's Montana and Arizona business ventures were but a prelude to a much greater railroad enterprise, one that connected Salt Lake City with booming Los Angeles and its Pacific Ocean harbor at San Pedro across a desert landscape overlooked or shunned by other railroad empire builders. Not surprisingly, this was as harsh a desert environment as one could find across the entire West, and it seemed to hold little promise of reward for any entrepreneur brave enough to extend tracks across it. Clark accepted the risk, and to supply water for his thirsty steam engines, he established in southern Nevada a way station the railroad called Las Vegas.[8]

The Salt Lake City–Los Angeles rail project launched by Clark became an active promoter of attractions within a desert domain that included California's Death Valley. Despite its furnace-like summer temperatures, it provided a comfortable winter retreat for moneyed Southern California residents, and its sere landscape and a below-sea-level basin called Badwater had a scenic appeal that was the delight of railroad wordsmiths.[9]

After Union Pacific acquired the Salt Lake Route in 1921 to gain access to Los Angeles and the Pacific coast, it continued to promote winter tours to Death Valley and summer tours to Zion and Bryce National Parks in Utah and the North Rim of the Grand Canyon in Arizona, all of which became popular topics for railroad publicists, as did Hoover (or Boulder) Dam upon its completion in the early 1930s, an attraction located only thirty-three miles from Las Vegas and accessible by motor coaches operated by Union Pacific Stages. Las Vegas itself amounted to little more than a railroad tank town—a term once used to signify a place so unimportant that it was nothing more than a stop to water steam locomotives—until after World War II, when legal gambling and related forms of entertainment transformed Clark County and made Las Vegas the largest city in Nevada.[10]

Clark's new railroad to Los Angeles, as well as the longer-established Southern Pacific and Atchison, Topeka & Santa Fe, two transcontinental lines with a long and intense interest in promoting California scenery and settlement, benefited from the twin fairs the Golden State hosted in 1915 to commemorate the recent opening of the Panama Canal. One extravaganza, the Panama-California Exposition, took place in San Diego's Balboa Park and focused on the growth of California, while the other, the *officially sanctioned* Panama-Pacific International Exposition, was held in San Francisco and was global in outlook. Both exhibitions inspired a flood of railroad publications, as had the earlier officially sanctioned world's fairs held in Chicago and Saint Louis.[11]

Facing, In 1915, the Milwaukee Road issued a brochure that diplomatically highlighted California's expositions held simultaneously in San Francisco and San Diego to commemorate the opening of the Panama Canal. The Milwaukee Road did not enter California, but it hoped to profit from fair traffic.

PANAMA-CALIFORNIA EXPOSITION SAN DIEGO 1915

PANAMA-PACIFIC EXPOSITION SAN FRANCISCO 1915

CHICAGO
MILWAUKEE & St. PAUL
RAILWAY

PANAMA-CALIFORNIA EXPOSITION
1915
THE COMPLETION OF THE PANAMA CANAL
SAN DIEGO

PANAMA-PACIFIC-INTERNATIONAL-EXPOSITION
SAN FRANCISCO 1915

CHICAGO
MILWAUKEE & St. PAUL
RAILWAY

Railroads of the United States and Canada could not have realized in 1915 that the world's fair held in San Francisco would be the last in North America at which most long-distance visitors arrived by train. Two years earlier, the Lincoln Highway became the first motor route extending from coast to coast across the United States. It was obviously not a short farm-to-market link like those promoted by the Illinois Central, Frisco, and other railroads earlier in the century. Further destined to undermine railroads' dominance of land transportation across the United States was the congressional passage of the Highway Act of 1916, a measure that for the first time in nearly a century gave federal dollars to support new highway construction. It was a harbinger of changes soon to come. An increasing number of visitors to subsequent world's fairs held in Chicago, New York, Montreal, and other big cities across North America would arrive by private automobile, and railroads had diminished interest in publicizing them.[12]

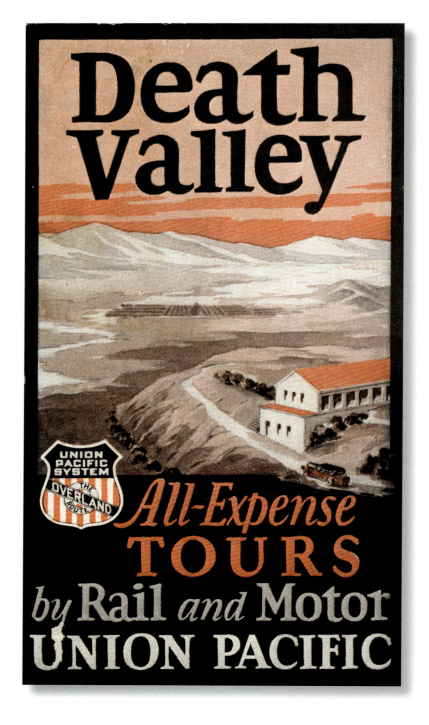

After the Union Pacific acquired the Los Angeles & Salt Lake line, it continued to advertise Death Valley vacations. Though the California location was a furnace during the scorching summer months, its oasis accommodations offered affluent residents of the Los Angeles area a delightful winter retreat.

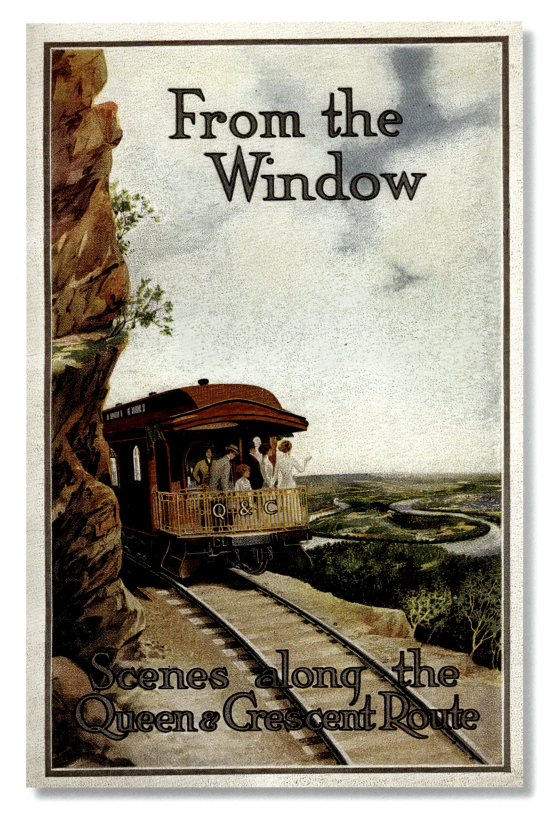

But after one leaves these different States and rides between the mountain ranges of Colorado, he commits a sin if he does not sit day and night by the car window.

—from Richard Harding Davis, *The West From a Car-Window* (1892)[1]

The Queen & Crescent used a graphic end-of-train image to emphasize the view from its train windows, or in this case from the platform, probably the best vantage point before railroad lawyers raised questions of safety and liability. The Queen & Crescent name spoke to its end cities of Cincinnati, Ohio, the Queen City, and New Orleans, Louisiana, nicknamed the Crescent City because of its location along a sweeping bend in the Mississippi River. The expansion-minded Southern Railway consolidated its ownership of the Queen & Crescent Route in 1926.

15

LOOKING AND SEEING

FROM CAR WINDOWS INTO THE GREAT OUTDOORS

Even as tracks redefined spatial relationships across North America and railroad wordsmiths assiduously repackaged expansive portions of the landscape to make them more appealing, rail carriers sought to transform trackside scenery into an enjoyable feature of any long-distance trip. The greater the distance, the more of a companion the view from the car windows became. "One of the attractive features of the Norfolk and Western is the continual variety of beautiful landscapes as viewed from the windows of the passing trains."[2]

In the late nineteenth century, train journeys across the western portion of the United States often required several days to complete. In Canada, a transcontinental journey from Montreal to Vancouver required an even greater commitment of time. "Surely nothing could be more pleasure-giving than to ride through a magnificent country, with a lovely, ever-changing panorama unveiling itself through the glass panels at your elbow."[3]

Long-distance travelers occupied themselves in various ways. Some turned inward and spent their time studying fellow passengers or perhaps engaging in idle chitchat with them. Some even admitted to flirting coyly with attractive strangers. Others sought to lose themselves in the pulp fiction and true crime stories that onboard news butchers offered for sale, or they dozed

or snacked on food purchased from the onboard salesmen or savored an elegant meal in the dining car. Finally, the moving panorama just beyond the car windows could prove interesting, especially if the vernacular landscape were interpreted in a booklet or folder that the railroad gave to passengers or that they could purchase for a nominal sum at a newsstand or from the train's roving seller of candy, cigars, and newspapers. In the early twentieth century, the emergence of movies inspired the Frisco to advertise the Ozark Mountain scenery beyond its train windows as "Every Mile a Moving Picture." Covering another part of the West and serving as "an entertaining companion for a transcontinental trip" was a handbook called *Sights and Scenes along the Union Pacific System*. It provided statistical and historical information about the locations seen en route.[4]

The darkness of night presented a problem for viewers of the passing landscape, but the Milwaukee Road rose to the challenge: it installed a marine searchlight on the rear platform of its Fast Mail overnight train between Minneapolis and Chicago. A skilled operator would rotate the beam of light to illuminate objects in the shadowy landscape up to three miles away, along either side of the tracks. "The road parallels the Mississippi River for over one hundred miles, and the illumination of the scenes along the river banks, the boats, passing trains, etc., will be an amusing feature of a trip on this train." One must wonder what trackside residents thought of the railroad's brilliant form of amusement.[5]

Railroad commuters seldom spent much time gazing out the window because their daily journeys were relatively short and trackside scenery had grown familiar. The one sight many commuters desired most to see after a day of work was home. By contrast, long-distance travelers had time on their hands, and often they passed through landscapes they had never seen before. For many travelers, the unfamiliar scenery offered an antidote to boredom as the landscape unspooled beyond the car windows like one of the large canvas panoramas that became a popular form of entertainment in the late nineteenth century.

The West from a train window was of special interest. Capable wordsmiths like American author Hamlin Garland sought to capture western grandeur in print. For an 1893 issue of the *Atlantic Monthly*, he penned an elaborate description of the Arizona desert landscape he observed from the window of a train, most likely one operated by the Atchison, Topeka & Santa Fe across the Painted Desert: "Dun plains speckled with sagebrush and blue-gray clumps of weeds, levels that run to huge cliffs of orange-colored stone—cliffs that rise against the deep blue sky like ruined walls of fortresses or castles." While crossing North Dakota a few days later, he noted, "As the morning advanced, the sunshine grew to a white radiance that flooded everything in a blinding, shadowless light. There was nothing to check it or temper it; no tree, no green grass, no hills. Only a russet plain set about with yellow or white little farmhouses. The town behind had no trees."[6]

Travelers might be curious about the passing scenes and perhaps wonder to themselves about the history of a particularly attractive community or the length of the tunnel from which their train had just emerged. Thus, beginning in the early 1850s a special genre of railroad literature devoted to descriptions of the passing landscape grew ever more popular—and visually attractive. The most compelling examples showcased the prose of professional writers and an array of captivating graphics.[7]

To some travelers, the time required to cross the western half of the United States must have seemed interminably long even if they kept a guidebook in hand. One feature of the transportation revolution of the 1920s was that transcontinental railroads successfully trimmed hours from their long-distance schedules. The new San Francisco Overland Limited the Union Pacific introduced in 1926 required "only" sixty-three hours to cover the distance between Chicago and the Pacific coast, and the same was true for the Los Angeles Limited. Travelers aboard the less posh Gold Coast Limited made the overland journey to San Francisco in sixty-eight hours, but the slower train cost them slightly less money. To meet the heightened competition for California travelers, the Rock Island and Southern Pacific Lines inaugurated their deluxe Golden State Limited, which completed its run from Chicago to Los Angeles in sixty-three hours. All these trains were hauled by steam locomotives, and the introduction of diesel power in the late 1930s would enable railroads to further reduce their running times.[8]

Initially, individuals published the trackside guides in hopes of making a profit from their sale to curious travelers. In the early 1850s, a few railroads began to publish trackside guides of their own. Their intent was not to make money but rather to help occupy a passenger's time by describing the human imprint on the trackside landscape canvas that nature provided. Often this took the form of brief geography and geology lessons, but capsule histories of the towns, bridges, and tunnels just beyond the tracks might also be featured, along with some entertaining anecdotes and a few corny jokes. The range of possibilities was almost endless, and the contents of the publication might even appear idiosyncratic because they depended entirely on what a railroad chose to discuss—or not.

Trackside guides, like some public timetables, typically called attention to the engineering marvels along the way, with railroad bridges and tunnels often portrayed in lavish detail. The Hoosac Tunnel in western Massachusetts was featured on the covers of Fitchburg Railroad timetables, as was the Eads Bridge across the Mississippi River on those of the Baltimore & Ohio Southwestern line. With the rise of safety consciousness in the

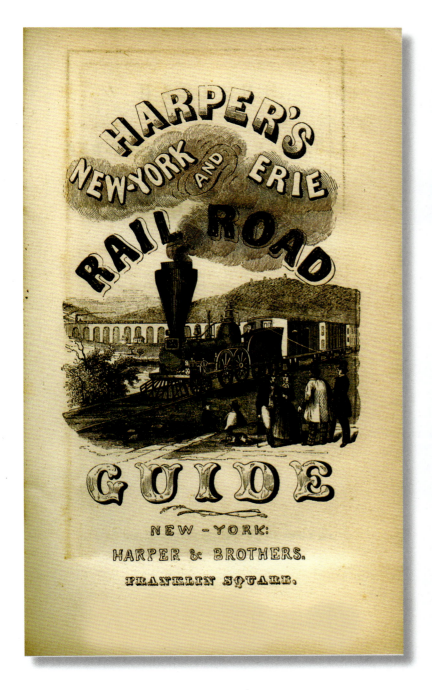

Harper's New York and Erie Railroad Guide of the 1850s was among the earliest publications devoted to helping travelers better appreciate and understand the landscapes passing by their train windows. Some guides were sold in stations or by onboard news butchers, but as time went on, railroads came to recognize the value of the publications and simply gave them away.

early twentieth century, rail companies occasionally saluted themselves by calling passengers' attention to the installation of electric signals designed to prevent collisions. They noted their purchase, too, of the latest steel passenger cars, which were safer in a derailment than the wooden carriages of earlier years.

Railroads, particularly the transcontinental lines, also liked to salute themselves by noting the many changes they had wrought across the West—and they invariably presented all such changes in a highly positive light. After the coming of railroads to the High Plains, the once enormous herds of bison shrank noticeably, yet Northern Pacific wordsmiths managed to present the railroad's ecological impact in upbeat terms. One such publication noted with a generous measure of self-congratulatory rhetoric that the company would no longer haul buffalo hides because the Northern Pacific desired to sustain the remaining bison population for future generations of hunters.

Given that it took several days to cross the two thousand miles separating Chicago or Saint Louis from the cities of the West Coast, rail publicists viewed long-distance passengers as members of a captive audience who might be tempted to settle the sparsely populated landscapes they viewed beyond the train window. Perhaps they could be interested in travel to a vacation destination, such as newly created Yellowstone National Park or one of its several sister parks elsewhere in the American West, each with its railroad patron.

By the beginning of the twentieth century, railroads large and small published trackside guides under various guises. Their quality varied, as did their titles. *En Route to the Southland*, a 1900 joint publication by the Louisville & Nashville and the Chicago & Eastern Illinois railroads, described various points of interest along their through line between Chicago and Nashville, Tennessee.[9] Some trackside guides provided long and windy examples of the rhetorical excesses of the Gilded Age, while other announced themselves in plain terms and might simply be titled "From Car Windows." Some guides were heavily illustrated with chromolithographs, while others preferred black-and-white engravings or photographs. During the early 1950s, the New York Central continued the long-standing tradition with a brochure aptly titled *Magic Windows*, which described sights along the railroad's 961-mile corridor between Chicago and New York.[10]

The cover of the Pennsylvania Railroad's 1905 *Through the Car Window* implied that the view from its trains offered a magical combination of fantasy and romance. There is something about this image, too, that suggests the appeal of motion pictures, a recent invention already revolutionizing popular culture.

RAILROAD LITERATURE AS A MENACE TO MORALS

During the nineteenth century, the term the American press often used to describe all types of railroad-generated printed paper was *railroad literature*, a broad category that included everything from public timetables to annual reports. But that was not all. To the confusion of interested readers more than a century later, newspapers of the 1880s and 1890s used an identical term to describe the lowbrow reading material that news butchers sold en route to entertain passengers easily bored by the passing landscape, a genre also known as day-coach literature.*

Some Americans regarded the pulp "literature" available for sale aboard trains as so wretched, so far beneath contempt, that they labeled it obscene and joined together to suppress it as a menace to public morals. The American Railway Literary Union and Pure Literature Bureau, an organization of high-minded individuals, sought to persuade rail officials to ban its sale aboard their trains. They described their self-appointed task as "purifying" the minds of readers.†

Some executives, most notably the management of the lofty Pennsylvania Railroad, did respond positively to moral suasion. Additional rail carriers soon did likewise. "The North-Western line today issued orders to cut off all paper-back novels on the main line and branch trains in Iowa," reported the *Minneapolis Journal* in 1905. It added that on trains of the Vanderbilt Lines, which included the New York Central, "no trashy stuff, detective stories or joke books will be handled." Presumably would-be purchasers of salacious pulp fiction and titillating true crime drama would henceforth seek to elevate their minds with one of the trackside scenery guides that were sold for a nominal sum or given away by railroads or with published sermons of contemporary American evangelist Dwight L. Moody.‡

* Frank Donovan Jr., "The Railroad in Literature as a Public Relations Medium," *Railway Age*, August 31, 1940, 307, 312. *Philadelphia Times*, January 8, 1881; *Sunday Truth* (Buffalo, NY), February 9, 1890; *London Chronicle*, reprinted in *Evening Star* (Washington, DC), October 31, 1910.

‡ *Minneapolis Journal*, July 21, 1905; *Pittsburgh Daily Post*, March 4, 1875; *Philadelphia Times*, January 8, 1881; *Sunday Truth*, February 9, 1890.

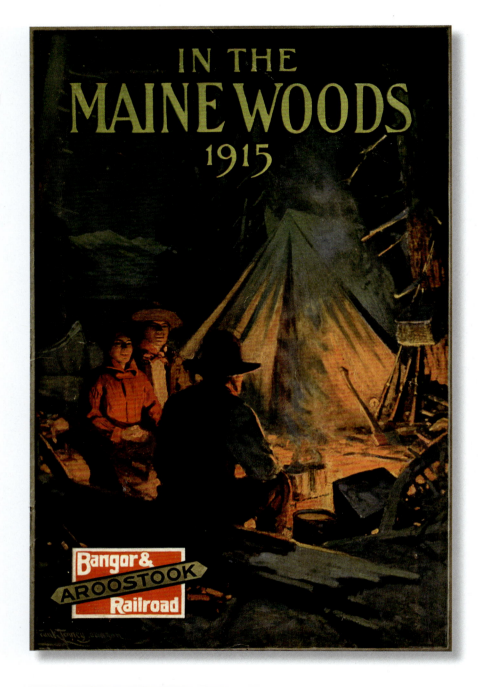

Bangor & Aroostook's annual *In the Maine Woods* was a substantial publication of nearly two hundred pages. Regardless of the year of publication, its text and commercial art were noteworthy.

Whatever their layout and design, railroad trackside guides endured until 1971, the year most carriers in the United States transferred the remnants of a formerly extensive network of passenger trains to Amtrak, the new quasi-governmental operator. Amtrak continued this publishing tradition for passengers aboard its long-distance trains for several additional years.

One extremely curious interaction with the passing landscape occurred in the early twentieth century in the California desert, where Southern Pacific tracks briefly but closely paralleled the Salton Sea. Onboard anglers would reportedly wait in keen anticipation for just the right moment to cast a line from their moving train in hope of reeling in a large carp. This sounds like one of the tall tales nineteenth-century newspapers would occasionally create to entertain readers. Another fishy tale of this type claimed that wild salmon attacked passengers aboard a stagecoach as it sought to cross a flood-swollen western river. More easily verified are the stories of passengers who shot at prairie dogs and herds of buffalo from their train windows to relieve the boredom of crossing the High Plains of Nebraska and Wyoming after the completion of America's first transcontinental railroad in 1869. Observers reported that the hunters seldom, if ever, hit their targets.[11]

Offering a more conventional approach to fishing and hunting was the Bangor & Aroostook Railroad's annual guide titled *In the Maine Woods*. Annual series such as this were published by several other railroads and were eagerly awaited by outdoors-minded readers during the years before World War II. In terms of extolling the virtues of fishing, no railroad excelled the zeal of the Grand Rapids & Indiana Railway, a Pennsylvania subsidiary that extended tracks north from Cincinnati to Michigan's Straits of Mackinac. It promoted itself as the "Fishing Line" and decorated its public timetables with piscatory graphics. For two cents, it sold anglers a brochure titled *Where to Go Fishing*: "Everyone who is addicted to the gentle and apostolic art of catching fish this time of the year commences to expect the arrival of the publication of the Grand Rapids and

Transcontinental railroads between Chicago and the West Coast typically scheduled their premier passenger trains to cross the flatlands by night. During the age of commercial air travel, America's heartland was frequently referred to as "flyover country," and though the phrase had not yet been coined during the heyday of rail travel, the notion that flatland equaled boring scenery still prevailed. Hence, the Chicago & North-Western's *Across Picturesque Illinois and Iowa* offered a notable exception.

Indiana Railway, with its usual wealth of illustrations and descriptions, which make a man go home and look up his tackle."[12]

Railroads of the American West competed with one another to provide travelers with trackside glimpses of Native Americans or with face-to-face contact during pauses to relieve the tedium of a transcontinental journey, as the Atchison, Topeka & Santa Fe traditionally did at its station in Albuquerque, New Mexico. During the summer of 1936, the Milwaukee Road's Olympian trains paused in Mobridge, South Dakota, to change crews and give passengers "an opportunity to witness an Indian Ceremonial Dance performed by four adult Indian couples and three Indian children. The dancers are completely costumed and painted for the performance of this ancient and authentic tribal rite."[13]

When scenery outside the car windows no longer held a traveler's interest and railroad literature grew boring, a passenger could always explore the train itself. After enclosed vestibules replaced open platforms to make passage from one car to another safe and easy, it became possible to explore nearly the full length of the train. For travelers with money, that might mean a stop in the dining car for a multicourse meal.[14]

Within the sleeping cars, the Pullman Company worked hard to maintain a uniformly high standard of comfort and cleanliness for its enormous fleet. During the first two-thirds of the twentieth century, Pullman also held a monopoly on overnight train travel accommodations. By contrast, railroad dining cars reflected the geographical and culinary diversity of rival carriers. Specialty items available aboard their diners served to advertise their passenger trains and the distinctiveness of their cuisine to prospective travelers. The Northern Pacific, for example, gained widespread fame for its large baked potatoes.[15]

The view through the train windows looked both ways, I hasten to add. While one aspect of publishing the railroad involved marketing the passing scenery, the thing I recall most vividly from my time watching Pennsylvania Railroad's passenger trains rush past our backyard in Greenfield, Indiana, during the 1950s is standing trackside and looking through the windows into the dining cars. The view was fleeting at best, but time and again I caught a glimpse of a world of unimaginable luxury. Now I realize that with the inauguration of each new passenger train, rail publicists were ready with illustrated brochures that emphasized the interior amenities awaiting travelers. There are hundreds, if not thousands, of brochures devoted to individual named trains. The names themselves evoked the magic of train travel, and the Twentieth-Century Limited, Broadway Limited, Empire Builder, and Super Chief were among the grandest and most marketable names in travel. None of these fashionable four flashed past my backyard, but the twice-daily rush of the Spirit of Saint Louis provided magic enough. Its sister trains, the Jeffersonian, Penn-Texas, and Indianapolis Limited, offered me a welcome visual bonus seven days each week.[16]

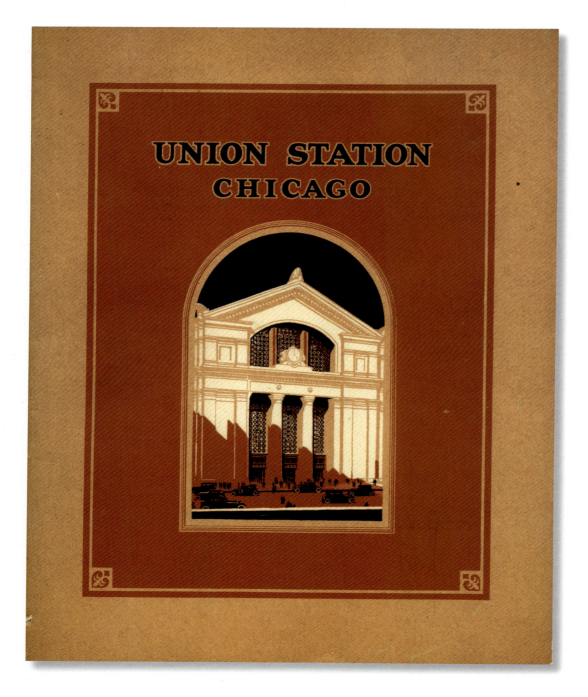

When the train came into the station George felt relieved. He scampered hurriedly aboard. . . . With the recollection of little things occupying his mind he closed his eyes and leaned back in the car seat. He stayed that way for a long time and when he roused himself and again looked out of the car window the town of Winesburg had disappeared and his life there had become but a background on which to paint the dreams of his manhood.

—from Sherwood Anderson, *Winesburg, Ohio* (1919)[1]

The dedication of Chicago Union Station in 1925 provided another occasion to publish the railroad. Commemorative folders were common accompaniments to the public celebrations of a new metropolitan rail station.

16

IN CATHEDRALS OF COMMERCE

CELEBRATING THE RAILROAD LANDSCAPE

Railroad stations large and small had many features in common. They all provided departing passengers and those awaiting the arrival of trains a shelter from inclement weather. They featured an agent—sometimes many agents—ready to sell tickets, and large wooden racks stocked with a colorful array of timetables and various promotional booklets provided by railroads from around the country. Larger stations featured separate windows to handle baggage, a duty discharged in country stations by the ambidextrous ticket agent, who also handled some freight and express as well as functioned as a telegrapher. More than anyone else (except perhaps the train conductor), a ticket agent represented the public face of the railroad.[2]

During the pre-automobile era, the country railroad station served as a vital center of community life, a gathering place for curious townspeople drawn by the arrival and departure of the daily trains, often only one in each direction, which may have provided the most exciting event of the day in a sleepy village. Local newspapers sometimes printed the names of arriving and departing passengers. At the station, too, customers eagerly awaited the arrival of goods they had ordered from a catalog emporium like Sears, Roebuck and Company, based in Chicago.

Before the dawn of radio, the click of a telegraph sounder as translated by a kindly ticket agent/telegrapher provided baseball fans inning-by-inning scores from World Series baseball games or the early returns from presidential elections. The station and its trains also functioned as the gateway for young men and women determined to leave behind the stultifying life of the village to seek their fortunes in the big city, as took place at the conclusion of Sherwood Anderson's classic novel *Winesburg, Ohio*.[3]

A country railroad station was typically a modest structure that featured a small but cozy waiting room, a bay window so that the agent could see approaching trains, and often a covered platform for the convenience of passengers. Architecturally, a station often bore the distinctive stamp of the railroad that built it. Many companies had standard sets of plans that varied according to how large a community a station was intended to serve.

Rail stations in large cities of the United States and Canada were not merely functional; each edifice was also intended to make a bold and powerful statement architecturally. Exterior columns and vast interior spaces spoke to the importance of

WHY AND HOW THE FLYER FLIES

cities like New York and Chicago, and the imposing building showcased the prowess of the railroad or group of railroads that constructed it. During the early twentieth century, the grand opening of North America's monumental rail stations inspired the publication of rail booklets to commemorate the special occasion.[4]

Cities of the Northeast, being first in the nation to be served by the pioneering generation of railroads, typically had more than one station, each constructed to serve the needs of a separate railroad. Baltimore, New York, and Boston to this day have multiple railroad stations. Indianapolis was introduced to its first railroad only in the late 1840s, but in 1853 the Indiana capital, soon destined to become a major midwestern hub, opened the nation's first union station, a structure intended to serve passengers using the trains of all railroads entering the city. Nothing could be more convenient for travelers who needed to transfer from one railroad to another.[5] By contrast, Chicago never had a single station, although since 1971 Union Station has finally lived up to its name by meeting the needs of long-distance Amtrak passengers traveling through the Windy City. Numerous

commuter trains that serve Chicago's many suburbs depart from Union Station and from the former Northwestern Station a few blocks away.[6]

In 1904, at the dawn of the interurban era, the city of Indianapolis gained a second station, one used exclusively by the numerous electric railways that in the early twentieth century years fanned out in all directions into the Indiana countryside. Its massive train shed covered no fewer than nine separate tracks used by as many as six hundred trains a day during the years immediately before World War I. The Traction Terminal spoke to the prevailing optimism that fueled the Midwest's brief but passionate love affair with electric interurban railways. The structure ranked as the largest interurban station in the world. However, beginning in the 1920s, intercity buses gradually elbowed aside the interurban cars until by early 1941 there were none left. The renowned Chicago architect Daniel Burnham designed the Traction Terminal, although that did not prevent the Indianapolis landmark from being razed in 1972. An architecturally unremarkable parking structure and hotel later occupied the site. On the other hand, the Burnham-designed Washington

One could argue whether the Saint Louis Union Station, Boston's South Station, or New York's Grand Central Station was the greatest rail terminus in the United States. All were imposing and well-used structures, but if "greatness" were measured by the number of individual railroads that used the station, Saint Louis was without a peer from the mid-1890s through the 1960s. Displayed here is a stock certificate issued by the Terminal Railroad Association of St. Louis, parent company of Union Station. The Boston and New York City stations always featured a far greater number of commuter trains than Saint Louis.

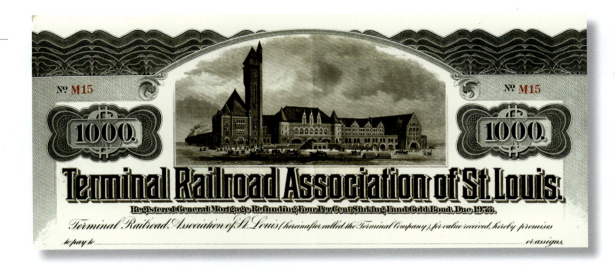

Union Station opened to travelers in 1907, and that monumental cathedral of commerce continues to be used by the trains of Amtrak and two separate commuter railroads.[7]

Saint Louis, which possessed an enormous municipal ego because of its favored location as America's gateway to the West, nursed a major grudge after upstart Chicago overtook it in population and importance in the 1880s. In past years the Mississippi River and its tributaries had blessed Saint Louis by functioning as a highway during the steamboat era but then cursed the city by serving as a moat to isolate it from rail lines constructed east of the river. Only with the completion of the Eads Bridge in the mid-1870s did Saint Louis gain direct railroad access to railroads and cities on the opposite side of the Mississippi. For several more years the city endured the inconvenience created by multiple rail gauges and thus the use of multiple rail stations.

In 1894 the doors opened on one of the grandest union stations in the world. Leading Saint Louis businessmen who backed the project sent their architect, Theodore Link, to the walled city of Carcassonne, France, for inspiration, and his turreted Romanesque design incorporated many imposing elements intended to convey the world-class stature of the Missouri city named for the French King Louis IX. The unspoken statement was that while Chicago had become a bigger city, Saint Louis was a great rail hub situated at the crossroads of North America. Its station

functioned as the belt buckle that conveniently joined together railroads serving all regions of the nation, from New England to the Deep South and from the Great Lakes to the shores of Southern California—even to distant Mexico City. Boston's North and South Stations and New York's Grand Central and Pennsylvania Stations all qualified as imposing cathedrals of commerce, but in terms of the number of individual railroad companies that utilized it, the Saint Louis Union Station was without peer.[8]

The idea of a single union station grew increasingly popular, and none was built except as a monument, a cathedral of commerce, intended to impress travelers with the greatness of the city and the preeminence of the railroads that served them there. While Indianapolis and Denver both had union stations that predated the imposing edifice erected in Saint Louis, Denver soon tore down its original union station and constructed a grander one, while Indianapolis remained content with the imposing one it erected in the 1880s to replace its humble first union station. The quest to build union stations that made architectural statements resulted in older ones being razed and imposing new structures being built in Kansas City and Washington, most notably, and later in Los Angeles and Cincinnati. For the union station constructed in Los Angeles the architects chose a Spanish colonial design, while for Cincinnati they fashioned

New York Central passenger traffic outgrew its original Grand Central Station, pictured here in 1896, and forced the railroad to open a larger and grander edifice in 1913, New York's current Grand Central Station.

one of the grandest railroad tributes to art deco. Both stations remain truly outstanding monuments, as does the Saint Louis Union Station, though today it houses an upscale hotel and an entertainment complex that features a state-of-the-art aquarium but no trains.[9]

It would not do for urban rail station interiors to appear shabby or cheaply decorated. The public image of a station's railroad users as well as the city it served were on display. Many travelers formed their first impressions of a city as they passed through its municipal front door. Elegance was important. When the new union station in Tacoma, Washington, opened its doors in 1911, the walls of its waiting room were finished "with marble brought from Italy. The floors are finished with marble mosaic and terrazzo, with an Italian marble border." In short, Tacoma's "approach" will aid "in giving a good impression to the visitor. It will attract the homeseeker as surely as will the city itself with its advantages. It will attract people to Tacoma and will care for them when they have become Tacomans."[10]

Just as station architecture conveyed a message to travelers, so too did the exterior landscaping. The Atchison, Topeka & Santa Fe considered the matter of "railroad gardening" to be so important in terms of station aesthetics and railroad advertising that it employed a "consulting landscape gardener." Its landscape specialist wrote, "Not only are the immediate surroundings of the station building elevated to a higher standard of beauty, but the example has a beneficial effect on the town or city in which the station is located." These aesthetic benefits, though they did not involve rail publishing, also provided "advertising value to the road."[11]

Much has been written about the fate of New York's magnificent Pennsylvania Station and the way its destruction energized the historic preservation movement across the United States, but decades earlier the imposing station George Gould erected in Pittsburgh had suffered a similar fate. Even before the ego-driven edifice first opened its doors in early 1904, the passenger department of the Wabash Railroad had published a folder to salute the expensive feat of civil engineering required to access it: a tunnel through Mount Washington and a massive cantilever bridge across the Monongahela River. The folder also contained a map intended to salute the "Gould System" as it spread its iron web across the middle portion of the United States and reached toward both the Atlantic and Pacific coasts.[12]

The imposing eleven-floor terminal cost George Gould at least $15 million in 2024 dollars. The architect of the Beaux Arts structure was Theodore Link, who designed the Saint Louis Union Station, which opened in 1894. His Pittsburgh handiwork closed in 1931, the terminal building succumbed to fire in 1946, and its purposeless access bridge was dismantled two years later.[13]

The list of architecturally imposing stations that continue to serve rail travelers across the United States and Canada is impressive, but most noticeably, it would not have included New York's Pennsylvania Station during the decades bracketed by the demolition of the street-level portion of its headhouse and train shed in 1963 and its metamorphosis in early 2021 with the opening of the $1.6 billion Moynihan Train Hall. In the same way, the Kansas City Union Station grew shabby with the decline of passenger trains during the 1960s, but then it was refurbished and today continues to accommodate Amtrak trains. It remains one of the most recognizable architectural icons of the bistate metropolis.[14]

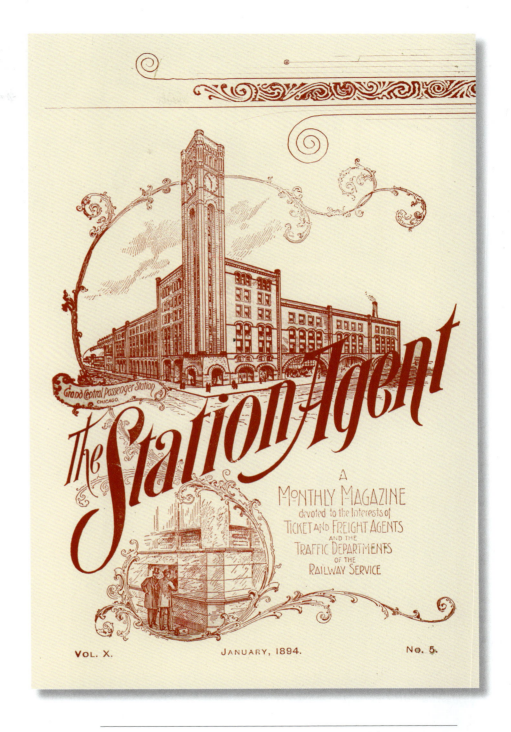

The Station Agent, a trade journal devoted to the interests of station and ticket agents, was published from the early 1890s into the 1920s and contains a wealth of information about rail travel during those pivotal years.

There is possibly no form of race restriction and race discrimination so far-reaching in the drawing of manhood; so potent in spreading race prejudice, or so insidious in its damnable influence as the jim crow car. . . . What is needed in this year of our Lord 1908 is earnest, effective action if the jim crow cars are to be derailed.

—from *York Dispatch* (Pennsylvania), January 23, 1908

This Chicago, Rock Island & Pacific graphic sought to burnish the appeal of its most luxurious train amenities among wealthy travelers of the early twentieth century.

17

DESIGN MATTERS

FROM JIM CROW TO PHOEBE SNOW

Just as the design of a metropolitan railroad station served a function but also conveyed a symbolic message, so too did rail car interiors. Early carriages were small and cramped, and their meager interior furnishings suggest that railroads made little if any effort to provide for passenger comfort, but by the 1890s American rail cars had evolved into "a commodious abode, uniting the appointments of luxurious private residence with the agreeable features of a modern club house." In other words, in the late nineteenth century car interiors grew redolent with the design embellishments that typified the excesses of the Gilded Age (also known as the latter part of the Victorian era). For many passengers, especially those who paid extra to travel aboard a sleeping car, the train interior was the equivalent to accommodations provided by a luxury hotel.[1]

Travel aboard certain trains also conveyed a message about a person's status. When the Northern Pacific launched its North Coast Limited in 1900, the railroad described it as "preeminently a train for cosmopolitan travel. It is indeed a high-toned train for high-toned travelers," but because it featured both standard Pullman cars and budget-level tourist sleeping cars, the railroad could claim that it was a train also for "the everyday, unpretentious element" that was satisfied with less luxurious and less expensive accommodations. The train also featured a "barber shop, buffet, and bath, which are open to all first-class passengers at a reasonable charge," while its posh observation car featured a library of "one hundred forty well-selected volumes" and current magazines and illustrated papers "encased in leather covers."[2]

Dining cars of the "North Coast Limited" were "manned by the best help it is possible to obtain. Breakfast and luncheon are *à la carte*, dinner is served *table d'hôte*, at the price of $1.00." During the mid-1920s, to cater to the often-finicky appetites of children, the Northern Pacific printed six different menu cards with Yellowstone Park themes. "There is Peter Rabbit, Sammy Squirrel, the Hold-up Bear, Piggy Porcupine, Billy Beaver, and Aunty Antelope." Each card featured rhymes on the reverse side to entertain "the tiny tots (and incidentally for the grown up) and make the set an attractive souvenir of the trip over this line." Dinner in the diner was a gustatory pleasure in an age when few people ever dined out.[3]

Railroads became known for the special dishes they served aboard their dining cars. The Northern Pacific, for example, publicly promoted itself as "the route of the great big baked potato." The purpose was twofold: to advertise a popular and tasty dining car staple and to attract attention to the agricultural products

More plebeian were the accommodations the Chicago, Alton & St. Louis sought to highlight in its chair car cutaway engraving from 1879. The passing of twenty years separated this Alton graphic from the previous Rock Island one, and during that time rail travel accommodations grew ever more luxurious, especially for passengers able and willing to pay the additional fee charged by the Pullman Palace Car Company for its elevated level of comfort.

of "Northern Pacific country." The railroad maintained its own poultry and dairy farms near Seattle. Other railroads serving the Pacific Northwest, notably the Union Pacific, promoted apple cuisine in a variety of giveaway brochures that featured fruit recipes.[4]

As memorable an experience as dinner in the diner was on many railroads, none excelled the meals provided by Fred Harvey and his patron, the Atchison, Topeka & Santa Fe Railway. "There are very many good eating-houses on railway lines throughout the United States, but we have never encountered such a succession of excellent meals on a railway line as on the route between San Diego and Kansas City," opined the editor of the *Official Guide* in 1892. Harvey restaurants and hotels welcomed hungry or sleepy travelers at numerous locations along Santa Fe tracks that connected Chicago with Texas and

California, and a Harvey House even served travelers in Saint Louis, a destination not located along Santa Fe tracks but one that for many years the railroad aspired to reach.[5]

Many of the Harvey restaurants and hotels fell on hard times as train travel declined after the mid-1950s, but in more recent years a few have been restored to their former glory, an outstanding example being the LaPosada in Winslow, Arizona, in which hotel guests can savor meals worthy of Harvey's exacting standards and then stroll the attractive grounds outside to watch the daily parade of trains, many of them headed east to Chicago or west to Los Angeles.

In the South, starting in the 1890s and continuing through the 1940s, the interior spatial arrangements of rail passenger cars mirrored the racial segregation mandated by state and local laws. The separation of white and Black passengers was referred to as Jim Crow, a term synonymous everywhere with racial discrimination.[6]

The United States Supreme Court had ruled in the 1890s in favor of "separate but equal" travel accommodations, though in subsequent years the "equal" proviso of the mandate was seldom strictly enforced by American railroads or intercity motorbus

The cover of a dining car menu from Southern Pacific trains of the early twentieth century illustrates the importance of commercial art when used to heighten the graphic appeal of a ubiquitous category of railroad publishing. Dining cars were a welcome addition to the passenger trains that once crisscrossed the United States and Canada, though the Atchison, Topeka & Santa Fe favored pausing its long-distance trains to enable passengers to dine trackside in one of the Fred Harvey Company's famed restaurants.

companies. Standard floor plans for many of the large bus stations built by Greyhound across the South during the 1930s and 1940s illustrate in unmistakable detail that many more restroom stalls were provided for white travelers than for Black. Racially segregated transportation endured until the mid-1950s, when the Interstate Commerce Commission ended it.[7]

Starting in the late nineteenth century, railroads grew especially eager to maintain good relations with their many female patrons. Better trains often featured a car for the exclusive use of women, if only to spare them from the thick clouds of cigar smoke men of the era were capable of puffing. Likewise, larger rail stations usually featured a separate waiting room for women traveling alone or with children. Questions of gender and interior spaces grew more complicated during the 1920s, when railroads debated whether a special lounge was needed to accommodate women smokers in stations and aboard trains: "Some observers say that smoking among women is only a fad; the girls are only showing off. Are female smokers going to become so numerous as to call for separate accommodations on local coach trains?"[8]

Along the Lackawanna

Lackawanna Railroad

It's time to go
With Phoebe Snow
And view the scenes
She loves to show
Each mile is quite
A new delight
Upon the Road
Of Anthracite

NEW YORK

BUFFALO **CHICAGO**

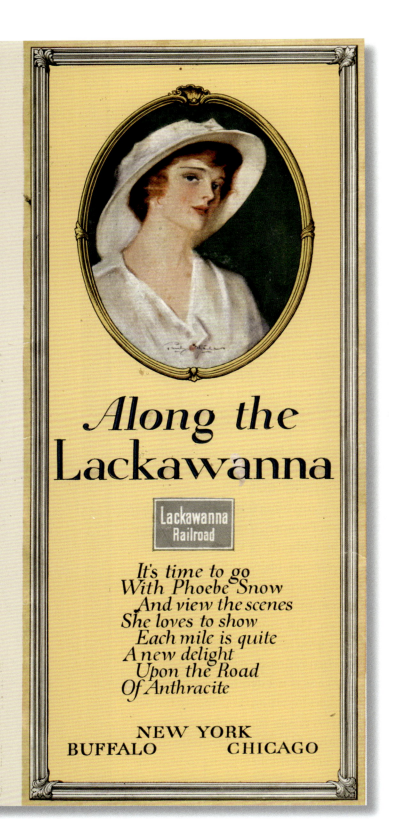

Rail publications increasingly recognized the influence women had in their family's choice of a vacation destination. Women appeared frequently on the covers of promotional brochures designed to entice people to travel to warm-weather resorts to escape the chill of winter. Some also appeared on brochures promoting the settlement of railroad lands. One eastern railroad, the Delaware, Lackawanna & Western, invented an attractive female character named Phoebe Snow to emphasize the cleanliness of its trains hauled by steam locomotives that burned hot and smokeless anthracite coal. The advertising ploy was clever because steam locomotives of the era typically consumed bituminous coal or heavy grades of oil. The resulting cinders and soot, when blown through car windows open to catch summer breezes in the days before air-conditioned passenger cars (which date from the 1930s), soiled many a white blouse or shirt.[9]

The Missouri-Kansas-Texas line in the early twentieth century promoted a counterpart to Phoebe Snow called Miss Katy. The two railroad ladies bore many similarities, but Phoebe Snow was an enduring symbol that appeared on Lackawanna-issued postcards and was for many years the name of the railroad's premier passenger train, but Miss Katy gradually faded from memory after the close of the Saint Louis World's Fair of 1904. Another familiar, much beloved, and long-enduring icon, this one intended to emphasize a good night's sleep aboard the trains of the Chesapeake & Ohio Lines, was Chessie, the railroad kitten. The railroad's advertising slogan was, naturally, "Sleep like a kitten."[10]

Facing, The Delaware, Lackawanna & Western's Phoebe Snow proved to be a potent and enduring advertising icon for the railroad, as were Betty Crocker, Aunt Jemima, and Uncle Ben for decades within the food industry. This trackside guide featuring the timeless railroad lady dates from the 1920s.

Above, The Missouri-Kansas-Texas introduced its Katy Girl shortly before the Saint Louis World's Fair of 1904. She debuted in company advertisements and on the cover of this 1903 timetable, but her public appearance was short lived.

AUTHORITY AND COURTESY

The two most public faces of any railroad were its ticket or station agents and its train conductors. A pleasant feature of any trip by rail, particularly one chosen to reach a vacation destination and not taken out of necessity, was interaction with a uniformed conductor. He wore the uniform not just to appear nattily dressed but also to establish his authority as boss of the train. The most visible portion of his work was to collect tickets, answer questions from passengers, and maintain good order throughout the train. He could, if required, eject a drunk or obnoxious person at the nearest station. Behind the scenes, he sought to ensure safe operations and, if possible, to maintain on-time arrivals and departures as listed in the timetables. Worth mentioning is that during the mid-1850s the conductors of the Erie Railroad adopted a uniform similar to the police of New York City. Some railroads outfitted conductors with intentionally showy uniforms that featured gold-lace trimmings and silver badges. "He swelled through the reeling aisles of the roaring train in princely pomp."*

The downside to a conductor's personification of authority was that to "very many people who travel, the conductor is a high and mighty being, to be timorously approached and gently entreated, if at all." Courtesy went with the job, but some people in authority would forget: sometimes when a conductor and his trainman assistant entered a car to collect tickets, "they slam the heavy door. When they go out they slam it again for luck. It was made to be shut. If nervous passengers choose to jump nearly out of their hides, all right; it's up to them."†

It became the task of railroad wordsmiths to write reminder pamphlets on good manners and civility for onboard crews. When managers of the St. Louis Southwestern Railway thought its train personnel needed lessons in courtesy, it assigned the task to in-house pamphleteers. The result was *The Advantages of Courtesy*, by which the Cotton Belt sought to improve interactions between employees and the traveling public along its line through southeastern Missouri, eastern Arkansas, and eastern Texas. The advice sounded like it came from an etiquette manual: "Of course, it may be necessary to discuss and emphasize this point, although lack of civility is the exception in railroad travel in this country, but the best proof of the advantages of courtesy is in the effect on the man himself who uses it. If any crusty person is doubtful of this point, he should try it on for a while, and see how much better it feels to be quit of the 'grouch.'"‡

For similar reasons, the Atlantic Coast Line issued special instruction booklets to teach onboard staff how to deal as diplomatically as possible with the troublesome and potentially contentious matter of racial segregation. Its luxury trains for the Carolinas, Georgia, and Florida originated in New York's Pennsylvania Station and sprinted across New Jersey, Pennsylvania, and Delaware before they reached the Mason-Dixon Line, a popularly regarded demarcation between North and South.

Florida trains continued through the historic border state of Maryland before entering the old Confederacy at the northern Virginia border formed by the Potomac River. The problem for onboard employees was the matter of state-mandated racial segregation and Jim Crow accommodations within the South. Laws encompassed stations and trains all the way from northern Virginia to the end of the tracks in southern Florida. Onboard personnel had the delicate task of encouraging passenger compliance with Jim Crow laws at some point south of the Mason-Dixon Line, but always without offending, if possible, the revenue passengers. Matters of race were infrequently mentioned in any rail publications, though illustrations that featured Black porters and dining car waiters occasionally appeared in the travel literature.§

*American Railroad Journal, September 1, 1855, 555–556; Railway News, December 1883, 3. The importance of crew uniforms was the subject of a 1913 Northern Pacific pamphlet titled Rules and Specifications Governing Uniforming of Employees (Saint Paul, MN: Northern Pacific Railway, 1913). The little guide provided detailed specifications regarding a proper uniform, including the materials and dimensions approved for pockets, lapels, collars, buttons, and buttonholes.

† Railway Age Gazette, February 25, 1910, 419.

‡ Official Guide, August 1912, xxx. Another in-house publication similar in intent was issued by the Efficiency Committee of the San Pedro, Los Angeles & Salt Lake Railroad under the pathological title "The Red Tape Worm." The publication described how the "system" in many offices "[had] developed into a monster which [strangled] efficiency." Official Guide, April 1915, xxv.

§ For a discussion of the legal mandate that required railroads of the South to maintain "separate but equal" facilities, see Railroad Gazette, November 25, 1904, 164; July 12, 1907, 51. One truly odd railroad-published artifact was a special ticket issued in 1886 that permitted Indians to ride outside the cars of Northern Pacific passenger trains but not inside. Approved Indian spaces included the outside platforms of the baggage, mail, and express cars of passenger trains and whatever space the conductor of a freight train might permit. This rare example of printed rail ephemera is preserved at the Washington State Historical Society in Tacoma.

Rail unions published trade journals that highlighted news and feature stories of interest to their members. The *Railway Conductor* had counterpart publications devoted to the interests of telegraphers, locomotive engineers, and ticket agents, among others.

This Northern Pacific advertisement from *Harper's Weekly* (May 5, 1900) is notable for the dignified appearance of one of its African American dining car employees. At the turn of the century and for years afterward, it was too common for advertisers to indulge in demeaning racial stereotypes.

"A handsome folder has been issued by the passenger department of the Great Northern Railway, describing their 'Oriental Limited.' This superb train is made up of a day coach, tourist sleeper, dining car, standard sleeper and compartment observation car. The illustrations give an excellent idea of the arrangement of the interior of the cars, and are supplemented by a birds-eye-view of the country traversed." That was 1906, when the interior passenger trains still reflected the decorative excesses of the Gilded Age.[11]

Beginning mainly in the 1920s, railroads increasingly hired specially trained interior designers to provide their car interiors a modern look. The "limousine-lounge cars" operated on the Columbine between Chicago and Denver were consciously decorated by the Union Pacific and Chicago & North Western in the style of the "'Adam' period." The Milwaukee Road preferred a colorful Spanish design for its new Olympian, introduced in 1927. When the Southern Railway advertised its all-Pullman Crescent Limited between New York and New Orleans, it touted car exteriors painted in two shades of green and interior decorations that featured "the latest developments of the Pullman car designers."[12]

During the opening decades of the twentieth century, one feature of train travel—a feature that took precedence over the advertising value of improvements in interior design—was better sanitation inside rail stations and passenger cars. The replacement of common vessels for drinking water with individual paper cups was a 1912 sanitation upgrade mandated by Uncle Sam for interstate railroads not already required to do so by the individual states. Another big step toward greater sanitation was curtailing the nation's habit that most annoyed foreign visitors to the United States: men spitting in public conveyances. "I would say—let the men follow the example of the women. The women do not spit on the floor and there is not the slightest excuse for the men doing it. Spitting is usually a nasty, dirty, filthy habit, and has no part with a gentleman."[13]

Train exteriors had long presented a design challenge because grime created by coal and oil-burning locomotives militated against the use of bright colors. During the age of steam, the Pullman Company favored olive drab for the exterior of its cars. Here, incidentally, was one area in which the electric interurban railways held a decided advantage over their steam-powered big brothers. The clean-running interurban cars maintained their bright exterior colors, and some companies became identified in that way. The Red Line, for example, was the familiar name of the Indianapolis & Cincinnati Traction Company, which served southeastern Indiana and attired its cars in crimson paint.

When diesel locomotives replaced steam on the passenger trains of the United States and Canada between the late 1930s and the 1950s, railroads felt free to adopt a variety of colorful exterior paint schemes. For example, Missouri Pacific showcased its attractively attired Eagle streamliners on the covers of public timetables, which during the 1950s recaptured the visual appeal of those published by the railroads of the United States before World War I.

Facing, The Missouri Pacific timetable cover dates from 1950 and thus lies well outside the scope of *Railroad Nation*, yet it showcases several items of note: the rebound in the use of color graphics after the shock administered by the United States Railroad Administration in 1918 and the bright exterior colors of locomotives and passenger trains made possible by conversion from steam to diesel propulsion.

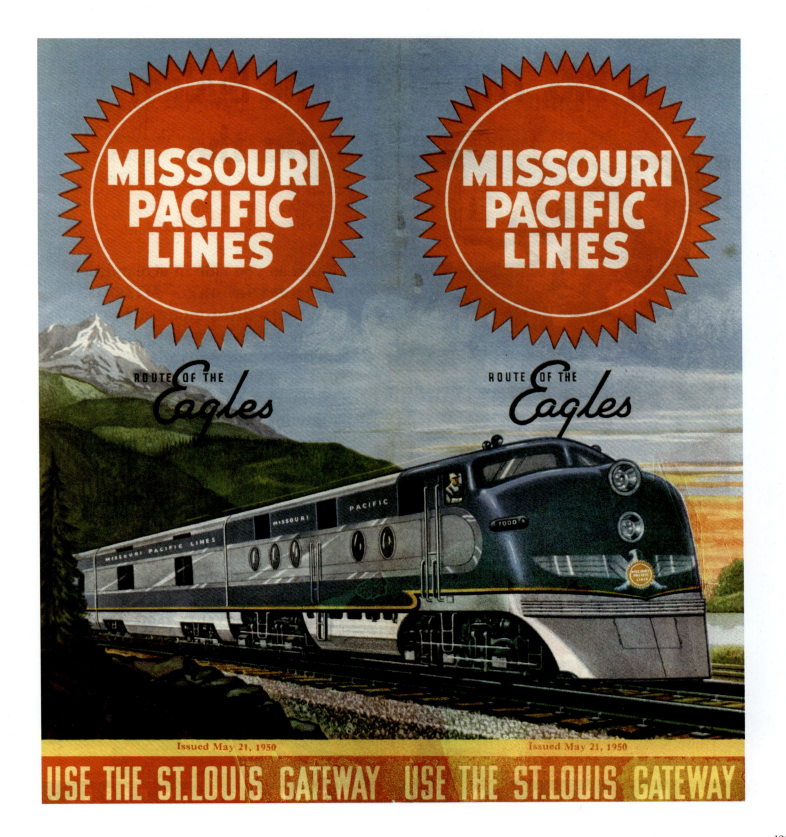

USE THE ST. LOUIS GATEWAY USE THE ST. LOUIS GATEWAY

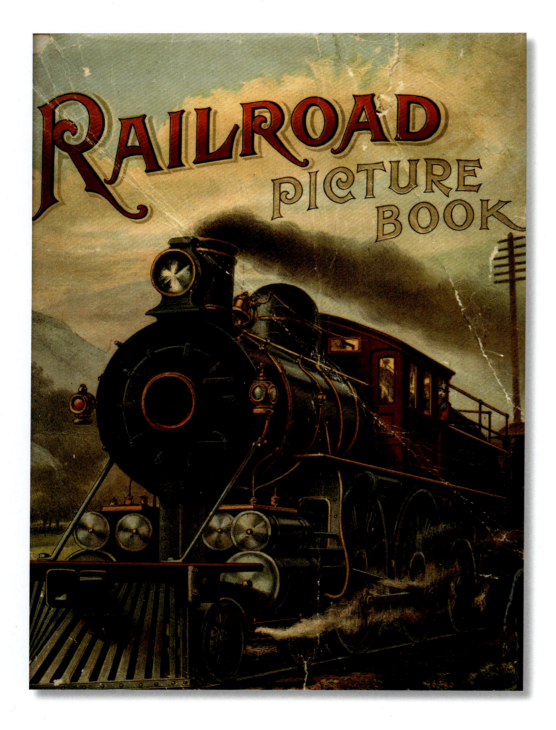

Thus, then, about thirty years ago, it was doubted whether locomotives could run at all upon iron railways; twenty years ago, the idea of their moving at a greater speed than ten miles in the hour was scoffed at as chimerical; fifteen years ago, the unexpected rate of thirty miles an hour was considered a wonder which no effort of practical science could surpass; and now a speed of nearly fifty miles an hour is in daily use, while the rate of a mile per minute is promised, and, in some special instances, has actually been exceeded.

—from *American Railroad Journal* (1845)[1]

Books featuring railroads were once very popular among young readers because children were often fascinated by trains, whether they rode them or simply saw one steaming noisily along the tracks. The cover image in this example emphasized speed as convincingly portrayed by a commercial artist.

18

THE QUEST FOR SPEED

In all they did, American railroads were in a hurry, but some citizens of the new nation seemed in an inordinately greater hurry. Their desire was to get to their destinations as quickly as possible. Because of the enormous spatial dimensions of the United States, a driving force behind the nation's passion for railroads was the quest to attain ever greater speeds. The same was true on the nation's great river highways. "In the 'flush times' of steamboating, a race between two notoriously fleet steamers was an event of vast importance," observed Mark Twain in his *Life on the Mississippi.* "The date was set for it several weeks in advance, and from that time forward the whole Mississippi Valley was in a consuming state of excitement. Politics and weather were dropped, and people talked only of the coming race."[2]

The ideal may have been speedy travel, but because of the economies required of builders of America's pre–Civil War railroads, the reality was that train travel between major cities of the United States was slow. The Richmond, Fredericksburg & Potomac Railroad advertised in 1836 that passengers aboard its train that left Richmond at 4:00 a.m. were scheduled to arrive in Washington, DC, at 7:00 p.m. Fifteen hours were required to cover a distance slightly greater than a hundred miles because the economies typical of early American railroads required through

travelers to use a combination of train, boat, and stagecoach—train in Virginia, boat along the Potomac River, and stagecoach in Maryland. An all-rail route completed shortly after the Civil War reduced the original travel time to a few hours and provided a vital link between railroads of the Northeast and the South.[3]

The rail connection across northern Virginia enabled through trains to speed vacation-minded travelers between New York, Philadelphia, Baltimore, and other cities of the Northeast and winter resorts in the Carolinas, Georgia, and Florida. During the 1920s, luxurious trains and steamship connections from Florida's Key West completed the 1,600-mile trip separating New York City from the exotic indulgences available in Havana, Cuba, in slightly less than forty-eight hours. Whenever better technology and improved rights-of-way enabled railroads to up the speed of a flagship train and shave an hour or two from the published schedules, it was an event worth advertising.[4]

"We are pre-eminently a locomotive people, and our very amusements are locomotive—the greater the speed, the greater the sport," mused the editor of the *American Railroad Journal* in 1846. To convey the impression of speed, a marketable asset

EXIT THE "CRAWLING AGE"

"But the days for coaching are past, and the '*crawling age*' of 'twelve miles the hour' teams, must give place to the days of steam. Few men are nowadays [in 1846] satisfied with a speed of less than double the best time made by the 'fast mail.' Such is the march of improvement!"*

Prose of the nineteenth century like the passage quoted above had many ways of saying something obvious, but always with the maximum use of words. The quotation is from the *American Railway Journal*. One of its numerous post–Civil War peers, the *American Railway Times*, made much the same observation but phrased it this way: "The utilitarian spirit of the age is strikingly exhibited in the intense desire to diminish the quantity of time necessary to pass from one spot of the earth's surface to another, and to communicate almost instantaneously with a remote distance." Wordsmiths seeking to describe the increased speed of trains during the last three decades of the nineteenth century seemed intent, ironically, on slowing readers by using the maximum number of words possible. They employed a similarly languid style of prose in their ornate pen pictures of Mother Nature's vacation attractions, fertile soils, and almost any other topic assigned to them.†

* *American Railroad Journal*, October 31, 1946, 696.

† *American Railway Times*, May 25, 1867, 166. See also Stephen Kern, *The Culture of Time and Space, 1880–1918* (Cambridge, MA: Harvard University Press, 1983). Of particular interest is chapter 5, which is titled "Speed."

among American rail travelers, some companies styled themselves "air lines" to suggest straight tracks conducive to fast-running trains. The words *air line* were first applied to American railroads during the 1840s and 1850s as a term of derision, but the attempted ridicule backfired. "It was at once adopted by the road thus stigmatized, and an 'Air Line' is now understood to be the most direct route that it is possible to attain between two given points." The most famous twentieth-century railroad to embrace this synonym for speed was the Seaboard Air Line Railroad, which sought to use the term to competitive advantage in its head-to-head battle with the Atlantic Coast Line for Florida tourists. In the late 1920s, when commercial aviation securities were the rage among Wall Street investors, some naive individuals mistakenly purchased Seaboard Air Line common stock.[5]

As a nation, Americans in their haste were willing to tolerate the dangers inherent in speed. The use of single tracks with occasional turnouts heightened the danger of a head-on collision, or a rear one if the train ahead was slow to take the sidetrack, as was the case in the tragedy of Casey Jones, a brave engineer immortalized in a lachrymose ballad especially popular in early twentieth-century America.

Even before the nation's first railroads, steamboats plying the Mississippi River and America's other great interior waterways frequently engaged in races despite the obvious danger of a boiler explosion. Some races, as Missouri's Mark Twain noted in his book *Life on the Mississippi*, were arranged several weeks in advance. Others were impromptu contests that resulted when one steamboat overtook a rival. Crews often kept a special stash of dry and especially hot-burning wood handy for such occasions, and they worked furiously to stoke the boiler to raise steam pressure to the maximum—or beyond.[6]

No matter how fast or efficient the steamboats were (when the river itself cooperated), trains were faster, and only the worst floods and winter snows might temporarily affect their daily efficiency. Americans also took pride in a speeding stagecoach, but no flesh-and-blood horse could match the speed or endurance of the iron horse. The quest for speed was the genesis of the fabled Pony Express, which commencing in 1860 could forward a letter two thousand miles between the nation's westernmost railhead at Saint Joseph, Missouri, and Sacramento, California, in less than two weeks, a span of time that compared favorably to a minimum of twenty-two days by steamship between New York and San Francisco (via the Isthmus of Panama) or twenty-one days by stagecoach between Saint Louis and San Francisco. In March 1861 the recently inaugurated Pony Express delivered a copy of President Lincoln's inaugural address to California in the record time of seven days and seventeen hours. However, even the fastest relay of horses proved no match for the infinitely greater speed of the first transcontinental telegraph, which put the Pony Express out of business on October 25, 1861.[7]

Railroads advertised the times of their fastest trains to attract passengers. For years the New York Central and Pennsylvania lines vigorously competed to run the fastest trains between New York and Chicago, which at their speediest meant about eighteen hours for the Twentieth Century Limited and its rival Broadway Limited. A steam locomotive of the New York Central widely publicized for its rapid running—among the first in the world to travel greater than one hundred miles per hour—formed the railroad's centerpiece at the 1893 world's fair in Chicago, and No. 999 subsequently appeared on a United States postage stamp. The New York Central's publicity coup was orchestrated by the railroad's general passenger agent and resident advertising genius George H. Daniels. His key collaborator was the company's photographer, Arthur P. Yates, who pioneered a technique to capture on the slow film of the day reasonably sharp images of locomotives at speed.[8]

Americans loved fast-running trains regardless of where they ran, even though with greater speeds came the increased danger of an accident. In Great Britain three separate railroads linked London to Scotland, and for a time during the late nineteenth century, all three companies engaged in a race to run the fastest trains. This proved counterproductive, however, when the traveling public grew concerned about the potential for a serious accident and shunned Britain's fast-running trains. By contrast, Americans in the early twentieth century seemed more willing to accept the risks that came with greater train speeds.[9]

One of the earliest and most notable efforts to run dedicated high-speed trains within the United States unfolded in dramatic fashion in the early twentieth century when promoters proposed in 1905 to construct a new and straight-as-an-arrow electric interurban railway to connect New York and Chicago in a mere ten hours. The widely advertised Chicago–New York Electric Air Line Railroad seemed too good to be true, and it was. A short segment was completed as a local interurban between Gary and nearby La Porte, Indiana, and its trains operated at ordinary speeds. Many mom-and-pop investors, lured by the widely advertised promise of extraordinary speed and the assurance of a lucrative return on their dollars, had in the end nothing to show for their misplaced confidence in the promoters' claims.[10]

One immutable force of nature that seasonally affected train speeds on railroads both electric and steam, especially those in the northern states, was the chill of winter. As a result, trains "cannot be run safely on as fast schedules in winter as in summer. The engineman cannot keep his head outside of the cab in cold

THE PUBLISHING LEGACY OF GEORGE H. DANIELS

George Henry Daniels (1842–1908) was a railroad publicist of remarkable talent. More than most of his turn-of-the century peers, he knew the rail industry from the ground up, literally. At the age of sixteen, the young Illinois native was a rodman who carried the tools and instruments used by civil engineers as they led construction of the North Missouri Railroad, later a key component the Wabash, St. Louis & Pacific, which hired Daniels in 1880 as its general passenger agent. At the company's Saint Louis headquarters, he oversaw the publication of numerous Wabash imprints and honed his skills as both a writer and a railroad spokesperson. He subsequently organized several regional traffic associations that provided him a broad range of railroad acquaintances across the Midwest.*

After he relocated to the East Coast in 1889, Daniels gained national fame as a publicist for the New York Central System, and today he is regarded as one of the fathers of American public relations. He oversaw the Central's monthly promotional magazine, called the *Four-Track News*. "Its regular issues consist of about 136 pages. Its contents are varied and entertaining. Its list of contributors contains the names of some of the most pleasing writers in the country, and its tone is cheerful and representative of the brisk, breezy age we live in." Among various turn-of-the century

counterparts to the *Four-Track News* was a hefty monthly periodical issued by the Saint Louis–San Francisco, a gangling rail system based in Saint Louis.†

Very likely the always personable Daniels remained in contact with his former Missouri colleagues even after he relocated to New York City. In the early twentieth century, the Saint Louis–San Francisco launched a monthly magazine that forcefully promoted the "soil and scenery" of the American Southwest—most notably within the states of Missouri, Oklahoma, Arkansas, and Texas. The text of the Frisco's counterpart to the *Four-Track News* was anything but subtle. Issue after issue pounded home the message that the railroad had opened a landed empire with farms free, or nearly so, to all would-be settlers. The publication evolved as it sought its niche, with one of its titles being the *Southwest Magazine*.

* *St. Louis Globe-Democrat*, July 2, 1908; *Buffalo (NY) Enquirer*, July 2, 1908; *Saxby's Magazine*, 1902, 49–51.

† *Scranton (PA) Truth*, September 5, 1904. In addition to publishing the *Four-Track News*, Daniels coined the name of the New York Central's most famous train, the 20th Century Limited, a luxurious hotel on wheels that, after its launch in 1902, ran overnight between New York and Chicago until 1967. Lucius Beebe, *20th Century: "The Greatest Train in the World"* (Berkeley, CA: Howell-North, 1962).

weather as he can in warm weather, and as the windows of the cab become frosted, the chances of his failing to see a signal increased." In addition, frigid weather slowed the labor of personnel at station stops along the way as they handled the mail and baggage carried aboard the headend cars. Because some passengers grew unhappy if trains ran chronically late compared to the times printed in public timetables, railroad competitors occasionally agreed in advance to slow their passenger trains and lengthen their scheduled times printed in public timetables they issued during the winter months.[11]

I end this chapter with the realization that there were some things railroad publicists did not care to emphasize. Over the years, safety as exemplified by all-steel passenger cars and trackside block signals were topics worth publicizing in a variety of special booklets; on the other hand, derailments and crashes went unmentioned in railroad publishing, although the more tragic the outcome, the more the event was exploited by daily newspapers.

In recent times, some features of rail travel are given a positive spin by contemporary publicists, but if a person searches for the truth behind their claims, a different reality might emerge. I think here of the exaggerated claims made in my own region by high-speed rail advocates who seem woefully ignorant of history and thus make spurious claims in print that are unworthy additions to publishing the railroad. Let me hasten to explain on the basis of my personal experience as an avid train rider and also as a seeker of the truth.

During the mid-1930s, the Green Diamond of the investor-owned Illinois Central made its debut on the run between Saint Louis and Chicago as one of the new generation of internal combustion streamliners. It was a ballast scorcher that regularly completed its 294-mile sprint in four hours and fifty-five minutes. Fast-forward nearly ninety years to Amtrak's internet-only public timetable, which lists its fastest train as covering the distance in four hours and forty-six minutes, and that is using the former Alton route fully ten miles shorter than that of the Green Diamond. It does not require higher mathematics to calculate

Portrait of George H. Daniels. Railroad advertising, the New York Central publicist firmly believed, circulated around the world to showcase the many attractions of the United States. In some nations, large maps prepared by American railroads hung on schoolroom walls.

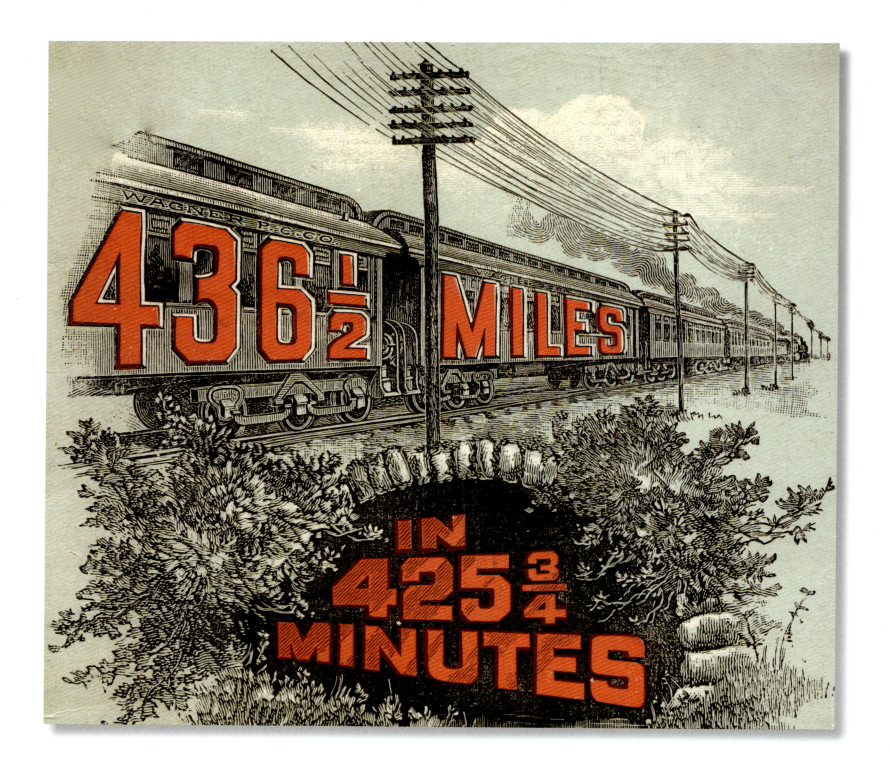

AIR RAIL AIR RAIL

NEW YORK
PHILADELPHIA
CHICAGO
CLEVELAND
PORT COLUMBUS
PITTSBURGH
BALTIMORE
INDIANAPOLIS
SAN FRANCISCO
WASHINGTON
KANSAS CITY
ST. LOUIS
LOS ANGELES
WICHITA
KINGMAN
WINSLOW
WAYNOKA
ALBUQUERQUE
CLOVIS

COAST TO COAST IN 48 HOURS

Facing, Speed was foremost in this turn-of-the-century issue of the New York Central's *Four-Track News.* The railroad's publicity genius, George H. Daniels, knew that speed sold tickets. The challenge for railroad companies at the dawn of the twentieth century was to balance speed with safety.

Above, No matter how fast a train ran, its speed fell short of commercial airliners, which flew ever faster during the late 1920s and 1930s because of design improvements such as streamlining. In 1929 various railroads teamed up with the nation's youthful airlines to provide the best of both worlds: aviation speeds during daylight hours and railroad comfort and safety during the hours of darkness. To advertise what became the most famous of these combinations, in 1929 the Pennsylvania Railroad published a colorful salute to the latest form of transcontinental travel. However, navigation and safety improvements in the air and on the ground soon enabled airlines to fly coast-to-coast without the aid of railroads. In the mid-1950s, travel within the United States by air topped that by rail for the first time.

THE SOUND OF SPEED

The coming of railroads to North America created a distinctive landscape for the eye and an equally distinctive soundscape for the ear. The *Railway News* in 1885 noted the need for "a sweet-voiced steam-whistle" when it complained about the "piercing, sleep-defying, and diabolical steam-whistle" that disturbed train travelers and "even the peaceful burgher dwelling within ear-shot of the railway." During the daylight hours, "the sound offends the ear and shocks the nervous. But at night it is hideous and satanic." The *Railway News* praised the recent invention of a new type of locomotive chime whistle employed on the Chesapeake & Ohio Railroad that sounded "smooth full and round and is not unlike the organ note so pleasant to the ear." Yes, even the sound of the railroad evolved during their early trial-and-error years.*

In 1837 the *American Railway Journal* sought to capture in print the sounds of speed by quoting from a British medical publication. The writer described a locomotive and its train of cars descending a grade as "dashing along like lightning, and with a uniform growl or roar, like a continuous discharge of distant artillery or thunder." The noise made it "impossible not to feel some sense of danger." Two trains "flying in opposite directions are scarcely less agitating to the nerves than the transit through the tunnels." After pausing for water, the locomotive is able "to renew its gigantic task."

"The steam-shriek is a new phenomenon on the railroad, and a very startling one it is" because "unlike the voice of man or any known animal," the sound of the whistle was so loud that it could easily be heard two miles away. "It is a most unearthly yell, or scream," as if emitted by some "monstrous animal while being gored to death."†

Fittingly, "Sounds" was the title that Henry David Thoreau gave his chapter in *Walden* on the nearby Fitchburg Railroad. He wrote, "The whistle of the locomotive penetrates my woods summer and winter, sounding like the scream of a hawk sailing over some farmer's yard, informing me that many restless city merchants are arriving within the circle of the town, or adventurous country traders from the other side." Listening from his lakeside retreat, Thoreau also described a railway locomotive in terms of the sounds it made: "I hear him in his stable blowing off the superfluous energy of the day, that he may calm his nerves and cool his liver and brain for a few hours of iron slumber." In the hands of a skilled wordsmith like Thoreau, the ornate prose of his era expressed a mellifluous sound not unlike the whistles of the Chesapeake & Ohio's steam locomotives described earlier in this sidebar.‡

* *Railway News*, July 16, 1885, 257. The comments from 1885 contained in this sidebar emphasize the importance of the sound of the railroad, a dimension of history often overlooked in print. See Mark M. Smith, *Listening to Nineteenth-Century America* (Chapel Hill: University of North Carolina Press, 2001); Richard Cullen Rath, *How Early America Sounded* (Ithaca, NY: Cornell University Press, 2003); Jane Brox, *Silence: A Social History of One of the Least Understood Elements of Our Lives* (Boston: Houghton Mifflin Harcourt, 2019).

† *Medico-Chirurgical Review and Journal of Practical Medicine*, reprinted in *American Railroad Journal*, December 30, 1837, 684.

‡ Henry David Thoreau, *Walden and Civil Disobedience*, ed. Sherman Paul (1854; repr., Boston: Houghton Mifflin, 1957), chap. 4. Because of its distinctive animal-like sounds, the iron horse was a popular subject for onlookers to anthropomorphize in print.

that we moderns now make the Saint Louis–Chicago journey nine minutes faster than our 1930s forebearers, and that is after an infusion of nearly two billion taxpayer dollars provided to the state of Illinois by the Obama administration to create a high-speed route. The dollars spent to upgrade track between Saint Louis and Chicago were supposed to enable Amtrak trains across Illinois to attain a top speed of 110 miles per hour.[12]

The modern world of high-speed trains dates from the first run of the Japanese bullet trains in the early 1960s. Japan and France have invested heavily in dedicated track and high-speed trains, and some Americans want to do likewise. But there is a serious stumbling block to the implementation of their dreams: high-speed trains in Japan, France, and other countries outside the United States connect with numerous secondary trains and thus conveniently extend the effective range of travel by rail. The United States until the 1960s enjoyed a vast and comprehensive network of intercity trains that could easily have made dedicated high-speed lines viable, but that marvelous network shrank dramatically during the fifteen years after the United

States launched construction of its interstate highway system in 1956. American passenger trains might have disappeared completely had not the federal government launched Amtrak in 1971 to save a remnant of the former system. Amtrak later added high-speed trains to its Northeast Corridor route, which connects Boston and Washington via New York, Philadelphia, and Baltimore. Amtrak's Acela trains, however, attain their top speed of 150 miles per hour only along a short segment of track between Baltimore and Philadelphia.[13]

Thus far, America's contributions to high-speed trains have been unimpressive and hardly worth publicizing, especially when compared to the speed standards that prevail elsewhere in the world. It is not uncommon for some French TGV trains to maintain 197 miles per hour over distances that correspond to America's Northeast Corridor. The United States is clearly a laggard in the world of high-speed trains, and with the notable exception of Florida's 110-mile-per-hour Brightline trains between Orlando and Miami, the nation's bungling and half-hearted efforts to date have almost been laughable.[14]

Facing, "How far is an hour?" asks an advertisement that dates from the late 1940s. An attempt to answer that question animates my interest in exploring matters of time and space in *Railroad Nation.* One obvious response is that during the nineteenth century, railroads steadily increased the distance that goods and passengers could travel in an hour, while airlines continued that quest during the twentieth century and ultimately triumphed over rail travel. Now, if only long-distance air travel today were as comfortable for budget travelers as trains once were. The personal discomfort occasioned by numerous long-distance flights in "steerage class" almost caused me to write a book on modern commercial aviation titled "Air Pains."

How **FAR** *is an hour?*

The compiler of the railroad folder was an artful gentleman, a skilled word-slinger, a charming litterateur. American letters can ill afford to restrict his field of activities. Unless he finds a similar field for his eloquence and imagination the railroad eulogist will be missed. He was given to exaggeration, but he was a far more entertaining fellow than the writer of best sellers. His work has given pleasure to myriads who will mourn his passing.

—from *Indianapolis News*, April 4, 1918

Chicago Great Western's *Minnesota's Ten-Thousand Lakes* is an evocative example of the type of artistic creativity that after World War I vanished from the imprints of many marginal passenger carriers that no longer saw value in promoting vacations. Especially was that true as more and more Americans acquired automobiles during the 1920s and 1930s and set forth on their own.

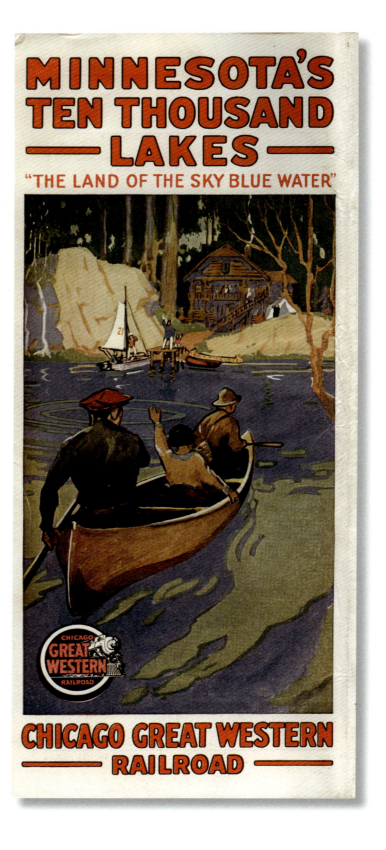

19

RAILROAD GRAPHICS CONSCRIPTED FOR THE DURATION

America's entry into World War I in April 1917 placed a weighty burden on the nation's railroads, one that coercive federal and state regulations had made even more onerous. Legislators at all levels of government during the so-called Progressive Era of the early twentieth century had successfully piled one railroad regulation atop another. On occasion, newly enacted federal and state regulations directly contradicted one another, but such was the zeal of politicians to win the applause of voters and muckraking journalists that any regulation, no matter how misguided or petty, seemed better than none at all.[1]

Two decades earlier, in the 1880s, railroads had acquired an unprecedented degree of near-monopoly power over transportation within the United States, and this frightened many Americans. The first meaningful federal response was the congressional creation of the Interstate Commerce Commission in 1888. America's first-ever federal regulatory agency initially did little more than publish a thick annual compilation of rail industry statistics, but for the remainder of the nineteenth century, that seemed enough to satisfy politicians, both Republicans and Democrats, who sought to allay the monopoly fears of their constituents. Congress subsequently passed the Sherman Anti-trust Act in 1890, which appeared powerful on paper but which until

the early twentieth century was just another toothless regulatory tiger full of growl but possessing little bite. Only when the young, energetic, and wholly accidental president, Theodore Roosevelt, challenged railroad power in the early twentieth century did anything change. Roosevelt became known as the "trust buster," and members of Congress emboldened by the changing mood of the electorate rushed to further rein in railroad operators.[2]

The consequence, intended or not, was that railroads lost luster as an attractive investment, and raising the dollars needed to modernize infrastructure and rolling stock grew increasingly difficult during the years from 1900 to 1917. The automobile industry sped ahead (aided by federal dollars for highway construction after 1916) and attracted all the money it needed to grow from infancy to early adulthood during the same span of time. Thus, from a railroad perspective, America's Progressive Era was wholly regressive.

Beset with "criticisms and attacks," railroads awoke rather belatedly to the importance of improved public relations, admitted the *Railway Age Gazette* in 1915: "The managements of individual railways permit, or cause to be done, many things which are impolitic or wrong and which incense the public, and much of the regulation proposed or adopted is provoked by such

BUFFALO
ROCHESTER
AND
PITTSBURGH
RY.

LOCAL TIME TABLE

H. E. HUNTINGTON,
GENERAL PASSENGER AGENT

BUFFALO
ROCHESTER
AND
PITTSBURGH
RY.

LOCAL TIME TABLE

H. E. HUNTINGTON,
GENERAL PASSENGER AGENT

conduct on the part of the railways." The industry had long distinguished itself by the mass of new promotional publications railroads issued each year, but now as never before it needed to sell itself to overcome public hostility and not simply to promote vacation possibilities or the settlement of railroad lands.[3]

After Congress committed the United States to the Great War in April 1917, it was no longer business as usual for the nation's railroads, and travelers by train were among the first Americans to experience the impact of the wartime revisions and cutbacks required to provide passenger cars to handle troop movements unprecedented in size. As numerous through sleeping car routes as well as entire passenger trains, including the Broadway Limited, flagship of the Pennsylvania Railroad, were axed from the public timetables, the remaining trains grew more crowded and noticeably less luxurious. The New York Central eliminated all observation cars from its named limiteds and specials.[4]

When Iowa's rail commissioners denied a public request for the Chicago Great Western to reinstate two trains it had to remove to support the war effort, they explained that "this country is now at war" and despite some pushback from travelers, "we cannot be expected to order the railroads to operate trains where their operation is a mere matter of convenience and not a matter of necessity."[5]

Railroad advertisements in late 1917 urged Americans to forgo their usual Christmas journeys, unless they were absolutely necessary, so that "soldiers on furlough and persons who

must travel may do so with a minimum of inconvenience." Familiar foods disappeared from dining car menus. After a request by the newly created United States Food Administration in early 1918, fifty-nine out of sixty-three dining car services pledged to forgo all wheat products to save flour for the war effort.[6]

The biggest wartime problem facing American railroads was the timely movement of an unprecedented tonnage of military freight. After the congressional war declaration of April 1917, federal authorities expected the nation's rail carriers to spring into action and deliver countless tons of wartime cargo to ports of embarkation along the East Coast, but the heavily regulated industry did not own a large enough fleet of freight cars or have a suitably modern infrastructure in place to handle the sudden surge of wartime business expeditiously. Critics claimed that freight waiting to be delivered to the port of New York was stuck aboard trains backed up all the way to Chicago. Of course, most people blamed railroad companies for the logjam, and President Woodrow Wilson persuaded a majority in Congress to create the United States Railroad Administration (USRA) in late December 1917 to unsnarl the knot and get vital wartime cargoes rolling again. For the first time ever, Uncle Sam ran the nation's railroads.

The federal government did not formally own the nation's rail network, but the bureaucrats of the newly created USRA did control virtually every aspect of their day-to-day operations. Within the next month or two, carriers across the United States discontinued numerous additional passenger trains as mandated by USRA director general William Gibbs McAdoo to conserve coal required by the war effort. With the noticeable reductions in overnight train accommodations, the formerly dreaded upper berth of a Pullman sleeper became a traveler's prized possession. Uncle Sam further mandated that competing lines bury long-standing rivalries and share facilities, as when Baltimore & Ohio trains relocated from their former terminus on the New Jersey side of the Hudson River into Pennsylvania Station in the heart of New York City. Likewise, the four railroad rivals running passenger trains between Saint Louis and Chicago were now required to operate them at noncompeting intervals spaced throughout the day.[7]

Fifty years and more of the steady improvement of railroad graphics came to an abrupt halt in early April 1918 as the result of overreach by one bureaucrat, the newly appointed federal czar of the rail industry. His name and official title were henceforth imprinted on every conceivable form of railroad paper, from tickets and timetables to dining car menus: "W. G. McAdoo, Director General of Railroads." Journalists took note of his passion to plaster his name in every imaginable place. "Personally we don't object to Mr. McAdoo succeeding his illustrious father-in-law to the presidency," noted one small-town Kansas newspaper that voiced the concerns of many Americans. "But the care that is taken to put his name out at every possible opportunity on the railroad literature seems to us, open minded and sympathetic as we are, as savoring of an attempt to make political capital out of a great national movement, which will never succeed as a one-man institution, nor mixed with politics."[8]

The nation's new rail boss was a lawyer who had gained widespread public attention a decade earlier by overseeing the difficult task of extending underwater tunnels between Newark, New Jersey, and New York City to create the Hudson & Manhattan Railway, a commuter line that operates today as PATH. The remarkable feat of engineering certainly advanced his career, but providing McAdoo an inside track to head the USRA was his status as President Woodrow Wilson's son-in-law. McAdoo became the "train dispatcher extraordinary for this amazing system, which resting in the palm of one super-director, is a visualization of power that will have no rival in time of peace." He would oversee an industry of 1,700,000 employees, 250,000 miles of track, 65,000 locomotives, and 2,500,000 cars.[9]

Congress created the USRA eight months after the nation formally joined the Allied cause in the Great War then raging across Europe. In April 1918, McAdoo approved a ban on the colorful graphics that railroads had routinely used for decades to enhance the eye appeal of their imprints and ordered that publications "exploiting train service, pleasure or health resorts, and the like, must be discontinued until further notice." In other words, the federal edict banned brochures, calendars, wall maps, and journal advertisements that boasted of one railroad's

Portrait of William Gibbs McAdoo, who served simultaneously as head of the United States Railroad Administration and as President Woodrow Wilson's secretary of the Treasury. To claim he was the busiest man in Washington during World War I is no exaggeration. McAdoo was no stranger to rail transportation, having previously served as president of the Hudson & Manhattan Railroad and built a street railway in Knoxville, Tennessee.

competitive advantage over its rivals. Timetable designs were to be standardized and their distribution restricted to avoid waste. Competition among railroads was squandering the nation's resources, reasoned McAdoo, and every conceivable example, including timetable graphics, must be eliminated.[10]

"Mr. McAdoo stated that during the period of government operation and control of railroads, it is apparent that the large expenditures hitherto made by the carriers for various forms of publicity are unnecessary, and that the custom of exploiting train service, pleasure or health resorts and the like, must be discontinued until further notice," reported *Railway Age* in its April 12, 1918, issue. "All advertising of luxurious trains, claims of superior service and extraneous matter of every description is to be omitted and the folders made purely informative." In the words of a Seattle newspaper, Uncle Sam had summarily excised the windy verbiage typical of booster publications: "Railroad literature advertising health resorts will no longer read like circus lithographs."[11]

McAdoo had apparently decided that because war was a grim business, the annual flood of paper coming from America's railroads should reflect its grimness. His thinking was consistent with the nation's semi-hysterical wartime crusade to prevent wasteful competition and foster efficiency. After the USRA's April edict, all timetables, regardless of the issuing railroad, appeared uniformly ugly in their military drab. Illustrations, and even bright colors, disappeared from covers, which featured black text on a light brown background. Graphic designers had no choice but to rein in their former creativity. According to *Printers' Ink*, a respected trade journal, the government-mandated products were "gloomy, standardized affairs, but at least they gave the schedules of trains."[12]

In the headline that accompanied the *Pittsburgh Post-Gazette*'s account of the USRA's encompassing edict, the newspaper lamented, "Gorgeous Railroad Timetables to Be Retired by Companies." The clock appeared to have been turned back

GENERAL INFORMATION

This railroad is in possession and control of the Government of the United States, and is being operated by the Director General of Railroads through the United States Railroad Administration.

Not Responsible. It is not responsible for errors in time tables, inconvenience or damage resulting from delayed trains or failure to make connection; schedules herein are subject to change without notice.

Buy Tickets before boarding trains and avoid payment of extra charge.

Children under 5 years of age free, when accompanied by parent or guardian; 5 years of age and under 12, one-half fare; 12 years of age or over, full fare.

Adjustment of Fares. In cases of dispute with Conductors or Agents, pay the fare required, take receipt and communicate with E. P. Cockrell, General Passenger Agent, Chicago.

Redemption of Tickets. Tickets unused, or partly used, will be redeemed under tariff regulations at proper value.

Baggage. 150 pounds of baggage will be carried free on each whole ticket and 75 pounds on each half ticket.

Baggage Maximums. No single piece of baggage exceeding **250** pounds in weight, or **72** inches in greatest dimension, or single shipment exceeding **$2,500.00** in value will be checked. Free allowances subject to tariff stipulations as to contents, weight, value and size.

Liability Limited. Excess value to be declared and paid for at time of checking.

Bicycles (not Motorcycles), **Baby Carriages, Dogs,** and **Guns** are transported in baggage cars subject to tariff regulations.

Lost Articles should be inquired for through General Passenger Department, Chicago, Superintendent, LaFayette, Ind., or nearest representative.

No responsibility is assumed for unchecked articles left in stations or cars.

Charges for Drawing-Rooms, Compartments and Sections. A minimum of one and one-half adult passage tickets will be required for the exclusive use of a section and two adult passage tickets will be required for the exclusive use of a drawing-room or compartment in all standard sleeping cars operated between all points on the Chicago, Indianapolis and Louisville R. R., also in all through standard sleeping cars operated between all points on the Chicago, Indianapolis & Louisville R. R., and points on or via other lines.

When members of the same family or party occupy one or more drawing rooms or compartments, extra tickets will not be required if the total number of tickets presented for the entire party is equivalent to two whole tickets for each drawing room or compartment and one and one-half tickets for each section.

Lost Tickets. If you lose your ticket you are out of pocket the value thereof. The railroad is under no obligation to give you another in its place nor to allow you to ride free. Give notice of your loss to the conductor. Pay your fare to him or purchase another ticket from first ticket station. Take conductor's or ticket agent's receipt for the amount paid. When you reach your destination write to the General Passenger Agent of the road of which you bought your ticket, enclose receipt and explain the circumstances. If your ticket is found and returned unused the railroad will refund your money.

Trains usually run on time, in accordance with time tables given herein, but no responsibility is assumed for consequences arising from delays, or from errors in the printed schedules.

Time from 12.01 midnight to 12.00 noon is shown by LIGHT faced figures, and time from 12.01 noon to 12.00 midnight by HEAVY faced figures.

PASSENGER TRAFFIC REPRESENTATIVES

Chicago, Ill................HERBERT WILEY, General Agent, Passenger Department, 608 So. Dearborn St.

French Lick Springs, Ind..F. R. HARRISON, District Passenger Agent

Indianapolis, Ind.........FRANK B. HUMSTON, Division Freight and Passenger Agent, Board of Trade Building

LaFayette, Ind............JOHN PRIEST, Traveling Passenger Agent North Street Station

Louisville, Ky.............E. H. BACON, Division Freight and Passenger Agent, Lincoln Trust Building

---

General Offices, Transportation Building,
Chicago, Ill.

Telephone, All Departments, Harrison 3309

CHAS. M. WOODMAN, Assistant General Passenger Agent......Chicago, Ill.

E. P. COCKRELL, General Passenger Agent....................Chicago, Ill.

Corrected to November 1, 1918

UNITED STATES RAILROAD ADMINISTRATION
W. G. McAdoo, Director General of Railroads

Chicago, Indianapolis & Louisville Railroad

MONON ROUTE

Time Tables

AVOID WASTE
KEEP THIS TIME TABLE

nearly a full century, to railroading's early years of drab and uninspired imprints. "The railroad folder will therefore devolve into a mere timetable," complained the *Buffalo Evening News.* "The effect of the order will put a crimp into the business of many printing establishments and another product of peaceful times made to feel the blight of war. Also an entertaining branch of American literature will be banished from national life." The USRA's abrupt curtailment of railroad literature, grumbled the *Indianapolis News,* was a "disturbing" example of federal authorities carrying a wartime economy program to its "logical extreme." Printing and publishing establishments within the United States employed about half a million people at the time, and thousands more worked in advertising, and McAdoo's directive thus affected many of their jobs. News outlets across the United States joined the public debate, and the *El Paso Herald,* seeking to strike a lighthearted note despite the grim tone of McAdoo's edict, declared: "Attacks of spring fever will be much lighter this year. There will be no railroad folders to make them virulent."[13]

In fairness to the director general, he implemented a drastic reduction in the print runs of timetables, but that was a reform many rail carriers had long wished to achieve. "Railroad time tables and folders are of all kinds; but they cost money and much more than they used to cost," noted the editor of the *Railway Age Gazette* in October 1917, three months before the federal takeover. "There was a time, not so many years ago, that time tables were issued in such large quantities that a large proportion of them had to be destroyed at each change of time. That condition has now been remedied on nearly every road, but there is still much waste." The journal noted that when travelers asked for a timetable for a train between two stations, ticket agents would invariably "pass out a complete booklet of almost all the trains on the system, when a very small folder giving only the trains in which the passenger is interested, would suffice. This is, of course, a tremendous waste." Likewise, the director general considered it unpatriotic for railroad rivals to squander the precious wartime resources required to make paper for brochures and other handouts that promoted vacation destinations or any land settlement schemes.[14]

Some newspaper editors disagreed with McAdoo's approval of the USRA's mandate, as did Secretary of the Interior Franklin K. Lane, a fellow member of Wilson's cabinet. Back in 1913, the initial year of the Wilson administration, Secretary Lane had vigorously promoted scenery as a valuable resource, a commodity that could be bought and sold like any other, except "that you can sell it over and over again without reducing the original bulk of the commodity." Given that Lane oversaw the national parks, his concept of scenery made sense. Some observers labeled it a new idea, and maybe it was within the isolated confines of the federal bureaucracy, but rail publicists had recognized the economic value of scenery for at least fifty years, or ever since the end of the Civil War in 1865.[15]

Lane's view of the positive value of scenery and his pushback against McAdoo's imposition of ugliness on railroad imprints won a rare exemption for USRA brochures that boosted national parks. The idea was that the USRA, as the sole issuer of national park publications, did not squander wartime resources, as multiple publications by railroad competitors supposedly would. However, a tagline in each USRA brochure continued to burnish McAdoo's name and title.[16]

McAdoo's political ambitions were clearly on display, but he failed to secure the Democratic Party's presidential nomination in 1920 and again in 1924, though at both conventions he led the field of candidates on the first ballot. One must wonder if McAdoo had "reverse charisma," with people liking him at first until his ego got in the way. In any case, in California the former rail czar found a second career as the general counsel for United Artists, the moviemakers. The voters of the Golden State sent him to Capitol Hill as one of their state's two United States senators in 1932. McAdoo's apparent "reverse charisma" contributed to his defeat for reelection six years later.[17]

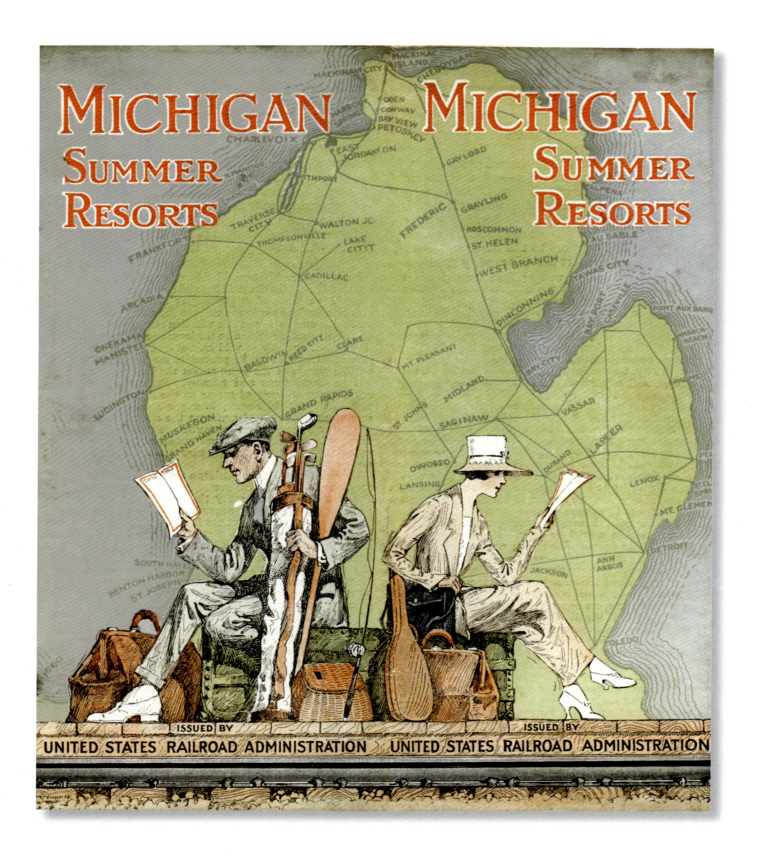

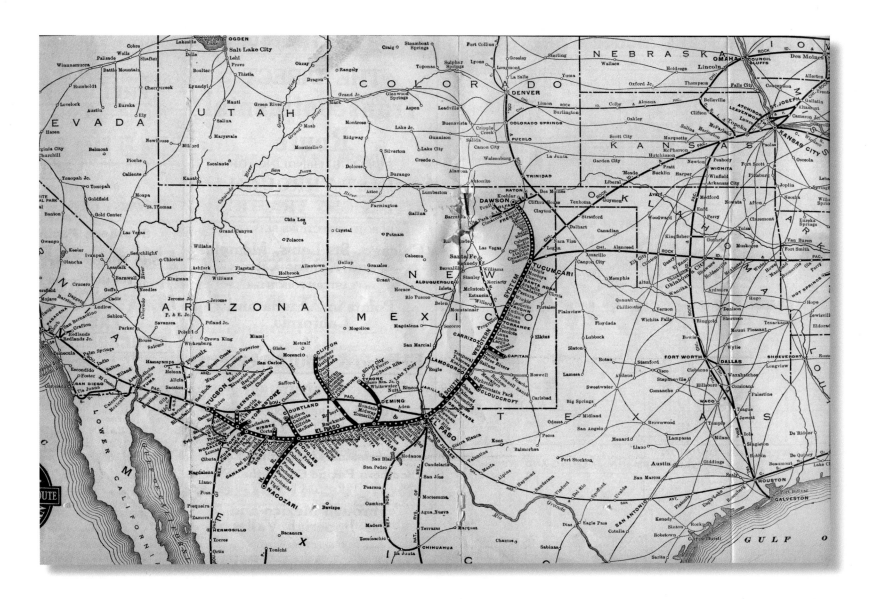

Facing, The United States Railroad Administration's *Michigan Summer Resorts* brochure appeared shortly before Uncle Sam returned rail carriers to their investor-owners in March 1920. Walker D. Hines, McAdoo's peacetime successor at the throttle of the USRA, took a more indulgent view of commercial art, and thus Uncle Sam published a series of attractive brochures devoted to national parks and other popular destinations.

Above, A timetable map the El Paso & Southwestern issued in 1924 reveals the railroad's relatively simple but efficient route structure during the years its tracks extended from Dawson, a Phelps Dodge coal town located in the Sangre de Cristo Mountains north of Tucumcari, New Mexico, to Tucson, Arizona, but with pre–World War I ambitions to build west to Los Angeles. Among its cargoes were trainloads of metallurgical coal hauled from Phelps Dodge mines in northern New Mexico to the copper company's big smelter in Douglas, Arizona, located just north of the international border. From there trains hauled the processed copper to an El Paso refinery for further purification, which yielded silver and gold as by-products.

McAdoo kept his heavy hand on the USRA throttle until shortly after the war ended in November 1918. His successor, Walker D. Hines, saw no reason to indulge his ego by plastering his name in every conceivable place likely to be seen by the traveling public, and he phased out the familiar tagline. An attorney and chairman of the board of the Atchison, Topeka & Santa Fe Railway when President Wilson tapped him to be McAdoo's assistant, Hines succeeded him in early 1919 to become the USRA's second (and final) director general.[18] His oversight during the USRA's transition to peacetime operations was not so strict as McAdoo's, nor was Hines consumed by political ambition as McAdoo was.[19]

The Great War ended in November 1918, but Uncle Sam kept the railroads in military uniform until March 1920 and only released them after a lengthy national debate over whether federal authorities should retain control of the rail carriers by transforming them into a government-owned enterprise. The debate ended with the March return of the railroads to their investor-owners. Within a matter of weeks, an array of colorful publications reappeared almost magically in rail stations and on timetable racks, and this simple act brought joy to many Americans who celebrated the nation's return to "normalcy."[20]

Already during the spring of 1919 when Walker D. Hines headed the USRA, rail advertising had been resurrected from its wartime grave with an appropriation of $800,000 to fund a limited campaign to boost national park visitation and some of America's more important health and pleasure resorts. The Great War had nonetheless changed the rail industry forever. The reasoning used to support a tentative return to publishing the railroad was that the industry needed passenger revenue, but "the public has not been traveling as it did in the prewar days," a development that alarmed "practical railroad men" within the USRA. The *International Railway Journal* insisted in August 1920 that "advertising can do a whole lot more for the railroads than it did in the past." Alas, the decline in passenger traffic, especially on local lines, only grew worse during the 1920s despite the best efforts of rail publicists.[21]

After Uncle Sam returned the nation's railroads to private ownership, some carriers chose never again to employ color graphics to add visual spice to timetable covers. In a world increasingly defined by highway competition and with rail industry operations tightly regulated by the Interstate Commerce Commission and other bureaucracies, some lines chose to maintain only a perfunctory level of passenger service through the 1920s and no longer published vacation or settlement brochures of any type.

Likewise gone with the war was the industry's former enthusiasm for the construction of new lines. Before the April declaration of war, a regional railroad, the El Paso & Southwestern, had considered forging yet another transcontinental link by connecting its tracks with those of the Chicago, Rock Island & Pacific at Tucumcari, New Mexico, and running trains through between Chicago and Los Angeles in booming Southern California. All that remained to achieve this dream was to extend its existing tracks five hundred miles west across the lightly populated desert landscape that separated Tucson, Arizona, and Los Angeles.[22]

In anticipation of becoming America's latest transcontinental railroad, the El Paso & Southwestern had apparently purchased land in Los Angeles on which to build a large station once its tracks arrived from Tucson, but the Great War and the austerity imposed by the USRA upended such plans. The railroad property in Los Angeles later became the site of the Los Angeles Union Passenger Terminal, a beautiful Spanish colonial structure that continues serve Amtrak passengers and Southern California commuters.[23]

The El Paso & Southwestern quietly merged with its onetime competitor, the Southern Pacific, in 1924. Tracks that in several places were located within sight of the international border with Mexico functioned as a secondary route for Southern Pacific trains traveling across the desert landscape that separated El Paso and Tucson, until the line was considered redundant and the rails pulled up. The El Paso & Southwestern depot in Tucson remains standing, and for several years the historic building found use as a popular restaurant.[24]

The return to normalcy is being indicated by many things. There is nothing that brings back to mind so vividly the "good old days" as to step into the Consolidated Ticket Office and take a look at the big case containing those highly colored folders, which the railroads were in the habit of issuing before the war.

—from *Shreveport Journal* (Louisiana), May 17, 1921

The Missouri Pacific's post–World War I *See the USA* brochure cover art conveyed the message that the grim days of government-mandated curtailments were over, colorful publications had come back, and the nation's scenic attractions once again beckoned to travelers.

20

AMERICA'S SECOND
TRANSPORTATION REVOLUTION

On October 1, 1920, the Southern Pacific Lines restored prewar luxuries to its Sunset Limited. The announcement was welcome news to travelers, but in almost every way there was no return to prewar times. Americans would never again see an annual uptick in rail mileage, as they had before 1916, and with the exception of World War II, they would not see rail ridership increase, as it usually did during the first seventeen years of the twentieth century. In fact, in terms of ridership the trend line pointed decidedly downward all through the 1920s, especially for local and branch-line rail passenger traffic.[1]

A compelling case can be made that during the past two centuries, North America experienced three revolutions in transportation that have positioned us where we are today. The first, as documented in detail by historian George Rogers Taylor, took place during the 1820s and 1830s and had as its centerpiece the steam-powered railroads that emerged during those two decades as vital conduits for passengers and freight. A second transportation revolution took place during the 1920s with the rapid rise of automobile ownership, the federal and state dollars lavished on the nation's fast-expanding network of all-weather highways, a noticeable decline in electric interurban traffic, and an equally worrisome falloff in steam railroad patronage aboard local trains that served sparsely populated rural areas. "The growth of motor transportation within recent years has been the most remarkable transportation development since the early construction of railroads."[2]

Until officials agreed to assign numbers to the federal highway network in 1926, America's most prominent motor corridors were promoted as named "trails." One of the coast-to-coast routes was the National Old Trails Highway, which east of Kansas City became US 40 and west became US 66, certainly the most celebrated motor route in American history. In an early 1920s brochure meant to advertise the route between Kansas City and Los Angeles, a gravel pathway that extended 1,886 miles across the sparsely populated Great Plains and the arid landscape of the Southwest, boosters assured motorists that "almost for the entire length of the highway, it is paralleled by the Santa Fe Railroad," which meant that tourists were never distant from towns that provided reasonably priced hotel accommodations and speedy access to automobile replacement parts in the event of a breakdown. Not only did railroads in this way blaze trails for highway travelers but their tracks helped visually orient early pilots carrying the mail.[3]

Toward the end of the transportation revolution of the 1920s, after Charles Lindbergh's epochal solo flight to Paris in 1927 made America conscious of aviation as no earlier flight milestones had done, several commercial airlines were launched. A few of these aviation ventures survived mergers and bankruptcies to become today's legacy carriers: American, Delta, and United. "Travel speeds, which made those of the fastest trains look slow by comparison, are the steady pace of modern transport airplanes," observed *Railway Age* in a 1933 article titled "Old Ways Are Not Good Enough."[4]

America's third revolution in transportation took place during the 1950s and 1960s with the construction of a modern interstate highway network starting in 1956 and the arrival of commercial aviation's jet age just three years later in 1959; both events contributed to a steady decline in railroad passenger traffic after mid-decade and all through the 1960s. Finally, the removal of mail from the railroads starting in 1958, a federal subsidy that had helped to underwrite the cost of many passenger trains that otherwise lost money, contributed to the transportation revolution of the 1950s and 1960s. Massive cuts of mail by rail occurred most notably in 1967.

With few exceptions, we are still living with the legacy of America's third revolution in transportation. After a dazzling interlude that featured supersonic jet transport, travelers have remained satisfied to ride aboard commercial jets that fly no faster today than they did in 1959, more than sixty years ago, but that are far less comfortable for passengers squeezed tightly into economy seats. The automobile of 2025 is functionally the same as an automobile of the 1920s, though modern vehicles offer significantly greater safety and mechanical reliability. In terms of propulsion, many more electric and hybrid-electric cars are cruising America's roads today than in the 1950s, but in a way this change represents little more than an update of automotive technology popular at the dawn of the twentieth century, when one-third of all motor vehicles then cruising the nation's streets and highways featured storage batteries to provide electrical energy.[5]

Let us return now to study further the transportation revolution of the 1920s, the only one of the three epochs that took place when railroads had the motivation and means to excel as publishers and thus maintained their rich and varied publishing legacy of earlier years. As noted in the previous chapter, when Uncle Sam returned the nation's railroads to their investor-owners in March 1920, the industry's enthusiasm for new construction had vanished, and it never would return to prewar levels. The network of railroad lines across the United States peaked in 1916 at 250,000 miles and then began to shrink, very slightly at first, during the postwar years.[6]

After the conflict ended, a host of new challenges bedeviled the industry. Foremost was the largely unregulated highway competition that resulted from the rapid growth of intercity bus and truck lines during the 1920s, but even more worrisome was the ever-rising number of private automobiles. "Nothing could better illustrate the revolution within recent years in the tastes and habits, and especially the traveling habits, of the American people, than the way in which the railways have been affected by it. Prior to 1920 there was an increase in their passenger business almost every year." Afterward and throughout the 1920s, nearly every issue of *Railway Age* noted the ongoing decline in passenger traffic. "It is 20,600,000 private automobiles, and not the 90,000 motor coaches, that are responsible for this continuing decline in railway passenger revenue," and no one could predict with assurance how much more rail travel would decline during the years ahead.[7]

Despite the noticeable impact of highway competition on rail earnings, the regulatory burden imposed during the Progressive Era remained in place and was justified by the outdated presumption of the industry's monopoly power. The big challenge for rail executives was how best to adjust to the unfamiliar new era of competition that, with the benefit of hindsight, can be labeled the transportation revolution of the 1920s: "Although still in its infancy, highway transportation has removed all doubt that it will eventually take an important place in our national transportation system."[8]

To fight the competition, railroads lavished attention on their long-distance trains, but to stem mounting losses from their many branch-line locals, companies often replaced steam-powered trains with "doodlebugs," or internal combustion rail motor cars. "In many places highway motor coaches can be substituted for unprofitable trains by cooperating with coach operators, or by the railways controlling the motor coach companies themselves." Perhaps, mused the editor of *Railway Age* in late 1927, the decline in local traffic was inevitable: "In a sparsely settled territory where all the traffic ever available justified a railroad running but two trains a day, one could scarcely expect a man to lose a whole day in making a 12-mile round trip by train, when he could make it in his car in an hour or two."[9]

With their return to private hands, many of the larger railroads of the United States resumed their roles as publishers, and their timetables regained much of their former eye appeal. Though railroads largely abandoned their promotion of western settlement, in no small part because their effort to populate and build traffic along their tracks had been so successful during the prewar years, they did continue to promote the settlement of Florida in the 1920s—as well as winter vacations in Florida, along the Gulf Coast, in the deserts of Arizona and Southern California, and deep into Mexico. Americans were traveling as never before. In the spring of 1928, the industry's leading trade journal advised, "It is not too soon to begin such advertising, since vacations are already being planned."[10]

Railroad publishing that promoted travel by train to mountain resorts throughout New England to escape the summer heat and humidity regained their former eye appeal. For the Southern Railway that meant encouraging people once again to vacation in Asheville and other places in the highlands of western North Carolina, while the Bangor & Aroostook resumed its annual appeal to hunters and fishermen to escape to the woods and lakes of northern Maine. Midwestern railroads resumed their promotion of cool lakeside retreats in Michigan and northern Wisconsin. Travelers were once again urged to board trains for the Rocky Mountain resorts of Colorado and Montana, Yellowstone National Park in Wyoming, and the Black Hills of South Dakota, a pleasant retreat given invaluable publicity when the president of the United States, Calvin Coolidge, chose to vacation there.

By the mid-1920s the highways of the United States had become good enough to support the creation of numerous intercity bus lines. The threshold to entry was very low, and apart from licensing and state-imposed safety regulations, all one needed to enter the bus business in many states was a vehicle or two. Among the first railroads to recognize the value of a bus subsidiary of their own was the Spokane, Portland & Seattle, which in the mid-1920s commenced to operate a fleet of thirty buses between Portland and Seaside, Oregon, to supplement its passenger trains.[11]

Within a matter of months, the Great Northern emerged as America's largest railway bus operator. Its subsidiary, Northland Transportation Company, operated 140 motor coaches along three thousand miles of highway to offer reliable coordinated service with its trains in Minnesota. By the close of the decade, dozens of major rail lines across the United States had launched intercity motorbus subsidiaries of their own, as did some of the smaller carriers like Maine's Bangor & Aroostook. One western railroad operated 275 buses.[12]

By late 1925 it was possible for a hearty and economy-minded soul to ride intercity buses from coast to coast (more or less). The transcontinental journey cost $127.14 but required *forty-one* different carriers and included two interurbans and several steam railroad rides to bridge gaps and connect with various bus lines then in operation. Even when the transcontinental journey could be made entirely by motor coach, it was a long and tiresome odyssey. By the late 1920s a few West Coast intercity carriers sought to ease the discomfort of long-distance highway travel with luxurious buses that featured private beds intended to pamper overnight riders.[13]

Financial privation during the early years of the Great Depression increased the desire of travelers for low-cost alternatives to railroads, which boosted the popularity of the intercity bus

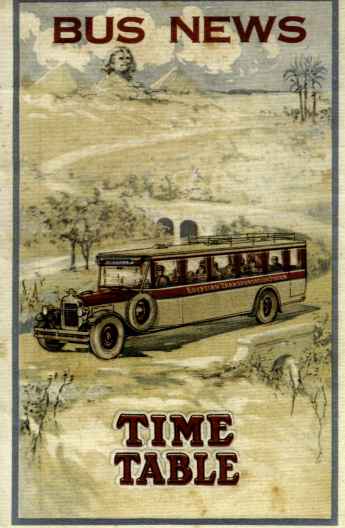

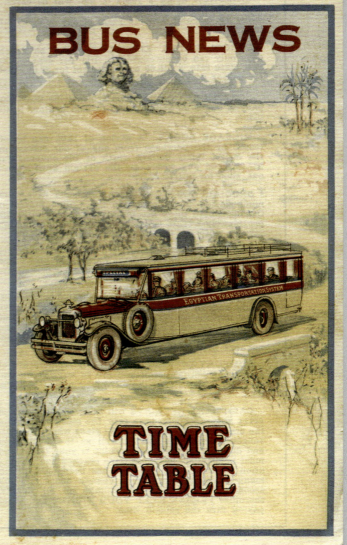

As a color for the exterior of the new train, canary yellow was selected after exhaustive tests. It was chosen as an additional safety measure. Canary yellow can be seen for a greater distance than any other color and its blended combination with golden brown trim constitutes one of the outstanding features of the train.

SUPER SPEED—WITH SAFETY—AND COMFORT

Facing, This example of commercial art from 1929 appeared on the timetable cover of an Illinois bus line called the Egyptian Transportation System. It was clearly an exercise in geographic fantasy worthy of high-spirited railroad publicists during their pre–World War I heyday and was perhaps inspired by their aesthetic indulgences. The inside joke that was the basis for the curious example of commercial art is that southern Illinois is known locally as Little Egypt because one of the region's important communities at the time was Cairo (which within the surrounding area is pronounced "Kay-row" and which, because it lacks pyramids and palm trees, bears no resemblance to the Egyptian capital).

Above, The Union Pacific saluted its futuristic (for the mid-1930s) M-10000 Train by publishing a colorful brochure. Several different railroads' nearly simultaneous introduction of streamlined trains powered by internal combustion engines foreshadowed the coming demise of steam and the triumph of diesel propulsion along the tracks of North America.

lines. By 1933 the nation's bus operators could brag that forty-five thousand communities and 10 percent of Americans had no rail service and were wholly dependent on highway alternatives: "What the motor truck has done for the economic welfare of the people, the motor bus has contributed to their social and cultural advancement."[14]

Perhaps because railroads were early operators of intercity bus lines, many motor coach operators emulated them by publishing visually attractive timetables and various brochures promoting vacation travel by bus. Some companies published route guides that explained to bus passengers some of the landscape features they observed outside the coach windows. "Cleanliness, comfort, and the beauty of the scenery bordering our highways have given to the American traveler the same advantages in bus travel that he secures when using his own car."[15]

The final additions to the changing transportation mix of the 1920s were the first commercial airlines with staying power. As with intercity bus operators, entrepreneurs who desired to launch an airline need only cross a low threshold, but to keep an airline aloft required a combination of good luck, intelligent management, profitable routes, and reasonably steady cash flow. Absent any one of those four, and an airline likely faced a bleak future. Adverse publicity from a crash might shake the confidence of travelers and investors alike and ground a once-promising airline venture.[16]

History does not usually divide neatly into decades, but the 1920s seem to offer an exception. During the opening months of 1920, Uncle Sam returned the railroads to their private owners. During the closing months of 1929, a stock market crash presaged hard times and a host of new economic challenges ahead. Looking back to 1920, one could say that during that decade the railroads faced competition as never before and that intermodal rivalry remade the industry, especially its passenger services, in dramatic ways that affected the attractive publications intended for public consumption.

One way that railroads during the 1920s responded to the rising tide of competition was to give greater emphasis to the interior design of long-distance passenger trains: "In several cases, for instance, colonial types of ornamentation and furnishings have been adapted with highly pleasing results." The inspiration in large measure of the "systematic utilization of aesthetic values" was the automobile, which had evolved from an "awkward looking contraption" into "a thing of beauty, and the latest models represent fine examples of the possibilities of the application of artistic principles to mechanical." Railroads, observed the editor of *Railway Age* in 1934, were likewise moving "in the direction of higher artistic standards without seriously narrowing the range of efficient engineering." The result was a revolution in styling.[17]

During the 1930s, the Union Pacific and Chicago, Burlington & Quincy each unveiled passenger trains during mid-decade that heralded the coming demise of steam on railroads around the world. Both featured internal combustion engines and innovative styling inside and out that mirrored the art deco motif popular during the Depression and among the designers of the first streamlined automobiles and airliners. Railroads, of course, hastened to publicize their latest contributions to speed, comfort, safety, and modernity.[18]

The Union Pacific's City of Salina and the Burlington's Zephyr both debuted in 1934. After a tour that wowed more than a million onlookers in sixty-five cities across the United States, the City of Salina shuttled daily between Kansas City, Missouri, and Salina, Kansas, for the next eight years. A rapid series of improvements to diesel-powered streamliners rendered the City of Salina obsolete, and during World War II it was scrapped "so that its precious aluminum [might] fight the nation's enemies." As for railroad publicists, their task now was to promote patriotism and, ironically, to discourage rail travel by civilians by asking a formerly unthinkable question: "Is your trip necessary?"[19]

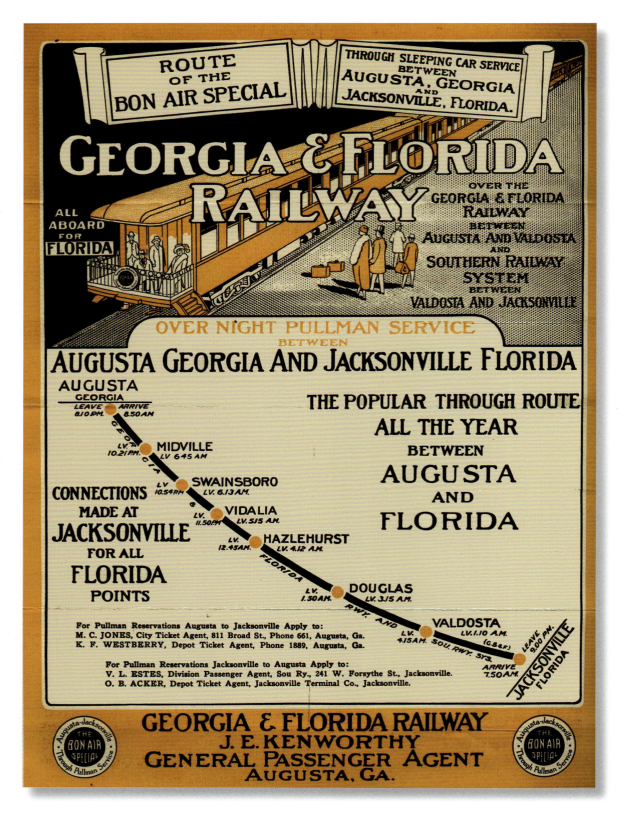

Of all modes of transport, the train is perhaps the best aid to thought. The views have none of the potential monotony of those on a ship or a plane, moving quickly enough for us not to get exasperated but slowly enough to allow us to identify objects.

—from Alain de Botton, *The Art of Travel* (2002)[1]

A map intended to promote the Georgia & Florida during the 1920s and 1930s indulged in the usual creative fantasy of straightening curves along the route of its Bon-Air Special as it plodded across Georgia between Augusta and Jacksonville, Florida.

CONCLUSION

PUTTING THINGS IN PERSPECTIVE

Publicizing the railroad, as distinct from various other types of publishing activity, was not limited to paper and artwork, as is exemplified by the exhibit cars operated by several different carriers. None of these forms of publicity could compare with the head-on collision of two locomotives staged in 1896 by the Missouri-Kansas-Texas Railway in central Texas, an oddball event immortalized by the ragtime king, Scott Joplin, in his "Great Crush Collision March," which he dedicated to the railroad.[2]

During the century of commercial art featured in *Railroad Nation*, no industry loomed larger in North America than the railroad. At the dawn of the twentieth century, railroad securities dominated the New York Stock Exchange. Likewise, railroads were by far the most significant providers of transportation across North America, and no other industry equaled it as a multifaceted publisher of anything and everything that suited its fancy. Previous chapters have highlighted several broad categories of publications that served the commercial interests of North America's rail industry, but as I noted earlier, publications occasionally defy easy classification, as do some illustrations.

On the conservative end of the visual spectrum was the Lehigh Valley, one of several railroads that gained recognition as a hauler of anthracite coal from the mines of eastern Pennsylvania to markets in New York City and Philadelphia. Year after year its twentieth-century timetable covers featured the same basic design, drab in its unimaginative imagery and drab in its unimaginative use of color—text on a dark green background. That said, the Lehigh Valley created visually arresting brochures to promote vacation travel. Perhaps the railroad's managers saw little value in spending thousands of dollars annually to print attractive timetables that the typical passenger used once or twice and then threw away.

At the other end of the publishing spectrum was the Missouri-Kansas-Texas, which seldom used the same timetable cover design twice. Moreover, some of its many different contributions to rail graphics leave modern readers wondering what messages management intended to convey with the assortment of brochures and pamphlets published during the 1870s and 1880s. Some of its oddball publications may have been intended solely to keep the Missouri-Kansas-Texas in the public consciousness of the southwestern states and territories it served.

If their primary purpose was to keep the railroad in the public consciousness, then the Katy—in fact, nearly all North American railroads—had thousands of allies in the newspapers published daily or weekly across the continent that regularly printed train times in every issue. Seldom, however, did any money change hands. Instead, until the practice was outlawed in the United States in the early twentieth century, railroads gave journal editors and publishers free passes for travel in exchange for printing their advertisements and schedules in the popular press and in this way, perhaps, promoting a positive image of the industry in their feature stories. Indeed, a seemingly endless stream of news articles about railroads did loom large in turn-of-the-century newspapers. Often a prominent portion of page 1 was devoted to railroad news, and not just to the occasional train wreck. Mundane news items told of promotions, retirements, and even births and deaths within the local community of railroaders. In a small community like Parsons, Kansas, which functioned as the beating heart of the Missouri-Kansas-Texas system, such details were of personal interest to readers, but rail news and feature stories appeared also in general interest newspapers published in cities and villages that had no close ties to the rail industry.

It was the same for the interurban electric railways that grew in prominence after 1900. Newspapers of the Midwest, a region in which interurban enthusiasm ran amok, devoted so much space to the industry that they often grouped many brief bits of news under text headings labeled "Interurban Items." Because the typical interurban railway was much like a city trolley enterprise on steroids and seldom covered distances greater than fifty miles, electric lines had no incentive to print settlement brochures of any type (mainly because the federal government had terminated its generous giveaway of land to steam railroads long before the first electric interurban turned a wheel). It was the same for vacation come-ons, and with cars that ran at frequent intervals, often every thirty minutes, timetables with eye appeal were unnecessary. A few electric interurban railways published colorful ones, but most were drab but functional listings printed on cheap paper.

During the heyday of railroad publishing, an unusual term gained currency among ticket agents (and within some police departments): *timetable fiend*, a mildly pejorative turn of phrase I mentioned briefly in chapter 12. During the late nineteenth century, newspapers commonly labeled photo enthusiasts Kodak fiends, a term that referenced the introduction in 1888 of Eastman Kodak film and cameras that made snapshot photography fun and accessible to anyone. The timetable variety of "fiends" were those individuals who raided recently stocked timetable racks and often cleaned them out, though they had no intention of traveling anywhere by train. Their journeys were wholly imaginary, made with the aid of published schedules. Some enthusiasts were attracted, no doubt, to the artwork or to the maps. One extreme example from 1878 was the "mysterious old gentleman who has been going around to the different hotels and appropriating the railway circulars that are placed there for the use of travelers." When Saint Louis police arrested the "timetable fiend," they recovered nearly five pounds of rail imprints stuffed into his pockets and boots: "Officers found his lodgings to be overflowing with paper he had accumulated over the years." What to do? "He cannot be convicted of larceny," observed a slightly bemused editor, "as railway circulars in hotels are placed there for free distribution."[3]

It is not possible to be a rail "timetable fiend" today because those useful paper documents no longer exist, apart from a variety of small ones published for commuter lines, and even some of those have been replaced by internet listings. Some of us are still fond of collecting timetables even if there are none on literature racks for us to raid. *Ephemera* is the term that best describes this category of historical documents. They were originally intended to be ephemeral, at least that seemed to be the presumption of publishers, who expected this form of paper to be used for a specific purpose for a limited time and then tossed away, as most were. A few were tossed into desk drawers and forgotten. That was fortunate because one way or another a representative number of the multimillion booklets, brochures, and public timetables published by the railroads of North America has survived. Examples are bought and sold daily on eBay, and timetable collectors occasionally pay $1,000 or more to add a rare piece of paper ephemera to their holdings.

There is a society of like-minded enthusiasts who salute the transportation publishing tradition of former years with their journal, the *Timetable Collector*. Similarly, ephemera enthusiasts, who are serious collectors of everything from historic valentines and the business trade cards formerly distributed by merchants of all types of goods to cigar and fruit crate labels, have their Ephemera Society of America, an organization formed in 1980 and now the publisher three times a year of a beautifully illustrated magazine titled the *Ephemera Journal*.

A Handy Shipping Service

PRACTICALLY everywhere you travel by railroad, you will find nearby this convenient, swift and dependable shipping medium —Railway Express service.

Whether it be a package or your pets or your luggage, or almost anything on earth you wish to have transported carefully and quickly, the Railway Express will be glad to take care of it for you.

They will carry it through to destination speedily, safely and at very reasonable cost.

Our nearest representative is eager to serve you.

RAILWAY EXPRESS AGENCY

INCORPORATED

"Dependable for Anything Sendable"

Printed in U. S. A.

WE SHIP BY
RAILWAY
EXPRESS

Sending Your Packages

Railway Express Agency served as the express handmaiden of the rail industry from 1919 to 1975. Its pea-green trucks facilitated the movement of parcels between the railroads and local pickup and delivery sites, including individual homes.

RAILROAD EPHEMERA EMULATORS

Because of years of railroad publishing, examples of graphic arts intended to promote sales already existed for the rising automobile industry to emulate. That is, the automakers as well as various businesses located along the evolving highway habitat continued the publishing tradition inaugurated by North America's rail lines, and over the years they too generated an enormous number of colorful brochures that fall under the definition of *ephemera*. These might include brochures published annually to advertise various makes of new automobiles and given away to potential customers in dealers' showrooms or flyers that urge motorists to eat at a particular restaurant or to sleep at a roadside motor court or motel. The array of paper giveaways includes the attractive maps that service stations once provided free to motorists to encourage the highway travel that made money for petroleum marketers like Texaco, Mobil, and numerous others.

A modern feature of the highway habitat is the welcome center located at the border of many states. These buildings typically feature display racks stuffed with promotional brochures intended to encourage motorists to visit historical sites or to stay at a particular motel or hotel—and, of course, to spend money within the state. The display racks are in many ways a throwback to those found in railroad stations during an earlier era.

As a boy in 1957, I became fascinated with railroad timetables and later with copies of the *Official Guide*, two forms of ephemera, though I did not realize that my little collection of printed paper came with such an impressive name. Over the years my stash of transportation ephemera grew steadily larger (even as the variety and availability of paper travel documents shrank). Thus, it seemed logical to include in *Railroad Nation* an example of bus and airline transportation ephemera with artwork apparently inspired by railroad publishers. The visual text provides a nice complement to the verbal text, a form of enhancement that designers of railroad brochures were encouraged to recognize and implement more than a century ago.

NEW YORK

by CLIPPER

PAN AMERICAN WORLD AIRWAYS
THE WORLD'S MOST EXPERIENCED AIRLINE

Many additional items of railroad ephemera remain outside the scope of *Railroad Nation*, which makes no pretense of being comprehensive. This group includes posters and calendars, two broad categories of published material intended for public consumption that are usually as bold in their use of commercial art as rail brochures, pamphlets, and timetables—and sometimes far more so.[4] In-house ephemera of interest to collectors include the passes given to railroad employees, exchanged among industry executives, and formerly distributed to newspaper editors, judges, and politicians as a subtle bribe. In one of their smarter moves, Progressive Era activists of the early twentieth century regarded this as influence peddling and successfully banned the giveaway of free passes to people outside the rail industry.

Again, despite my necessary omissions, I hope that *Railroad Nation* provides a representative sample of the commercial art that the rail industry used to transform time and space across North America. Some fifty years ago, most North American railroads shucked their long-distance passenger trains, often with a sense of relief, and Amtrak in the United States and Via Rail in Canada thereupon assumed responsibility for maintaining a skeletal travel network in each country. In places like the Northeast Corridor between Washington and Boston via Philadelphia and New York, Amtrak trains are fast and frequent and provide a valuable service that in connecting one downtown with another is competitive with air travel. Similar successful segments exist in densely populated portions of California.[5]

As for publishing the railroad today, little need exists. Amtrak jettisoned a systemwide timetable in favor of an online site that lists train times and sells tickets. In much the same way, airline and bus timetables and other promotional materials have largely vanished. With the COVID-19 crisis, many air carriers jettisoned the flight magazines once found in seat-back pockets. In similar fashion, service station giveaway maps disappeared during the energy crisis of the early 1970s. Various commuter rail lines still distribute paper timetables, as do some transport providers abroad, but these too will likely join the lengthening list of vanished but collectible reminders of past practices.

From paper timetables and airline magazines to phone booths and cassettes, useful items regularly come and go as a result of changing technologies and changing popular tastes and fashions. Postcards, introduced in the early twentieth century, were once the rage as a means of personal communication, but email and smartphones offer a better two-way exchange today. I only wonder what types of ephemera will disappear next.

Quite apart from their mostly vanished publishing activity, the railroads of North America in one way or another still support long-distance passenger trains, even if not with enthusiasm. Travel by train remains for me a truly magical experience regardless of the geographical location, though nowadays I prefer riding the rails of Great Britain and continental Europe and the long-distance limiteds operated by Amtrak across the United States since 1971, which still bear legacy names like Empire Builder, California Zephyr, and Sunset Limited, though these trains seem to have devolved into a shadow of what they once were.[6]

In Britain, journeys that begin or end within one of the modern cathedrals of commerce like London's incomparable Paddington or St. Pancras stations offer an unfailing source of pleasure and occasional inspiration and insight to this retired history professor who continues to enjoy the creativity involved in researching, writing, and illustrating a new book to share with interested readers. May *Railroad Nation* inspire happy travels, even if only in readers' imaginations.[7]

The Midland Railway's historic St. Pancras Station in London remains an alluring cathedral of commerce, and especially so because from under its capacious train shed the international trains of Eurostar dash beneath the English Channel to link the capital cities of the United Kingdom and France.

Commerce is the child of transportation. Every forward step in the progress of the human race has been the direct result of improvement in methods of communication.

—from Commercial Travelers Club, *Trade and Travel* (1895)[8]

The artwork used to showcase the Southern Railway's *Augusta Special* brochure of 1916 evokes the sense of anticipation that rail travelers felt as they prepared to board a long-distance passenger train.

The Reading Railroad profited from a dense network of tracks spread across the anthracite coal country of eastern Pennsylvania, but it also advertised the many scenic attractions served by its passenger trains. These included not only the many historical sights contained in Philadelphia but also the Revolutionary War battlefield park of Valley Forge. This image was featured on the front cover of its 1925 *Pleasant Places* brochure.

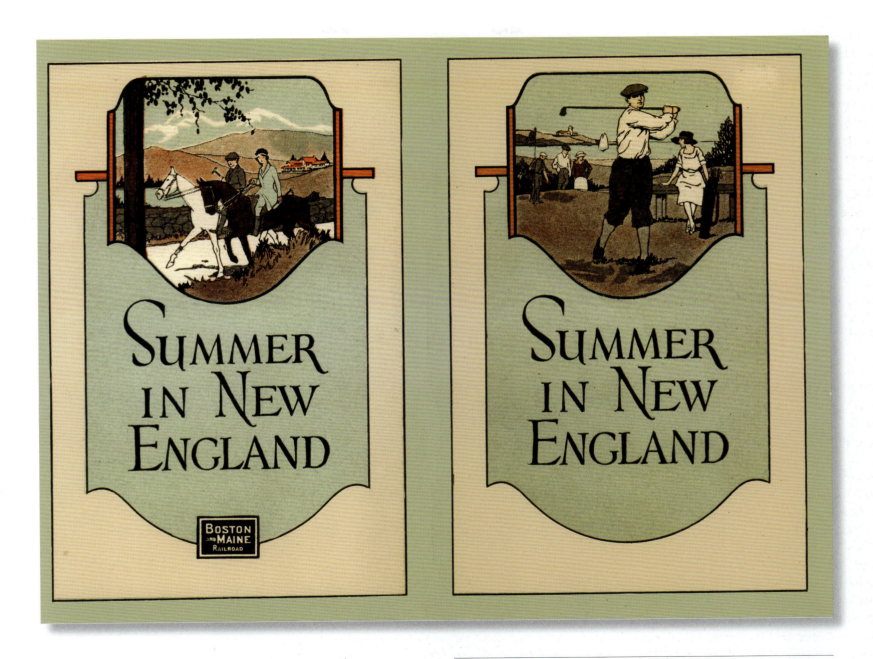

The several large railroads that served the six New England states—including the New Haven, Boston & Maine; Boston & Albany; Vermont Central; Rutland; and Maine Central—had little reason to promote settlement, but all published attractive brochures devoted to vacation travel. The Boston & Maine's *Summer in New England* (1924) is one result of their rivalry.

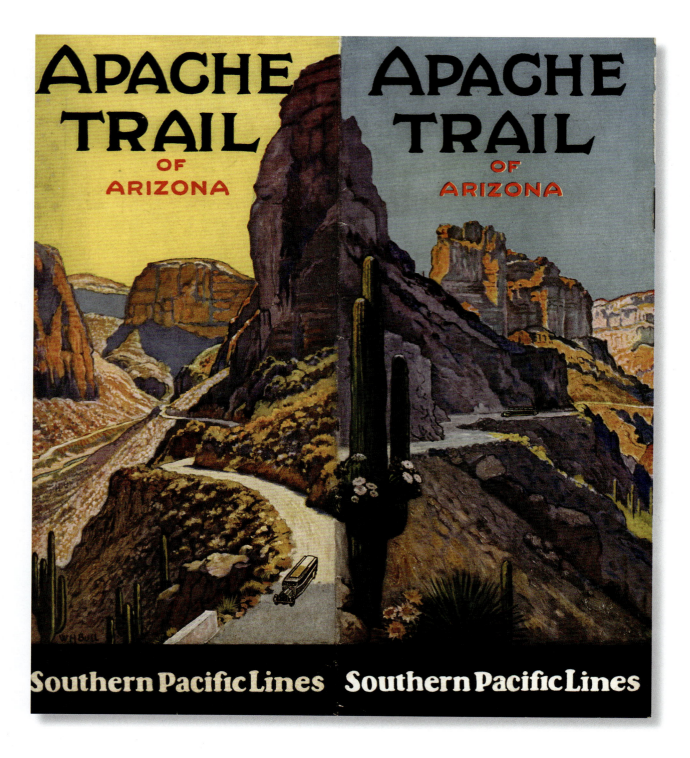

I end my admittedly personal exploration of railroad time and space and the commercial art it inspired with a bold cover image the Southern Pacific used during the 1920s to promote its Apache Trail detours through the dramatic desert landscape of central Arizona. This is my favorite among the many compelling images used to enliven railroad imprints as I sought to showcase them for readers of *Railroad Nation*.

NOTES

PREFACE AND ACKNOWLEDGMENTS

1. Ian Kennedy and Julian Treuhertz, *The Railway: Art in the Age of Steam* (New Haven, CT: Yale University Press, 2008). See also Gareth Rees, *Early Railway Prints: A Social History of the Railways from 1825 to 1850* (Oxford: Phaidon, 1980); C. Hamilton Ellis, *Railway Art* (Boston: New York Graphic Society, 1977); Sandra D'Emilio and Suzan Campbell, *Visions and Visionaries: The Art & Artists of the Santa Fe Railway* (Layton, UT: Peregrine Smith, 1991); David Hockney and Martin Gayford, *A History of Pictures: From the Cave to the Computer Screen* (New York: Abrams, 2016). In response to the contrary claim that railroad landscapes were, in fact, unsightly, one railroad publication said that "the making of a railroad is necessarily an ugly work" and its excavation is "likely to destroy the harmony and natural beauty of the landscape for a time, but when once constructed there is nothing to offend the eye." It concluded its essay on railroad aesthetics with another bold claim: "Our railways are a majestic construction, grand and awe-inspiring to behold in their wonderful winding courses, and are suggestive of vast power, great genius and enterprise and myriad labor." *West Shore Railroad Suburban Times*, September 1890, 2. The art showcased in the Kennedy and Treuhertz book would certainly support this claim.

2. The Frisco Line, as was its chosen nickname in 1901, underwent periodic reorganizations, a process common to many railroads over the years. For legal reasons, at such times they made minor modifications to their formal corporate titles. In later years it was the Saint Louis-San Francisco Railway Company. Likewise, another Saint Louis–based carrier was at various times the Missouri, Kansas & Texas Railway System or the Missouri-Kansas-Texas Railroad Company. I seek to use a consistent corporate moniker throughout *Railroad Nation*.

3. Jay T. Last, *The Color Explosion: Nineteenth-Century American Lithography* (Santa Ana, CA: Hillcrest, 2005). The *International Railway Journal* offers a treasure trove of information about the railroad as publisher (with numerous examples of the evolution of railway advertisements from 1892 through the 1920s). Its original title was *International Passenger and Ticket Agents' Journal*, which is why the monthly devoted so much attention over the years to railroad ticket sellers and station agents and their role as the primary dispensers of information and literature to the traveling public.

4. *Official Guide*, July 1892, xix. A similar publication—in fact, the Bangor & Aroostook Railroad's most impressive annual offering for several decades—was titled *In the Maine Woods*. Its contents were "of the sort that arouse all the latent instincts of the primitive man, to lock his desk and get into the woods with rod and gun." A key feature of the Maine guidebook was its photographs, "of which there are many, showing bits of landscape, mountain and lake, hunting and fishing scenes, game, guides, and sportsmen, taken on the spot." *Official Guide*, April 1900, xxvii.

5. Edward Hungerford, "Railroad Advertising," *Railway Age Gazette*, May 14, 1915, 1012–1014. At this time Hungerford was the advertising manager for Wells, Fargo. Among his numerous

books was *The Modern Railroad* (1911). See also Alfred D. Chandler Jr., *The Railroads: The Nation's First Big Business* (New York: Harcourt, Brace & World, 1965); James A. Ward, *Railroads and the Character of America, 1820–1887* (Knoxville: University of Tennessee Press, 1986); Maury Klein, *Unfinished Business: The Railroad in American Life* (Hanover, NH: University Press of New England, 1994).

6. Tad Burness, *Classic Railroad Advertising: Riding the Rails Again* (Iola, WI: Krause, 2001); Keith Lovegrove, *Railroad Identity, Design and Culture* (New York: Rizzoli, 2005).

7. Walker D. Hines, *War History of American Railroads* (New Haven, CT: Yale University Press, 1928).

8. For more on Downing and his remarkable railroad career, which spanned the years 1935–1979, see Robert Downing, "Managerial Leadership in Transportation" (presentation, Robert W. Downing lecture series, Lexington Group, Saint Paul, MN, 2002). Also valuable is Downing, interview by Don L. Hofsommer, 1993, transcribed by Gregory P. Ames, John W. Barriger III National Railroad Library, Saint Louis.

9. William S. Greever, *Arid Domain: The Santa Fe Railway and Its Western Land Grant* (Stanford, CA: Stanford University Press, 1954). I use the term *Official Guide* throughout *Railroad Nation*, though the publication's title varied during the decades after it first appeared in June 1868 as the *Travelers' Official Railway Guide of the United States and Canada*. In 1957 when a kindly ticket agent at the Indianapolis Union Station gifted me with my first copy, its title had evolved to *The Official Guide of the Railways and Steam Navigation Lines of the United States, Porto Rico, Canada, Mexico and Cuba*. It added timetables for Cuba in 1899 after the Spanish-American War.

10. Edward W. Nolan, *Northern Pacific Views: The Railroad Photography of F. Jay Haynes, 1876–1905* (Helena: Montana Historical Society Press, 1983).

11. Christopher Rund, Fred W. Frailey, and Eric Powell, *The Indiana Rail Road Company: America's New Regional Railroad*, rev. ed. (Bloomington: Indiana University Press, 2012); Maurice W. Kirby, *The Origins of Railway Enterprise: The Stockton and Darlington Railway, 1821–1863* (Cambridge: Cambridge University Press, 1993); David Gwyn, *The Coming of the Railway: A New Global History, 1750–1850* (New Haven, CT: Yale University Press, 2023).

12. Carlos Arnaldo Schwantes, *Going Places: Transportation Redefines the Twentieth-Century West* (Bloomington: Indiana

University Press, 2003); Carlos A. Schwantes, *Just One Restless Rider: Reflections on Trains and Travel* (Columbia: University of Missouri Press, 2009).

13. Carlos A. Schwantes, *Railroad Signatures Across the Pacific Northwest* (Seattle: University of Washington Press, 1993); Carlos A. Schwantes and James P. Ronda, *The West the Railroads Made* (Seattle: University of Washington Press, 2008).

INTRODUCTION

1. Alfred D. Chandler Jr., *The Railroads: The Nation's First Big Business* (New York: Harcourt, Brace & World, 1965). My favorite historical overview is H. Roger Grant, *Railroads and the American People* (Bloomington: Indiana University Press, 2012), to which he has more recently added two companion volumes: *Electric Interurbans and the American People* (Bloomington: Indiana University Press, 2016); and *Transportation and the American People* (Bloomington: Indiana University Press, 2019).

2. Ellen Fletcher Rosebrock, *South Street: A Photographic Guide to New York City's Historic Seaport* (New York: Dover, 1977).

3. K. D. Kurutz and Gary F. Kurutz, *California Calls You: The Art of Promoting the Golden State, 1870 to 1940* (Sausalito, CA: Windgate, 2000). On the art of railroad posters, I defer to Michael E. Zega and John E. Gruber, *Travel by Train: The American Railroad Poster, 1870–1950* (Bloomington: Indiana University Press, 2002). Also of value are Beverley Cole and Richard Durack, *Railway Posters, 1923–1947* (York, UK: National Railway Museum, 1992); Terri J. Edelstein, ed., *Art for All: British Posters for Transport* (New Haven, CT: Yale University, 2010); J. T. Shackleton, *The Golden Age of Railway Posters* (Secaucus, NJ: Chartwell Books, 1976); Max Gallo, *The Poster in History* (New York: W. W. Norton, 2001); and Anna Villari and Dario Cimorelli, *Manifesti Posters: Traveling around Italy through Advertising, 1895–1960* (Milan: Silvana Editoriale Spa, 2010).

4. Tom D. Kilton, "The American Railroad as Publisher, Bookseller, and Librarian," *Journal of Library History* 17, no. 1 (Winter 1982): 39–64. See also E. J. Hart, *The Selling of Canada: The CPR and the Beginnings of Canadian Tourism* (Banff: Altitude, 1983); Marc H. Choko and David L. Jones, *Posters of the Canadian Pacific* (Richmond Hill, ON: Firefly Books, 2004).

5. Jay T. Last, *The Color Explosion: Nineteenth-Century American Lithography* (Santa Ana, CA: Hillcrest, 2005); Philip B. Meggs and Alston W. Purvis, *Meggs' History of Graphic Design,*

4th ed. (Hoboken: John Wiley & Sons, 2006). Electric interurban railways were not noted for their color printing activity except for Indiana's Chicago South Shore & South Bend Line. See Ronald D. Cohen and Stephen G. McShane, eds., *Moonlight in Duneland: The Illustrated Story of the Chicago South Shore and South Bend Railroad* (Bloomington: Indiana University Press, 1998).

6. Michael Twyman, "Chromolithography: The European Legacy," *Ephemera Journal* 10 (2003): 3–26; John Grossman, "Chromolithography and the Cigar Label: Sometimes the Label Was Better Than the Cigar," *Ephemera Journal* 9 (2002): 3–17. An excellent source of information on "created tourist traffic" is the *International Railway Journal*, which during the pre–World War I years devoted a monthly page to the Publicity Department. It regularly showcased examples of railroad travel imprints in feature stories enlivened by numerous black-and-white photographs of their cover graphics. See, for example, George Foxhall, "Heraldry of the Railroads," *International Railway Journal*, March 1914, 10; James M. Lingle, "Apportionment," *International Railway Journal*, January 1911, 12; Howard Elliott, "Railway Publicity," *International Railway Journal*, February 1911, 10. In 1911 Elliott was president of the Northern Pacific Railway, which because of its many different imprints over the years ranked as one of the foremost exemplars of railroad publishing.

7. Worth noting are Tad Burness, *Classic Railroad Advertising: Riding the Rails Again* (Iola, WI: Krause, 2001); C. Hamilton Ellis, *Railway Art* (Boston: New York Graphic Society, 1977); Pamela Walker Laird, *Advertising Progress: American Business and the Rise of Consumer Marketing* (Baltimore: Johns Hopkins University Press, 1998).

8. Editorial, *Omaha World-Herald*, June 7, 1921. The Nebraska newspaper concluded its editorial with these words: "Folder vacations are simply divine, and one retreats to his downy and virtuous couch simply tired out with traveling—and it hasn't cost him a dime!"

9. The first railroad in the trans-Mississippi West to promote day outings to escape the grime of the city was the Pacific Railroad of Missouri in 1852. Its illustrated pamphlet titled *A Guide to the Sceneries of St. Louis County* is described in Steven Rowan, *The Baron in the Grand Canyon: Friedrich Wilhelm von Egloffstein in the West* (Columbia: University of Missouri Press, 2012). A typical publication is *Excursion Guide of the Virginia Midland Railway* (n.p.: Virginia Midland Railway, 1882).

SECTION I: RAILROAD TIME AND SPACE

1. *American Railroad Journal, and Advocate of Internal Improvements,* June 9, 1832, 375.

2. *American Railroad Journal, and Advocate of Internal Improvements,* December 9, 1837, 657.

3. *American Railroad Journal,* November 9, 1850, 703. Henry Varnum Poor edited the publication during the 1850s, by which time it had shortened its name.

4. Grenville M. Dodge, *Paper Read before the Society of the Army of the Tennessee at Its Twenty-First Annual Reunion at Toledo, O., Sept. 15, 1888* (New York: Unz, 1899), 42.

5. Houston East & West Texas Railway, *Texas* (Houston: Houston East & West Texas Railway, 1894), 18.

1. TIMELINE AND OVERVIEW

1. Henry Villard, *Memoirs of Henry Villard, Journalist and Financier, 1835–1900* (Boston: Houghton, Mifflin, 1904), 1:96; Alexandra Villard de Borchgrave and John Cullen, *Villard: The Life and Times of an American Titan* (New York: Doubleday, 2001).

2. John W. Starr Jr., *Lincoln and the Railroads: A Biographical Study* (New York: Dodd, Mead, 1927); Thomas Crump, *Abraham Lincoln's World: How Riverboats, Railroads, and Republicans Transformed America* (London: Continuum, 2009); Jason Emerson, *Giant in the Shadows: The Life of Robert T. Lincoln* (Carbondale: Southern Illinois University Press, 2012); James D. Dilts, *The Great Road: The Building of the Baltimore & Ohio, the Nation's First Railroad, 1828–1853* (Stanford, CA: Stanford University Press, 1993); Paul Wallace Gates, *The Illinois Central Railroad and Its Colonization Work* (Cambridge, MA: Harvard University Press, 1934).

3. Mary Helen Dohan, *Mr. Roosevelt's Steamboat: The First Steamboat to Travel the Mississippi* (New York: Dodd, Mead, 1981).

4. Jay Feldman, *When the Mississippi Ran Backwards: Empire, Intrigue, Murder, and the New Madrid Earthquakes* (New York: Free Press, 2005).

5. Joel Overholser, *Fort Benton: World's Innermost Port* (Fort Benton, MT: privately printed, 1987); William E. Lass, *A History of Steamboating on the Upper Missouri* (Lincoln: University of Nebraska Press, 1962).

6. Michael Robbins, *The Railway Age in Britain and Its Impact on the World* (1962; repr., Baltimore: Penguin Books, 1965); Jack

Simmons, *The Railways of Britain: An Historical Introduction*, 2nd ed. (London: Macmillan, 1968).

7. Ronald E. Shaw, *Canals for a Nation: The Canal Era in the United States, 1790–1860* (Lexington: University Press of Kentucky, 1990).

8. James E. Vance Jr., *The North American Railroad: Its Origin, Evolution, and Geography* (Baltimore: Johns Hopkins University Press, 1995).

9. Wyatt Winton Belcher, *The Economic Rivalry between St. Louis and Chicago, 1850–1880* (New York: Columbia University Press, 1947); Jeffrey S. Adler, *Yankee Merchants and the Making of the Urban West: The Rise and Fall of Antebellum St. Louis* (Cambridge: Cambridge University Press, 1991).

10. James Neal Primm, *Lion of the Valley: St. Louis, Missouri, 1764–1980*; 3rd ed. (Saint Louis: Missouri Historical Society Press, 1998).

11. Brian McGinty, *Lincoln's Greatest Case: The River, the Bridge, and the Making of Modern America* (New York: Liveright, 2015).

12. Richard White, *Railroaded: The Transcontinentals and the Making of Modern America* (New York: W. W. Norton, 2011); David Haward Bain, *Empire Express: Building the First Transcontinental Railroad* (New York: Viking, 1999); Stephen E. Ambrose, *Nothing Like It in the World: The Men Who Built the Transcontinental Railroad, 1963–1869* (New York: Simon & Schuster, 2000).

13. Albro Martin, *James J. Hill and the Opening of the Northwest* (New York: Oxford University Press, 1976); Seth H. Bramson, *Speedway to Sunshine: The Story of the Florida East Coast Railway* (Erin, ON: Boston Mills, 1984).

14. Liston Edgington Leyendecker, *Palace Car Prince: A Biography of George Mortimer Pullman* (Niwot: University Press of Colorado, 1992).

15. Thomas Kessner, *The Flight of the Century: Charles Lindbergh and the Rise of American Aviation* (New York: Oxford University Press, 2010). In 1926, incidentally, the year Robert Todd Lincoln died, the Chicago & Alton Railroad's Passenger Department distributed a special leaflet to honor the birthday of his martyred father. It contained Lincoln's Gettysburg Address and his Farewell Address. The commemorative leaflet contained a description of Lincoln's years in Springfield, Illinois, an important stop for Alton passenger trains, including its Abraham Lincoln and Ann Rutledge. In addition, the railroad granted travelers a free stopover in Springfield of up to ten days to give them "an opportunity to view mementoes and visit locations made famous by association with the martyred president." *Official Guide*, May 1926, xxxii.

2. COMING TO TERMS WITH THE WONDER OF THE AGE

1. *American Railroad Journal*, June 16, 1849, 373

2. John Higham, *From Boundlessness to Consolidation: The Transformation of American Culture, 1848–1860* (Ann Arbor, MI: Clements Library Associates, 1969).

3. Nathaniel Philbrick, *Sea of Glory: America's Voyage of Discovery, the U. S. Exploring Expedition, 1838–1842* (New York: Penguin Books, 2003).

4. Richard Shelton Kirby, Sidney Withington, Arthur Burr Darling, and Frederick Gridley Kilgour, *Engineering in History* (New York: McGraw-Hill, 1956). The Society of Civil Engineers, a professional organization in the United Kingdom, obtained a charter of incorporation from the British Crown in 1834. The situation in the United States was that "some enterprising carpenter or mason of the neighborhood, becoming possessed of a level and compass, styles himself an engineer," or so claimed the *American Railroad Journal, and Advocate of Internal Improvements*, October 18, 1834, 641. The publication, barely two years old, had been forced to add "internal improvements" to its weekly coverage because in those early and tentative years its editor, D. K. Minor, discovered that the journal could not survive on news and essays devoted only to railroads. In the interest of simplicity, I will refer to this publication elsewhere as the *American Railroad Journal*.

5. One of the earliest and most influential guides that circulated on both sides of the Atlantic was a large book by Nicholas Wood, *A Practical Treatise on Rail-Roads, and Interior Communication in General; With Original Experiments and Tables of the Comparative Value of Canals and Rail-Road* (London: Knight & Lacey, 1825). On England's role as the world's railway pioneer, see Stuart Hylton, *The Grand Experiment: The Birth of the Railway Age, 1820–45* (Hersham, Surrey, UK: Ian Allen, 2007). At least a dozen "civil engineers" from the United States traveled to Britain between 1825 and 1840 to observe rail developments there and gain skills needed to build American railroads. See Darwin H. Stapleton, "The Origin of American Railroad Technology, 1825–1940," *Railroad History*, no. 139 (Autumn 1978): 65–77.

6. Fortunately, we have a beautifully translated version of Gerstner's observations published in English by Stanford

University Press. Franz Anton Ritter von Gerstner, *Early American Railroads*, ed. Frederick C. Gamst, trans. David J. Diephouse and John C. Decker, 2 vols. (Stanford, CA: Stanford University Press, 1997); originally published as *Die inner Communicationen* (1842–1843).

7. *Herapath's Journal*, August 21, 1858, 866. England's respected rail journal advocated a law to limit lines to a length of 150 miles or less.

8. The von Gerstner book was published in English as the result of the collaborative effort of several interested individuals, while the English translation of Chevalier's observations is the product of one scholar's fascination with the era that gave us the insights of both Tocqueville and Chevalier. Fortunately for those of us whose ability to read French is limited, my history colleague Steven Rowan translated into English an unabridged version of Chevalier's observations originally published under the lengthy title of *History and Description of the Routes of Communication in the United States and of the Works That Depend on Them*, an achievement never before attempted. To complement his translation, Rowan included a brief biography of Chevalier, who deserves to be far better known today for his encyclopedic observations of North American transportation and communication technology during their formative years. For readers requiring less detail, historian John William Ward edited an English-language version of Chevalier's later *Letters on North America* under the title *Society, Manners and Politics in the United States* (1961; repr., Ithaca, NY: Cornell University Press, 1969).

9. James D. Dilts, *The Great Road: The Building of the Baltimore & Ohio, the Nation's First Railroad, 1828–1855* (Stanford, CA: Stanford University Press, 1993); George Rogers Taylor, *The Transportation Revolution, 1815–1860* (1951; repr., New York: Harper & Row, 1968); Horatio Allen, *The Railroad Era: First Five Years of Development* (New York: Horatio Allen, 1884); Charles Frederick Carter, *When Railroads Were New* (New York: Henry Holt, 1909); Frederick Albert Cleveland and Fred Wilbur Powell, *Railroad Promotion and Capitalization in the United States* (New York: Longmans, Green, 1909). The words *first true railroad* refer to the fact that the Stockton & Darlington, Liverpool & Manchester, and Baltimore & Ohio were common carriers that transported freight of all types *and passengers*. In England, tramways and plateways had been used in earlier years to haul a single commodity like coal. David Gwyn, *The Coming of the Railway: A New Global History, 1750–1850* (New Haven: Yale University Press,

2023). In the United States precursors include the Quincy Granite Railway in Massachusetts and the Mauch Chunk coal road in Pennsylvania. *American Railway Times*, January 14, 1871, 14.

10. *American Railroad Journal*, May 30, 1835, 321. One matter of some debate during these early years was whether to call the new mode of transportation the railway or the railroad. Even the British initially wavered on the correct terminology before settling on *railway*, as did the Canadians, while the United States tended to favor *railroad* but with conspicuous exceptions. Some major rail carriers switched back and forth between the two terms during times of financial reorganization, an all-too-common fate, especially during the nineteenth century. Delta, "A Few Words on Railways," *Railway Magazine*, April 1836, 96–100. Like its American counterpart, the British publication found it initially difficult to settle on a working title, with its early issues appearing as the *Railway Magazine and Annals of Science*. From 1843 to 1893 it was *Herapath's Railway and Commercial Journal*.

11. W. J. Rorabaugh, *The Alcoholic Republic: An American Tradition* (New York: Oxford University Press, 1979). For a contemporary account of commerce along the Erie Canal, see the *American Railroad Journal*, March 7, 1835, 129–132. Providing an excellent account of how the city of New York functioned as the intermediary between the commerce and trade of the North Atlantic and that of the American Midwest is Robert Greenhalgh Albion, *The Rise of New York Port, 1815–1860* (New York: Charles Scribner's Sons, 1939). Carrying the story forward is Carl W. Condit, *The Port of New York: A History of the Rail and Terminal System from the Beginnings to Pennsylvania Station* (Chicago: University of Chicago Press, 1980); and Carl W. Condit, *The Port of New York: A History of the Rail and Terminal System from the Grand Central Electrification to the Present* (Chicago: University of Chicago Press, 1981).

12. *Baltimore American*, quoted in *American Railroad Journal*, May 9, 1835, 273. Pennsylvania's canal, as reported here, was, in fact, a hybrid combination of waterways and rail links. Providing a detailed history of this ultimately unworkable technological compromise is Albert J. Churella, *The Pennsylvania Railroad*, vol. 1, *Building an Empire, 1846–1917* (Philadelphia: University of Pennsylvania Press, 2013).

13. Promotion of a cause, whether the construction of railroads and canals or of a new society, dates back at least to the pamphleteers of America's Revolutionary War era. Although their brochures seldom featured any artwork, canal promoters were

skilled wordsmiths who set the tone for railroad boosters. Carlos A. Schwantes, "Promoting America's Canals: Popularizing the Hopes and Fears of the New American Nation," *Journal of American Culture*, January 1979, 700–712. Research for this graduate school essay introduced me to the vast collection of transportation pamphlets and other early American ephemera held by the Clements Library of the University of Michigan.

14. An excellent overview of the railroad's trial-and-error decades is Alvin F. Harlow, *Steelways of New England* (New York: Creative Edge, 1946).

15. Publicola, "Social Influence of Roads and Railways," *American Railroad Journal*, February 6, 1836, 66. During the early years of canal and railroad construction, it was common for American writers to use pseudonyms, as pamphleteers had done during the Revolutionary War to conceal their identity from the British, who would have considered them traitors. John Herapath estimated that the cost per mile of track in the United States was £5,000, versus £18,000 for Great Britain. Herapath, *Railway Magazine*, February 1837, 100. On the American defense of their cost-effective method of railroad construction, see *Herapath's Journal*, June 8, 1850, 553.

16. *Edinburgh Review*, quoted in *American Railroad Journal*, December 26, 1846, 821. The cheap construction of America's early railroads is examined at length in the *Journal of the Franklin Institute of the State of Pennsylvania*, November 1840, 296–301. One noteworthy exception to the European observers' generalizations was the Hoosac Tunnel, which extended five miles under the mountains of western Massachusetts. The project took twenty-five years to complete. See William B. Meyer, "The Long Agony of the Great Bore," *Invention & Technology* 1, no. 2 (Summer 1985): 53–56.

17. Harriet Martineu, *Society in America* (London, 1837), 180–181; *American Railway Times*, August 8, 1863, 254; *American Railroad Journal*, June 9, 1832, 375.

18. Schwantes, "Promoting America's Canals," 700–712.

19. Simon Garfield, *The Last Journey of William Huskisson* (London: Faber & Faber, 2002). In addition to Dilts, *Great Road*, see John F. Stover, *History of the Baltimore and Ohio Railroad* (West Lafayette, IN: Purdue University Press, 1987). After nearly five years of rail operations in Great Britain and the United States, the *American Railroad Journal* reported that maintaining the Liverpool & Manchester to the high standards typical of British railways had been five times more expensive than for the Baltimore & Ohio. "The Liverpool road was made in the most substantial manner, with very little curvature. The Baltimore and Ohio is very much curved, which increases the expense of maintaining the parallelism of the rails." *American Railroad Journal*, May 23, 1835, 308.

20. At the time, a Tennessean, Andrew Jackson, occupied the White House. He boarded a Baltimore & Ohio car at Ellicott's Mills on June 6, 1833, for a pleasure trip to Baltimore and thus was the first president of the United States to ride a train. The *Montgomery (Alabama) Advertiser* (January 17, 1904) recounts how copies of the *Rail-Road Advocate* were preserved. Scattered editions of the historic journal are now posted on the internet. For an extended contemporary account of the Liverpool & Manchester Railway, see *American Railroad Journal*, May 30, 1835, 322–324.

21. *Railroad Journal, and Advocate of Internal Improvements*, December 8, 1832, 785; August 25, 1837, 527; September 2, 1837, 545. The publication's title was at first as tentative as some of America's rail construction projects. The journal quickly abandoned the term *Rail-Road* and for a time styled itself as the *Railroad Journal, and Advocate of Internal Improvements*. Presumably it temporarily dropped the word American from its title because so much of its news content originally came from Great Britain, and specifically from the *London Mechanics' Magazine*.

22. Another early railroad that used incline planes was the Mohawk & Hudson in upstate New York. As of 1837, the rail line was sixteen miles long and used two incline planes powered by stationary engines to surmount an elevation of 439 feet. *American Railroad Journal*, December 9, 1837, 660.

23. The first twenty-five volumes of the *American Railroad Journal* (1832–1852) are readily available for purchase on DVD. In 1887 the *American Railroad Journal* evolved into the *Railroad and Engineering Journal*, and in 1892 it transformed again, into the *American Engineer and Railroad Journal*. On using locks versus building more powerful locomotives to surmount grades, see *American Railroad Journal*, May 30, 1835, 322. The alternative of an incline plane proved popular in England but less so in the United States, although during the 1830s and 1840s the *American Railroad Journal* dutifully described its pros and cons. See, for example, *American Railroad Journal*, September 23, 1848, 609–610. By this date the masthead subtitle of the publication had dropped its previous reference to "internal improvements" and added "Iron Manufacturer's and Mining Gazette." When Henry Varnum Poor

became its editor in the early 1850s, the *American Railroad Journal* finally confined itself almost exclusively to railroad topics.

24. Craig Miner, *A Most Magnificent Machine: America Adopts the Railroad, 1825–1862* (Lawrence: University Press of Kansas, 2010); John F. Stover, *Iron Road to the West: American Railroads in the 1850s* (New York: Columbia University Press, 1978).

25. A lengthy overview titled "Engineering Education" appeared in the *American Railway Review*, April 25, 1861, 241.

26. Ben Marsden, *Watt's Perfect Engine: Steam and the Age of Invention* (New York: Columbia University Press, 2002); Thomas Crump, *A Brief History of the Age of Steam: The Power That Drove the Industrial Revolution* (New York: Carroll & Graf, 2007); Jonathan Glancey, *Giants of Steam: The Great Men and Machines of Rail's Golden Age* (London: Atlantic Books, 2012).

27. Charles Dickens, *American Notes* (London: Chapman & Hall, 1842), 43–45; Robert G. Athearn, *Westward the Briton* (1953; repr., Lincoln: University of Nebraska Press, n.d.), chaps. 2, 7; Trevor K. Snowdon, *Diverging Tracks: American versus English Rail Travel in the 19th Century* (Jefferson, NC: McFarland, 2019).

28. *American Railway Times*, August 18, 1866, 262; January 14, 1871, 14.

3. SPATIAL REORIENTATION

1. John P. Davis, *The Union Pacific Railway: A Study in Railway Politics, History, and Economics* (Chicago: S. C. Griggs, 1894), 16.

2. *St. Louis Intelligencer*, quoted in *American Railroad Journal*, December 18, 1852, 804.

3. *American Railroad Journal*, June 24, 1854, 398. On Washington's birthday in 1854, the Chicago & Rock Island celebrated its historic reach west to the Mississippi River, a first for the railroads of the United States. H. Roger Grant describes the landmark event in *A Mighty Fine Road: A History of the Chicago, Rock Island & Pacific Railroad Company* (Bloomington: Indiana University Press, 2020), 13–15. The completion of the Ohio & Mississippi Railroad to the east bank of the Mississippi River at Illinoistown (later East Saint Louis) in 1857 warranted an even grander celebration and a massive commemorative book: William Prescott Smith, *The Book of the Great Railway Celebrations of 1857* (New York: D. Appleton, 1858). The Eads Bridge over the Mississippi and into Saint Louis was completed seventeen years later on July 4, 1874. Until then, railroads east and west of the great waterway used the Wiggins Ferry Company.

4. *New York Journal of Commerce*, quoted in *American Railroad Journal*, October 27, 1849, 678. One example of the nationwide debate is Calvin Colton, *A Lecture on the Railroad to the Pacific: Delivered August 12, 1850, at the Smithsonian Institute, Washington* (New York: A. S. Barnes, 1850). Colton, a minister by profession, supported a Pacific railroad and claimed that the project enjoyed the support of Divine Providence and would likely "change the current of human affairs, and gravely affect the condition of nations." Colton, 3. Here was another example of the nation's current fascination with its Manifest Destiny as well as its mission to Christianize the world.

5. *American Railroad Journal*, July 2, 1853, 422–423; William H. Goetzmann, *Army Exploration in the American West, 1803–1863*, rev. ed. (1959; repr., Austin: Texas State Historical Association, 1991). Offering an in-depth look at one of the routes the army surveyed are Paul D. McDermott, Ronald E. Grim, and Philip Mobley, *Eye of the Explorer: Views of the Northern Pacific Railroad Survey, 1853–54* (Missoula, MT: Mountain, 2010).

6. With spread-eagle prose typical of the 1850s enthusiasm for a railroad across the West, the Cincinnati publication prophesied, "Where the buffalo and the Indian roam, will be traversed in every direction by the fiery locomotive, bearing tens of thousands not only between the Atlantic and Pacific shores of America, but between Europe and Asia." *Railroad Record*, June 23, 1853, 257–258. At least the *Railroad Record* acknowledged the Indigenous peoples of the West, a reality many railroad settlement promoters simply ignored when they described the western landscape as "empty." No rail journal of the 1850s, not even the *American Railroad Journal*, was a more insistent promoter of a transcontinental railroad than the *Railroad Record*. Perhaps that was inevitable given that the former publication was based on the East Coast in New York City and the latter in Cincinnati, a city that saw itself as a potential rail gateway to the West (in competition with Saint Louis, Chicago, and Memphis). Its envisioned route would occupy the middle ground among its urban competitors by utilizing the Ohio River (or soon-to-be-built railroad connections) to reach Cairo, Illinois, and then crossing the Mississippi River by means of a ferry. Cincinnati's quest proved quixotic, but from its first issue in 1853 until its demise in 1873, the *Railroad Record* remained a far better source than any other publication for news of railroads across the Midwest and into Missouri and Arkansas.

7. The idea of a transcontinental railroad that ran to the West Coast of the United States and then extended the nation's

commercial reach via ship across the Pacific Ocean to China and India was voiced frequently during the late 1840s and 1850s. *American Railroad Journal*, April 25, 1846, 260. See also Peter A. Hansen, Don L. Hofsommer, and Carlos Arnaldo Schwantes, *Crossroads of a Continent: Missouri Railroads, 1951–1921* (Bloomington: Indiana University Press, 2022).

8. *Herapath's Journal*, January 13, 1849, 41.

9. F. S. Cotterill, "The National Railroad Convention in St. Louis, 1849," in *St. Louis from Village to Metropolis: Essays from the Missouri Historical Review, 1906–2006*, ed. Louis S. Gerteis (Columbia: State Historical Society of Missouri, 2009), 103–115. See also *American Railroad Journal*, November 3, 1849, 690–693; November 17, 1849, 722; December 1, 1849, 759.

10. *American Railroad Journal*, January 13, 1855, 17–19.

11. *American Railroad Journal*, March 10, 1855, 149; Robert R. Russel, *Improvement of Communication with the Pacific Coast as an Issue in American Politics, 1873–1864* (Cedar Rapids, IA: Torch, 1948); Julius Grodinsky, *Transcontinental Railway Strategy, 1869–1893: A Study of Businessmen* (Philadelphia: University of Pennsylvania Press, 1962); Oscar O. Winther, *The Transportation Frontier: Trans-Mississippi West, 1865–1890* (New York: Holt, Rinehart & Winston, 1964); Robert Edgar Riegel, *The Story of the Western Railroads: From 1852 through the Reign of the Giants* (1926; repr., Lincoln: University of Nebraska Press, 1964); Balthasar Henry Meyer, dir., *History of Transportation in the United States before 1860* (Washington, DC: Carnegie Institution of Washington, 1917).

12. *American Railway Times*, June 29, 1867, 202. Final-spike ceremonies, both the extravagant and the modest, would be held across the American and Canadian Wests between Promontory in 1869 and the completion of the Inside Gateway at Bieber, California, on November 10, 1931. Perhaps the longest-running rail construction project in the history of the United States was the link forged between San Francisco and Portland, an enterprise that required twenty-one years from start to finish because of local politics, financial shortfalls, and the rugged mountains of Northern California and Southern Oregon. A final-spike ceremony took place in Ashland, Oregon, on December 17, 1887, when Charles Crocker struck the blows that fired celebratory cannons at both ends of the line. *Official Guide*, January 1888, xvii.

13. Stephen E. Ambrose, *Nothing Like It in the World: The Men Who Built the Transcontinental Railroad, 1863–1869* (New York: Simon & Schuster, 2000); David Haward Bain, *Empire Express:*

Building the First Transcontinental Railroad (New York: Viking/Penguin Group, 1999); Richard White, *Railroaded: The Transcontinentals and the Making of Modern America* (New York: W. W. Norton, 2011).

14. Wyatt Winton Belcher, *The Economic Rivalry between St. Louis and Chicago, 1850–1880* (New York: Columbia University Press, 1947); Olivia Mahoney, *Go West! Chicago and American Expansion* (Chicago: Chicago Historical Society, 1899).

15. John H. Coatsworth, *Growth against Development: The Economic Impact of Railroads in Porfirian Mexico* (DeKalb: Northern Illinois University Press, 1981).

16. Peter Hopkirk, *The Great Game: The Struggle for Empire in Central Asia* (New York: Kodansha International, 1994); Sarah Searight, *Steaming East: The Hundred-Year Saga of the Struggle to Forge Rail and Steamship Links between Europe and India* (London: Bodley Head, 1991). Russia completed its trans-Siberian railroad in mid-1904. That year, the longest transcontinental line in the world functioned as part of a Russian attempt to assert imperial might in the Far East by plunging into a war with Japan that ended in military disaster for Russia. Steven G. Marks, *Road to Power: The Trans-Siberian Railroad and the Colonization of Asian Russia, 1850–1917* (Ithaca, NY: Cornell University Press, 1991); Deborah Manley, ed., *The Trans-Siberian Railway: A Traveller's Anthology* (London: Century Hutchinson, 1988). Great Britain never completed a Cape to Cairo railway because its primary proponent, Cecil John Rhodes of South Africa, died in 1902 and a German colony in East Africa blocked the way. George Tabor, *The Cape to Cairo Railway* (London: Genta, 2003). Finally, a rail line intended to function as an empire builder for pre–World War I Germany was the Berlin-Baghdad Railway. Sean McMeekin, *The Berlin-Baghdad Express: The Ottoman Empire and Germany's Bid for World Power* (Cambridge, MA: Belknap Press of Harvard University Press, 2010).

17. *Railway Register*, quoted in *Official Guide*, July 1889, xxix.

4. GOD'S TIME VERSUS RAILROAD TIME

1. J. C. Swayze, *Hill & Swayze's Confederate States Rail-Road and Steam-Boat Guide* (Griffin, GA: Hill & Swayze, 1862), 2.

2. *Confessions of Saint Augustine*, Book XI, trans. Henry Chadwick (New York: Oxford University Press, 1992).

3. Ian R. Bartky, *Selling the True Time: Nineteenth-Century Timekeeping in America* (Stanford, CA: Stanford University Press, 2000); Michael O'Malley, *Keeping Watch: A History of American Time* (New York: Penguin Group, 1990); Kevin Lynch, *What Time Is This Place* (Cambridge, MA: MIT Press, 1972). In September 2002, *Scientific American* devoted an entire issue to "A Matter of Time," which does a superb job of unraveling some of timekeeping's numerous complexities.

4. When a newspaper published in Idaho Territory compared differences in time between the mountain village of Idaho City and metropolitan New York and San Francisco, it twice repeated the word *about* in reference to the hours and minutes. Approximate timekeeping was good enough for an isolated region still linked by freight wagons and stagecoaches but not railroads. *Idaho World*, June 17, 1865, 2.

5. Carlos A. Schwantes, *Long Day's Journey: The Steamboat and Stagecoach Era in the Northern West* (Seattle: University of Washington Press, 1999). See also Joseph Mills Hanson, *The Conquest of the Missouri* (New York: Murray Hill Books, 1909); William E. Lass, *A History of Steamboating on the Upper Missouri* (Lincoln: University of Nebraska Press, 1962); *Navigating the Missouri: Steamboating on Nature's Highway, 1819–1935* (Norman, OK: Arthur H. Clark, 2008). One classic firsthand account of steamboat life on inland waters is Mark Twain, *Life on the Mississippi* (1883; repr., New York: New American Library, 2001).

6. *Railway Review*, November 15, 1884, 589; William E. Dodge, *Old New York: A Lecture* (New York: Dodd, Mead, 1880). Dodge's partner in the New York countinghouse was Anson G. Phelps, and on the other side of the Atlantic in Liverpool, his partner was Daniel James. Through partnerships like this was trade conducted from one continent to another in the 1830s and 1840s. The simple partnership arrangement made no business sense for an enterprise as complex and capital intensive as a railroad, even a short one, and hence the rise of the railroad corporation. For more information about the evolution of a typical trading partnership, see Carlos A. Schwantes, *Vision and Enterprise: Exploring the History of Phelps Dodge Corporation* (Tucson: University of Arizona Press, 2000). On the evolution of Sunday observance, see Craig Harline, *Sunday: A History of the First Day from Babylonia to the Super Bowl* (New York: Doubleday, 2007).

7. Chester F. Sanger, "Sunday Travel and the Law," *Bay State Monthly*, January 1885, 231–235. Sunday trains, or lack thereof, became a particularly contentious matter in religiously conservative Scotland, and the British Parliament took up the question of whether to operate mail trains on Sunday. *Herapath's Journal*, July 13, 1850, 677. *Railway World* for March 15, 1890, devoted pages 242 and 243 to summarizing the crazy-quilt pattern of Sunday laws that prevailed at that time across the United States. Connecticut, for example, prohibited railroads from running trains between sunrise and sunset on Sundays "except for necessity or mercy." In several other states, the restriction on train operations was Sunday from midnight to midnight. Wyoming exempted railroads from Sunday restrictions, while Arkansas law apparently ignored railroad operations but imposed penalties for Sunday horse racing, cockfighting, and baseball, and Georgia could imprison for six months anyone who took a Sunday bath "in view of any road leading to a house of worship."

8. *New York Presbyterian*, quoted in *American Railroad Journal*, June 7, 1856, 356–357. See also *Railway World*, August 29, 1891, 819–820. The president of a large Chicago-based railroad once commented: "I do not feel right to go into my slip on Sunday and listen to a good sermon, realizing all the while that thousands of our men are out on their trains, away from their homes and working; but as long as the public sentiment demands these trains how are we to help ourselves?" L. S. Coffin, "Sunday Railway Trains," *Railway Review*, January 2, 1897, 9–10.

9. *American Railroad Journal*, December 23, 1854, 801. Poor edited the publication from 1849 to 1862. He achieved fame for his financial analysis, and his name lives on today in Standard and Poor's 500 Index, usually abbreviated as the S&P 500.

10. Sunday travel (or not) was a contentious issue in Great Britain too. The country's leading railway publication, *Herapath's Journal*, dared to respond to critics who claimed that God punished Sunday train operators by depressing the value of their securities: "If railways are down in the market because their Directors are irreligious (?) enough to run trains on Sunday, how singular it is that railways should have stood so high in 1845 when there was as much or more travelling on Sundays." *Herapath's Journal*, February 10, 1849, 126. Regarding Sunday mail trains, see *Herapath's Journal*, March 23, 1850, 296; and July 20, 1850, 697. In its vigorous opposition to the Sunday restriction of train operations, the publication warned: "Scottish manners and prejudices cannot be engrafted upon Englishmen, and we should advise the attempt not to be made." *Herapath's Journal*, June 8, 1850, 554–555. See also David Brooke, "The Opposition to Sunday Rail Services in North-Eastern England, 1834–1914," *Journal of Transport*

History, November 1963, 95–109; Charles Worcester Clark, "The Day of Rest," *Atlantic Monthly*, September 1889, 366–375.

11.   Great Britain, being a far smaller and much more linear nation north to south than the United States or Canada, adopted a single time standard for its railroads. A measure of uniformity commonly known as "railway time" emerged in the 1830s and 1840s, but with the Time Act of 1880, Parliament made Greenwich time legally binding on all the railroads of Great Britain. Simon Bradley, *The Railways: Nation, Network and People* (London: Profile Books, 2015).

12.   This odd tidbit of time history comes from the Santa Fe's listing in my November 1883 copy of the *Travelers' Official Guide of the Railway and Steam Navigation Lines in the United States and Canada*, a predecessor title to the January 1958 *Official Guide* I acquired as a gift from a ticket agent at the Indianapolis Union Station. It was the first of a lifetime collection of *Official Guides*. Decades later I was particularly eager to acquire the November 1883 issue on eBay because it was the last one published before the adoption of standard time that month. Records of the General Time Convention debates are housed at the Hagley Museum and Library in Wilmington, Delaware. See also Charles F. Dowd, *System of National Time and Its Application, by Means of Hour and Minute Indexes, to the National Railway Time-Table; Also a Railway Time Gazetteer* (Albany: Weed, Parsons, 1870). Dowd wrote, "It is not at all uncommon for extended Railways to adopt several different standards of time upon their own route, and quite frequently two or more clocks are found in the same depot pointing out very different times. . . . Any traveler, therefore, upon leaving home, loses all confidence in his watch, and is, in fact without any reliable time." Dowd, 3. In Omaha, as Dowd noted for example, local time was one hour faster than railway time.

13.   *Official Guide*, December 1923, xxix; Carlene Stephens, "'The Most Reliable Time': William Bond, the New England Railroads, and Time Awareness in 19th Century America," *Technology and Culture*, January 1989, 1–23. Studies of how time was organized globally include Derek Howse, *Greenwich Time and the Discovery of the Longitude* (New York: Oxford University Press, 1980); and Ian R. Bartky, *One Time Fits All: The Campaigns for Global Uniformity* (Stanford, CA: Stanford University Press, 2007).

14.   An excellent study focusing on one region of the United States is Aaron W. Marrs, "Railroads and Time Consciousness in the Antebellum South," *Enterprise & Society* 9 (September 2008): 433–456.

15.   *Railway Review*, November 24, 1883, 690. The journal also noted the role Sandford Fleming, a Canadian, played in bringing standard time to the railroads of North America. See Clark Blaise, *Time Lord: Sir Sandford Fleming and the Creation of Standard Time* (New York: Pantheon Books, 2000). Many people can claim to be the "father of standard time," but certainly the editor of the *Official Guide*, William Frederick Allen, a well-documented and particularly insistent advocate, merited the praise the *Railway Review* gave him.

16.   On the history of the *Official Guide of the Railways*, at one time the world's largest monthly publication, see Harold H. Baetjer, *A Book That Gathers No Dust* (New York: National Railway Publication Company, 1950).

17.   *Railway Review*, November 24, 1883, 690. As recently as November 6, 2016, the *New York Times* published an opinion essay by James Gleick titled "Time to Dump Time Zones," an arrangement described as "confusing, awkward and arbitrary." Trains operating across Russia between Moscow and Vladivostok operate on Moscow time and make no use of time zones.

18.   The question of adopting a twenty-four-hour clock was debated but rejected by the railroads of the United States. Hence, its typical timetables indicated p.m. hours with heavy-faced type and a.m. with light. *Railway Review*, September 15, 1883, 538. Among numerous reasons given for the rejection of a twenty-four-hour clock was that it would be "impossible to get men to understand the new notation." On the other hand, Sandford Fleming, the Scottish-born Canadian engineer who was another of the fathers of standard time, and William Cornelius Van Horne, president of the Canadian Pacific, favored it. Van Horn reported that a three-year trial by his company found it "highly satisfactory." He added, "No confusion whatever resulted from its adoption or has grown out of its use, and I have yet to hear of the first objection to it on the part of the public." The Intercolonial Railway (a 906-mile railway across eastern Canada) adopted the twenty-four-hour time notation in 1887 without a word of complaint from its employees or the traveling public. *Railroad and Engineering Journal*, May 1889, 225–226.

19.   Michael Downing, *Spring Forward: The Annual Madness of Daylight Saving Time* (Berkeley, CA: Counterpoint, 2005); David Prerau, *Seize the Daylight: The Curious and Contentious Story of Daylight Saving Time* (New York: Thunder's Mouth, 2005).

20. Also aiding the cause of railroad standardization during the 1880s was the Master Car-Builders Association. See *Railway Review*, December 13, 1884, 638. The Railway Master Mechanics Association worked for years to promote the standardization of nuts, bolt heads, screw threads, and, most importantly, the wheel flanges that kept trains on the tracks. *Locomotive Engineering*, March 1892, 81; *American Engineer and Railroad Journal*, March 1893, 105–107.

5. THE BATTLE OF THE GAUGES

1. *Railway World*, June 7, 1890, 531; October 24, 1891, 1014–1015.
2. In Great Britain during the mid-1840s, a special parliamentary commission thoroughly studied the gauge question. Its findings were summarized in North America in successive monthly issues of the *Journal of the Franklin Institute of the State of Pennsylvania* beginning in October 1846.
3. *American Railroad Journal*, July 31, 1845, 485.
4. Zerah Colburn, "Breaks of Gauge," *American Railroad Journal*, February 11, 1854, 91–92.
5. At this time, the four-foot, eight-and-a-half-inch gauge was considered narrow. The other five "standards" ranged upward in size to six feet on the New York & Erie. *American Railroad Journal*, June 25, 1853, 405. A truly narrow gauge "standard" of three feet emerged only in the early 1870s. The Denver & Rio Grande, which dated from 1870 and was based in the mountains of Colorado, emerged as the poster child for a new group of advocates. Its corporate secretary predicted: "We confidently expect even on the short section to be completed this summer to make such a showing as to establish the 3-feet gauge as preeminently the 'gauge of the future' for railways of this country, or at least of the new West." *American Railway Times*, July 8, 1871, 211.
6. *American Railroad Journal*, September 23, 1854, 606.
7. Because the port city of Liverpool and the cloth manufacturing center of Manchester ranked as two of the most important and most visible results of the Industrial Revolution, the twenty-mile-long railway link between them gained far more prominence around the world than the equally important Stockton & Darlington, and the person most responsible for both the Liverpool & Manchester's track gauge and its prize-winning locomotive design was George Stephenson. Maurice W. Kirby, *The Origins of Railway Enterprise: The Stockton and Darlington Railway, 1821–1863* (Cambridge: Cambridge University Press, 1993); Christopher McGowan, *The Rainhill Trials: The Greatest Contest of Industrial Britain and the Birth of Commercial Rail* (London: Little, Brown, 2004); Simon Garfield, *The Last Journey of William Huskisson* (London: Faber & Faber, 2002); L. T. C. Rolt, *George and Robert Stephenson: The Railway Revolution* (London: Longmans, 1960).

8. *American Railroad Journal*, November 19, 1853, 747. The Indianapolis & Cincinnati line expected to link with the Ohio & Mississippi in Lawrenceburg, but the latter company used a broad gauge of six feet between the rails, which would have made seamless interchange difficult. The Northern Cross, the initial rail line completed in Illinois (beginning in 1837), a state eventually crisscrossed by a dense network of tracks, ran fifty-nine miles from the state capital at Springfield to the east bank of the Illinois River at Meredosia, where water connections were available to Alton and Saint Louis. Simon Cordery, *The Iron Road in the Prairie State: The Story of Illinois Railroading* (Bloomington: Indiana University Press, 2016).
9. *Railroad Record*, June 1, 1865, 177.
10. George W. Hilton, *American Narrow Gauge Railroads* (Stanford, CA: Stanford University Press, 1990).
11. Over the years, the gauge question inspired considerable comment in the *American Railroad Journal*, with Zerah Coburn serving as a prominent proponent of standard-gauge tracks. See, for example, *American Railway Journal*, March 11, 1854, 151–152. Until the creation of a uniform system of tracks, Canadian railroads adopted either the standard gauge or the "medium broad" one of five feet, six inches. *American Railroad Journal*, May 1, 1852, 282; *American Railway Review*, June 28, 1860, 389; J. M. Trout and Edw. Trout, *The Railways of Canada for 1870–1* (Toronto: Monetary Times, 1871), 62–65. On these pages the authors dealt at length with the gauge question in Canada, and they promoted the adoption of the same standard gauge that prevailed across much of the northern United States to facilitate commerce between the two nations. The case for standard gauge was especially compelling for the Great Western line that ran through Ontario north of Lake Erie to link Buffalo and Detroit. "This can never be exclusively a Canadian line, it will be more an American one," the authors said, concluding that "a change of gauge at the frontiers would, therefore, be bad policy." Nowhere did they argue that Canada's track gauge ought to differ from that in the United States to forestall any invasion attempts from the south.

12. *Railway Review*, February 27, 1886, 98–99. See also George Rogers Taylor and Irene D. Neu, *The American Railroad Network, 1861–1890* (1956; repr., Urbana: University of Illinois Press, 2003).

13. Douglas J. Puffert, *Tracks across Continents, Paths through History: The Economic Dynamics of Standardization in Railway Gauge* (Chicago: University of Chicago Press, 2009); C. C. Singleton and David Burke, *Railways of Australia* (Sydney: Angus and Robertson, 1963). On the array of spatial relationships that railroad gauge standardization made possible, see James E. Vance Jr., *The North American Railroad: Its Origin, Evolution, and Geography* (Baltimore: Johns Hopkins University Press, 1995).

14. M. John Lubetkin, *Jay Cooke's Gamble: The Northern Pacific Railroad, the Sioux, and the Panic of 1873* (Norman: University of Oklahoma Press, 2006); Sig Mickelson, *The Northern Pacific Railroad and the Selling of the West* (Sioux Falls, SD: Center for Western Studies, Augustana College, 1993). One notable publisher of a series of guides intended to inform the first generation of transcontinental train travelers was George Crofutt, who claimed that by 1878 he had sold more than three hundred thousand copies of his *Overland Tourist*. J. Valerie Fifer, *American Progress: The Growth of Transport, Tourist, and Information Industries in the Nineteenth-Century West* (Chester, CT: Globe Pequot, 1988).

15. Keith L. Bryant Jr., *History of the Atchison, Topeka and Santa Fe Railway* (New York: Macmillan, 1974); Walter R. Borneman, *Rival Rails: The Race to Build America's Greatest Transcontinental Railroad* (New York: Random House, 2010); John Sedgwick, *From the River to the Sea: The Untold Story of the Railroad War That Made the West* (New York: Avid Reader, 2021).

16. The Atchison, Topeka & Santa Fe's extensive Atlantic & Pacific land holdings across northern New Mexico and Arizona were originally intended to boost construction of a Frisco predecessor across southwestern Missouri. For a study of this convoluted transaction, see William S. Greever, *Arid Domain: The Santa Fe Railway and Its Western Land Grant* (Stanford, CA: Stanford University Press, 1954).

17. The Western Pacific inaugurated through passenger trains over its route during the summer of 1910. *Official Guide*, July 1910, xxvii. The delay between the completion of construction and the commencement of through trains was typical and provided time for a railroad to perfect its track, the roadbed, and other features of its new support structure.

18. *Railway Age Gazette*, October 16, 1916, 586. See also Howard V. Worley Jr., *Wabash Pittsburgh Terminal Railway* (Saxonburg,

PA: Howdy Productions, 2004); Edwin P. Hoyt, *The Goulds: A Social History* (New York: Weybright & Talley, 1969).

19. *Railway and Marine News and Pacific Commerce*, November 9, 1925, 17. For years, the Southern Pacific provided the sole rail link between California and the Pacific Northwest states of Oregon and Idaho. In 1929, long after George Gould's involvement with the Western Pacific ended, the railroad achieved a second destiny by joining with the Great Northern Railway to provide an "Inside Gateway" alternative to Southern Pacific's Northwest line. See Roger Vaughn, *Arthur Curtiss James: Unsung Titan of the Gilded Age* (n.p.: Story Arts Media, 2019), chap. 14. At that time, and before the Great Depression affected his fortune, James was described as "one of the most powerful figures in the present railroad world, but not so well known as some of his more demonstrative contemporaries." *Railway & Marine News*, July 1930, 30.

20. The Missouri Pacific formed the backbone of Gould's ambitious transcontinental system, but in 1911 America's would-be rail baron lost control of that railroad too. The Missouri Pacific's most significant subsidiaries were the St. Louis, Iron Mountain & Southern and the Texas & Pacific. *Railway and Marine News and Pacific Commerce*, November 9, 1925, 17.

21. Richard J. Orsi, *Sunset Limited: The Southern Pacific Railroad and the Development of the American West, 1850–1930* (Berkeley: University of California Press, 2005); Barbara J. Rozek, *Come to Texas: Enticing Immigrants, 1865–1915* (College Station: Texas A&M University Press, 2003); Claire Strom, *Profiting from the Plains: The Great Northern Railway and Corporate Development of the American West* (Seattle: University of Washington Press, 2003). Railroads promoting the settlement of Montana made grandiose claims about the farmlands available in the eastern portion of the state, with tragic results for settlers who believed them. See Jonathan Raban, *Bad Land: An American Romance* (New York: Vintage, 1996).

6. THE COMPASS OF OPPORTUNITY

1. Emma H. Adams, *To and Fro, Up and Down in Southern California, Oregon, and Washington Territory, with Sketches in Arizona, New Mexico, and British Columbia* (Cincinnati: Cranston & Stowe, 1888), 375. Adams added, "No sooner has one set of magnificent enterprises—such as tunneling a mountain range, founding a city, building an important railway, dredging the Columbia for fifty miles—been printed into being, by the lively journalists,

than away speed the go-aheads to inaugurate as many more." Another traveler amazed by the shrill boosterism common on the Pacific Slope was Frances Fuller Victor, who while riding aboard a Northern Pacific train across the dry landscape of eastern Washington in the early 1890s took note of a booster's injunction to "Keep Your Eye on Pasco," one of the upstart communities arising along the tracks. The problem, Victor noted in her acerbic rejoinder, was that when you stepped off the train in Pasco and gazed about "for anything upon which to keep your eye," it would be blown full of sand and would refuse "to risk more than the briefest glimpse afterwards." Boosters claimed they would redeem the surrounding landscape of sandy sagebrush wasteland with irrigation, "but in the interim, keeping one's eyes on Pasco is a painful experience." Frances Fuller Victor, *Atlantis Arisen; or, Talks of a Tourist about Oregon and Washington* (Philadelphia: J. B. Lippincott, 1891), 351–352.

2. That claim is given visible form by the massive Gateway Arch, which today dominates the Saint Louis waterfront.

3. Bob Lettenberger, "Beer and Trains," *Trains: The Magazine of Railroading*, May 2023, 30–39.

4. L. U. Reavis, *Saint Louis: The Future Great City of the World* (Saint Louis: C. R. Barns, 1876); Reavis, *The Great Empire of the West beyond the Mississippi* (Saint Louis: Nixon-Jones, 1882). The several Gould railroads based in Saint Louis also included the Wabash, which reached across the heartland from Kansas City and Omaha to Chicago, Detroit, and Buffalo. H. Roger Grant, *"Follow the Flag": A History of the Wabash Railroad Company* (DeKalb: Northern Illinois University Press, 2004).

5. *Official Guide*, October 1911, xxxi.

6. Peter A. Hansen, Don L. Hofsommer, and Carlos A. Schwantes, *Crossroads of a Continent: Missouri Railroads, 1851–1921* (Bloomington, Indiana University Press, 2022).

7. The early twentieth century also witnessed the completion of two new transcontinental lines across the United States, in addition to the two new railroads across Canada. The wealthy midwestern carrier Chicago, Milwaukee & St. Paul bridged the Missouri River in South Dakota and commenced construction west to Seattle and Tacoma, the Puget Sound gateways to the Pacific Ocean and Asia. George Gould pushed construction of the Western Pacific from Salt Lake City to San Francisco Bay in the expectation that it would form a link in his proposed rail line across the United States. Many books have been written about the nineteenth-century transcontinental railroads of the United States, but a convenient summary featuring a gorgeous array of graphics is Center for Railroad Photography and Art, *After Promontory: One Hundred and Fifty Years of Transcontinental Railroading* (Madison, WI: Center for Railroad Photography and Art and Indiana University Press, 2019).

8. *Official Guide*, December 1910, xxvii. The Great Northern, the would-be merger partner of the Northern Pacific until blocked in the Northern Securities case of 1904, also operated a show car in 1910. It operated in much the same manner as its Northern Pacific counterpart, featuring exhibits, lecturers, news writeups and advertisements in local newspapers, and promotional literature, "and in the near future free moving picture shows [would] be adopted instead of lantern slides." *Evening Telegram* (Portland, OR), May 4, 1910.

9. *Official Guide*, September 1911, xxx. Louis W. Hill, who succeeded his father as head of the Great Northern Railway, operated a special hotel train in conjunction with the Minnesota State Automobile Association's third annual endurance run from Saint Paul to Helena, Montana, during the summer of 1911. The train was timed to rendezvous with motorists at the end of each day and provide hot meals, lodging, and "entertainment upon the arrival of the road-weary party." The Great Northern train contained auto supplies and tires and even a darkroom for photographers.

10. See, for example, Drake Hokanson, *The Lincoln Highway: Main Street across America* (Iowa City: University of Iowa Press, 1988).

7. RAILROAD IMPERIALISM AND NATION BUILDING

1. J. M. Trout and Edw. Trout, *The Railways of Canada for 1870–1* (Toronto: Monetary Times, 1871), 31–32. See also Pierre Berton, *The Impossible Railway: The Building of the Canadian Pacific* (New York: Alfred A. Knopf, 1972); Hugh A. Dempsey, ed., *The CPR West: The Iron Road and the Making of a Nation* (Vancouver: Douglas and McIntyre, 1984); John Murray Gibbon, *Steel of Empire: The Romantic History of the Canadian Pacific, the Northwest Passage of Today* (Indianapolis: Bobbs-Merrill, 1935). Providing a classic overview of the history of Canada is W. L. Morton, *The Kingdom of Canada: A General History from Earliest Times*, 2nd ed. (Toronto: McClelland & Stewart, 1969).

2. Leonard Bertram Irwin, "Pacific Railways and Nationalism in the Canadian-American Northwest, 1845–1873" (PhD diss., University of Pennsylvania, 1939).

3. Robert F. Legget, *Railways of Canada* (Vancouver: Douglas & McIntyre, 1987).

4. *Herapath's Journal*, January 2, 1858, 14. Starting with an essay on Canada and providing a useful comparative approach to railroad imperialism around the world are Clarence B. Davis and Kenneth E. Wilburn Jr., eds., *Railway Imperialism* (New York: Greenwood, 1991). The term All Red Route described the steamship and rail combination that enabled London to remain in contact with the empire's far-flung colonies. Red is the color that mapmakers used to designate British possessions around the world.

5. Canadian National Railways dates from 1919 and was privatized in 1995. G. R. Stevens, *History of the Canadian National Railways* (New York: Macmillan, 1973); R. B. Fleming, *The Railway King of Canada: Sir William Mackenzie, 1849–1923* (Vancouver: UBC Press, 1991); Frank Leonard, *A Thousand Blunders: The Grand Trunk Pacific Railway and Northern British Columbia* (Vancouver: UBC Press, 1996); Donald MacKay, *The Asian Dream: The Pacific Rim and Canada's National Railway* (Vancouver: Douglas & McIntyre, 1986).

6. Additional Chicago-based railroads that straddled the Mississippi River but that had no ambition to cross the United States from coast to coast were the Chicago & Alton; the Chicago & North Western; the Chicago, Burlington & Quincy; and the Chicago, Milwaukee, St. Paul & Pacific.

7. *American Railway Times*, May 26, 1866, 163. The original Panama Railroad ran through a far northern portion of the nation of Colombia, an area that only later, in 1903, became the independent country of Panama. Peter Pyne, *The Panama Railroad* (Bloomington: Indiana University Press, 2021). The Pyne account is the most recent and most thorough of several book-length studies of North America's first transcontinental railroad. These include Duncan S. Somerville, *The Aspinwall Empire* (Mystic, CT: Mystic Seaport Museum, 1983); Joseph L. Schott, *Rails across Panama: The Story of the Panama Railroad, 1849–1855* (Indianapolis: Bobbs-Merrill, 1967); and F. N. Otis, *Illustrated History of the Panama Railroad* (New York: Harper & Brothers, 1862).

8. Raymond A. Rydell, "The Cape Horn Route to California, 1849," *Pacific Historical Review*, May 1948, 149–163. See also David McCullough, *The Path between the Seas: The Creation of the Panama Canal, 1870–1914* (New York: Simon & Schuster, 1977); John Haskell Kemble, *The Panama Route, 1848–1869* (Columbia: University of South Carolina Press, 1990).

9. James B. Hedges, *Building the Canadian West: The Land and Colonization Policies of the Canadian Pacific Railway* (New York: Macmillan, 1939); E. J. Hart, *The Selling of Canada: The CPR and the Beginnings of Canadian Tourism* (Banff: Altitude, 1983); Doug Owram, *Promise of Eden: The Canadian Expansionist Movement and the Idea of the West, 1856–1900* (Toronto: University of Toronto Press, 1980).

10. Barbara Chisholm, ed., *Castles of the North: Canada's Grand Hotels* (Toronto: Lynx Images, 2003).

11. In more recent times the Canadian Pacific slimmed down to concentrate on its railroad operations by selling its airline (now part of Air Canada), its steamship franchise to Princess, and its chain of hotels to Fairmont. For many years it had also functioned as the parent company of the Minneapolis, St. Paul & Sault Ste. Marie (Soo Line). To that property it added the eastern end of the defunct Milwaukee Road to achieve a considerable presence across the upper Midwest of the United States. The Canadian Pacific extended its presence much farther south with its 2023 acquisition of Kansas City Southern.

12. William R. Summerhill, *Order against Progress: Government, Foreign Investment, and Railroads in Brazil, 1854–1913* (Stanford, CA: Stanford University Press, 2003); Martin Cooper, *Brazilian Railway Culture* (Newcastle upon Tyne: Cambridge Scholars Publishing, 2011); Clodomiro Pereira Da Silva, *Railroads in the State of São Paulo (Brazil)* (São Paulo: Department of Agriculture, Commerce and Public Works of the State of S. Paulo, 1903).

13. Winthrop R. Wright, *British-Owned Railways in Argentina: Their Effect on the Growth of Economic Nationalism, 1854–1948* (Austin: University of Texas Press, 1974); Frederic M. Halsey, *Railway Expansion in Latin America* (New York: Moody Magazine and Book, 1916); Edgar A. Haine, *Railways across the Andes* (Boulder: Pruett, 1981).

14. A sampling of books on the railways of Africa and Asia would include George Tabor, *The Cape to Cairo Railway and River Routes* (London: Genta, 2003); Thomas L. Kennedy, *The Cape to Cairo Rail Journey* (n.p.: Thomas L. Kennedy, 2015); Charles Miller, *The Lunatic Express: An Entertainment in Imperialism* (1971; repr., London: Penguin Books, 2001); Ian J. Kerr, *Engines of Change: The Railroads That Made India* (Westport, CT: Praeger,

2007); Dan Free, *Early Japanese Railways, 1853–1914: Engineering Triumphs That Transformed Meiji-Era Japan* (Tokyo: Tuttle, 2008); and Augustus J. Veenendaal Jr., *Narrow Gauge in the Tropics: The Railways of the Dutch East Indies, 1864–1942* (Bloomington: Indiana University Press, 2022). Noteworthy for the extent of its coverage and its many illustrations is the five-volume set compiled by Leo Weinthal, *The Story of the Cape to Cairo Railway and River Route, from 1887 to 1922* (London: Pioneer, 1923). Contributors include Theodore Roosevelt and Winston Churchill.

15. John Bigelow, "The Railway Invasion of Mexico," *Harper's New Monthly Magazine*, October 1882, 745–757.

16. Providing an overview of Mexican railroads at their dawn is the *American Railway Times*, September 25, 1869, 307. More recent accounts include John H. Coatsworth, *Growth against Development: The Economic Impact of Railroads in Porfirian Mexico* (DeKalb: Northern Illinois University Press, 1981); Michael Matthews, *The Civilizing Machine: A Cultural History of Mexican Railroads, 1876–1910* (Lincoln: University of Nebraska Press, 2013); Teresa Van Hoy, *A Social History of Mexico's Railroads: Peons, Prisoners, and Priests* (Lanham, MD: Rowman & Littlefield, 2008); and Daniel Lewis, *Iron Horse Imperialism: The Southern Pacific of Mexico, 1880–1951* (Tucson: University of Arizona Press, 2007). See also Bernard Moses, *The Railway Revolution in Mexico* (San Francisco: Berkeley, 1895); Fred Wilbur Powell, *The Railroads of Mexico* (Boston: Stratford, 1921).

17. Keith Bryant Jr., *Arthur E. Stilwell: Promoter with a Hunch* (Nashville: Vanderbilt University Press, 1971); David M. Pletcher, *Rails, Mines, and Progress: Seven American Promoters in Mexico, 1967–1911* (Ithaca, NY: Cornell University Press, 1958), Chapter 8 on Stilwell, 260–295.

18. John Leeds Kerr, *Destination Topolobampo: The Kansas City, Mexico & Orient Railway* (San Marino, CA: Golden West Books, 1968); Don Burgess, ed., *Sierra Challenge: The Construction of the Chihuahua al Pacífico Railroad* (Taos, NM: Barranca, 2013); *Mexico's Copper Canyon, State of Chihuahua* (n.p.: Guia México Desconocido, n.d. [ca. 2000]).

19. In recent decades, the two big Canadian railroads both reached far south across the United States. The Canadian National, which for years had controlled the Grand Trunk Western, which extended from Ontario across Michigan and northern Indiana to Chicago, added the Illinois Central to give it access to the Gulf Coast port of New Orleans. Don L. Hofsommer, *Grand Trunk Corporation: Canadian National Railways in the United States, 1971–1992* (East Lansing: Michigan State University Press, 1995). A Canadian transcontinental railway of decidedly different orientation was the line completed north to Hudson's Bay in 1929, which was supposed to give the Dominion another outlet to the Atlantic Ocean—except during those months when water in the Far North froze solid. Ian Bickle, *Turmoil and Triumph: The Controversial Railway to Hudson Bay* (Calgary: Detselig, 1995).

8. MAGICIAN'S WAND

1. *Milwaukee Railway System Employees' Magazine*, September 1914, 5. Similar sentiments appear in the *Milwaukee Railway System Employees' Magazine*, April 1916, 5–7, and *Milwaukee Magazine*, March 1930, 7.

2. Walter V. Woehlke, "Transplanting the Garden of Eden," *Sunset*, June 1911, 587. The article references Oregon's Rogue River Valley and describes how the introduction of apple orchards wrought a positive transformation of the landscape and its inhabitants. Articles that described how railroads transformed the natural landscape into moneymaking orchards and farms—replacing the native bunchgrass of eastern Washington, for example, with apples and grain—appeared frequently in the Development Section of *Sunset*. For two additional examples of the formulaic approach to repackaging the landscape, see A. J. Wells, "Twin Towns of the Touchet," *Sunset*, October 1908, 561–567; John Scott Mills, "Riches of an Inland Empire," *Sunset*, October 1910, 471–476. The former article highlights the transformation that took place in eastern Washington north of the city of Walla Walla, and the latter focuses on the reworked landscape surrounding Idaho Falls in eastern Idaho.

3. Among America's early land-promotion brochures is *A Guide to the Illinois Central Railroad Lands* (Chicago: Illinois Central Railroad, 1859). An 1856 version of the same basic prospectus, bearing the title "The Illinois Central Rail-Road Company Offers for Sale Over 2,000,000 Acres Selected Farming and Wood-Lands," did not feature any of the woodcuts used to illustrate the 1859 guide. The pioneer land giveaway was the brainchild of Illinois senator Stephen A. Douglas, who in 1850 replaced Senator Thomas Hart Benton as chair of the Interior Committee and used his new position of power to promote Illinois railroads as vigorously as Benton had attempted to do for his home state of Missouri in the late 1840s. See Peter A. Hansen, Don L. Hofsommer, and Carlos A. Schwantes, *Crossroads of a Continent: Missouri*

Railroads, 1851–1921 (Bloomington: Indiana University Press, 2022).

4. General studies include Leslie E. Decker, *Railroads, Lands, and Politics* (Providence, RI: Brown University Press, 1964); Lloyd J. Mercer, *Railroads and Land Grant Policy: A Study in Government Intervention* (New York: Academic, 1982). Books about individual railroads and their land grants are notable for their depth and detail: William S. Greever, *Arid Domain: The Santa Fe Railway and Its Western Land Grant* (Stanford, CA: Stanford University Press, 1954); Paul Wallace Gates, *The Illinois Central Railroad and Its Colonization Work* (Cambridge, MA: Harvard University Press, 1934); Richard C. Overton, *Burlington West: A Colonization History of the Burlington Railroad* (Cambridge, MA: Harvard University Press, 1941); Richard J. Orsi, *Sunset Limited: The Southern Pacific Railroad and the Development of the American West* (Berkeley: University of California Press, 2005); Claire Strom, *Profiting from the Plains: The Great Northern Railway and Corporate Development of the American West* (Seattle: University of Washington Press, 2003).

5. *Charter of the Northern Pacific Railroad Company, July 2, 1864* (Boston: J. H. Eastburn's, 1866). For a convenient overview of railroad land grants, see William S. Greever, "A Comparison of Railroad Land-Grant Policies," *Agricultural History*, April 1951, 83–90. In all, the federal government used land to encourage the construction of at least seventy separate railroads. The Great Northern is often thought to have completed its transcontinental line from Saint Paul to Seattle in 1893 without the aid of a land grant, but one of its predecessor companies did receive three million acres of federal land through the territory of Minnesota in 1857. John B. Rae, "The Great Northern's Land Grant," *Journal of Economic History* 12 (Spring 1952): 140–145.

6. Jay Cooke, *The Northern Pacific Railroad's Land Grant* (Philadelphia: Jay Cooke, 1870), 3.

7. Examples of Cooke's relentless boosterism are *The Northern Pacific Railroad: Its Route, Resources, Progress and Business* (Philadelphia: Jay Cooke, 1871); and *The Northern Pacific Railroad: Its Land Grant, Traffic, Resources, and Tributary Country* (Philadelphia: Jay Cooke, 1873). Details of Northern Pacific's legal dealings with its Philadelphia fiscal agent are provided in *Northern Pacific R. R. Co. Agreement Concluded May 20th, 1869, and Supplementary Agreement between Northern Pacific R. R. Company, and Jay Cooke & Co.*, a pamphlet available at the Washington State Historical Society in Tacoma.

8. Jan Taylor, "Marketing the Northwest: The Northern Pacific Railroad's Last Spike Excursion," *Montana: The Magazine of Western History* 60, no. 4 (Winter 2010): 16–35, 93–94.

9. Alexandra Villard de Borchgrave and John Cullen, *Villard: The Life and Times of an American Titan* (New York: Doubleday, 2001).

10. David M. Emmons, *Garden in the Grasslands: Boomer Literature of the Central Great Plains* (Lincoln: University of Nebraska Press, 1971); Jan Blodgett, *Land of Bright Promise: Advertising the Texas Panhandle and South Plains, 1870–1917* (Austin: University of Texas Press, 1988); Barbara J. Rozek, *Come to Texas: Enticing Immigrants, 1865–1915* (College Station: Texas A&M University Press, 2003). Specific examples include Houston East & West Texas Railway, *Texas* (Houston: Houston East & West Texas Railway, 1894), 12; Robert E. Strahorn, *The Resources and Attractions of Idaho Territory* (1881; repr., Moscow: University of Idaho Press, 1990); and Olin D. Wheeler, *Indianland and Wonderland* (Saint Paul: Northern Pacific Railroad, 1894).

11. Joseph J. Finn, "Railroad Passenger Advertising," *Railway Age*, November 20, 1948, 202–204. A case study that examines railroad competition for settlers is Carlos A. Schwantes, ed., "Problems of Empire Building: The Oregon Trunk Railway Survey of Disappointed Homeseekers, 1911," *Oregon Historical Quarterly* 83 (Winter 1982): 371–390.

12. *Official Guide*, June 1907, xxxii. Grants of land intended to encourage railroad construction were not limited to the federal government's contribution of approximately 225 million acres. Nine states gave railroads nearly 50 million additional acres. The subject is a controversial one. See Robert S. Henry, "The Railroad Land Grant Legend in American History Texts," *Mississippi Valley Historical Review* 32 (September 1945): 171–194. Henry's essay caused considerable stir among historians, both pro and con, with the debate continuing as "Comments on 'The Railroad Land Grant Legend in American History Texts,'" *Mississippi Valley Historical Review* 32 (March 1946): 557–576. Offering a decidedly negative view of the giveaway are Derrick Jensen and George Draffan, *Railroads and Clearcuts: The Legacy of Congress's 1864 Northern Pacific Railroad Land Grant* (Spokane, WA: Inland Empire Public Lands Council, 1995).

13. *Official Guide*, June 1907, xxxii; October 1909, xxviii. For additional information on this plucky carrier of the Upper Midwest, see Don L. Hofsommer, *The Tootin' Louis: A History of the*

Minneapolis and St. Louis Railway (Minneapolis: University of Minnesota Press, 2005), esp. chap. 9.

14. *Official Guide*, May 1910, xxxi.

15. Homeseeker's Bureau, *The Old Timer and the Homeseeker* (Portland, OR: Homeseekers' Bureau, 1911).

16. *Sunset* magazine, which is still published for West Coast readers, originated shortly before the dawn of the twentieth century as a booster publication sponsored by the Southern Pacific System. Paul C. Johnson, ed., *The Early Sunset Magazine, 1898–1928* (San Francisco: California Historical Society, 1973). Numerous examples of its Homeseekers' Bureau publications are contained in the William Bittle Wells Collection at the University of Oregon in Eugene. For a sampling of illustrations drawn from the Wells Collection, see Carlos A. Schwantes, *Railroad Signatures across the Pacific Northwest* (Seattle: University of Washington Press, 1993).

17. J. A. Jasberg, "The Best Type of Settler," in *Proceedings of the Fourteenth Annual Meeting of the American Railway Development Association* (Denver, 1912), 52–54.

18. The North-Western's wordsmith noted that "practically any American citizen—or foreigner who has established a permanent residence in the United States and filed satisfactory First Citizen papers—has a right to secure 160 acres of federal land." Chicago & North-Western, *Isn't It Time You Owned a Farm?* (Chicago: Chicago & North-Western, 1911), 3.

19. Jonathan Raban, *Bad Land: An American Romance* (New York: Vintage Books, 1996); Roy V. Scott, *Railroad Development Programs in the Twentieth Century* (Ames: Iowa State University Press, 1985).

20. Studies of railroad salesmanship include J. Valerie Fifer, *American Progress: The Growth of the Transport, Tourist, and Information Industries in the Nineteenth-Century West Seen through the Life and Times of George A. Crofutt, Pioneer and Publicist of the Transcontinental Age* (Chester, CT: Globe Pequot, 1988); and Sig Mickelson, *The Northern Pacific Railroad and the Selling of the West: A Nineteenth-Century Public Relations Venture* (Sioux Falls, SD: Center for Western Studies, 1993).

9. INVENTING NEW VACATION DESTINATIONS

1. *Railway World*, December 26, 1891, 1226.

2. Delving into the differences between travel and tourism is Garrett Eckbo, "The Landscape of Tourism," *Landscape* (Spring–Summer 1969): 29–31. As for vacation travel, "Americans are not in the habit of doing things by halves." Thus it was with their annual break from the stresses of work, be they physical or mental: "Vacation has become popular, and what is popular goes. It is to the credit of the railroads that they have done so much to stimulate this habit." *International Railway Journal*, September 1906, 12.

3. Peter Bailey, "'A Mingled Mass of Perfectly Legitimate Pleasures': The Victorian Middle Class and the Problem of Leisure," *Victorian Studies* 21, no. 1 (Autumn 1977): 7–28; Cindy S. Aron, *Working at Play: A History of Vacations in the United States* (New York: Oxford University Press, 1999); Orvar Löfgren, *On Holiday: History of Vacationing* (Berkeley: University of California Press, 1999); John A. Jakle, *The Tourist: Travel in Twentieth-Century North America* (Lincoln: University of Nebraska Press, 1985); Earl Pomeroy, *In Search of the Golden West: The Tourist in Western America* (New York: Alfred A. Knopf, 1957); Marguerite S. Shaffer, *See America First: Tourism and National Identity, 1880–1940* (Washington: Smithsonian Institution Press, 2001).

4. Wisconsin Central Line, *Summer of 1888* (n.p.: Passenger Department, 1888), 4. Booklets issued by a competitor, the Chicago & North Western, highlighted the hotels, boardinghouses, and camps that catered to "sportsmen and those in search of recreation in the woods and streams of Wisconsin, Minnesota and the northern Michigan peninsula." *Official Guide*, October 1906, xxxi; June 1909, xxxi.

5. *Official Guide*, August 1905, xxix–xxi.

6. *Official Guide*, July 1926, xxxii; *Milwaukee Magazine*, July 1927, 3–4. The former town of Salesville became Gallatin Gateway, Montana.

7. Thornton Waite, *Yellowstone by Train: A History of Rail Travel to America's First National Park* (Missoula, MT: Pictorial Histories, 2006); C. W. Guthrie, *All Aboard for Glacier: The Great Northern Railway and Glacier National Park* (Helena, MT: Farcountry, 2004). Congress established Yosemite National Park in 1890, Mount Rainier in 1899, Crater Lake in 1902, Glacier in 1910, and Grand Canyon in 1919. The first national park established east of the Mississippi River was Acadia on the scenic coast of Maine, which dates from 1919. By 1929, far more visitors to America's twenty-one national parks arrived by automobile than by train, though the percentages varied by location. For Crater Lake, fully 98 percent of all visitors arrived by automobile, while for

Yellowstone it was 83 percent. *Railway Age*, December 14, 1929, 1390.

8. *Official Guide*, July 1939, 29. "The Great Northern Railway has supplemented the Government work in developing the park." Of course, Great Northern became the most avid promoter of the 1,400-square-mile park "embracing some of the grandest scenery on the continent." One of its early brochures was titled *See America First—Glacier National Park. Official Guide*, October 1911, xxx; November 1911, xxx; March 1912, xxix.

9. Alfred Runte, *Trains of Discovery: Railroads and the Legacy of Our National Parks*, 5th ed. (Lanham, MD: Roberts Rinehart, 2011).

10. Wisconsin Central Line, *Summer of 1888*, 4; Lloyd W. McDowell, "Westward Comes the Tourist," *Railway and Marine News*, May 1923, 12–15.

11. The New York Central's pamphlet noted one of the remarkable social trends of the past decade: "For the hundreds, who, ten years ago, left home for a summer outing; there are now thousands." *Saturday Evening Post*, reprinted in New York Central, *The Summer Boarder* (New York: New York Central, 1904).

12. *Official Guide*, December 1923, xxix.

13. Gregg M. Turner and Seth H. Bramson, *The Plant System of Railroads, Steamships and Hotels: The South's First Great Industrial Enterprise* (Laurys Station, PA: Garrigues House, 2004); Kelly Reynolds, *Henry Plant: Pioneer Empire Builder* (Cocoa, FL: Florida Historical Society, 2003).

14. Sidney Walter Martin, *Henry Flagler: Visionary of the Gilded Age* (Lake Buena Vista, FL: Tailored Tours, 1998); David Freeman Hawke, *John D.: The Founding Father of the Rockefellers* (New York: Harper & Row, 1980).

15. *Railway Journal*, February 1912, 5.

16. Seth H. Bramson, *The Greatest Railroad Story Ever Told: Henry Flagler & the Florida East Coast Railway's Key West Extension* (Charleston, SC: History, 2011).

17. *Official Guide*, August 1914, xxix.

18. *Flagler Museum: An Illustrated Guide*, 3rd ed. (Palm Beach: Flagler Museum, 2002).

19. To promote development along their tracks from Minnesota west to Washington, both the Northern Pacific and Milwaukee Road operated exhibit cars. The Chicago & Eastern Illinois operated a "fruit train" across Indiana and Illinois that featured exhibits and demonstrations of better marketing methods for the area's fruits and vegetables. *Official Guide*, March 1924, xxx;

Railway Age, August 21, 1926, 329–330. Among demonstration trains operated by other railroads were those devoted to "better farming," "good seeds," "sugar beets," and "beef production."

20. David Nolan, *Fifty Feet in Paradise: The Booming of Florida* (San Diego: Harcourt Brace Jovanovich, 1984); Gregg M. Turner, *A Milestone Celebration: The Seaboard Railway to Naples and Miami* (Bloomington, IN: AuthorHouse, 2004).

21. Les Standiford, *Last Train to Paradise: Henry Flagler and the Spectacular Rise and Fall of the Railroad That Crossed an Ocean* (New York: Crown, 2002); Gregg M. Turner, *A Journey into Florida Railroad History* (Gainesville: University Press of Florida, 2008).

10. MATCHLESS PLEASURELANDS AND SEASONAL VARIATIONS

1. Henry J. Winsor, *The Great Northwest: A Guide-Book and Itinerary* (New York: G. P. Putnam's Sons, 1883), 8.

2. *International Railway Journal*, January 1911, 13.

3. Richard A. Van Orman, *A Room for the Night: Hotels of the Old West* (Bloomington: Indiana University Press, 1966); A. K. Sandoval-Strausz, *Hotel: An American History* (New Haven, CT: Yale University Press, 2007); *United States Hotel Guide and Railway Companion for 1867* (New York: James Miller, 1867).

4. Otto Ernest Rayburn, *The Eureka Springs Story* (1954; repr., Eureka Springs, AR: Wheeler, 1982); Gregory S. Gatsos, *History of the West Baden Springs Hotel* (Bedford, IN: Gregory S. Gatsos, 2008).

5. *Official Guide*, June 1916, xxvi–xxvii. "Summering places" in Michigan and Wisconsin had the same appeal for residents of Detroit, Chicago, and many other cities of the Midwest "eager to escape" by train to lakeshore hotels, hunting lodges, and tents. Not to be overshadowed by its larger competitors along both sides of Lake Michigan, the Detroit & Mackinac Railway issued a brochure in 1916 to call attention to the summer resorts of Lake Huron. As an added feature, the publication also provided information on how to obtain a farm in Michigan. Presumably, vacationers with time on their hands could ponder the railroad's inducement to return to the land. *Official Guide*, July 1916, xxv.

6. *Official Guide*, January 1905, xxix. See also Marshall Sprague, *Newport in the Rockies: The Life and Good Times of Colorado Springs* (1961; repr., Athens: Swallow Press/Ohio University Press, 1987); Denver & Rio Grande Railway Company, *Health,*

Wealth and Pleasure in Colorado and New Mexico (Chicago: Belford, Clarke, 1881).

7. *Official Guide*, February 1910, xxix. Every region of the United States featured resorts of one type or another. New England and the states of the South were particularly popular because these areas were closest to the major population centers of the East Coast. On the other hand, the resorts of the Pacific Northwest, a distant region for most Americans, went largely unrecognized by vacation seekers from elsewhere. C. E. Johns, "Resorts of the Pacific Northwest," *Railway and Marine News*, September 1928, 10, 20.

8. *Western Resorts Reached via the Union Pacific System* (Omaha, NE: Union Pacific, 1896), 171–173. Also of interest was Union Pacific's *Health and Pleasure along the Line of the Oregon Railroad & Navigation Company* (n.p.: Union Pacific, 1903), a pamphlet that promoted the healing waters of Bingham Springs and Hot Lake in eastern Oregon, places especially therapeutic "to persons 'run down' by overwork or too close confinement in office or counting-room" (p. vi). The water of Hot Lake, the pamphlet promised, "is delightful to the taste, having something of the exhilarating effect of champagne. It has cured innumerable invalids, who had tried in vain all the noted resorts of this country and of Europe" (p. vii).

9. *Official Guide*, March 1911, xxxv. One of the first things the White Sulphur Springs & Yellowstone Park Railway did when completed was to add its timetable and a map to the mass of rail listings already comprising the *Official Guide*.

10. *Official Guide*, December 1926, xxxii.

11. *Official Guide*, May 1910, xxxi. Hot Springs National Park was established in 1921, but the Arkansas resort community existed well before that date. Martinsville, Indiana, located at the end of an electric interurban railway line from Indianapolis, offers another example of a community that was at one time home to sanitariums famous for mineral waters reputed to cure a variety of ailments. The largest such facility in the United States, if not the world, was the Battle Creek Sanitarium, run by Dr. John Harvey Kellogg, who invented the cornflake as a healthy substitute for the typical American breakfast loaded with fatty meats. His brother, Will K. Kellogg, a marketing genius, gave the world an enduring favorite in Kellogg's Corn Flakes. Sanitariums and mineral spas figured prominently in the health history of the late nineteenth and early twentieth centuries, and the heavily stressed business tycoons of that era were among their frequent clients. See Richard W. Schwarz, *John Harvey Kellogg, M. D.: Pioneering Health Reformer* (1970; repr., Hagerstown, MD: Review & Herald Publishing Association, 2006). Offering a dark and highly cynical fictional counterpoint to the Kellogg story and the health phenomenon it represented is T. Coraghessan Boyle, *The Road to Wellville* (Boston: Little, Brown, 1981).

12. *Official Guide*, March 1912, xxix; Billy M. Jones, *Health-Seekers in the Southwest, 1817–1900* (Norman: University of Oklahoma Press, 1967); Gene Fowler, *Crazy Water: The Story of Mineral Wells and Other Texas Health Resorts* (Fort Worth: Texas Christian University Press, 1991); David L. Richards, *Poland Spring: A Tale of the Gilded Age, 1860–1900* (Hanover, NH: University Press of New England, 2005).

13. *Official Guide*, September 1906, xxxii.

14. *Official Guide*, June 1906, xxxii. A complete compilation of the titles of railroad publications devoted to vacation attractions (collectively described as a "library of travel") would be difficult, if not impossible, to prepare. However, the opening pages of each month's *Official Guide* offer running commentary on many of the latest rail promotional publications.

15. *Official Guide*, February 1909, xxvii. One Louisville & Nashville publication was the aptly titled *Winter Time in Summer Land*. The editor of the *Official Guide*, always determined to report each month's new examples of publishing the railroad, wrote: "The cover is in a dainty design, and is a fine example of color printing." He added that the Louisville & Nashville had also published *Cuba, the Pearl of the Antilles, and the Gem of the Seas*, "a delightfully written and finely illustrated book, setting forth the attractions of our nearest neighbor in the West Indies."

16. Les Standiford, *Last Train to Paradise: Henry Flagler and the Spectacular Rise and Fall of the Railroad That Crossed an Ocean* (2002; repr., Palm Beach: Henry Morrison Flagler Museum, 2012); Sidney Walter Martin, *Henry Flagler: Visionary of the Gilded Age* (Lake Buena Vista, FL: Tailored Tours, 1998); Kelly Reynolds, *Henry Plant, Pioneer Empire Builder* (Cocoa: Florida Historical Society Press, 2003).

17. *Official Guide*, June 1906, xxxiii.

18. *Official Guide*, June 1907, xxxi; *Official Guide*, July 1907, xxxiii. The Mississippian and its through Pullman car from Chicago are mentioned in the *Official Guide* (December 1924, xxix) nearly two decades after its editor praised the railroad vacation brochures promoting the coasts of Oregon and Georgia, but the train and winter vacations along the Gulf Coast do not seem to

have warranted a special brochure. Very likely, the small railroad chose to skip the expense of printing. Besides, by 1924 an ever-increasing number of motorists were using private automobiles instead of passenger trains to reach vacation destinations (p. xxix). Certainly, one of the smallest railroads to issue summer vacation brochures was the East Tennessee & Western North Carolina, which in conjunction with the Linville River Railway, another narrow-gauge carrier, promoted the mountain scenery and numerous resorts of their remote service area. "Fishing, mountain climbing, golf and other outdoor sports may be enjoyed, and many fine scenic highways attract the visiting motorist." These words appeared in 1926, but eventually the motorists and the "fine scenic highways" eliminated the need for charming backwoods passenger trains. *Official Guide*, June 1926, xxxiv.

11. PRINT WORKS

1. David Jury, *Graphic Design before Graphic Designers: The Printer as Designer and Craftsman* (London: Thames & Hudson, 2012); Domenico Porzio, ed., *Lithography: 200 Years of Art, History and Technique* (New York: Harry N. Abrams, 1983), first published in Italian in 1982. A sampling of the numerous books dealing with the colorful world of rail poster graphics includes J. T. Shackleton, *The Golden Age of the Railway Poster* (Secaucus, NJ: Chartwell Books, 1976); Thierry Favre, *Railway Posters* (Woodbridge, Suffolk: Antique Collectors Club, 2011); and Marc H. Choko and David L. Jones, *Posters of the Canadian Pacific* (Richmond Hill, ON: Firefly Books, 2004). Placing railroad posters in their historical context are John Barnicoat, *Posters: A Concise History* (London: Thames & Hudson, 1972); Max Gallo, *The Poster in History* (New York: W. W. Norton, 2001), first published in Italian in 1972; and Alain Weill, *The Poster: A Worldwide Survey and History* (Boston: G. K. Hall, 1985).

2. C. C. Howard, "Cultivation and Solicitation," *Official Guide*, December 1934, 48.

3. *Record and Bergen County Herald* (Hackensack, NJ), January 23, 1904.

4. C. Talbot Southwick, "The Railroad Pamphlet," *Printing Art*, December 1904, 207–214. For an extended account of how railroad promotional booklets were made, see F. I. Whitney, "The Making of a Railroad Booklet," *American Printer*, December 1904, 280–281. Whitney, general passenger agent for the Great Northern Railway, believed that over the years the value of such publications had increased "as the crudities have been obliterated until to-day it has attained a popularity which is scarcely equaled by any other form of advertising." As for printed timetables, he believed it was "a waste of money to make them artistic and literary." Obviously, few industry peers agreed with Whitney: the decade after 1904 witnessed some of the most attractive rail timetables ever published. The amount of money railroads spent on printing in 1909 comes from *Railway Employees' Magazine*, March 1912, 25.

5. *Western Resorts Reached via the Union Pacific System* (n.p.: Union Pacific System, 1896). A list of the Northern Pacific's 1901 contributions to publishing the railroad is at the Washington State Historical Society in Tacoma, although it probably does not cite all available titles.

6. *Official Guide*, July 1910, xxvii. The Oregon Short Line was a Union Pacific subsidiary that connected with the original transcontinental railroad at Granger, Wyoming, and ran northwesterly across Idaho to provide access to the Pacific Northwest states of Oregon and Washington. For further information see Jeff Asay, *Union Pacific Northwest: The Oregon-Washington Railroad and Navigation Company* (Edmonds, WA: Pacific Fast Mail, 1991).

7. Simon Garfield, *Just My Type: A Book about Fonts* (New York: Gotham Books, 2011); Steven Heller and Louise Fili, *Vintage Type and Graphics* (New York: Allworth, 2011); Frank H. Atkinson, Charles J. Strong, and L. S. Strong, *Vintage Commercial Art & Design* (Mineola, NY: Dover, 2011); Allan Haley, *Alphabet: The History, Evolution and Design of the Letters We Use Today* (London: Thames & Hudson, 1995). Worth noting is another ubiquitous type of graphic representation, the railroad logo. Ian Logan and Jonathan Glancey, *Logomotion: Railroad Graphics and the American Dream* (London: Sheldrake, 2020).

8. *Official Guide*, June 1900, xxvii. The third edition of the Northern Pacific's thick publication called *Montana* totaled fifty thousand copies. *Official Guide*, August 1912, xxx. Intended to encourage new settlers, it featured a large-scale map of the state.

9. Jay T. Last, *The Color Explosion: Nineteenth-Century American Lithography* (Santa Ana, CA: Hillcrest, 2005); K. D. Kurutz and Gary F. Kurutz, *California Calls You: The Art of Promoting the Golden State, 1870–1940* (Sausalito, CA: Windgate, 2000). Providing historical context to railroad commercial art are Philip B. Meggs and Alston W. Purvis, *Meggs' History of Graphic Design*, 4th ed. (Hoboken, NJ: John Wiley & Sons, 2006); Richard Howells and Joaquim Negreiros, *Visual Culture*, 2nd ed. (Malden,

MA: Polity, 2012); and David Holloway and John Beck, eds., *American Visual Cultures* (London: Continuum, 2005).

10.   Poole Brothers in 1911 saluted its printing skills by distributing a portfolio containing examples of its numerous railroad publications. Among these were Oregon Short Line's *Where Gush the Geysers*, the Dominion Atlantic's *Vacation Days in Nova Scotia*, and Chicago, Milwaukee & Puget Sound's *Across the Continent*. One publication called *The Land of Opportunities* showcased how North America's rail carriers, both large and prominent and relatively obscure, embraced printed publicity during its heyday in the early twentieth century, because the issuing railroad was the Clinchfield Route, which traced a remote and hardscrabble corridor through deepest Appalachia. *Official Guide*, September 1911. Books on the history of advertising include Pamela Walker Laird, *Advertising Progress: American Business and the Rise of Consumer Marketing* (Baltimore: Johns Hopkins University Press, 1998); Roland Marchand, *Advertising the American Dream: Making Way for Modernity, 1920–1940* (Berkeley: University of California Press, 1985); and Charles Goodrum and Helen Dalrymple, *Advertising in America, The First 200 Years* (New York: Henry N. Abrams, 1990). Among the early twentieth-century trade journals devoted to the printing industry in the United States were the *American Printer* (New York); the *Inland Printer* (Chicago); and the *Printing Art* (Cambridge, Massachusetts).

11.   The Homeseekers' Bureau issued settlement brochures as part of its "community publicity" plan from 1907 until 1911. Numerous examples of its handiwork are described in the *Official Guide*, November 1910, xxx; April 1911, xxx; June 1912, xxxii. The papers of William Bittle Wells and the Bureau of Community Publicity he oversaw are archived at the University of Oregon in Eugene.

12.   Paul C. Johnson, ed., *The Early Sunset Magazine, 1898–1928* (San Francisco: California Historical Society, 1973). By no means were all promoters of the West affiliated with railroads, nor were all given to florid descriptions. One publicist, William H. Maher, wasted no words dancing around the topic of human greed when he titled his booster pamphlet *The Golden West, "Where Money Grows on Trees"* (Toledo, OH, 1911). Like railroad map fantasies, so it was with exaggerated booster claims, and many Americans no doubt grew skilled at separating fiction from truth.

13.   Stewart H. Holbrook, *Far Corner: A Personal View of the Pacific Northwest* (New York: Macmillan, 1952), 4.

14.   G. Henry Stetson, "Railway Publicity," *International Railway Journal*, January 1911, 12; Carlos A. Schwantes, "The Milwaukee Road's Pacific Extension, 1909–1929: The Photographs of Asahel Curtis," *Pacific Northwest Quarterly*, January 1981, 30–40.

15.   *Official Guide*, April 1906, xxxi.

16.   *Milwaukee Magazine*, January 1927, 9, 11; Chicago, Milwaukee & St. Paul Railway, *Montana: Along the New Line to the Pacific Coast* (Chicago: Chicago, Milwaukee & St. Paul Railway, 1912). Readers may discern that I am drawn to the Milwaukee Road, a quirky transcontinental railroad I never had the chance to ride, but I did write about its reach west to Puget Sound as illustrated by Seattle photographer Asahel Curtis in an illustrated essay: Schwantes, "The Milwaukee Road's Pacific Extension, 1909–1929: The Photographs of Asahel Curtis."

17.   Mark H. Salt, *Buffalo (NY) Courier*, May 28, 1911. The publication of brochures to encourage land settlement was by no means limited to the big transcontinental lines. Many smaller railroads contributed to an impressive body of literature. The Houston East & West Texas Railway, which in 1894 published a small booster pamphlet on the resources served by its tracks, included this admonition on its title page: "Read and send to some one you wish to do a favor."

18.   *Official Guide*, March 1909, xxviii.

19.   Southwick, "Railroad Pamphlet," 209; *Official Guide*, June 1906, xxxiii; September 1906, xxxii. In addition to the big three publishers, hundreds of specialized railroad printing firms existed across the United States. One large regional establishment was the Woodwood & Tiernan Company of Saint Louis. "We do an immense amount of railroad printing," explained one of its sales representatives, "and the outside public can have little idea of the enormity of this branch of business." *Memphis Commercial*, May 31, 1891.

20.   *Official Guide*, December 1923, xxix.

21.   *Official Guide*, September 1901, xxiv. One of the best examples of the creative reach of railroad publicists is the Union Pacific's 1899 pamphlet titled *Some of Wyoming's Vertebrate Fossils*, which said the "original inhabitants of Wyoming are attracting great attention from all geologists and paleontologists, and the new discoveries that are constantly being made there are adding materially to scientific knowledge." *Official Guide*, July 1899, xxx. The Union Pacific and its subsidiaries also published a *Corn Primer* as well as brochures that promoted apple growing and consumption. Union Pacific, *Corn Primer* (Portland:

Oregon-Washington Railroad & Navigation, 1916); *150 Recipes for Apple Dishes* (Omaha, NE: Agricultural Department, Union Pacific System, 1925). The Northern Pacific's counterpart brochure was *Apple Talk: Recipes for 55 Ways to Serve the Apple* (Saint Paul: Northern Pacific Railway, 1915).

22. *Official Guide*, September 1901, xxiv; May 1930, 17; *Restful Recreation Resorts* (Portland: Oregon Railroad & Navigation, 1904).

23. *Official Guide*, May 1927, xxxvi; June 1931, 40.

24. Chicago, Burlington & Quincy, *A Bouquet from the Garden of the Gods* (Chicago: Chicago, Burlington & Quincy, 1884), 1–2.

25. *Official Guide*, November 1929, 4; May 1930, 16; April 1931, 45.

26. *Official Guide*, August 1912, xxx.

12. TIMETABLE TYRANNY

1. Jules Verne, *Around the World in 80 Days* (1873; repr., New York: Charles Scribner's Sons, 1922), 25. Also of interest are Allen Foster, *Around the World with Citizen Train: The Sensational Adventures of the Real Phileas Fogg* (Dublin: Merlin, 2002); and *Railway World*, July 18, 1891, 674.

2. Chester G. Hearn, *Tracks in the Sea: Matthew Fontaine Maury and the Mapping of the Oceans* (Camden, ME: International Marine/McGraw-Hill, 2002); Dava Sobel, *Longitude: The True Story of a Lone Genius Who Solved the Greatest Scientific Problem of His Time* (New York: Walker, 1995); Andro Linklater, *Measuring America: How an Untamed Wilderness Shaped the United States and Fulfilled the Promise of Democracy* (New York: Walker, 2002); Carol Sheriff, *The Artificial River: The Erie Canal and the Paradox of Progress, 1817–1862* (New York: Hill & Wang, 1996); Peter L. Bernstein, *Wedding of the Waters: The Erie Canal and the Making of a Great Nation* (New York: W. W. Norton, 2005); Gerard Koeppel, *Bond of Union: Building the Erie Canal and the American Empire* (Philadelphia: Da Capo, 2009). Koeppel notes that in the state assembly of New York, "the prospect of country surveyors engineering the nation's greatest construction project brought ridicule and alarm." Koeppel, 182.

3. Franz Anton Ritter von Gerstner, *Early American Railroads*, ed. Frederick C. Gamst, trans. David J. Diephouse and John C. Decker, 2 vols. (Stanford, CA: Stanford University Press, 1997); originally published as *Die inner Communicationen* (1842–1843).

4. *Champaign (IL) Daily News*, March 21, 1903.

5. A copy of the timetable/advertisement appears in *Railway Age*, November 20, 1948, 202. See also *International Railway Journal*, June 1920, 13.

6. My own interest in railroad and other transportation timetables dates back to 1957, when a kindly ticket agent at the Indianapolis Union Station gave this twelve-year-old boy a copy of the *Official Railway Guide*. A few months earlier I had discovered railroad timetables on a rack in the same station. The *Official Guide* gave a quantum leap to my understanding of the rail network across North America. One result nearly twenty years later was Carlos A. Schwantes, "The Joy of Timetables," *Journal of Popular Culture* 9, no. 3 (Winter 1975): 604–617. As I recall, the editor, inspired perhaps by the popularity of a recent book titled *The Joy of Sex* (1972), chose the title, and I acquiesced because I was a young member of the history profession eager to get an article published.

7. G. Royde Smith, *The History of Bradshaw: A Centenary Review of the Origin and Growth of the Most Famous Guide in the World* (London: Henry Blacklock, 1939); Charles Lee, *The Centenary of "Bradshaw"* (London: Railway Gazette, 1940); Vic Bradshaw-Mitchell, *Bradshaw's History* (Midhurst: Middleton, 2012); John George Freeman, *Three Men and a Bradshaw: An Original Victorian Travel Journal*, ed. Ronnie Scott (London: Random House Books, 2015). The *Bradshaw* guide ceased publication in 1961.

8. "It is a puzzle to most people to decipher the ordinary time table of a trunk line railroad. Infinitely more complex is the problem of arranging that schedule." *International Railway Journal*, March 1903, 28–19. Daily newspapers occasionally offered readers a behind-the-scenes look at the labor-intensive work required to construct accurate timetables. For three of the best accounts, see the *Washington Star*, reprinted in *St. Louis Globe-Democrat*, May 12, 1895; *Chicago Inter-Ocean*, September 15, 1899; W. G. Maddox, "How Timetables Are Made," *International Railway Journal*, June 1922, 13–14.

9. *Doggett's Railroad Guide and Gazetteer for 1848* (New York: John Doggett Jr., 1848), 11.

10. J. C. Swayze, *Hill & Swayze's Confederate States Rail-Road and Steam-Boat Guide* (Griffin, GA: J. C. Swayze, n.d., ca. 1863), 21.

11. *Official Guide*, May 1918, xxiii. The *Official Guide* for May 1943 (p. 14) contains a seventy-five-year retrospective account of

the publication. Giving the newborn publication a valuable boost was the October 1868 meeting in Saint Louis of the American Association of General Passenger and Ticket Agents, which endorsed the *Official Guide* as its professional standard. *Official Guide*, April 1894, xxv.

12. National Railway Publication, *Travelers' Official Railway Guide for the United States and Canada, June 1868* (1868; repr., New York: National Railway Publication Company, 1968). Its name and its geographical coverage changed over the years, but for convenience I refer to it throughout *Railroad Nation* as the *Official Guide*.

13. Other competitors to the *Official Guide* in 1868 included Disturnell's *Railroad, Steamboat and Telegraph Guide* (established in 1846); Doggett's *Railroad Guide and Gazeteer* (1848); Dinsmore's *American Railway Guide* (1850); and Lloyd's *American Guide* (1857). During the remainder of the nineteenth century and the first two decades of the twentieth century, the National Railway Publication Company gained control of its several competitors and folded them into the *Official Guide*. This information comes from the one hundredth anniversary retrospective provided by the *Official Guide*, June 1968, I-9.

14. *Russell's Official National Motor Coach Guide* (also called the *Official Bus Guide*) was a monthly publication issued by Russell's Guides of Cedar Rapids, Iowa. Before the company focused on a guide devoted exclusively to intercity bus transportation across the United States and Canada, it published a variety of regional timetable compilations that included schedules for electric interurban railways as well as steam railroads. These compact and easily portable guidebooks likely appealed to traveling salesmen, who were especially heavy users of public transport during the first three decades of the twentieth century, before the widespread use of automobiles. See Timothy B. Spears, *100 Years on the Road: The Traveling Salesman in American Culture* (New Haven, CT: Yale University Press, 1995). One common term used during the early years was *commercial traveler*. A somewhat eclectic guide to a salesman's life on the railroad was Commercial Travelers Club, *Trade and Travel: An Illustrated Volume Descriptive of the Commercial, Financial, Transportation and Hotel Interests of the United States* (New York: Commercial Travelers Club, 1895).

15. Information on Potter's labor of love comes from Frances Robinson, "Trainspotters and Other Train Lovers Take

Timetable to Heart," *Wall Street Journal Online*, May 2, 2014. See also Jill Hamilton, *Thomas Cook: Holiday-Maker* (Gloucestershire: Sutton, 2005); Susan Major, *Early Victorian Railway Excursions* (Barnsley: Pen & Sword Transport, 2015). Conversations with John Potter and Tom Hoback over a leisurely dinner at The George, a historic hotel in Stamford, were always a special treat during my several annual visits to study the railways of Great Britain. Fortuitously, Stamford is also home to one of the most attractive small railway stations in England, as well as to Robert Humm and his incredible bookstore. He is without doubt the largest seller of transportation books in the world, and no visit to Britain would be complete without a pause for tea, biscuits, and good conversation with the remarkable Mr. Humm.

16. Luke Sharp, "A Time-Table Vacation," *Detroit Free Press*, January 27, 1889.

17. *Buffalo (NY) Evening News*, April 16, 1918; Sharp, "Time-Table Vacation"; *Omaha Daily News*, May 6, 1918. Collectors were well known to railroad ticket agents: "We have hundreds of such men and women who come to the office after every piece of literature the railroad prints, from the local time-tables to the book descriptions of a southern or western jaunt. Their thirst for this kind of literature can never be satiated; it seems to have the same influence as alcoholic stimulants—the more they get the more they want." *Pittsburgh Dispatch*, reprinted in *Railroad Telegrapher*, August 24, 1895, 11.

18. Luke Sharp, "Time-Table Vacation." The word *fiend* as a term to describe all types of enthusiasts endured for a couple of generations; as late as December 30, 1923, the *Boston Globe* headlined a feature story "Time-Table Fiend Knows How You Can Get Anywhere." *Omaha Daily News*, May 6, 1918. Another term that newspapers formerly used to describe avid collectors of railroad publishing was *print squirrel*. *Commercial Appeal* (Memphis), October 13, 1917.

19. *Fort Worth Record-Telegram*, September 20, 1924. "Don't throw away the timetable when it has served its immediate and primary purpose. Look it through. Then perhaps the children will find material in it for geography study at school." The appeal of railroad timetables remains strong among collectors, though few new imprints are published these days, apart from urban commuter lines. See Henry Grabar, "The Lost Excitement, Pathos, and Beauty of the Railroad Timetable," *Atlantic*, November 22, 2013 (theatlantic.com/technology/archive).

13. RAILROAD CARTOGRAPHY AS THE LIE OF THE LAND

1. *Official Guide*, February 1911, xxviii. At the time the official title of the railroad was the Chicago, Milwaukee & St. Paul. It was known familiarly as "the St. Paul." Its extension from Mobridge, South Dakota, to the Pacific coast was originally titled the Chicago, Milwaukee & Puget Sound, and under that name it issued its initial timetables and brochures. When the overly ambitious railroad emerged from bankruptcy in the mid-1920s, it became the Chicago, Milwaukee, St. Paul & Pacific, familiarly known as the "Milwaukee Road," the designation I use for the sake of convenience throughout this book. Detailed maps were typically not included in the timetables that railroads distributed to commuters. These were usually small and easy-to-pocket, and most of them contained only a list of train times and possibly a few locally oriented advertisements to help offset the cost of publication.

2. American Baptist Home Mission Society, undated pamphlet (ca. 1883).

3. "Railroad advertisements not always are constructed on a strict basis of truth. There is a paucity of things interesting and beautiful along some of the lines of steel that traverse this great American continent, and a fertile imagination is required to bring out to the best advantage those objects which have about them an element of interest and a semblance of beauty." *Inland Printer*, October 1899, 143.

4. Derek Hayes, *The First Railroads: Atlas of Early Railroads* (Buffalo, NY: Firefly Books, 2017); Julian Holland and David Spaven, *Mapping the Railways* (2011; repr., Glasgow: Collins, 2013); Andrew M. Modelski, *Railroad Maps of North America: The First Hundred Years* (Washington, DC: Government Printing Office, 1984); Mark Ovenden, *Railway Maps of the World* (New York: Viking/Penguin Group, 2011). See also James R. Akerman and Robert W. Karrow Jr., eds., *Maps: Finding Our Place in the World* (Chicago: University of Chicago Press, 2007).

5. Katharine Harmon, *The Map as Art: Contemporary Artists Explore Cartography* (New York: Princeton Architectural Press, 2009); Katharine Harmon, *You Are Here: Personal Geography and Other Maps of the Imagination* (New York: Princeton Architectural Press, 2004).

6. *New York Herald*, reprinted in *Inland Printer*, August 1895, 500. I am indebted to Gregory Ames for calling this lampoon to my attention in his own delightfully composed essay "Forgetting St. Louis and Other Map Mischief," *Railroad History*, no. 188 (Spring–Summer 2003), 34.

7. Harold H. Baetjer, *A Book That Gathers No Dust* (New York: National Railway Publication Company, 1950); H. Roger Grant, Don L. Hofsommer, and Osmund Overby, *St. Louis Union Station: A Place for People, a Place for Trains* (Saint Louis: Saint Louis Mercantile Library, 1994). The other Fred Harvey restaurant not located along the Santa Fe Route was in Cleveland, Ohio.

8. *Bradshaw's General Railway and Steam Navigation Guide for Great Britain and Ireland*, April 1910, reprinted by David & Charles. This copy of *Bradshaw's*, a massive book of 1,190 pages, compares favorably in length with the *Official Guide*, which one month in the late 1920s topped out at nearly two thousand pages and could legitimately claim to be the largest monthly periodical in the world. G. Royde Smith, *The History of Bradshaw: A Centenary Review of the Origin and Growth of the Most Famous Guide in the World* (London: Henry Blacklock, 1939). Numerophobia is an affliction recognized today by the Cleveland Clinic and other medical authorities.

14. MEET ME IN SAINT LOUIS AND ELSEWHERE

1. For further details of this long-running municipal rivalry, see Peter A. Hansen, Don L. Hofsommer, and Carlos Arnaldo Schwantes, *Crossroads of a Continent: Missouri Railroads, 1851–1921* (Bloomington: Indiana University Press, 2022). See also Wyatt Winton Belcher, *The Economic Rivalry between St. Louis and Chicago, 1850–1880* (New York: Columbia University Press, 1947). Two uncommonly fine histories of the rival cities are James Neal Primm, *Lion of the Valley: St. Louis Missouri, 1764–1980*, 3rd ed. (Saint Louis: Missouri Historical Society Press, 1998); and William Cronon, *Nature's Metropolis: Chicago and the Great West* (New York: W. W. Norton, 1991).

2. Offering the most thorough coverage by far of the railroad exhibits at the Louisiana Purchase Exposition is *Railway and Engineering Review, 1904 World's Fair Number*, December 31, 1904.

3. Thornton Waite, *Fairs and Railroads: Railroads at World's Fairs, Expositions, and Railroad Fairs* (Missoula, MT: Pictorial Histories, 2010). Every world's fair appears to have inspired one or more books detailing its history and significance. For the Paris's Exposition Universelle of 1889, which bequeathed to France one of its the most recognizable and enduring icons, see

Jill Jonnes, *Eiffel's Tower and the World's Fair Where Buffalo Bill Beguiled Paris, the Artists Quarreled, and Thomas Edison Became a Count* (New York: Viking, 2009). For other notable world's fairs, see James Gilbert, *Whose Fair? Experience, Memory, and the History of the Great St. Louis Exposition* (Chicago: University of Chicago Press, 2009).

4. Robert W. Rydell, *All the World's a Fair: Visions of Empire at American International Expositions, 1876–1916* (Chicago: University of Chicago Press, 1984); Robert W. Rydell, *World of Fairs: The Century-of-Progress Expositions* (Chicago: University of Chicago Press, 1993); Robert W. Rydell, John E. Findling, and Kimberly D. Pelle, *Fair America: World's Fairs in the United States* (Washington: Smithsonian Books, 2000).

5. *Locomotive Engineering*, June 1893, 242.

6. Clark represented Montana in the United States Senate between 1901 and 1907, having first tried to bribe his way into office and been rejected by senators when his vote-buying scandal became public. He second attempt was successful, or at least his fellow senators looked the other way. As Mark Twain, one of America's keenest observers of the Gilded Age corruption, was supposed to have quipped, "We have the best government money can buy." My interest in pursuing historical connections was inspired in large measure by James Burke, *Connections* (New York: Simon & Schuster, 2007).

7. David F. Myrick, *Railroads of Arizona*, vol. 6, *Jerome and the Northern Railroads* (Berkeley, CA: Signature, 2010).

8. Though his brother J. Ross Clark seems to have spied the potential for the desert railroad first, William Andrews Clark supplied the dollars needed to launch construction of the San Pedro, Los Angeles & Salt Lake Railroad in 1905. He regarded it as a valuable conduit for carrying his Montana copper to the Pacific coast port of San Pedro, an arrangement that would grow even more lucrative when an interoceanic canal could be completed across Panama. See John R. Signor, *The Los Angeles and Salt Lake Railroad Company: Union Pacific's Historic Salt Lake Route* (San Marino, CA: Golden West Books, 1988).

9. *Official Guide*, November 1929, 4.

10. *Official Guide*, June 1906, xxxiii; November 1929, 4; December 1933, 42. In 1923, the Union Pacific opened a new branch line to Cedar City, Utah, where it acquired the El Escalante Hotel to serve as a base for tourists traveling to Zion National Park and several natural attractions of southern Utah and northern Arizona. *Railway and Marine News*, October 1923, 14; May 1924, 1–2;

Official Guide, June 1924, 11. See also Hal Rothman, *Neon Metropolis: How Las Vegas Started the Twenty-First Century* (New York: Routledge, 2003).

11. San Diego's displays focused on California, while the exhibits of San Francisco's Panama-Pacific Exposition "[represented] the culture and invention of the entire world." *Official Guide*, June 1915, xxv–xxvi. North America has hosted numerous big expositions over the years, and while some were loosely described as "world's fairs," only a few qualified as officially sanctioned. These "official" ones were held in Philadelphia in 1876, Chicago in 1893, Saint Louis in 1904, San Francisco in 1915, Chicago in 1933 and 1934, San Francisco in 1939 and 1940, New York in 1939 and 1940, Seattle in 1962, and Montreal in 1967.

12. It would be difficult to say which world's fair held in North America generated the greatest amount of railroad publicity, in terms of both timetable illustrations and specialty brochures. I may be slightly biased, but I believe the number and diversity of rail publications devoted to the Louisiana Purchase Exposition held in Saint Louis in 1904 was never equaled before or since. It was, in addition, the last officially sanctioned world's fair held before the dawn of automobile competition, with its ever-increasing impact on long-distance travel formerly monopolized by railroads.

15. LOOKING AND SEEING

1. Richard Harding Davis, *The West from a Car-Window* (New York: Harper & Brothers, 1892), 225.

2. *Official Guide*, June 1914, xxix; Carlos A. Schwantes, "The View from the Passenger Car Vestibule: Travelers Interact with the Passing Landscape," *Railroad Heritage* 14 (2005): 10.

3. *West Shore Railroad Suburban Times*, September 1890, 2. See also Angela Miller, *The Empire of the Eye: Landscape Representations and American Cultural Politics, 1825–1875* (Ithaca, NY: Cornell University Press, 1993); Richard H. Gassan, *The Birth of American Tourism: New York, the Hudson Valley, and American Culture, 1790–1830* (Amherst: University of Massachusetts Press, 2008). Travel guides date back at least to the sixteenth-century pilgrimage to the Holy Land: "Pilgrims seem to have been very anxious to accomplish the journey out and home with the least possible amount of fatigue or inconvenience." Hence, a popular guide published in 1515 explained "how the thing might be done

comfortably and economically." *Railway World*, February 8, 1890, 125.

4. *Official Guide*, August 1916, xxiii.

5. *Official Guide*, August 1913, xxix. North America's expansive vernacular landscape, an integral part of any long-distance train journey and a prominent feature in railroad promotional literature and commercial art, has itself been the subject of several thought-provoking studies, including John Brinckerhoff Jackson, *Discovering the Vernacular Landscape* (New Haven, CT: Yale University Press, 1984); John Brinckerhoff Jackson, *American Space, the Centennial Years: 1865–1876* (New York: W. W. Norton, 1972); and Michael P. Conzen, ed., *The Making of the American Landscape* (London: HarperCollinsAcademic, 1990). This trio of books suggests the need for a study specifically devoted to the making of North America's railroad landscape, a need met twice over in books by John R. Stilgoe. See Stilgoe, *Metropolitan Corridor: Railroads and the American Scene* (New Haven, CT: Yale University Press, 1983); Stilgoe, *Train Time: Railroads and the Imminent Reshaping of the United States Landscape* (Charlottesville: University of Virginia Press, 2007). A counterpart study for the United Kingdom is Gordon Biddle, *Railways in the Landscape: How They Transformed the Face of Britain* (Barnsley, South Yorkshire: Pen & Sword Books, 2016). Encouraging readers to see vernacular landscapes afresh are the many books written by geographer Yi-Fu Tuan. See Tuan, *Topophilia: A Study of Environmental Perception, Attitudes, and Values* (1974; repr., New York: Columbia University Press, 1990); Tuan, *Landscapes of Fear* (New York: Pantheon Books, 1975). Finally, for one of the most insightful and thorough studies of the landscape beyond the train windows and of passengers' perceptions of it, see Wolfgang Schivelbusch, *The Railway Journey: Trains & Travel in the 19th Century* (New York: Urizen Books, 1977), first published in German in 1978.

6. Hamlin Garland, "Western Landscapes," *Atlantic Monthly*, December 1893, 805–809. During the slower-paced 1890s, American readers reveled in the elaborate prose that Garland used in his descriptions of the trackside West. Not surprisingly, railroad promotional brochures typically showcased a similar style of unhurried writing. The languid prose was so typical for the time that when the Rock Island Route published in 1900 an illustrated pamphlet called *Colorado, the Magnificent*, the review in the *Official Guide* took note of the "terse style" used to describe "the salient features" of a train trip through the Rocky Mountains. *Official Guide*, July 1900, xxvii. During the golden age of railroad

publications devoted to settlement and scenery, from the 1880s through 1917, monthly issues of the *Official Guide* provided brief (always positive) reviews of several thousand distinct pieces of literature. I know of no other source that provides as definitive a list of imprints devoted to publishing the railroad.

7. Offering an especially useful overview of "railroad literature" is Tom D. Kilton, "The American Railroad as Publisher, Bookseller, and Librarian," *Journal of Library History* 17, no. 1 (Winter 1982): 39–64. Providing an in-depth interpretation of one of the earliest guidebooks devoted to describing the railroad landscape as well as related topics is Matthew N. Johnston, *Narrating the Landscape: Print Culture and American Expansion in the Nineteenth Century* (Norman: University of Oklahoma Press, 2016). One early text described by Johnston was reprinted in 2017 under its original cumbersome title: William Guild, *A Chart and Description of the Boston and Worcester and Western Railroads; in Which is Noted the Towns, Villages, Stations, Bridges, Viaducts, Tunnels, Cuttings, Embankments, Gradients, &c., the Scenery and its Natural History and Other Objects Passed by this Line of Railway* (Boston: Bradbury & Guild, 1847). Among the largest and most thorough of the many trackside guides (comprising a total of 276 pages) was Henry J. Winsor, *The Great Northwest: A Guide-Book and Itinerary for the Use of Tourists and Travellers over the Lines of the Northern Pacific Railroad, the Oregon Railway and Navigation Company and the Oregon and California Railroad* (New York: G. P. Putnam's Sons, 1883).

8. *Official Guide*, December 1926, xxxii; May 1928, xxix. The San Francisco Overland Limited was operated jointly by the Chicago & North Western, Union Pacific, and Southern Pacific, and the Los Angeles Limited was operated jointly by the Chicago & Northwestern and Union Pacific, the segment of the journey from Salt Lake City to Los Angeles being the former Los Angeles & Salt Lake, a name adopted in 1916 to replace its cumbersome San Pedro, Los Angeles & Salt Lake Railroad title. Railroads serving the Pacific Northwest shortened their running times between Chicago and Seattle to sixty-eight hours. For the Milwaukee Road, that meant trimming its former schedule by two hours.

9. *Official Guide*, September 1900, xxv.

10. *Official Guide*, June 1951, xiv.

11. *Anaheim (CA) Gazette*, November 29, 1900; *Imperial (CA) Press*, August 26, 1905; Carlos A. Schwantes, *Long Day's Journey: The Steamboat and Stagecoach Era in the Northern West* (Seattle: University of Washington Press, 1999).

12. *Official Guide*, May 1910, xxi. In an odd sort of way, the in-house magazines airlines placed in seat-back pockets before the COVID-19 pandemic, while bearing only a superficial resemblance to the traditional railroad route guide, maintained the tradition of interesting members of a captive audience in possible vacation destinations, all of which, of course, were served by the airline publisher. At one time airlines published their own map guides to the passing scenery, but such cartography became meaningless with the coming of the jet age and planes that flew so high as to reduce any scenery below to mere patterns on the land. M. C. Hühne, *Airline Visual Identity, 1945–1975* (n.p.: Callisto, n.d.); Jim Heimann and Allison Silver, *20th Century Travel: 100 Years of Globe-Trotting Ads* (n.p.: Taschen, n.d.).

13. *Official Guide*, July 1936, 30.

14. The best and most comprehensive study of passenger rolling stock is John H. White Jr., *The American Railroad Passenger Car* (Baltimore: Johns Hopkins University Press, 1978). See also August Mencken, *The Railroad Passenger Car: An Illustrated History of the First Hundred Years with Accounts by Contemporary Passengers* (1957; repr., Baltimore: Johns Hopkins University Press, 2000); Joe Welsh and Bill Howes, *Travel by Pullman* (Saint Paul, MN: Motorbooks, 2007).

15. William A. McKenzie, *Dining Car to the Pacific: The "Famously Good" Food of the Northern Pacific Railway* (Minneapolis: University of Minnesota Press, 2004); Thomas J. Greco and Karl D. Spence, *Dining on the B & O: Recipes and Sidelights from a Bygone Age* (Baltimore: Johns Hopkins University Press, 2009); Jim A. Loveland, *Dinner Is Served: Fine Dining aboard the Southern Pacific* (San Marino, CA: Golden West Books, 1996); James D. Porterfield, *Dining by Rail: The History and Recipes of America's Golden Age of Railroad Cuisine* (New York: St. Martin's, 1993); Will C. Hollister, *Dinner in the Diner: Great Railroad Recipes of All Time* (Corona del Mar, CA: Trans-Anglo Books, 1975); Sharon Hudgins, ed., *Food on the Move: Dining on the Legendary Railway Journeys of the World* (London: Reaktion Books, 2019). On a closely related topic, see William Woys Weaver, *Culinary Ephemera: An Illustrated History* (Berkeley: University of California Press, 2010).

16. A *Railway Age* article celebrated the fiftieth anniversary of the Twentieth Century Limited. *Railway Age*, June 16, 1952, 51–52. The New York Central's most famous train was launched in 1902 and connected New York and Chicago in the then phenomenal time of twenty hours. The idea was an example of the fertile mind and creative showmanship of the railroad's chief publicist, George H. Daniels. In 1922 the railroad inaugurated the tradition of rolling out the "red carpet," literally, for guests who boarded the train at Grand Central Station in New York.

16. IN CATHEDRALS OF COMMERCE

1. Sherwood Anderson, *Winesburg, Ohio: A Group of Tales of Ohio Small-Town Life* (New York: Modern Library, 1919), 301, 303.

2. H. Roger Grant, *The Station Agent and the American Railroad Experience* (Bloomington: Indiana University Press, 2022).

3. H. Roger Grant and Charles W. Bohi, *The Country Railroad Station in America* (Boulder: Pruett, 1978). A monthly periodical, the *International Railway Journal*, was published from the 1890s into the 1920s, and it serves as an incomparable source of information about stationmasters, ticket agents, and rail travel in general.

4. Anderson, *Winesburg, Ohio*. See also Harry Holland, *Travellers' Architecture* (London: George H. Harrap, 1971).

5. James R. Hetherington, *Indianapolis Union Station: Trains, Travelers, and Changing Times* (Carmel: Guild Press of Indiana, 2000). The original Indianapolis structure was replaced by a larger and grander union station in 1888. This granddaddy of union stations is still standing, but I found that a recent visit to its great hall offered a depressing contrast to the lively scene of activity I remember from the 1950s. The room appears empty except on those occasions during which it is rented for a wedding or banquet. Across Illinois Street in yet another portion of the once-sprawling railroad complex is the Crowne Plaza Hotel, unique for having converted some classic heavyweight passenger cars into favored bedrooms.

6. Today's Union Station and the former Chicago & Northwestern Station (now renamed the Ogilvie Transportation Center and entirely given over to the commuter trains serving suburban communities located north and northwest of Chicago) are the survivors from the former array of five downtown rail stations. Joseph P. Schwieterman, *Terminal Town: An Illustrated Guide to Chicago's Airports, Bus Depots, Train Stations, and Steamship Landings, 1939–Present* (Lake Forest, IL: Lake Forest College Press, 2014).

7. Ever since I first saw the Traction Terminal, I remained captivated by the massive dimensions of the world's largest interurban station. In the early 1950s my mother would dress in

her finest outfit and take my brother Dave and me to the Central Swallow bus station in Greenfield for a day's outing to the big city of Indianapolis. The interurban trains that once threaded their way along Greenfield's main street had ceased running in the early 1930s, but their onetime hub station in Indianapolis endured. To a small boy the structure seemed massive enough to house a blimp or two in addition to the many intercity buses that in those days still used the structure. The building itself was conveniently placed, perhaps for reasons of politics, just half a block east of the Indiana Capitol. The interurban trains once ran through Greenfield to connect Indianapolis with Dayton, and though I regret never being able to see or ride one, they are the subject of Jerry Marlette, *Terre Haute, Indianapolis and Eastern Traction Company* (Indianapolis: Dog Ear, 2011).

8. H. Roger Grant, Don L. Hofsommer, and Osmund Overby, *St. Louis Union Station: A Place for People, a Place for Trains* (Saint Louis: Saint Louis Mercantile Library, 1994).

9. Given the defining presence of railroad stations in urban architecture, it is appropriate that many excellent books have been written about the topic generally and about specific landmark stations: Christopher Brown, *Still Standing: A Century of Urban Train Station Design* (Bloomington: Indiana University Press, 2005); Julian Cavalier, *Classic American Railroad Stations* (San Diego: A. S. Barnes, 1980); David Naylor, *Railroad Stations: The Buildings That Linked the Nation* (New York: W. W. Norton, 2012); Brian Solomon, *Railway Depots, Stations & Terminals* (Minneapolis: Voyageur, 2015); Jeffery Spivak, *Union Station Kansas City* (Kansas City: Kansas City Star Books, 1999); *Cincinnati Union Terminal: The Design and Construction of an Art Deco Masterpiece*, vol. 1 (Cincinnati: Cincinnati Railroad Club, 1999). An encyclopedic treatment of the railroad stations and other examples of public architecture for just one state, Georgia, is Wilber W. Caldwell, *The Courthouse and the Depot: A Narrative Guide to Railroad Expansion and Its Impact on Public Architecture in Georgia, 1833–1910* (Macon, GA: Mercer University Press, 2001).

10. *Official Guide*, May 1911, xxxi. Intercity passenger trains no longer use the Tacoma Union Station, but at least the imposing 1911 structure still stands and houses the United States District Court.

11. A. Reinisch, "Railroad Gardening," *Railroad Gazette*, March 17, 1905, 262–263. "More attention is being paid each year to the appearance of passenger station grounds and railway right of way in general." The Pennsylvania, among others, provided an incentive "for keeping the right of way neat" by awarding prizes to track gangs for their good work. *Railway Age Gazette*, July 12, 1912, 39.

12. *Official Guide*, April 1902, xxvi.

13. H. Roger Grant, *"Follow the Flag": A History of the Wabash Railroad* Company (DeKalb: Northern Illinois University, 2004), 105–108; Howard V. Worley Jr., *Wabash Pittsburgh Terminal Railway* (Saxonburg, PA: Howdy Productions, 2004). For an in-depth history of Link's Saint Louis Union Station, by some measures the largest in the United States, see Grant, Hofsommer, and Overby, *St. Louis Union Station*.

14. For a reminder of what was lost with the station's destruction, see Lorraine B. Diehl, *The Late, Great Pennsylvania Station* (New York: American Heritage, 1985); Hilary Ballon, *New York's Pennsylvania Stations* (New York: W. W. Norton, 2002).

17. DESIGN MATTERS

1. *Railway World*, December 26, 1891, 1226; August Mencken, *The Railroad Passenger Car: An Illustrated History of the First Hundred Years with Accounts by Contemporary Passengers* (1957; repr., Baltimore: Johns Hopkins University Press, 2000); Trevor K. Snowdon, *Diverging Tracks: American versus English Rail Travel in the 19th Century* (Jefferson, NC: McFarland, 2019).

2. Olin D. Wheeler, *Wonderland 1904* (Saint Paul, MN: Northern Pacific Railway, 1904), 63–67.

3. Wheeler, *Wonderland 1904*, 64; *Official Guide*, August 1926, xxxii.

4. William A. McKenzie, *Dining Car to the Pacific: The "Famously Good" Food of the Northern Pacific Railway* (Minneapolis: University of Minnesota Press, 2004); *International Railway Journal* (December 1913), 10.

5. *Official Guide*, May 1892, xxi. See also Marta Weigle and Barbara A. Babcock, eds., *The Great Southwest of the Fred Harvey Company and the Santa Fe Railway* (Phoenix: Heard Museum, 1996); Stephen Fried, *Appetite for America: How Visionary Businessman Fred Harvey Built a Railroad Hospitality Empire That Civilized the Wild West* (New York: Bantam Books/Random House, 2010); George H. Foster and Peter C. Weiglin, *The Harvey House Cookbook: Memories of Dining along the Santa Fe Railroad* (Atlanta: Longstreet, 1992); Lesley Poling-Kempes, *The Harvey Girls: Women Who Opened the West* (New York: Paragon House, 1989). The Fred Harvey Company also offered a variety of popular

tours. Paul and Kathleen Nickens, *Touring the West with the Fred Harvey Co. & the Santa Fe Railway* (Atglen, PA: Schiffer, 2009); D. H. Thomas, *The Southwest Indian Detours: The Story of the Fred Harvey/Santa Fe Railway Experiment in "Detourism"* (Phoenix: Hunter, 1978); Richard H. Frost, *The Railroad and the Pueblo Indians: The Impact of the Atchison, Topeka and Santa Fe on the Pueblos of the Rio Grande, 1880–1930* (Salt Lake City: University of Utah Press, 2016).

6. A classic account of the Jim Crow era in race relations is C. Vann Woodward, *The Strange Career of Jim Crow* (New York: Oxford University Press, 1955).

7. Despite the manifest insult of Jim Crow accommodations across the South, two integral features of any long-distance rail journey across the United States were African American Pullman porters and dining car waiters. See Jack Santino, *Miles of Smiles, Years of Struggle: Stories of Black Pullman Porters* (Urbana: University of Illinois Press, 1989); Larry Tye, *Rising from the Rails: Pullman Porters and the Making of the Black Middle Class* (New York: Henry Holt, 2004); Eric Arnesen, *Brotherhoods of Color: Black Railroad Workers and the Struggle for Equality* (Cambridge, MA: Harvard University Press, 2001).

8. *Railway Age*, August 28, 1926, 356.

9. Sheldon S. King, *The Route of Phoebe Snow: A Story of the Delaware, Lackawanna and Western Railroad* (Flanders, NJ: Railroad Avenue Enterprises, 1986). On the fate of Phoebe Snow, see H. Roger Grant, *Erie Lackawanna: Death of an American Railroad, 1938–1992* (Stanford, CA: Stanford University Press, 1994). On the experience of train travel, see Wolfgang Schivelbusch, *The Railway Journey: Trains and Travel in the 19th Century* (New York: Urizen Books, 1977), first published in German in 1978.

10. Thomas W. Dixon Jr., *Chessie, the Railroad Kitten* (Lynchburg, VA: TLC, 1988). Chessie made her debut in 1933.

11. *Official Guide*, June 1906, xxxii.

12. *Official Guide*, November 1927, xxx; November 1929, 4. Aboard its new Empire Builder (inaugurated in 1929) the Great Northern Railway promised "a home-like atmosphere" and "genuine hospitality." *Railway and Marine News*, April 1930, 19. On the importance of interior design in the new passenger trains of the late 1920s and early 1930s, see *Railway Age*, June 30, 1934, 965–966.

13. J. N. Hurty, "Railway Sanitation," *Railroad Age Gazette*, July 9, 1909, 53–54. Dr. Hurty was secretary of the Indiana State Board of Health. On paper drinking cups, see *Railway Age Gazette*, November 1, 1912, 823; November 8, 1912, 896). To maintain pure

and cool drinking water aboard trains of its Los Angeles division, the Southern Pacific used distilled water to make blocks of ice, which men clad in white coats and rubber gloves sawed into small pieces and added to coolers placed aboard the outbound trains. The onboard water coolers were frequently steam cleaned, and Southern Pacific personnel analyzed the purity of the railroad's water supply every six months. *Railroad Age Gazette*, October 31, 1918, 820. For amplification of some of the matters discussed only briefly here, see Amy G. Richter, *Home on the Rails: Women, the Railroad, and the Rise of Public Domesticity* (Chapel Hill: University of North Carolina Press, 2005).

18. THE QUEST FOR SPEED

1. *American Railroad Journal*, July 10, 1845, 442.

2. Mark Twain, *Life on the Mississippi* (1883; repr., New York: New American Library, 2001), 145–146.

3. *Official Guide*, November 1899, xxviii.

4. *Official Guide*, April 1927, xxxi.

5. *American Railroad Journal*, July 25, 1846, 474; September 24, 1853, 615.

6. Louis C. Hunter, *Steamboats on the Western Rivers: An Economic and Technological History* (1949; repr., New York: Dover, 1993); Harry Sinclair Drago, *The Steamboaters: From the Early Side-Wheelers to the Big Packets* (New York: Dodd, Mead, 1967); William J. Petersen, *Steamboating on the Upper Mississippi* (1968; repr., New York: Dover, 1995).

7. The Missouri partnership behind the Pony Express was Russell, Majors & Waddell, which had also found success in frontier freighting and stagecoaching. Oscar Osburn Winther, *Via Western Express & Stagecoach: California's Transportation Links with the Nation, 1848–1869* (1945; repr., Lincoln: University of Nebraska Press, 1979); Alexander Majors, *Seventy Years on the Frontier* (1893; repr., Minneapolis: Ross & Haines, 1965).

8. Given the extremely slow speed of photographic film in the 1890s, an image of a fast-running locomotive was a source of popular amazement. Daniels made five thousand enlargements of a Yates image of locomotive No. 999 and the Empire State Express running at speed and distributed them all over the world, a form of publishing the railroad that greatly enhanced the reputation of the New York Central & Hudson River line.

9. J. T. Burton Alexander, *Runs in Three Continents: A Short Record of Actual Performances on Some European, Canadian,*

Australian, and American Railways (London: Elliot Stock, 1900). Alexander's book, which is basically a compilation of speed data gleaned from a seemingly random sampling of trains from around the world, speaks to the world's growing obsession with fast-running trains. Mark Aldrich, *Death Rode the Rails: American Railroad Accidents and Safety, 1828–1965* (Baltimore: Johns Hopkins University Press, 2006); Steven W. Usselman, *Regulating Railroad Innovation: Business, Technology, and Politics in America, 1840–1920* (Cambridge: Cambridge University Press, 2002).

10. Thomas R. Bullard and William M. Shapotkin, *Faster than the Limiteds: The Story of the Chicago–New York Air Line Railroad and Its Transformation into Gary Railways* (Chicago: Central Electric Railfans' Association, 2004). From the library of the late H. Roger Grant I acquired a set of the *Air Line News*, a monthly publication issued by the interurban railway's promoters between 1906 and 1913, with each issue intended to encourage mom-and-pop investors to purchase additional stock in the enterprise. What a tragedy!

11. *Railway Age Gazette*, September 20, 1912, 498–499.

12. I admit to being very cynical about what federal dollars accomplished in Illinois. I have ridden Amtrak many times between Saint Louis and Chicago, and what I find most impressive about the line is the many miles of expensive fencing. For certain, the fence contractors must have made a bundle of money. As for speed: once on a trip from Chicago to Saint Louis our Amtrak train halted in Alton and waited for more than thirty minutes for a dispatcher to clear its way for the final few miles into Saint Louis. According to our conductor, the dispatcher for the next shift had overslept. If this was true, then all tax dollars spent to foster high-speed operations could be defeated by a traffic bottleneck at either end or by a sleepy dispatcher. A list of articles and essays debating the pros and cons of high-speed trains for the United States is too lengthy to compile here. I will cite only the following handful easily available on the internet: M. E. Singer, "Chicago–St. Louis: Missing Ingredients," *Railway Age*, June 22, 2023; Kevin Baker, "21st Century Limited: The Lost Glory of America's Railroads," *Harper's*, July 2014; Andrew Gumbel, "Trains to Nowhere: Can California's High-Speed Rail Project Ever Get Back on Track?," *Guardian*, May 29, 2022; Minko Kim, "Why High-Speed Bullet Trains Won't Work in the U.S. Right Now," *Scientific American*, September 5, 2023.

13. Harold A. Edmonson, ed., *Journey to Amtrak: The Year History Rode the Passenger Train* (Milwaukee: Kalmbach, 1972);

Craig Sanders, *Amtrak in the Heartland* (Bloomington: Indiana University Press, 2006); and Geoffrey H. Doughty, Jeffrey T. Darbee, and Eugene E. Harmon, *Amtrak, America's Railroad: Transportation's Orphan and Its Struggle for Survival* (Bloomington: Indiana University Press, 2021).

14. Geoffrey Freeman Allen, *The World's Fastest Trains: From the Age of Steam to the TGV*, 2nd ed. (Sparkford, UK: Patrick Stevens Limited, 1992); Brian Solomon, *Bullet Trains* (Osceola, WI: MBI, 2001); Brian Perren, *TGV Handbook*, 2nd ed. (Harrow Weald, UK: Capital Transport, 1998).

19. RAILROAD GRAPHICS CONSCRIPTED FOR THE DURATION

1. Michael McGerr, *A Fierce Discontent: The Rise and Fall of the Progressive Movement in America, 1870–1920* (New York: Oxford University Press, 2003); Steven W. Usselman, *Regulating Railroad Innovation: Business, Technology, and Politics in America, 1840–1920* (Cambridge: Cambridge University Press, 2002).

2. Albro Martin, *Enterprise Denied: Origins of the Decline of American Railroads, 1897–1917* (New York: Columbia University Press, 1971); Robert E. Gallamore and John R. Meyer, *American Railroads: Decline and Renaissance in the Twentieth Century* (Cambridge, MA: Harvard University Press, 2014).

3. *Railway Age Gazette*, August 27, 1915, 376–377. "It was not so many years ago that the promotion of railroad business consisted almost entirely of formal announcements of arrival and departure of trains, occasionally featuring special excursions and cut-rate opportunities. Then a few scenic attractions were thrown in occasionally to leaven the lump, but without material advantage." Finally, during the 1880s and 1890s, according to the *International Railway Journal*, the industry discovered that "railroad service could be merchandised exactly like any other service," which meant that "trains were named, their advantages and attractions were pointed out with selling enthusiasm, and the equipment of the roads, their protection to passengers, the safety, reliability and speed of their trains were all discussed." *Saturday Evening Post*, reprinted in *International Railway Journal*, August 1916, 10.

4. *Official Guide*, December 1917, xxiii. Remember that these reductions in service took place before the more draconian ones imposed in 1918 by the United States Railroad Administration.

5. *Railway Age Gazette*, November 23, 1917, 938. "Mere matters of convenience, which are desirable in times of peace and for the

purposes of peace, will have to wait until peace comes. The application is hereby dismissed." The logic enunciated by the Iowa rail commissioners was identical to that invoked in countless ways across the United States during World War I to justify federal and state mandates that resulted in civilian privation.

6. *Railway Age Gazette*, December 28, 1917, 1193; *Railway Age*, April 26, 1918, 1094. In February 1918, American railroads saved 251,138 pounds of wheat flour.

7. For one patron's explanation of why upper berths in a Pullman car were dreaded by most travelers, see *Railway Age Gazette*, October 19, 1917, 679.

8. *Erie (KS) Record*, November 8, 1918. "'Billy McAdoo' is some advertiser," noted one California newspaper. "Hitherto the name of the road such as 'Southern Pacific' was enough, and the various railroad presidents did not find it necessary to run their names all over everything connected with the business. But it is different with a prospective United States presidential candidate." *Visalia Times-Delta*, August 18, 1918.

9. *New York Tribune*, February 3, 1918; *Palm Beach (FL) Post*, December 22, 1918; *Electric Railway Journal*, September 24, 1910, 478.

10. *Railway Age*, April 12, 1918, 969. According to the Interstate Commerce Commission, railroads in 1916 spent nearly $8 million on advertising.

11. *Seattle Star*, April 3, 1918; *Railway Age*, April 12, 1918, 969.

12. *Printers' Ink*, reprinted in *International Railway Journal*, December 1920. Once World War I ended, it did not take long for partisan politics to assess the impact of the United States Railroad Administration and its first director general. Republican senator Lawrence Yates Sherman of Illinois declared in early 1920 that the USRA campaign to save paper was hypocritical because McAdoo as director general used endless reams in the political "propaganda" he distributed as railway literature in his not-so-subtle bid to become president of the United States: "Mr. McAdoo paid his campaign bills at the expense of the government and he passes as an example of public virtue." *St. Louis Globe-Democrat*, February 6, 1920.

13. *Advertising & Selling*, April 1918, 13; *Buffalo (NY) Evening News*, April 16, 1918; *Pittsburgh Post-Gazette*, April 4, 1918; *Indianapolis News*, April 4, 1918; *Printers' Ink*, April 11, 1918; *El Paso Herald*, April 23, 1918, 73. The *Post-Gazette* was one of several newspapers across the United States that disagreed with McAdoo's banishment of railroad commercial art, but they all did so very carefully lest they be accused of criticizing the war effort, a federal crime during those days of overheated patriotism. A newspaper in Evansville, Indiana, editorialized that McAdoo "was taking the joy out of life," because "thousands of people take wonderful trips through the country with the aid of the illustrated railway folder. Many of them make that trip in imagination, lack of funds preventing them from making it otherwise. But the fact that they are unable to visit the wonderful places so vividly and interestingly portrayed in pictures and description does not detract from their enjoyment." *Evansville Journal*, April 25, 1918.

14. *Railway Age Gazette*, October 19, 1917, 675. "As for the passenger, he usually does not specifically desire to be handed an expensive time table just to glance at the time of a single train."

15. *Official Guide*, August 1915, xxvi. One additional result of McAdoo's edict: "Exit the Imaginary Vacation," sighed the headline in an *Omaha Daily News* story about the abrupt disappearance of the colorful and freely available railroad imprints of years past. "Secretary McAdoo has ruled that railroad folders are to be purely informative. They are not to advertise trains de luxe, superior service or the charms that lie at the other end of the journey." With the restrictions he placed on the design and availability of railroad imprints, the director general "dealt a deadly blow to the imaginative vacationer who spends an imaginary salary on an imaginary trip." *Omaha Daily News*, May 6, 1918.

16. Among the USRA's free brochures available in 1919 were seventeen different titles that publicized national parks and monuments ranging from Yellowstone and Yosemite to Hot Springs and Mesa Verde, many with full-color covers. Recall that McAdoo had resigned as the nation's rail czar early that year and been replaced by railroad executive Walker D. Hines.

17. McAdoo for whatever reason proved a genius at shooting himself in the foot politically. In 1923 he was the front-runner for the Democratic Party's presidential nomination the following year, but his candidacy suffered a severe blow when it came to light that he had accepted $25,000 from one of the principals in the Teapot Dome scandal, money he claimed to have returned once he learned the identity of his sordid benefactor. At the 1924 convention, McAdoo made an even bigger mistake when he refused to repudiate support from the then-powerful Ku Klux Klan.

18. Walker D. Hines, *War History of American Railroads* (New Haven, CT: Yale University Press, 1928); Rudolph L. Daniels,

The Great Railroad War: United States Railway Operations during World War I (Branchville, NJ: Garbely, 2017).

19. "Walker D. Hines will make one deviation from the policy of his predecessor which though not highly important is, nonetheless, interesting. He will keep his name off most of the railway literature. Before Mr. McAdoo had retired as director general his name adorned every time table, poster and even ticket, in addition to the various forms of stationery." *Nebraska State Journal* (Lincoln), January 24, 1919.

20. On the distribution of timetables during the United States Railroad Administration, see "Economical and Efficient Handling of Time Table Folders," *International Railway Journal*, August 1919, 9. Even before the federal takeover in early 1918, American railroads had begun to curtail timetable distribution as a wartime economy measure: "The old rack that once stood in the corner filled with this literature, to be taken on a 'help-yourself basis,' is gone." *International Railway Journal*, November 1917, 22.

21. *International Railway Journal*, May 1919, 13, 14; *International Railway Journal*, August 1920, 14. See also Edward Hungerford, "Our Railroads Start Back," *International Railway Journal*, August 1920, 2, 6.

22. The inspiration behind the construction of the El Paso & Southwestern line was James Douglas, the president of Phelps Dodge, a mining giant in the American Southwest and northern Mexico. Dissatisfied with the service provided by the Southern Pacific, he oversaw construction of a new railroad originally intended to move ore from the Copper Queen Mine in Bisbee, Arizona, to Phelps Dodge's distant metal processors and customers. For further details, see Carlos A. Schwantes, *Vision and Enterprise: Exploring the History of Phelps Dodge Corporation* (Tucson: University of Arizona Press, 2000). The El Paso & Southwestern would probably qualify as North America's final transcontinental railroad had its tracks reached Los Angeles, but there were at least two other contenders for that title. One was the Canadian line completed north to Hudson's Bay, an arm of the Atlantic Ocean, in 1929, and the other was the Montreal to Texas Gulf Coast system that Leonor F. Loree sought to forge in the mid-1920s by combining existing railroads, including the Delaware & Hudson, which he had headed since 1907, and the Kansas City Southern, of which he was chairman of the board. The Interstate Commerce Commission blocked his audacious move. Harold C. Burr, "Railroad Men Who Made the Grade: Leonor F. Loree," *Brooklyn Daily Eagle*, January 2, 1927.

23. *Railway Age*, May 6, 1939, 768–769. See also Bill Bradley, *The Last of the Great Stations: 40 Years of the Los Angeles Union Passenger Terminal* (n.p.: Interurbans, 1979); Marlyn Musicant, ed., *Los Angeles Union Station* (Los Angeles: Getty Research Institute, 2014).

24. One stop on the El Paso & Southwestern line was Columbus, New Mexico, where in 1916 the ragtag troops of the Mexican revolutionary Pancho Villa crossed the international boundary and shot up the town, a provocative act that led President Wilson to dispatch General John J. Pershing and approximately six thousand members of the United States Army in hot pursuit. They could not capture the wily Villa, and after the United States joined the Great War in Europe the following year, the importance of America's intervention into Mexico's troubled borderlands diminished. Paul J. Vanderwood and Frank N. Samponaro, *Border Fury: A Picture Postcard Record of Mexico's Revolution and U.S. War Preparedness, 1910–1917* (Albuquerque: University of New Mexico Press, 1988).

20. AMERICA'S SECOND TRANSPORTATION REVOLUTION

1. *Official Guide*, October 1920, 29.

2. *Railway Age*, December 12, 1925, 1075–1076. The article emphasized that "the motor vehicle has come to stay and should be dealt with on its merits by the railways, whether as a competitive or auxiliary means of transportation." See also George Rogers Taylor, *The Transportation Revolution, 1815–1860* (1951; repr., New York: Harper & Row, 1968); Gregory Lee Thompson, *The Passenger Train in the Motor Age: California's Rail and Bus Industries, 1910–1941* (Columbus: Ohio State University 1993); John A. Jakle and Keith A. Sculle, *Supplanting America's Railroads: The Early Auto Age, 1900–1940* (Knoxville: University of Tennessee Press, 2017); Albert E. Meier and John P. Hoschek, *Over the Road: A History of Intercity Bus Transportation in the United States* (Upper Montclair, NJ: Motor Bus Society, 1975).

3. *Log of National Old Trails Highway* (Albuquerque, NM: Albuquerque Auto Trades, Circa 1922), 1–2; F. Robert van der Linden, *Airlines & Airmail: The Post Office and the Birth of the Commercial Aviation Industry* (Lexington: University Press of Kentucky, 2002); Barry Rosenberg and Catherine Macaulay, *Mavericks of the Sky: The First Daring Pilots of the U.S. Airmail* (New York: HarperCollins, 2006).

4. *Railway Age*, July 16, 1927, 88; "Old Ways Are Not Good Enough," *Railway Age*, October 28, 1933, 590–592. For histories of the rise of commercial aviation in the United States, see Carl Solberg, *Conquest of the Skies: A History of Commercial Aviation in America* (Boston: Little, Brown, 1979); T. A. Heppenheimer, *Turbulent Skies: The History of Commercial Aviation* (New York: John Wiley & Sons, 1995); Joseph J. Corn, *The Winged Gospel: America's Romance with Aviation, 1900–1950* (New York: Oxford University Press, 1983); Sam Howe Verhovek, *Jet Age: The Comet, the 707, and the Race to Shrink the World* (New York: Penguin Group, 2010).

5. Lawrence Goldstone, *Drive: Henry Ford, George Selden, and the Race to Invent the Auto Age* (New York: Ballantine Books, 2016); I. B. Holley Jr., *The Highway Revolution: How the United States Got Out of the Mud* (Durham, NC: Carolina Academic Press, 2008); Phil Patton, *Open Road: A Celebration of the American Highway* (New York: Simon & Schuster, 1986); Earl Swift, *The Big Roads: The Untold Story of the Engineers, Visionaries, and Trailblazers Who Created the American Superhighways* (Boston: Houghton Mifflin Harcourt, 2011).

6. Federal legislation in 1916 and 1921 provided money for highway construction. In addition, during the post–World War I years from 1918 to 1921, some $140 million of military surplus machinery was donated to the states to support highway construction and maintenance. The federal giveaway included twenty-three thousand army trucks. *Public Roads*, November 1921, 22. "With the improvement in highways during the past few years the automobile has become an important factor in both local and long haul passenger transportation." C. M. Burt, "Effect of Automobile Travel," *Railway Age*, October 11, 1924, 643–644.

7. *Railway Age*, August 11, 1928, 249; August 25, 1928, 394.

8. *Railway Age*, August 30, 1924, 356. Inflation had begun to bedevil railroads before World War I, even as early as 1915, but it grew much more worrisome during the years 1917 through 1919, two years of conflict and one of turmoil immediately following the armistice. But for railroads to raise their fares to cover their rising expenses presented a problem: "It will give enormous impetus to the movement, already well under way, to make each man furnish his own private means of rapid transit between cities, for it is the final step in giving the automobile a definite advantage in the way of cheapness." *Des Moines Register and Leader*, quoted in *Railway Age Gazette*, December 24, 1915, 1180–1181. For additional discussion of the transportation revolution of the 1920s, see Carlos Arnaldo Schwantes, *Going Places:*

Transportation Redefines the Twentieth-Century West (Bloomington: Indiana University Press, 2003), chap. 6.

9. *Railway Age*, December 10, 1927, 1145; August 25, 1928, 394. In 1929, for the first time in history, "the railways are handling more passenger business in sleeping and parlor cars than in day coaches." These figures "are highly significant as a reflection of the revolution in travel that has occurred within recent years." *Railway Age*, June 1, 1929, 1267. Long-distance train travel held up well during the 1920s despite growing highway competition. Some major railroads even reported that the number of long-distance journeys by rail was increasing. Local trains, which could no longer compete successfully with private automobiles and intercity buses, became chronic money losers, and "abandonment is considered seriously." One option intended to stanch the flow of red ink was to substitute gas-electric rail motor cars, single-unit trains popularly labeled "doodlebugs," for steam-powered trains. If they did not make money, they could at least cut the cost of operating local trains. Another option was for railroads to operate intercity bus subsidiaries, as many began to do during the second half of the 1920s. W. R. McKeen Jr., "Gasolene Motor Cars," *Railroad Gazette*, June 15, 1906, 652–653; L. C. Josephs Jr., "A Field for Gasoline Railway Motor Cars," *Railway Age*, October 1921, 627–628; John F. Layng, "The Future Ahead for the Branch Line," *Electric Railway Journal*, September 26, 1925, 511–516; *Railway Age*, October 24, 1925, 738; *Railway Age*, May 22, 1926, 1395–1399. For a statistical analysis of the abandonment of 6,400 miles of American railroads during the 1920s, see *Bus Transportation*, May 1931, 231.

10. *Railway Age*, April 28, 1928, 950. One new advertising medium that railroads were slow to utilize was radio. The pioneer in this field was the Great Northern, which became the sponsor of a weekly program broadcast by a network of thirty-eight radio stations. *Railway Age*, January 19, 1929, 184.

11. *Railway Age*, February 27, 1926, 548–550. See also Edward F. Loomis, "Railroads Become a Factor in the Bus Field," *Bus Transportation*, October 1925, 482–484. Loomis observed, "Whereas eighteen months ago not a single railroad in the country operated a bus, directly or indirectly, now almost daily the news tells either of the formation of rail subsidiaries to operate buses or of indorsements of the bus as a rail auxiliary by railroad officials." Loomis, 482.

12. *Railway Age*, May 22, 1926, 1401–1403; *Highway Magazine*, February 1930, 34–35. In the late 1920s, some industry observers

referred to the new occupation of bus driver as "Bus Captain." Lewis R. Freeman, "The Bus Captain," *Bus Transportation*, August 1929, 436–438. During a tour of China in 1906 I heard our local handler repeatedly refer to our driver as "Bus Master Shin."

13. Lewis R. Freeman wrote a multipart account of his quest to cross the continent by motor coach, with the concluding installment featuring a statistical tabulation of his journey titled "From Chicago to Los Angeles on Common Carrier Lines," *Bus Transportation*, June 1926, 295–298. Earlier portions of his lengthy travel narrative appeared in *Bus Transportation*, March 1926, 139–141; May 1926, 251–252. For a lengthy discussion of the Nite Coaches operated by Pacific Greyhound between Los Angeles and San Francisco, see *Bus Transportation*, July 1932, 303–304. The implementation of various forms of luxury bus travel between New York and Chicago is described in *Bus Transportation*, April 1930, 205.

14. A. L. Cricher, "45,000 Communities Rely Solely on Motor Transportation," *Bus Transportation*, January 1933, 55–57. "Less than 10 years ago the public passenger vehicles of the highways were practically unheard of." *Public Roads*, December 1925, 213.

15. Cricher, "45,000 Communities Rely Solely on Motor Transportation," 57. By the late 1920s, or so highway advocates claimed, the United States had improved only 20 percent of its three million miles of roadways. The highway industry was "still in its swaddling-clothes." In other words, "the magnitude of the constant developments in highway engineering during the past ten years would seem almost to belie the fact that the surface has scarcely been scratched." *Highway Magazine*, February 1930, 34–35.

16. Railroads adapted to the new age of air transportation as best they could. Best known was the 1929 coast-to-coast route that featured air travel during daylight hours and night travel aboard the sleeping cars of the Pennsylvania and Santa Fe railroads. Lesser known is the air-rail combination that linked New York City with Mexico City, a journey of forty-eight hours eastbound and sixty-seven hours in the opposite direction because the westbound trip required an overnight stop in Brownsville, Texas. Also operating at that time was the Air Capital Limited, an overnight train the Frisco operated between Saint Louis and Wichita, Kansas, which was fast becoming a center of aircraft production. *Official Guide*, October 1929, 13; *Railway Age*, November 15, 1930, 1017; Charles Layng, "Competition Stirs Railways," *Railway Age*, January 3, 1931, 42–44, 118. For an informative

firsthand account of early commercial air travel, see Daniel B. Trefethen, "My First Trip as an Air Tourist," *Pacific Airport News*, June 1928, 9–10. The first *all-air* coast-to-coast travel commenced in late 1929 between New York and Los Angeles and required twenty-four hours' flying time and one overnight stop en route. *Pacific Aviation News*, November 1929, 11.

17. *Railway Age*, December 29, 1928, 1283; May 19, 1934, 726.

18. Robert C. Reed, *The Streamline Era* (San Marino, CA: Golden West Books, 1975); Bob Johnston and Joe Welsh, *The Art of the Streamliner*, with Mike Schafer (New York: MetroBooks, 2001); Donald J. Heimburger and Carl R. Byron, *The American Streamliner: Prewar Years* (Forest Park, IL: Heimburger House, 1996); Ric Morgan, *The Train of Tomorrow* (Bloomington: Indiana University Press, 2007); Jeffrey L. Meikle, *Twentieth Century Limited: Industrial Design in America, 1925–1939* (Philadelphia: Temple University Press, 1979).

19. *Railway Age*, May 27, 1933, 761–762; April 25, 1942, 832; *Oregon Motorist*, August 1935, 8–9. A description of the circumstances surrounding the emergence of another of Union Pacific's pioneer streamliners can be found in Carlos A. Schwantes, ed., "Riding on the City of Portland, 1935," *Oregon Historical Quarterly* 85 (Summer 1984): 194–207; *Railway Age*, October 13, 1934, 427–428. Although diesel locomotives headed the streamlined passenger trains introduced in the late 1930s, the revolution in railroad motive power had its origins a decade earlier. See William C. Dickerman, "Modern Trends in Motive Power," *Railway Age*, April 29, 1933, 622–623. The author was president of the American Locomotive Company. The concept of streamlined passenger trains dated back to the turn of the century and the Adams Air-Splitting Train of the Baltimore & Ohio. *Railroad Gazette*, June 8, 1900, 368.

CONCLUSION

1. Alain de Botton, *The Art of Travel* (New York: Pantheon Books, 2002), 56.

2. Sheet music for Joplin's "Great Crush Collision March" was published in 1895.

3. *Yorkville (NY) Enquirer*, March 28, 1878. On August 14, 2011, the *New York Times* reported on an interesting connection between timetables and children with autism: "People with autism have difficulty processing and making sense of the world, so they are drawn to predictable patterns, which, of course, trains

run by." Especially popular are subway trains, their runs being frequent and times generally predictable, but also some museums have learned that their timetable collections are magnets for visitors with autism. For some youngsters with autism spectrum disorders, the sight of a train is wildly exciting; for others it has a calming effect. What distinguishes the condition, notes the *New York Times*, is the intensity of their response.

4. For example, see Ronald D. Cohen and Stephen G. McShane, *Moonlight in Duneland: The Illustrated Story of the Chicago South Shore and South Bend Railroad* (Bloomington: Indiana University Press, 1998).

5. Harold A. Edmonson, ed., *Journey to Amtrak: The Year History Rode the Passenger Train* (Milwaukee: Kalmbach Books, 1972).

6. Kevin Baker, "21st Century Limited: The Lost Glory of America's Railroads," *Harper's Magazine*, July 2014, 43–58.

7. Christian Wolmar, *Cathedrals of Steam: How London's Great Stations Were Built and How They Transformed a City* (London: Atlantic Books, 2020); Christopher Brown, *Still Standing: A Century of Urban Train Station Design* (Bloomington: Indiana University Press, 2005).

8. Commercial Travelers Club, *Trade and Travel: An Illustrated Volume Descriptive of the Commercial, Financial, Transportation and Hotel Interests of the United States* (New York: Commercial Travelers Club of New York, 1895), 36.

INDEX

The railroads of the United States had a lengthy and sometimes bewildering history of financial reorganization that sometimes resulted in a carrier's slight change of corporate title, such as from "railroad" to "railway" and even to "rail road." Thus, depending on the year, it was correct to speak of the Saint Louis & San Francisco Railway or the Saint Louis-San Francisco Railway. This index makes no attempt to differentiate between "railroad" or "railway" or even "system" as used at various times in corporate titles. Thus, all railroad corporate titles indexed below are italicized to avoid any confusion.

Carlos A. Schwantes is the author or editor of twenty books and numerous professional journal articles. During his fifty-year career in the classroom, he frequently taught classes both on Missouri as the Gateway to the West and on the railroads of the United States.

FOR INDIANA UNIVERSITY PRESS

Tony Brewer *Artist and Book Designer*

Dan Crissman *Editorial Director and Acquisitions Editor*

Anna Francis *Assistant Acquisitions Editor*

Anna Garnai *Editorial Assistant*

Katie Huggins *Production Manager*

David Miller *Lead Project Manager/Editor*

Dan Pyle *Online Publishing Manager*

Stephen Williams *Assistant Director of Marketing*

Jennifer Witzke *Senior Artist and Book Designer*